Geographies of Power

For
Jennifer (AH)
and
Leslie C. Wright (MWW)

Geographies of Power

Placing Scale

Edited by
Andrew Herod
and
Melissa W. Wright

Blackwell
Publishing

Editorial Offices:
350 Main Street, Malden, MA 02148-5018, USA
108 Cowley Road, Oxford OX4 1JF, UK
550 Swanston Street, Carlton South, Melbourne, Victoria 3053, Australia
Kurfürstendamm 57, 10707 Berlin, Germany

First published 2002 by Blackwell Publishers Ltd

Library of Congress Cataloging-in-Publication Data

Geographies of power: placing scale/edited by Andrew Herod
and Melissa W. Wright.
      p. cm.
Includes bibliographical references and index.
   ISBN 0–631–22557–9 (alk. paper) – ISBN 0–631–22558–7 (alk. paper)
   1. September 11 Terrorist Attacks, 2001. 2. Terrorism–United States.
3. Globalization. 4. International relations. 5. World
politics–1995–2005. I. Herod, Andrew, 1964– II. Wright, Melissa W.
   HV6432.G68 2002
   303.48′2–dc21

                                                                    2002000891

A catalogue record for this title is available from the British Library.

Set in 10 on 12 pt Palatino
by Kolam Information Services Pvt. Ltd., Pondicherry, India
Printed and bound in the United Kingdom by MPG Books Ltd, Bodmin, Cornwall

For further information on
Blackwell Publishing, visit our website:
www.blackwellpublishing.com

Contents

Figures

Contributors

Kevin R. Cox is Professor of Geography at the Ohio State University. His interests are in the politics of local and regional development and in method, broadly conceived. He is the author of four books and his work has appeared in a range of social science journals.

Altha J. Cravey is Associate Professor of Geography at the University of North Carolina in Chapel Hill. As a former construction electrician and member of the International Brotherhood of Electrical Workers, she became interested in geographies of gender, work, and globalization. Author of *Women and Work in Mexico's Maquiladoras* (1998), she publishes on globalization topics in Mexico and the US South.

Jeff R. Crump is currently Associate Professor in the Housing Studies Program at the University of Minnesota. He received his Ph.D. in geography (1989) at the University of Nebraska–Lincoln. His research interests include public housing and urban policy, immigration and housing, and labor geography.

J. K. Gibson-Graham is the pen-name of Julie Graham (Professor of Geography, University of Massachusetts, Amherst) and Katherine Gibson (Professor of Human Geography, Research School of Pacific and Asian Studies, Australian National University). J. K. Gibson-Graham is the author of *The End of Capitalism (As We Knew It): A Feminist Critique of Political Economy* (1996) and co-editor of *Class and Its Others* (2000) and *Re/Presenting Class* (2001).

Andrew Herod is Associate Professor of Geography at the University of Georgia. He is the author *of Labor Geographies: Workers and the Landscapes of Capitalism* (2001), editor of *Organizing the Landscape:*

Geographical Perspectives on Labor Unionism (1998), and co-editor of *An Unruly World? Globalization, Governance and Geography* (1998).

Ken Hillis is Assistant Professor of Communication Studies at the University of North Carolina at Chapel Hill. Synthesizing political economy and cultural studies approaches, his work focuses on visual culture, and the history, theory, and criticism of new technologies and digital media. Ken is also an Adjunct Professor of Geography at UNC. He is the author of *Digital Sensations: Space, Identity, and Embodiment in Virtual Reality* (1999). His current book project, *Rituals of Transmission*, examines relationships among on-line technologies, digital celebrity, fetishism, and identity.

Andrew Kirby is Professor of Social Sciences at Arizona State University West. He edits the international journal *Cities, the International Journal of Policy and Planning*, and is engaged in several projects dealing with social and ecological change in Phoenix. He teaches in the fields of urban studies, social theory, and popular culture, and his recent publications include papers on world systems theory and on state theory in *Political Geography*. His last book was *Power/Resistance*.

Hilda E. Kurtz is Assistant Professor of Geography at the University of Georgia. Her research explores the geography of social movements, both in the social construction of movement grievances and the geographic constitution of movement strategies and outcomes. In addition to interrogating the politics of scale, her research considers the role of women and the construction of citizenship claims within the movement for environmental justice. Her earlier work on differentiated meanings of community gardens/gardening is published in *Urban Geography*.

Alan Latham is Lecturer in Geography at the University of Southampton. His research focuses on the social and economic dynamics of urban public culture. In particular he is interested in the ways that locally embedded practices are linked within transnationally ordered networks. His work has appeared in a number of edited collections and international journals, such as *Society and Space, Environment and Planning A*, and *Area*.

Helga Leitner is Professor of Geography and a faculty member in the Institute of Global Studies and the Interdisciplinary Center for the Study of Global Change at the University of Minnesota. She has published two books, and has written numerous articles and book chapters on the political economy of urban development and urban entrepreuneurialism, the politics of citizenship and immigrant incorporation, and the politics of scale. Her current research interests include geographies of governance and citizenship, and interurban policy and activist networks.

Susan P. Mains is Lecturer in Human Geography at the University of the West Indies, Mona. Her current work explores media representations of transnationalism, race, and immigration, drawing on case studies in the US, Jamaica, and the UK. She previously worked as a researcher at the British Film Institute, publishing work on her ongoing projects examining representations of race, gender, and place in UK media and centering on the US–Mexico border.

Eugene J. McCann is Assistant Professor of Geography at the Ohio State University. His research interests are in urban geography and urban politics, particularly in the discourses and representational practices at the heart of urban struggle and their relationships to space, place, and scale. His current work is on the relationships between the 'cultural' and the 'economic' in urban studies.

Claire Pavlik is Assistant Professor in Geography at the University of Iowa. Her research in economic geography focuses on structural changes in healthcare and the impacts these changes have on access to care. Her current projects include examining the roles that organizational and electronic networks, including telemedicine, play in institutional strategy, and how changes in healthcare policy shift the location of healthcare delivery and the boundaries between paid and unpaid work.

Michael Petit is Mellon Teaching Fellow at the Center for Teaching, Learning, and Writing and a 2001–2 Seminar Fellow at the John Hope Franklin Institute for Interdisciplinary Studies, Duke University. He teaches courses in writing, literature, and popular culture. His current research project examines the emergence of sodomitical and sapphic identities in the eighteenth-century British novel. He is also the author of the book *Peacekeepers at War* (1986), an examination of US foreign policy in Lebanon.

Eric Sheppard is Professor of Geography and member of the Interdisciplinary Center for the Study of Global Change and the Institute for Social, Ecological, and Economic Sustainability at the University of Minnesota. He is a former editor of *Antipode* and currently co-editor of *Environment and Planning A*. His current research interests include interurban policy and activist networks, the spatiality of globalization, and geographies of the information society. He is co-author of *A World of Difference* (1998) and *A Companion to Economic Geography* (2000).

Melissa W. Wright is Assistant Professor of Geography and Women's Studies at Penn State University. She has published articles in *Environment and Planning A, Antipode, Public Culture, Cultural Anthropology, Social Text,* and *Hypatia: A Journal of Feminist Philosophy.*

Acknowledgments

All of the chapters (with the exception of that by Kevin Cox) were first presented at the 1999 Georgia Conference on "Theorizing Space and Time at the End of the Millennium" which was held April 9–11 in the Department of Geography, University of Georgia. We would like to thank all of the contributors whose work appears in this edited volume for making this collective effort run smoothly. We would also like to thank Paul Plummer (now at the University of Bristol) for his help as a co-organizer of the conference and Julie Graham and Kathy Gibson ("J. K. Gibson-Graham") for agreeing to present their work as the plenary address. We must also give recognition to Dean Wyatt Anderson of the Franklin College of Arts and Sciences of the University of Georgia for providing us with the funds to support the conference, together with the office staff of the Department of Geography for their help in making sure everyone got where they were supposed to be. At Blackwell we would like to thank Sarah Falkus, Katherine Warren, Joanna Pyke, Brian Johnson, Angela Cohen, Jane Hotchkiss, and Cameron Laux.

Placing Scale: An Introduction

Andrew Herod and Melissa W. Wright

We write this introduction at a time when references to things "global" appear to have gained more currency than ever. Most recently, a selectively defined "terrorism" has joined economic restructuring, climate change, environmental degradation, and the AIDS pandemic as issues that warrant "global attention." Hence, global terrorists are seen to be stalking the globe, a global economy is viewed as enveloping everyone in the circuitry of capitalist networks, and global warming is regarded as touching us all. That we have different experiences of these sorts of global phenomena, such that one person's terrorist is another's hero or that the warming climates so devastating for some are a godsend to others who will experience rainfall in once desiccated landscapes, does not alter the widespread belief in the globality of such events. To arrive at this global position is no small achievement, for the global scale is the acme of scales and the power to proclaim the globality of any event is the power to put the world on alert. In such a globalist discourse, the global is presented as the scale apparently from which there is no escape, the place at which there exists no option of disengagement, no safe-haven or untouched corner from which to watch events unfold in different parts of the planet. Presented as global issues, terrorism, capital mobility, climate change, and pandemics of disease are all phenomena for which we pause and consider their impacts.

Given, then, that globalism seems to be the *plat du jour* and that there has been much talk in recent years about an apparent rescaling of contemporary social, economic, and political life, with this collection of essays the individual contributors and ourselves as editors seek to explore the nexus of power and space behind what has come to be known as the "scale question." Collectively, we ask several sets of questions concerning how our world is scaled, how we think about such scaling, and how social actors go about attempting to scale their own activities in ways that allow them to exercise power or that facilitate their denial of power to others. In asking such questions, we bear in mind David Livingstone's (1992: 304) astute comment that "to dictate definition is to wield cultural power." Thus, we ask, how is it that certain events achieve the status of globality while others seem inexorably locked into the local? Why, for instance, was the September 11, 2001 bombing of the World Trade Center regarded as an act of "global" terrorism instead of regarded as an act perpetrated within the sovereign jurisdiction of the United States and thus a "national" or even "local" (New York City) crime? Was it because pictures of the burning twin towers were instantly flashed around the world? If so, then why are the pictures of war victims in, say, Kashmir or Central America which find their way to the world's television sets not considered to be representations of "global" events in the same way? Was it because the WTC victims included people from very many different countries of the world? If so, then why are not the kidnappings and murders of foreign tourists and business people in places such as the Philippines, Colombia, Egypt, and Russia not "global" events in the same way? Was it because of the magnitude of deaths? If so, then why are the thousands of people who are murdered every year in the United States (an estimated 15,517 during 2000, according to the Federal Bureau of Investigation [FBI 2001]), not to mention the hundreds of thousands in other countries across the planet, not considered likewise to be part of a "global" news story? How, in other words, do we determine that terrorist cells – or environmental problems or worker abuses or anything else – around the world represent global threats instead of different kinds of local ones?

Put another way, why was a September 9 bomb attack on an Israeli railway station in the northern coastal town of Nahariya called "regional" violence? Why was the bomb hurled, a few days earlier, at a Catholic girls' school in Belfast called "local" violence? When does an act of violence warrant the formation of an international coalition whose intent is to repel its perpetrators from all corners of the planet? When does a locally situated event merit a global response? Equally, what difference does it make to think of the same event (the bombing of a particular location) in different scalar ways, as a "local" as opposed to as a "global" event? And how are networks of social actors – whether "terrorists" or environmentalists or labor unionists or corporate executives – themselves constituted at different scales and what does this allow them to do or not to do with regard to their social praxis? What, for example, does it mean to talk of a "globally" organized corporation or political organization? The fact that such questions are not so easily answered lends credence, we would suggest, to the keen observation made by the feminist editors of the recent text *Between Woman and Nation* that, rather than thinking of processes of (re)scaling (such as those of globalization) as being seamless and unified, it is the "contradictory and paradoxical character of both totality and disunification that must be accounted for in any [such] analysis" (Kaplan et al. 1999: 3).

Of course, the power behind the labels for discerning between global and local events and subjects is not news to activists who have long battled the politics of scalar discourses. Human rights organizations, for instance, have worked hard to impress the global relevance of their causes – such as working conditions in multinational firms, the pandemic of rape, the international child-sex industry, domestic violence, and planetary environmental degradation – upon a worldwide audience. Yet transforming local organizations into ones with a global constituency and global reach is never easy without some form of supranational structure. Certainly, the United Nations Human Rights Commission has facilitated the efforts of some human rights organizations, such as Amnesty International and Human Rights Watch, to turn local abuses into international concerns. But even with wide international agreement that human rights is a global issue, human rights activists encounter a number of obstacles that inhibit the globalization of their causes, not least of which is that the language of "universal human rights" which many such activists pursue itself implies a global acceptance of a (usually) Western-defined notion of just what constitutes such human rights. Nevertheless, there are global successes for such activists. For instance, the 1995 World Conference on Women in Beijing illustrated how women from all walks of life can meet across the diverse terrain of their localized differences to bring their concerns regarding economic exploitation, emergent patriarchies, reproductive rights, the antagonisms between fundamentalisms and feminisms, and issues of race and imperialism into the global spotlight. Likewise, the protests in Seattle, Prague, and Genoa against the powerful symbols of globalization such as the WTO, IMF, and NAFTA – and against the undermining of a vaguely defined human rights which such entities are accused of facilitating – have revealed how a fight against any event or entity designated as "global" is instantly a fight of global proportion, even if conducted in particular and specific locations. The protestors in these cities have shocked the global corporate community and many governments with their ability to galvanize faith in the existence of a worldwide, anticorporate activism. In the process of transforming "local" disturbances into global activism they have helped to shatter the myth that human rights – or other concerns – could not transcend the local scale. This scalar leap across the semiotic landscape of the local into the global is a powerful leap indeed, as it allows "their protest over there" to become "our protest over here." Those protests, just like the global events to which they are directed, have made us collectively pause. Perhaps, then, David Harvey is on to something when he urges us to trespass the discursive regimes that separate "the local" from "the global" in our efforts to "redefine in a more subtle way the terms and spaces of political struggle open to us in these extraordinary times" (Harvey 2000: 18).

Placing the Scale Question

It would be something of a truism to say that social life is fundamentally scaled and issues of geographic scale are central to how social life is structured and plays out. Equally, how we think about scale fundamentally shapes how we understand social life and its attendant spatiality. Of course, such revelations in and of themselves are not novel, for geographers and others have long looked at various social and natural processes from multiple scales, arguing that what seems evident at one scale may be absent at another – phenomena may appear evenly dispersed across the landscape at one scale but quite concentrated when viewed from another. During the past decade or so, however, there has been an intense theorization of the problematic of scale within the social sciences, largely in response to the tremendous transformations which our world has been experiencing – deindustrialization, the growth of international capital flow, the rise of global communications systems, and easier transportation between places, to name just a few – and the feeling that something new is happening to the way in which social life is scaled. Given that we are largely products of what has come before us, the authors drawn together in this book to address problematics of scale, then, are engaging, in one form or another, with this body of work. Naturally enough, this means that this book's contents have been shaped – whether consciously or not – by the way in which this body of work has evolved. Consequently, while we do not intend to provide a litany of who has said what in this wide-ranging discussion about issues of scale, it is necessary, we feel, to say a few words about some of the major themes around which this work has revolved, so that we may better "place" this current volume. Certainly, we do not claim that we can provide anything but a partial account, but there are a number of matters that this body of work has addressed and which are important to touch upon, albeit briefly.

Three sets of considerations, we believe, are particularly significant. Perhaps the most central of these has concerned debates over the ontological status of scale, specifically whether scale is a material thing that can be "seen" in the landscape or whether it is merely an arbitrary mental device which allows us to make sense of our existence. Hence, some writers have argued that certain scales (the "national," the "global") are real enough but just seem naturally to present themselves as ways of organizing social praxis, whereas others have argued for what Neil Smith (1990) has termed the "social production of scale," wherein scale is conceived of not as a natural metric by which to order the world but one which emerges out of the struggles and compromises between different social actors. Hence, the national scale (in the form of the nation-state), for instance, was only really secured in the seventeenth century with the Treaty of Westphalia (which ended Europe's Thirty Years War) and was only imposed on much of the rest of the world in the nineteenth.[1] Still other writers have argued that scales do not actually exist, in and of themselves, except as convenient mental devices for ordering the world. Such disagreements over the ontological status of scale largely reflect broader divides between those who adhere to materialist epistemologies and those who adhere to idealist epistemologies. Arguably, they have been most evident in debates over the status of "the region." Thus, for instance, whereas for Smith (1990) the regional scale is constituted by the territorial division of labor, for John Fraser Hart (1982: 21) regions are simply "subjective artistic devices... shaped to fit the hand of the individual user." While, in practice, efforts to delimit where one region ends and another begins may be equally difficult for both materialists and idealists, such methodological questions should not be confused with ontological questions concerning the status of the region – for materialists regions exist in the landscape, for idealists they do not.

A second set of issues has concerned how scale is thought about, especially with regard to the metaphors that are marshaled in attempts to conceptualize the ways in which our world is scaled. Such issues reflect recent concerns within the social sciences about language and highlight the influence particularly of poststructuralism and the practices of deconstruction. Certainly, the use of metaphors should not surprise us, for metaphors can be powerful devices for understanding things. However, as deconstruction has taught us, language and metaphor are not innocent. For example, in using metaphor we implicitly recognize that at the very moment at which we say that one object or process is "like another," we are actually saying that it is different from that other object or process, even while we transfer the characteristics of one object or process onto the other. By way of illustration, when the geologist Alfred Wegener first began to write about what would later be called plate tectonics, he used imagery from glaciology and oceanography to describe how continents, "like floating icebergs, drifted farther and farther apart" (quoted in Giere 1988: 230), a metaphor that allowed him to conceptualize the process of continental movement yet which simultaneously constrained him to doing so through an understanding of the dynamics of icebergs and oceans, which have physical and chemical properties quite different from the Earth's crustal plates. Put another way, Wegener's understanding of plate tectonics was both enabled by his use of the iceberg metaphor while it was simultaneously constrained by the limits of early twentieth century knowledge concerning the very dynamics of icebergs.

With regard to geographic scale, then, there are several metaphors that we can employ to help us conceptualize scale in quite different ways. For instance, one way in which scale has frequently been thought of is in terms of the bounding of areal units, with the "urban scale" or the "regional scale" or the "national scale" or the "global scale" being seen to encircle all those within a particular territorial expanse. Thinking in such a manner of scale as a technology of bounding certainly has its uses, for effectively it allows us to divide up space around particular cultural and political markers. Hence, in such a conceptualization of scale it is the scale of the region that binds together, and distinguishes between, places and people considered, say, New Englanders or Southerners, while it is the national scale that allows us to distinguish between, for instance, things French and things German. Implicitly, though, a number of quite different metaphors appear to emerge from such a conceptualization of scale as a device for bounding space. The first of these is that of a ladder, where one climbs up the scalar rungs from the local through the regional and national to the global, or down these rungs from the global through the national and regional to the local. In such a metaphor, the rungs (scales) are connected together by the sidepieces of the ladder yet are quite distinct, the one from another – each rung is a separate entity, even as each is intimately connected to the other rungs to give the whole its structure.

A second metaphor which could just as easily be used to describe the understanding of scale as a tool for bounding space at different geographical resolutions, though, is that of scale as a series of concentric circles, with "smaller" scales such as the local being represented by circles which are closer to the central point (representing the location of the observer) and "larger" scales represented by bigger circles located further from the central point. Moving between scales, then, would be a process of traversing from a central point outwards to ever larger scales in which the global scale, being the most distant circle, is seen to enclose all other scales and yet be "farthest" from the location of the observer. As can be imagined, which of these two metaphors we choose to use will dramatically shape how we think about the scaled relationships between different places and the social actors within those places. In the ladder metaphor, for instance, the global scale is at the top and the local is at the bottom – the global is seen to be, in some senses, "above" the local but is not seen to encompass it. In contrast, using the circle metaphor leaves us in a situation in which the global is neither above nor below the local scale but most definitely is seen to quite literally encircle it. Equally, we might think of such a scaling of our world in terms, perhaps, of Russian Matryoshka ("nesting") dolls – each constituent doll and each constituent scale is separate and distinct and can be considered on its own, but the piece as a whole is only complete with each doll/scale nesting together, such that the dolls and scales fit together in one and only one way (a larger doll/scale simply will not fit inside a smaller one). As with the circle metaphor, there is no scale that is "above" another in the vertical sense that the ladder metaphor suggests, though the global scale (the outside doll) is "larger" than all the other scales and does contain within itself all these other "smaller" scales.

These, of course, are not the only metaphors upon which we could draw to make sense of our scaled world. Indeed, the inundation of our lives by computers appears to have spawned growing use of the metaphor of the network, which now seems to pervade our thinking about social relationships. Thus, as Mulgan (1991: 19–20) has suggested:

> The spread of electronic networks has been matched by a widespread use of the network as a logical device or metaphor, something that is good to think with ... Computers have done much to spread familiarity with the idea of logical rather than physical space, with their topological representations of flow diagrams, branching trees and other patterns ... Examples of this change include systems theories of society and cognitive psychology, both of which model systems in logical space. And whereas in the eighteenth and nineteenth centuries the workings of the brain or of societies were conceived as analogous to those of the loom or the steam engine, both are today conceived as complex networked systems for producing and processing information.

Hence, whereas thinking about scale in terms of bounded units of space may lead us to particular conceptualizations of the relationships between places, use of the network metaphor may help articulate a very different sense of scale and the scaled relationships within which people and places are bound, a sense in which specific places are seen as simultaneously global and local (and regional and national) without being wholly one or the other. Thus, Bruno Latour (1996: 370) has suggested that the world's complexity cannot be captured by "notions of levels, layers, territories, [and] spheres," and should not be thought of as being made up of discreet levels of bounded spaces which fit together neatly, as if scales could be stacked one above the other or fitted together in much the same way that Matryoshka dolls are contained one within another. Instead, he avers, the world needs to be understood as being networked together, as being "fibrous, thread-like, wiry, stringy, ropy, capillary[,]" descriptors that generate quite disparate understandings of the relationships between places and of scale.

Latour's description of how places are networked together, then, invokes very different metaphors for understanding how our world is scaled than do those discussed above. For instance, if we accept his description then we might choose to think of scale in terms of the root system of a tree or perhaps in terms of the tunnels made by earthworms in which the roots or tunnels overlap and are intertwined through different strata of soil. Certainly, some roots and tunnels lie in deeper soil strata than do others, but within the root or tunnel system as a whole it may be quite difficult to determine precisely where the boundaries of one layer of roots or tunnels (what we might see as one "scale") end and those of another begin, unlike the case of the ladder's rungs or the concentric circles or the Matryoshka dolls. Furthermore, it is possible for surface roots to dig deep down into the soil and for deeper roots to send shoots towards the surface. In such a representation, it makes little sense to talk of scale in terms of bounded spaces or in terms of the metrics of the clearly defined hierarchies of Euclidean space. Indeed, what exactly does it mean to talk of a "larger" scale or a "higher" scale if we use the metaphor of earthworm burrows? Does it make sense to talk any more of the global scale as "encompassing" the local if both are seen to be "located" at the respective ends of such burrows?

Obviously, there are yet other metaphors within our reach. In comparing all of these metaphors, however, we do not try here to suggest that one is necessarily better or worse than any other in some absolute sense. Such metaphors do not so much represent different material situations (so that one can be picked as being empirically more correct than another) as they represent different ways of thinking about and describing the material reality of our changing world. Thus, we should not confuse the changing of the metaphors we use to describe our world with a changing of the material relationships between places in that world. At the same time, though, the way the world appears to be scaled *is* a direct reflection of how we choose to represent it scale-wise. Hence, while changing our metaphor does not change the way the world is materially, it does change the ways in which we engage with our world and how we think about the possibilities for changing it, for systems of tree roots, ladders, concentric circles, and Matryoshka dolls are quite different images for shaping our thoughts about the world!

Following further the concern for the language which we use to think about scale, it is also apparent that much writing about scale has tended to be somewhat dualistic in its orientation, especially with regard to processes of globalization. Hence, globalization is most usually contrasted against the localization of social life, whether that is in terms of arguments about the "glocalization" of the nation-state in which the nation-state's powers are said to have been undermined by a transfer of capacities both to supranational and to local political entities, whether it is in terms of arguments about the glocalization of corporations in which transnational corporations must be global in reach but must tailor their products to local tastes (what Mair [1997] has called firms' need for "strategic localization"), whether it is in terms of arguments about the evisceration of the power of the local within a globalized world political economy, or whether it is in terms of arguments that globalization paradoxically brings with it the resurgence of localism, be that expressed in terms such as those used by Harvey (1989: 294) – who suggests that "[a]s spatial barriers diminish so we become much more sensitized to what the world's spaces contain," so that local variations in profit rates become much more important to global capital than ever before – or those of the cultural Jihad (Barber 1995) which the McDonaldization of the world appears to be catalyzing. Certainly, the global and the local are also sometimes each contrasted with other scales such as the national or the regional but, as the apparent two extremes of the scalar discourse, it is the global and the local which, we would suggest, are most usually thought of in dualistic terms. Indeed, one might even go so far as to suggest that discourses of both globalization and of localization *require* dualistic thought to give them capacity – the global gains its identity through being contrasted with the local, and vice versa. Thus, many representations of globalization require perceiving of the local as relatively impotent – that is, after all, why actors need to "go global." Equally, those representations which laud the continued or even increased power of the local – doing so either as a way of undermining the rhetoric of globalization (rhetoric which tries to subjugate the local) or of associating the local with a vibrant politics of difference (the case with much postmodern identity politics) – also often incorporate such dualistic thinking by suggesting that the local is, in fact, a refuge from the tyranny of the global and the discourse of globalization. In the case of postmodern identity politics, this latter appears to be particularly ironic, given the important work in that vein that has sought to question dualistic modes of thought.

If questions about the ontological status of scale and about the representations of scale that we use to think about how our world is structured are two central interrogatories which have driven critical reflection upon the problematic of scale during the past decade or so, a third set of questions involves what might be called the politics of actually producing scale. Thus, what exactly does it mean to talk of a "rescaling" of social praxis? What exactly are the social, cultural, economic, and political practices in which corporations, labor unions, environmental activists, and others engage to "produce scale"? For some, questions of the politics of producing scale have meant thinking about how social actors reorganize themselves from one spatial resolution to another. Hence, corporations are often said to "go global" by "scale jumping" from operating solely within the bounds of a particular nation-state to operating in multiple regions around the world. Likewise, local labor unions may "go national" in a dispute by seeking resources from sympathizers in other parts of a particular country or by developing collective bargaining agreements at the national level. Equally, they may choose to "go local" by breaking out of national collective bargaining agreements so that they can take advantage of local conditions when they bargain. In such cases, then, the process of rescaling is often presented as one in which social actors in a sense "relocate" their operations from one scale to another through this practice of jumping scales. In others, the concern has been to analyze not how social actors jump from one scale to another but to explore how they negotiate their ways through different scales or how they operate on multiple scales at the same time. Practices of scale jumping and negotiation, then, can be interpreted as instances of social actors producing new scales of economic and political organization for themselves in a process of "becoming" – becoming national, for instance.

However, whereas some commentators have suggested that scale jumping or scale negotiation are instances of social actors remaking the geographical resolutions of their own organization through their praxis and that this then represents a production of scale, others have suggested that, paradoxically, such representations of the rescaling of our contemporary world have rather uncritically incorporated a view of scale which prioritizes the scales themselves rather than the processes which constitute them, so that scales serve largely as the skeletal structure within which, and between which, social life takes place. For such critics, it is as if scales such as the "global" and the "local" – together with other scales – have been conceived of as already-existing spatial resolutions (even if socially produced) between which, and among which, social actors simply relocate themselves (Herod 2001: 126). While there is a recognition that scales themselves are real enough things and that they are not simply given by nature or some divine entity, representations of scale jumping and negotiating, then, can tend towards reifying scales themselves as objects that have a life of their own. In such a representation, the notion that social actors have successfully jumped from one scale of organization to another as part of their spatial praxis or that they have negotiated their way between, say, the local and the global scale, or that they have successfully managed to operate at several spatial scales simultaneously, misses the point that scales do not exist except through the social practices by which they are, in fact, constituted. To talk of jumping from one scale of organization to another can be seen to separate scales as social products from the social practices that create them, such that scales are in some ways seen as capable of existing independently of the social practices through which they are constantly reconfigured. For such critics, then, social actors do not "jump" from one scale to another but, rather, they actually *constitute* scale through their social praxis. Put another way, if we were to seek parallels in the literature discussing the "production of space," such a distinction would be the difference between talking about how social actors operate *in* and *across* space, and how they actually *produce* space as an integral part of their social praxis.

Of course, regardless of how the politics of producing scale is thought of, this politics must recognize the uneven resources of power, money, information, and time upon which different social actors rely in their pursuit of the production of scale. There is, then, no equivalent of the World Trade Organization for activists, who rarely enjoy the luxury of a meeting of their constituent members or the granting by nation-states of *carte blanche* to their efforts in forging binding agreements. By contrast, transnational corporations, buoyed by discourses of the global merit to free trade and the minimizing of barriers to international capital flows, have experienced comparative ease in making the case that their welfare is an issue of global concern which requires government facilitation of their global efforts. Moreover, they enjoy the clout and effective power that supranational governmental organizations, such as the World Trade Organization and International Monetary Fund, bring to their perspective. Equally, the impediments placed by, say, international immigration laws restricting the movement of people (especially poor people) across borders, together with the innumerable laws making it hard to engage in political organizing across international borders, add to the real difficulties faced by activists who are often working with impoverished and politically disenfranchised communities that are separated by linguistic and cultural differences. Effectively, such laws seek to localize poor peoples at a supposed time of growing planetary spatial integration of capital flows, goods and services, information, and wealthy people. Apparently, despite the one-world rhetoric of neoliberalism, some people face tremendous obstacles in linking their worlds and becoming fully-fledged citizens of the "global village" about which we hear so much.

Structure of the Book

Finally, we want to say a word or two about the structure of what follows. Specifically, we have tried to organize the chapters below around the three themes of "theorizing scale," "rhetorics of scale," and "scales of praxis." We would be the first to admit that these divisions are somewhat artificial and would probably collapse upon close examination. However, we have chosen this method of organization in the hope that it will give at least some structure to what follows, structure that will help the reader join us in thinking about issues of geographic scale and their import from a number of different angles. In particular, in the first section we have put together four chapters that address, in different ways, issues of the global–local dualism around which much thought concerning scale has often revolved. We feel that such an interrogation is especially needed at a time when the discourse of "globalization" appears to have infiltrated virtually every other discourse that has bearing upon our lives. The second section includes three essays that all examine how rhetorics of scale have been deployed at various times and with various consequences. The final section contains three essays, all exploring how various social actors have tried to construct scales of social, political, and economic organization that have helped them in the pursuit of their spatial objectives.

Our goal, then, has been to present a number of perspectives into how the politics of scale weave into our experience of place. This politics is inherently geographical. It is the politics governing our perception of the distance between ourselves and the systems of power that enmesh us. How we understand this distance is instantly and always a question of power and geography, and its exploration requires an inquiry into the spatial dynamics linking individual agency to structures of power. Some scholars have explored this distance as an issue of the discursive regulation that directly affects our sense of agency and our visions for structural change. Others have focused more forcefully on the material dimensions to structures of governance and their enforcement. Here, we present essays that span these approaches into investigations of place and power through the rubric of scale. In so doing, our intent is not to provide a cipher through which to understand the problematic of scale but, rather, to encourage further dialogue into how conceptions and visions of scale inform all aspects of social life. At a time when the world seems to be lining up around alliances over a thing called "global terrorism," we believe this discussion could not be more pressing.

NOTE

1   Among its provisions, the 1648 Treaty of Westphalia legally established the notion of the territorial integrity of each nation-state (even those which had been defeated in war) and the primacy of the nation-state over its citizenry. Although often ignored in practice, the Treaty also held that states should not interfere in the internal affairs of other states.

REFERENCES

Barber, B. 1995: *Jihad vs. McWorld*. New York: Ballantine.
FBI (Federal Bureau of Investigation). 2001: Crime in the United States, 2000. Press release, dated Oct. 22, FBI National Press Office, United States Dept. of Justice, Washington, DC. Available at www.fbi.gov/pressrel/pressrel01/cius2000.htm (accessed 10/25/01).
Giere, R. N. 1988: *Explaining Science: A Cognitive Approach*. Chicago: University of Chicago Press.
Hart, J. F. 1982: The highest form of the geographer's art. *Annals of the American Association of Geographers*, 72 (1), 1–29.
Harvey, D. 1989: *The Condition of Postmodernity*. Oxford: Blackwell.
Harvey, D. 2000: *Spaces of Hope*. Berkeley: University of California Press.

Herod, A. 2001: *Labor Geographies: Workers and the Landscapes of Capitalism.* Guilford: New York.

Kaplan, C., Alarcón, N., and Moallem, M. (eds) 1999: *Between Woman and Nation: Nationalisms, Transnational Feminisms, and the State.* Durham: Duke University Press.

Latour, B. 1996: On actor-network theory: A few clarifications. *Soziale Welt,* 47, 369–81.

Livingston, D. 1992: *The Geographical Tradition: Episodes in the History of a Contested Enterprise.* Oxford: Blackwell.

Mair, A. 1997: Strategic localization: The myth of the postnational enterprise. In K. Cox (ed.), *Spaces of Globalization: Reasserting the Power of the Local,* New York: Guilford, 64–88.

Mulgan, G. J. 1991: *Communication and Control: Networks and the New Economies of Communication.* New York: Guilford.

Smith, N. 1990: *Uneven Development: Nature, Capital and the Production of Space* (2nd ed.). Oxford: Blackwell.

Part I

Theorizing Scale

Introduction: Theorizing Scale

Andrew Herod and Melissa W. Wright

There has been much made in recent theorizing in the social sciences and humanities about processes of globalization. Indeed, it is arguable that "globalization" has become the intellectual and political leitmotif of the past two decades. Whether as material process or as ideological cover for neoliberalism, globalization appears to have colonized the lifeworld of many intellectuals, politicians, business leaders, labor union officials, political activists, and "ordinary" men and women in the street. Frequently, the process of globalization is portrayed as one in which the global scale of existence and social operation has become the only scale which really matters any more, such that whomever can control the global can effectively outmaneuver and dominate those operating at all other scales. Particularly with regard to capital, the ability of corporations to "go global" is often seen as the trump card which will allow the imagineers of a neoliberalized planetary economy to secure most readily their goals and so to inscribe a new world economic and political order with its attendant histories and geographies. Likewise, those groups such as labor unions and environmental activists who are opposed to neoliberal corporate agendas regularly talk about the necessity of developing global strategies with which they can challenge such agendas, although the rhetoric of such groups often simultaneously seems implicitly to concede the global scale to capital even as it seeks to challenge capital's command over the global – whereas for some the well-worn slogan of "think globally, act locally" may highlight the possibilities and potentialities of local action, for others it seems to suggest that "acting globally" is something which only capital and its organizations appear able to pull off, with the rest of us confined only to the ability to act locally.

It is within this context, then, that the set of essays in this first section of the book are located. In particular the following essays interrogate some of this received (and perceived) wisdom concerning globalization by questioning how we think about "the global" in relation to a variety of issues. They seek both to question how the global has been conceptualized in much writing about globalization and what some of the consequences of this are for the ways in which we experience processes of globalization. For example, in the first chapter in this section J. K. Gibson-Graham critically examines the global-local binary around which much discussion of globalization has revolved. Her essay delves into the asymmetrical dynamic linking concepts of "the global" to its binary and oppositional twin, "the local." By reviewing how the global is associated with strength, domination, and action, while the local is invariably coded as weakness, acquiescence, and passivity, Gibson-Graham illustrates the imbalance by which the global is accepted as the scale at which capital is seen to hold political and economic sway over the ever-impotent local. In such a representation of the changes taking place in our contemporary world, she argues, the global "appears as a telos on the move in the ongoing process called 'globalization'" while the local appears static and immobile, insufficient and inherently subordinate. The result, she suggests, is a conceptualization of the world that overwhelms any vision for achieving political change at the local scale. In opposing such a conceptualization, and as part of an effort to build a politics which might just challenge the global stance assumed by neoliberal prescriptions for our collective futures, Gibson-Graham outlines two strategies for action, these being deconstruction and what she calls practices of resubjectivation.

With regard to the first of these strategies, Gibson-Graham attempts to dislodge the comfortable heuristic that has positioned the global and the local within a binary hierarchy of power. More precisely, through the process of deconstruction she attempts to shake loose the local from its association with weakness, subordination, and passivity, while simultaneously undermining the connections between the global and power, mastery, and activity. Such a strategy, she suggests, allows us to recognize that such constructions are not fixed as the result of some kind of divine fiat but emerge, rather, from the very discourse of globalization itself. Indeed, discourses of globalization, whether of a neoliberal or proletarian internationalist bent, require just such a dualism to give them purchase – without such a dualism, there would be little impetus for processes of globalization, for it is the ability to go global which is seen as giving us the power to do things which would be beyond our reach if we were to remain local. Significantly, part of the power of the neoliberal dis-course about globalization has been its ability to associate the global/local dualism with another powerful dualism, that of capital-ism/noncapitalism, such that virtually every activity taking place within what are known as "capitalist economies" is perceived to be "capitalist" activity. In such a view, imagining noncapitalist activities becomes extremely difficult: following the logic of the global/local dualism, "capitalist" ventures are seen to penetrate and colonize all economic activities, whereas "noncapitalist" activities are assumed to be feeble, forceless, and doomed to failure when placed into competi-tion with the "realities" of "the" [singular] capitalist market.

Following from this process of deconstruction, with regard to the second strategy – creating new political and economic subjects in the face of globalization – Gibson-Graham recounts a series of work-shops and local interventions conducted in the north east of the United States and in south east Australia. These were aimed at creat-ing a discourse of economic and social development "in which the economy is diverse (rather than primarily capitalist) and economic dynamics are multiple (rather than limited to the quest for profitabil-ity and the law of the market) and overdetermined (rather than nat-urally dominant)." Through these projects, Gibson-Graham and her colleagues have attempted to create a space for practices and for a politics that are "anticapitalocentric" – that is to say, practices and a politics that challenge the belief in the global hegemony of capital-ism, that facilitate recognition of, and engagement with, "noncapital-ist" forms of economic development, and that foster alternative economic subjects. In challenging the identity of the economy as sin-gularly capitalist, and in challenging the subjection of localities to the global, she submits, the framework in which globalization (together with the attributes so frequently associated with the global) formerly appeared to make sense as a single economic process disappears. In its stead emerges the possibility of creating a transformative politics which does not rely upon a singular strategy to counter neoliberal globalization – that of mobilizing globally – but which presents mul-tiple avenues for challenging neoliberalism, including (but not limited to) "going global."

If the chapter by Gibson-Graham focuses upon destabilizing the global/local dualism with regard to the project of creating a trans-formative politics of economic development, the second chapter in this section, by Eugene McCann, examines how such a dualism has been incorporated within recent urban scholarship – particularly that concerning what has become known as the "global/world cities literature" – and what some of the consequences of this are for theorizing contemporary urban geographies. The crux of McCann's argument is that, whether consciously or not, much of the literature which has focused within urban studies during the past twenty years or so on the phenomenon of global/world cities – that is to say, those cities which have a disproportionate share of corporate headquarters and advanced producer-service firms – has reproduced a dualistic mode of understanding and representation. Specifically, McCann suggests that much urban theorizing has tended to be bifurcated between, on the one hand, research on the world's largest cities (London, New York, Los Angeles) which are said to have exhibited signs of "globalness" and, on the other, research on cities which, almost by definition, are deemed to be "ordinary," "less global," or "local" cities. Indeed, it is these latter which are used as the benchmarks for determining just how global the former group of cities is – as in Gibson-Graham's piece, we see how dualistic thinking serves to define one thing in regard to what is conceived of as its opposite. Hence, the experiences of cities such as London, New York, and Los Angeles are taken to be templates with which urban processes everywhere can be understood.

Certainly, we would not expect processes of globalization to play out evenly across the urban landscape – after all, this would ignore the very uneven development of landscapes that is the hallmark of capitalism – and, for sure, this is not McCann's argument. Rather, McCann submits that the way in which the global/world cities literature has constructed a dualism between those cities that have been understood to be showing evidence of globalization and those that have not has led to some problematic comprehensions of contemporary urban change. For McCann, then, the question is not whether or not processes of globalization have played out in a geographically and historically uneven manner but, instead, how the global/world cities literature has taken particular pieces of evidence as signs of globalness and then sought to evaluate other cities' globalness using such metrics. Put another way, the global/world cities argument relies upon a tautology that insists that the evidence of a city's globality lies in those things cited to represent such evidence. In other words, if particular kinds of evidence are all that we are looking for, then that is all that we will see. In turn, the absence of those kinds of global indicators in other places effectively removes them from scrutiny, since the very absence of such evidence is taken to mean they are, as yet, unaffected by globalization. Herein lies the logic of the synecdoche by which the bits and pieces of places come to represent the whole.

For McCann such synecdochal thinking results in two significant implications. First, how we understand processes of globalization as they play out in, and have impacts upon, particular cities appears to be merely a reflection of what we determine to be evidence of globalization itself. In short, a different metric for determining globalness will give us a different hierarchy of cities most affected by globalization, perhaps substituting Cleveland for Los Angeles, Cleethorpes for London, and so forth. Second, it ignores the fact that in other "less global" cities (at least as determined by the metrics used in mainstream global/world cities research) processes of globalization may indeed have an impact upon the built environment, yet in ways that we do not recognize due to the fact that our metric places observational and conceptual blinkers upon us. The solution to such problems is not to attempt to find some "objective" metric of globalism that will allow us to determine more effectively in some optimum fashion cities' globalness. Instead, we must recognize that what we see will always be shaped by how we understand "globalization" and its embodiments. Rather than resorting to the chimera of "objective" measures by which to better determine globalness/nonglobalness, we must reexamine how we conceptualize scale and the language with which we talk about globalization. Much as is the case with the chapter by Gibson-Graham, then, McCann's chapter ends with a discussion of how a new analytical language for understanding place may be useful in developing an urban studies that does not implicitly privilege the global scale of analysis.

Following from this questioning of how much literature in the humanities and social sciences has theorized scale (particularly with regard to globalization and the global), the chapter by Kevin Cox considers how globalization has been seen to be influencing the nation-state, particularly within what has come to be known as the "regulation approach" to understanding the relationship between capital and the state. Rather provocatively, Cox suggests that, as adopted by many to understand material practices under globalization, the regulation approach has, in fact, significant shortfalls with regard to its theorization of the rescaling of the activities of the state. Thus, Cox avers that arguments which suggest that a new "scalar fix" is emerging for the state as a result of processes of globalization – a new scalar fix variously described as the "hollowing out of the state" or "glocalization" – have failed to incorporate the complexity of what is occurring, particularly with regard to claims about what is happening at the sub-national scale. For example, Cox submits that while it may be true that some national governments are showing interest in developing self-propelling growth regions – which might be taken as evidence of a hollowing out of the nation-state or glocalization – "this has by no means had as a necessary concomitant devolution of authority" which the hollowing out and glocalization theses assume. The cause of these shortfalls, he maintains, is regulation theory's fostering of a problematic separation of the economic from the political and its incorporation of a rather simplistic view of matters spatial.

By way of contrast to a regulation theory approach, Cox proposes that three concepts – capital's geographic division of labor, the contradiction between capital's need for fixity and for mobility, and the scale division of labor – taken together provide at least some partial steps towards understanding the state's changing scalar fixes in a much more productive and theoretically rigorous manner. The combining of these three concepts, he proposes, provides a way of examining how territorially based alliances of state and capital (and, we might also add, labor), which are dependent upon localized social relations, struggle to defend and/or improve their positions in the geographic division of labor. In the process, commodity chains are often lengthened and scale divisions of labor experience transformation. Thus, Cox asserts, whereas "an account of the role of relations of local dependence and the formation of coalitions to defend and enhance the flow of value through local social relations is conspicuously lacking" in regulation theory-inspired accounts of hollowing out/glocalization, it is only by taking them into account that struggles over the new scalar fixes of the state which appear to be emerging can really be understood. Furthermore, such a focus on struggle shifts analytical attention from regulation theory's concern with spatial order – that is to say, with how the state seeks to impose regulatory fixes through which both macro- and microeconomic balance may be maintained – and redirects the analytical gaze to questions of how the economic landscape is fashioned in particular ways through processes of conflict and compromise, victory and defeat.

The final chapter in this section takes us back, in some ways, to issues with which we started, namely theorizing the relationship between the global and the local and, in particular, thinking about the language and metaphors that are used to do so. In this final chapter, then, Alan Latham argues that much theorizing about the effects of globalization and the rescaling of everyday life has failed to capture the complexity of what is occurring, largely because it has tended to see scale in terms of fixed levels or spatial resolutions, a view which draws upon linear, Euclidean views of space. In contrast, he suggests that a more productive way of conceptualizing contemporary processes of globalization as they relate to scale is that of actor-networks. Such an approach, Latham argues, can help articulate a sense of the ways in which specific places are constructed simultaneously as both global and local without being wholly either. Thus, drawing on the work of Michel Serres and Bruno Latour, he submits that the world is made up of myriad intertwinings of actor-networks or, as Latour puts it, the world is "fibrous, thread-like, wiry, stringy, ropy, capillary." Implicitly, this is a nonlinear and non-Euclidean representation of scale and space. Changing from a language which talks about the science of stable and well-defined distances (and, we might add, stable and well-defined geographic scales) to one which talks of nearness and rifts takes us from thinking about space and scale in terms of geometry and towards thinking about space and scale in terms of topology.

In order to explore such issues, Latham examines processes of urban change in Auckland, New Zealand. Specifically, he looks at how an old Victorian and Edwardian retail and service strip which had fallen on hard times by the 1960s has been transformed into an affluent, cosmopolitan area of fashionable restaurants. Through looking at the life story of the French/New Zealand owner and chief chef of one particular restaurant, Latham interrogates questions of globality and localness, asking questions about how "global" and how "local" is either this owner or the restaurant of which he is the proprietor. For instance, in some ways this restaurant could be seen as globalizing the epicurean opportunities in this part of Auckland, for its owner/chief chef is a classically trained French chef cooking Mediterranean fusion cuisine in a gourmet pizza restaurant. On the other hand, however, the fact that this particular restaurant owner employs local inhabitants as staff, uses locally obtained produce, and has sought to develop a sense of the *habitus* of his clientele so that he may better cater to their tastes can also be read as an effort by this foreign proprietor to localize himself. As Latham suggests, the activities of this particular social actor can be read both as globalizing Auckland's culinary landscape and as the chef's attempt to localize himself within the social networks of the city. The question thus arises: has our owner/chef gone global by moving from France to New Zealand and bringing with him the skills and culinary repertoire of his homeland, or has he gone local as he has embedded himself within the urban fabric of Auckland, or, indeed, has he gone national as he has situated himself within the New Zealand nation-state? Answering such questions, Latham avers, requires thinking not in terms of static levels between which actors negotiate their lives but, rather, in terms of how social practices are not "tightly tied to a single territory but are on the move, circulating through the world, separating and combining in complex and highly fluid ways." A topological approach, rooted in actor-network theory, he concludes, provides "a way of making sense of these kinds of non-scalar spatialities, as well as an avenue through which to break down apparent divisions between scales into more analytically useful accounts."

1

Beyond Global vs. Local: Economic Politics Outside the Binary Frame

J. K. Gibson-Graham

Rumination 1

Recently we gave a talk at a US university on "Imagining and Enacting Noncapitalist Futures" – a discussion of our action research projects in the Pioneer Valley of New England, USA and the Latrobe Valley of SE Australia. We were aware of a senior Marxist geographer sitting in the back row, listening attentively. Near the end of the question and answer period, after some urging, he made his intervention. Our material was interesting, he said, but it wasn't compelling. We failed to acknowledge the power of global economic dynamics and the force of political conservatism that could squash alternative economic experiments of the kind we had described. We seemed oblivious to the many historical examples of local endeavors that had ended in disbandment, defeat, and disgrace.

Cast, yet again, as the Pollyannas of the profession, we initially accepted this cold blast of "realism" as a sobering footnote to our presentation about imagining and becoming. But in retrospect we are less willing to allow this belittling reaction to stand unchallenged. Where, we ask ourselves, does the desire to speak the power of global forces originate? Why was this person's global perspective, his "everything dealt with" analysis, so convincing to others in the room?[1] And why did so many young people in the audience want to retain a critical or even cynical stance and to accept his view that the forces of globalization were inevitably more powerful than progressive, grassroots, local interventions?

Rumination 2

After a presentation at an Australian university where we talked about the work of ENGENDER, a Singapore-based NGO engaged in alternative livelihood projects with women in South East Asia, an incredulous Pacific historian derided us: "Do you really think that by earning $1,000 a year from selling village craft goods to international tourist resorts, rural Indonesian households will be able to prevent their daughters from being exploited in the Nike factory across the Straits?"

This response resonated with that of our disciplinary master. The historian appeared to scorn the hopefulness attached to the telling of small stories at the local level. Indeed, he was offended by the airspace we devote to such material. "Why waste the time of serious people with such trivia?" he seemed to say.

Rumination 3

On many occasions we have used the story of Mondragon to illustrate the possibilities and potentialities of local experiments. The Mondragon Co-operative Corporation (MCC) is a complex of industrial co-operatives in the Basque region of Spain that is famed for its almost 40,000 workers, as well as its successes in international markets and the panoply of service sector co-ops (in addition to the industrial co-ops) that provide banking, venture capital, research and development, and educational, health, and retailing services to co-op members and others. On one occasion, a senior industrial geographer came up to discuss the Mondragon case with us after a presentation that had focused largely upon our own community-based action research. Our friend was clearly relieved that we had made mention of Mondragon, a noncapitalist organization that was large and impressive, compared to the small-scale experiments that seemed – according to a cultural geographer in the audience – like "old-style, feel-good community development." Moreover, it was clear that the MCC's recent foray out of the Basque region to set up factories in international locations (North Africa, Europe, and Thailand) was somehow reassuring to this progressive and committed individual. That the MCC appeared to be "upscaling" just like capitalist multinationals was a cause for celebration. Had the very successful network of co-operatives remained local, regional, or even national, their power would have been questionable in his eyes.

Why, we have begun to wonder, do local projects stimulate these kinds of reactions? In all of them, as in our own responses, we recognize something visceral. The disavowal or denunciation of attempts to elaborate a localized economic politics seems to emanate from a bodily state, not simply a reasoned intellectual position. For many, it seems, recourse to the obviousness of global power provides a form of comfort, one that we find difficult to replicate or displace.

Familiarity Breeds Contempt: The Local Versus the Global

We are all familiar with the denigration of the local as small and relatively powerless, defined and confined by the global: the global is a force, the local is its field of play; the global is penetrating, the local penetrated and transformed. Globalism is synonymous with abstract space, the frictionless movement of money and commodities, the expansiveness and inventiveness of capitalism and the market. But its Other, localism, is coded as place, community, defensiveness, bounded identity, *in situ* labor, noncapitalism, the traditional.[2]

Of course, in such a representation localities are not passive, or not entirely so. They interact in the process of transformation, creating a heterogeneous landscape of globalization – but somehow global dominance is untransformed in the interaction. Thus, it is the global that appears as a telos on the move in the ongoing process called "globalization." The association of globalization with capital lends energy to the global and compounds the subordination of the local. Not only are localities subsumed as interior to the global, but noncapitalist economic activities involving households, collectives, independent producers, barter networks, etc. – all ostensibly local – are seen as contained and ultimately dominated by a global capitalist economy.

For instance, in their depictions of "geographical rescaling," writers such as Erik Swyngedouw, Neil Smith, and David Harvey invoke the association between capital, power, and the global. Thus Swyngedouw (1997: 170, inserts ours) argues that:

> Changes in scales of production/reproduction can go either upwards or downwards, but will always express new power relations and shift the balance more to one side than another. Over the past decades, it has been mainly capital that "jumped" upwards [to the global scale], while in many cases (and with varying degrees of resistance) the regulation of labor moved downwards [to the local scale].

Upscaling (globalization) seems to be the prerogative of capital and downscaling (localization) the forced option for labor. According to

Smith (1993) and Swyngedouw (1997), then, the new "gestalt of scale" is one in which the global is appropriating more power.[3] Add to this Harvey and Swyngedouw's (1993) assessment that

> oppositional groups, whether organized around working-class, gender, environmental or other politics, are usually much better and empowering in their strategies to organize in place, but often disempowered and fragmented when it comes to building alliances and organizing collaboration over space. (quoted in Swyngedouw 1997: 176)

In their view globalization ("the global control of money flows and competitive whirlwinds of 'glocal' industrial, financial, cultural and political corporations and institutions") *requires* that local struggles be conducted on a larger scale, using "co-ordinated action, cross-spatial alliances and effective solidarity" (Swyngedouw 1997: 176).

However, Harvey, Swyngedouw, and Smith seem captured by the vision that power inheres in greater size and spatial extensiveness and that real opposition must involve formal interplace organization.[4] The limits of large entities (including the manifold failures of MNCs and large nation-states to enact their will) and the effectivity of small ones (chaos theory's affirmation of the saying that a butterfly flapping its wings can affect the weather half a world away) are not sufficient to dislodge their belief in the boundless power of the global and the relative impotence of the local. Their interest in globalization is to understand it, expose it, and, hopefully, transform it, but they are not attracted to the local as a site of realistic challenge and possibility.[5]

In the book *Empire* (which is their name for the emerging global form of governance/subjection), Michael Hardt and Antonio Negri (2000: 206) concur with this vision of the appropriate scale for an oppositional politics:

> We believe that toward the end of challenging and resisting Empire and its world market, it is necessary to pose any alternative at an equally global level. Any proposition of a particular community in isolation, defined in racial, religious, or regional terms, "delinked" from Empire, shielded from its powers by fixed boundaries, is destined to end up as a kind of ghetto. Empire cannot be resisted by a project aimed at a limited, local autonomy.

Place-based politics and the localization of struggles are denigrated by them (2000: 45) as inherently regressive:

> This Leftist strategy of resistance to globalization and defense of locality is also damaging because in many cases what appear as local

identities are not autonomous or self-determining but actually feed into and support the development of the capitalist imperial machine. The globalization and deterritorialization operated by the imperial machine is not in fact opposed to localization or reterritorialization, but rather sets in play mobile and modulating circuits of differentiation and identification. The strategy of local resistance misidentifies and thus masks the enemy.

It is not, then, that local struggles are insufficiently powerful to counter global forces, in Hardt and Negri's view, but that local struggles actually cede power to an expansive capitalism by fragmenting the "global multitude" and blinding them to the "real alternative and the potentials for liberation that exist *within* Empire" (2000: 46). Unless resistance operates in certain global ways, it is tainted and reactionary. Local activism, when it involves defense of locality, invites forms of identification that privilege differentiation. Supported by postmodern theory, this kind of politics merely yokes uniqueness into a hegemonic power field – Empire.[6]

Rumination 4

In our related action research projects in different parts of the world we have employed a vision of diverse community economies as a way of conversing about alternative development pathways that do not conform to the new global (capitalist) "order." We are eager not to have these projects sequestered in a second-class domain – seen as worthy and interesting, perhaps, but as failing to challenge the power of global forces. Yet our language repeatedly exposes us to familiar difficulties and dangers. "Community" is often associated with place, with the local, and also with the confined and constrained. And "diversity" conjures images of a fragmentary politics of identity – the very enemy of the "collective resistance" that is the only hope of many antiglobalization theorists. We are treading on treacherous ground here, fractured by the fault line of global versus local.

Perhaps it is the power differential embedded in the binaries of global and local, space and place, that is responsible for the hostile or incredulous responses we receive (and indeed we do try to receive rather than simply to repel them). As with any such binary formulation within Western knowledge systems, superior power is already distributed to the primary or master term. Inevitably, then, projects of valuing the subordinate term come up against the always already-unequal allocation. Given this condition, local stories are patently ridiculous as ammunition for challenging the dominance and power of the global.

But since the local is the space of politics for most economic activists, it seems that we need to question its positioning as interior to the global and as a second best (or worse) political terrain. This repositioning of the local has already been done any number of times – but in the so-called era of globalization it is continually being undone and needs to be done again.

Challenging the Global/Local Binary

We have identified two strategies for challenging the power of the global/local binary. The first involves the tools of deconstruction, the theoretical intervention that has been so effective in shaking loose static identities that constrain thought and politics (Gibson-Graham 2000). The other involves practices of resubjectivation, a set of embodied interventions that attempt to confront and reshape the ways in which we live and enact the power of the global. While the former strategy is the more familiar, the latter seems to us more likely to be efficacious, since it addresses the deep affective substrate of our subjection to globalization.

Turning first to the resources of deconstruction, we find "global" and "local" positioned in a familiar hierarchy wherein each derives meaning from the other. The global is represented as sufficient, whole, powerful, and transformative in relation to which the local is deficient, fragmented, weak, and acted upon. Critics have attempted to destabilize this identity structure in a number of ways. In surveying this well-trodden critical ground yet again, we have resorted to a set of annotated signposts, dividing the challenges into those that see global and local as different "perspectives," those that see them as somehow "the same," and those that see both sides of the binary as referring to specific processes that are always in motion. (Like all distinctions, this categorization enhances visibility but disintegrates upon inspection.)

Perspectives

1. *The global and the local are not things in themselves, nor are "globalness" and "localness" inherent qualities of an object. They are interpretive frames – scales of analysis, for example (Gibson-Graham 1999a).*

One way to loosen the differential hold of the global and the local is to see them both as scales of analysis or interpretive frames, inherently empty of content. This move opposes the tendency to objectify both local and global, to perceive "localness" or "globalness" as essential or real qualities of an object. But does this really help us? As soon as we talk of scales of analysis we must distinguish between "different" scales. As geographers we are taught that at the global (technically, the "small") scale geographic details are sacrificed for broad patterns of differentiation and homogeneity. And at the local (or "large") scale broad patterns may not be visible but fine details can be registered. Thus, a higher "level of abstraction" is attached to the more extensive scalar view and concreteness is associated with the more limited scalar perspective. Already, differential valuations are entailed. Deep in our epistemic bones we prefer abstraction to concreteness and are ready to give more power to general and extensive processes than to specific and intensive ones. Western Enlightenment thought tempts us to attach meaning to otherwise "empty" scales of analysis and the global comes out a winner again.

2. *The global and the local each derive meaning from what they are not. The global is "something more than the national or regional … anything other than the local," and while the local once "derived its meaning from its contradiction to the national," now "nations and entire extra-national regions may qualify as references for the local"* (Dirlik 1999: 4).

This is a familiar deconstructive move highlighting the dependence of each term on the other (thus rendering the master term no longer sufficient and complete). Yet this move is readily subverted. Dirlik points to the historical shift in the meaning of the local, such that now whole national groupings can, in relation to the global, be seen as "local." What is defined as "other than the local" appears to be setting the agenda for what constitutes the local, rendering larger and larger entities "small." The original binary is reinstated with the global conceptualized in a grander (and therefore more powerful) way.

3. *Local and global "offer points of view on networks that are by nature neither local or global, but are more or less long and more or less connected"* (Latour 1993: 122).

The global and local are but different "takes" on the same universe of networks, connections, abstractness, and concreteness. Are they, though, merely different ways of focusing on this universe, or do they have a content that is specific to themselves? Shorter and less connected versus longer and more connected networks imply a concrete difference that resonates with conceptions of power differentials. Greater size and extensiveness imply domination and superior power in our Western discursive universe. How can we not see global networks as enrolling and enlisting more power than local ones?

The same

1. The global is local, in that it refers to processes that touch only certain (local) parts of the globe.

The global does not exist, or at least not in any stable and generic relation to other scales. Scratch anything "global" and you find locality – grounded practices in factories, stock exchanges, retail outlets, and communities. The contemporary formation of regional trading blocs is a process of regionalization and regulation, rather than one of unfettered globalization and deregulation, while multinational firms are actually multilocal rather than global, though the statistics on their profits and internal and external transactions are used as indicators of globalization.

2. The local is global, and place is a "particular moment" in spatialized networks of social relations. The uniqueness of place is not defined only by what is "included within that place itself" but "includes relations which stretch beyond – the global as part of what constitutes the local" (Massey 1994: 5).

The suggestion that place be seen as a "particular moment" in a set of relations whose uniqueness is given by the concrete specificity of interconnections highlights the overdetermination of a particular site. Here, the local or place is not a thing but a way of seeing and focusing – an "entry point," if you like.

Processes

The global and local are processes, not locations. Globalization and localization produce all spaces as hybrids, as "glocal" sites of both differentiation and integration (Dirlik 1999: 20).

The local and the global are not fixed entities but are contingently produced, always in the process of being re-produced and never completed. Thus, places contain processes that can be globalized. Local initiatives can be broadcast to the world and adopted in multiple places across space – the Grameen bank, for instance, is replicated in countless low-income neighborhoods across the world. And global processes always involve localization – the arrival of the McDonald's outlet on the next block, the local link-up to cable TV, the building of a factory on customary-owned land. This focus upon process opens up the binary to politics, to interventions that can interact to change the nature of globalization and localization (Escobar 2001).

From this brief foray into current deconstructive analyses, it is clear that global and local are recognized as existing within a structured formation that differentially distributes power to one term. Challenges to the global/local binary attempt to break down the dualist structure of difference, allowing us to see that the global is not global, the local is not local, and the local is not powerless or even less powerful. They argue for the unfixity and multiple meanings attached to each term, and resituate them as processes whose courses are unknown and potentially malleable.[7] The recognition that the differential positioning of the global with respect to the local emerges from the *discourse* of globalization, and that this discourse is produced and purveyed by theorists, becomes the starting point for a politics outside the binary frame.

What emerges from this abbreviated review of attempts to destabilize the global/local binary, however, is an overriding sense that the power differential is never completely eradicated by deconstructive reason and re-presentation. Power, it seems, is either already distributed and possessed or able to be mobilized more successfully by "the global" (whatever that may be). The efforts to render global and local as somehow the "same" end up allowing the global to retain its power, and the representational shift associated with seeing the local and the global as processes, as always unfixed, is curiously circumscribed by a sense of imbalance. Dirlik (1999: 42, italics ours), for example, in his discussion of the glocal, notes that "most phenomena are both global and local, but they are *not all local and global in the same way.*" Does not the italicized phrase create an opening for unequal power to be reinserted?

Arif Dirlik's work has prompted us to push a little at this point as we find it both appealing and disturbing.[8] Like many others interested in destabilizing the hegemony of capitalist globalization, Dirlik is interested in place as a political project. He sees (2001: 15) "the struggle for place in the concrete [as] a struggle against power, and the hegemony of abstraction." Conversely, the global project is a struggle in the concrete for power and the "essential placelessness of capitalism" (2001: 16). But having done so much to argue for a politics of place "in the face of globalization," he is ultimately convinced that "the globalization of the local does not compensate in terms of politics, economy and culture for the localization of the global" (1999: 42).[9] In the enactment of globalization and localization there is inevitably an unequal exchange of power – the one does not compensate fully for the other:

> What appears today as something of an exchange, in which both sides participate, may turn out to be less of an exchange because it is *unequal* exchange, because one side will see its life transformed by television while the other side will through the same television invade the world and create a new structural context for its operations. (Dirlik 1999: 42)

Along with Escobar (2001), Dirlik argues (1999: 45) that the political primacy and autonomy of place is the "irreducible basis" upon which to "produce translocal or, better still, transplace alliances and co-operative formations" – what others have called "grassroots globalization" or "globalization from below."[10] Drawing upon the vision of power as the capacity to mobilize across space (Allen 1999), he believes that the local networks of place-based politics must be developed at the same (global) scale if they are to offer effective resistance to global forces. Despite his intentions and different starting point, Dirlik ends up sounding not unlike Harvey or, for that matter, Hardt and Negri.[11] If even the most ardent advocates of place as a ground of politics fall back into agreement with the imperative to "upscale," where is the space of hope and effectivity for those of us who wish to enact a local economic politics?

Subjection to Globalization

Whether they present their analyses as truths requiring certain actions or as deconstructive arguments that challenge a discourse for political ends, it seems that most theorists do not see *themselves* as powerfully constituted by globalization. The realists see *the world* as taken over by global capitalism, the new Empire. The deconstructionists see *a dominant discourse* of globalization that is setting the political and policy agenda. In different ways they both stand outside globalization and "see it as it is" – yet the power of globalization seems to have colonized their political imaginations.

Judith Butler (1997: 11) notes the deep complicity between power and its subjects:

> A power *exerted on* a subject, subjection is nevertheless a power *assumed by* the subject, an assumption that constitutes the instrument of that subject's becoming.

Is it possible that the power of globalization (obvious to many as having taken over either the world or discourse) has also taken over the bodies of its critics? Could this affective subjection exerted on/assumed by the intellectual and activist be standing in the way of elaborating a politics beyond the binary frame? These questions have begun to tease our (self)reflection.

We are very much drawn to the idea of place as a political project (despite the cautionary and condescending language of Hardt and Negri). At this moment, when power is ceded to globalization by all and sundry, it seems both timely and important to reshape the effectivity of the local (Gibson-Graham 2003). But what does "politics" involve in a local context? Must local struggle emulate global institutions and forces, as so many assert, in order to be powerful and effective?[12] Is the defense of locality or place-based struggle necessarily more regressive or reactive than the championing of globally networked initiatives?

As feminists, we are reminded of the incredible power of discussions around kitchen tables and village wells that formed much of the political practice of a women's "movement" of global proportions. It is important not to underestimate the magnitude and extent of this movement. It transformed and continues to transform households, lives, and livelihoods around the world to different degrees and in different ways, rendering the life experiences of many women literally unrecognizable in the terms of a generation ago.[13] The "upscaling" or globalization of a feminist politics did not necessarily involve formal organization, coordinated actions, and alliances (although some of these followed upon the "second wave"). Indeed, the movement has remained largely discursive, often personal, un- or under-resourced. Perhaps it is the continually revitalizing and transformative energy of this relatively unorganized movement that encourages us to pursue a different kind of politics, outside the global/local binary.

We are enticed to think not about how the world is subjected to globalization (and the global capitalist economy) but how *we are subjected* to the discourse of globalization and the identities (and narratives) it dictates for us. In *The End of Capitalism (As We Knew It)*, we gained insight into how economic subjects might be subjected within globalization discourse by examining the work of Sharon Marcus on rape. Marcus (1992) points to the important role of language, narrative, and discursive constructions of sexual identity in circumscribing women's ability to act powerfully during the rape event. This resonated for us with the limited options for economic identity and power offered to local subjects by a capitalocentric discourse of globalization.[14] We likened freeing ourselves from the discourse of globalization to women shaking away their embodied self-understanding as always already victimized within the discourse of rape.

It seems to us that a politics of the local (an antiglobalization politics that is not simply "grassroots globalization") will go nowhere without subjects who can experience themselves as free from capitalist globalization. Our project of revaluing the local as a site of politics is not about "liberation" from subjection as such, but about creating new discourses that *subject* in different ways, thus enabling subjects to assume power in new forms.[15] Liberating the subject from the economic identities provided by the discourse of globalization requires creating alternative economic identities that subjects can take on (Gibson-Graham 1994).

Ultimately, then, the political project is one of resubjectivation, a process that is both prior to, and concomitant with, the building of alternative economic institutions and practices. Our strategies for resubjectivation involve two major steps. The first involves creating a discourse of the diverse economy, where noncapitalist activities are visible and viable in the economic terrain. The second engages in the micropolitics of enabling subjects to inhabit that terrain – taking on novel economic identities within a diverse economy and assuming the powers these new identities bestow.

Resubjectivation 1: Creating a New Symbolic – A Discourse of the Diverse Economy

In seeking to represent economic difference, we have come up against the poverty of economic language, which avails us few concepts with which to describe economic diversity and few resources for interpellating alternative economic subjects. The paucity of language is particularly problematic if we understand economic discourse as performative, producing rather than reflecting the reality it describes. Echoing Latour on performativity, Michel Callon (1998: 2) argues that "economics, in the broad sense of the term, performs, shapes, and formats the economy, rather than observing how it functions." If, then, the economy could be represented as diverse and decentered, and this representation were widely accepted, the power of capitalist globalization (with all the unidirectionality, domination, and singularity it implies) could be dispersed and redefined. New economic subjects could emerge, ones not subjected to a capitalist economy as workers, entrepreneurs, investors, and the unemployed.

Creating a discourse of economic difference in which the economy is diverse (rather than primarily capitalist) and in which economic dynamics are multiple (rather than limited to the quest for profitability and the law of the market) and overdetermined (rather than naturally dominant) (Graham 1992) is not a task we take on lightly. There is no readily available language with which to represent the variety of production relations, transactions, markets, property and other relations and practices that make up our economic world. Take the market, for example, the mechanism that is most often seen as producing globalization and the victimization of the local. Altvater (1993: 80–1) has this to say:

> When "the market" is invoked today, nearly fifty years after the construction of the postwar order, the main referent must be to the world market – to the markets for goods and services, capital (or "loci of production"), money and credit. The world market is the site of economic reproduction of the global capital relation, as well as of the political organization of hegemony. An opening to the world market is thus synonymous with integration into the global process of economic reproduction and a historically determined system of hegemony.

Hardt and Negri (2000: 190) harmonize on the same theme, arguing that

> the capitalist market is one machine that has always run counter to any division between inside and outside. It is thwarted by barriers and exclusions; it thrives instead by including always more within its sphere. Profit can be generated only through contact, engagement, interchange, and commerce. The realization of the world market would constitute the point of arrival of this tendency. In its ideal form there is no outside to the world market: the entire globe is its domain ...the world market might serve adequately...as the diagram of imperial power.

Kevin Danaher (2001: 12) makes a related argument:

top-down globalisation is characterised by a constant drive to maxi-
mise profits for globe-spanning corporations. It forces countries to
"open up" their national economies to large corporations, reduce social
services, privatise state functions, deregulate the economy, be "efficient" and competitive, and submit everything and everyone to the
rule of "market forces." Because markets move resources only in the
direction of those with money, social inequality has reached grotesque
levels.

These representations portray the market as singular, mysterious,
normal, lawful, imbued with expansive authority and force. Yet, as
we examine the diversity of markets and ways in which individuals
and enterprises of any form (co-operatives, small businesses, capitalist businesses, feudal enterprises, etc.) interact with markets, we see
how they are constructed, protected, played with, manipulated,
bounded, undermined, institutionalized, deinstitutionalized, personalized, niched, and so on. Can we talk of *the* market? Only if we are
willing to obscure these differences. Not all markets are for capitalist
commodities, nor are they all naturally expansive or dominant.[16] Yet
where is our language to express market dynamics differently? And
what about the non-market economic transactions that are also key to
our economy, such as gifts, in-kind exchanges, barter, internal transactions within enterprises, and contracted payments? What of the
multiple noncapitalist ways in which surplus labor is produced, appropriated, and distributed within the different kinds of economic
organizations that produce and purvey goods and services?

It is clear that economic literacy is dominated by the singularity of
capitalist production, wage labor, and "the" capitalist market. Yet,
when we think of the immense variety of ways in which goods and
services are produced and transacted in society, these economic identities and sites are but the paltry tip of a complex iceberg.

In figure 1.1 we have sketched out how we have begun to think of
the "diverse economy" in terms of multiple types of transactions,
forms of labor, and ways of organizing surplus production and
appropriation. The right-hand column on forms of organization is
inspired by Marx's distinction between capitalist and various noncapitalist forms of surplus appropriation and distribution. As Marx was
primarily interested in the rise of capitalist class relations, most of his
discussion in *Capital* explores the way in which surplus labor (in
value form) *produced* by workers is *appropriated* by the capitalist (or
board of directors of a capitalist firm) and *distributed* through a variety of payments (including interest payments, rent, taxes, management salaries, and dividends, as well as payments to the capitalist's

accumulation fund). He did, however, also describe noncapitalist class processes (for example, feudal, slave, independent or individual, and communal or communist) where the production, appropriation, and distribution of surplus is differently arranged. Whereas in an independent class process, for example, an individual produces, appropriates, and distributes her own surplus, in a communal class process the producers jointly decide what should be considered necessary and surplus labor, and they are the appropriators and first distributors of surplus (Gibson-Graham et al. 2000, 2001).

Transactions	*Labor*	*Organizational form*
MARKET	**WAGE**	**CAPITALIST**
ALTERNATIVE MARKET *Local trading systems* *Alternative currencies* *Black market*	*ALTERNATIVE PAID* *Co-operative* *Self-employed* *Indentured*	*ALTERNATIVE CAPITALIST* *Environmental ethic* *Social ethic*
NONMARKET *Barter* *Household flows* *Gifts*	*UNPAID* *Volunteer* *Housework* *Family care*	*NONCAPITALIST* *Communal* *Independent* *Feudal* *Slave*

Figure 1.1 A diverse economy

When we begin to use this rudimentary language of class and organizational difference, the economic landscape is suddenly transformed. A huge sector of noncapitalist economic activity in households, voluntary organizations, "third world" countries, cooperatives, prisons, small businesses, and communities looms large on the economic horizon and we can begin to question the superiority of global capitalism in terms of its size and extensiveness. The voices of noncapitalist practices begin to be heard in an intelligible tongue – one perhaps recognized by economic development practitioners or feminist economists or theorists of the informal sector. No longer represented in the language of community service, household arrangements, welfare, voluntarism, or black economies, the multifarious practices of the diverse economy can be re-cognized in a new language of economy. A discourse of economic difference begins to emerge.

The aim of reading the landscape for economic difference is not only to highlight all those "silent" or "invisible" sites and forms of labor whose effectivity in "the economy" are usually ignored, but also to show how these forms of labor interact with, and produce alongside, wage labor and capitalist production. This brings to the foreground the interdependence of "capitalist" and diverse "noncapitalist" economic practices. For us, one effect of representing the economy as multiply identified and complexly overdetermined is to open up the possibility that "local" noncapitalist economic practices "matter" (and can be seen, for example, as crucial "drivers" of development) and should therefore be a focus of an invigorated economic politics.[17]

Another effect of this representation is to allow a more sympathetic and empowered reading of already-existing examples of what we call "intentional economies" – communities and enterprises that have been explicitly developed as noncapitalist sites in which people are actively subjected to different discourses of economy.[18] A discourse of the diverse economy emboldens a noncapitalocentric reading of intentional economies and helps us to unravel the ways in which strategic interventions in markets, production, and property relations have successfully created local subjects who are not interpellated by capitalist globalization. Thus, the Mondragon co-operatives thrive because there is no lack of subjects who are committed to supporting this alternative economic development pathway. But these subjects did not arrive on the scene, ready-made. They have been created through a long history of interconnected cultural and social practices, including Basque language maintenance and schooling in co-operative principles.[19] Throughout its history, the Mondragon movement has been aware of the need to produce subjects who could assume the "subjection" of co-operativism. Our challenge is to get our language of economic diversity to do the same.

Resubjectivation 2: Enabling Identification – The Micropolitics of Subjection within a Diverse Economy

It is not enough to say that the subject is constituted in a symbolic system. It is not just in the play of symbols that the subject is constituted. It is constituted in real practices – historically analyzable practices. There is a technology of the constitution of the self which cuts across symbolic systems while using them. (Foucault 1984: 369)

Our action research projects work in what might be called the under-determined terrain of the noncapitalist economy (Sharp 2000).[20] The language project outlined above is a strategic attempt to create a new symbolic field where economic practices might be re-presented in an anticapitalocentric way. This is an intervention to perform the prevalence, or perhaps even dominance, of diverse noncapitalist activities within an economy usually represented as hegemonically "capitalist." But this intervention cannot by itself create subjects of the diverse economy – people who can assume identity and agency via their subjection within a new symbolic system. A major challenge in our projects has been to engender novel identifications among potential subjects of "noncapitalist development."

We have employed a number of different strategies to release subjects from the body-snatching grip of globalization discourse. Not all have relied upon argumentation and exemplification. Indeed, we have become increasingly aware of the importance of cultivating a visceral receptivity to new becomings as a way of empowering local projects of alternative development.[21] One strategy has been to create conversational spaces where groups experience the affective power of re-cognition as well-known practices are re-presented as alternative economic activities. Another has been to engage community members in learning the language of economic difference and creating opportunities to practice speaking it in supportive contexts, encouraging this language to enter into the unconscious where it can unleash dreams, fantasies, and projections. A third has been to involve people in projects and working groups in the community economy.[22]

Creating space for identification

As part of one project we conducted focus groups in a rural agricultural region (Shepparton) and a resource-based region (Latrobe Valley) in southeast Australia. Participants explored the social and economic impacts of the past 15–20 years of economic restructuring – involving capitalization and growth in Shepparton and disinvestment and decline in the Latrobe Valley (Gibson et al. 1999). In both contexts the locality was represented as acted upon by global and national forces beyond its control and the community was seen as having to "cope." The mood of the group was respectful and relatively subdued as various stories and analyses were aired, broken only by occasional eruptions of emotion.

But when participants were asked to think of stories of success and hope in their regions, we observed a palpable shift in mood, an acceleration of pace, and heightened excitement – no matter that the responses were halting and disorganized, with no obvious narrative structure to follow. As each example was related, other stories came to mind, yielding ever more varied interpretations of "success." Among the many examples mentioned were: a voluntary community jazz club; The Bridge, a youth drop-in center; Dasma, a garbage recycling business that employs people who are intellectually disabled; an antisalinity community drains project; the Rumbalara Football and Netball sporting club for indigenous Australians; and Wood-Worx, a woodworking concern run by unemployed workers using recycled timber donated by "local" multinational corporate actors (Gibson et al. 1999: 30–3). All were instances of economic and social enterprises within the noncapitalist or alternative capitalist sectors. All were potential sites of new forms of subjectivation. And all were projects that cultivated the *local* subject, allowing people to become subjects rather than objects of development.

The changed mood and disposition of bodies that accompanied this creative and imaginative exercise prompted us to organize another event in which the examples they had mentioned (and others) could be showcased and re-presented as elements of a diverse economy. We were eager to build upon the receptivity to "thinking otherwise" that had emerged in the focus groups and to harness it in a number of ways. In particular, we were interested in intervening in the political debate that had recently erupted over the "crisis" of the bush. Rural and regional Australia was portrayed in the popular media as an economic and social disaster area and in this context a new political party ("One Nation," led by Pauline Hanson) had emerged to mobilize economic nationalist, anti-immigration, and racist sentiments within the Australian electorate. A notable effect had been the acceleration of regional competition for new capital investment and government handouts that policy-makers in each place hoped would pull the regions out of "crisis." It seemed important to create a space where new becomings might be fostered that could counter this reactive and self-interested politics of place.

Using the video facilities of regional universities in three eastern Australian states (Queensland, New South Wales, and Victoria) we organized a video conference in which community spokespeople from eleven organizations spoke for ten minutes each about their history and activities (Gibson-Graham 1999b; www.communityeconomies.org/projects/videoconf.html). The audience in each location consisted of activists, community members, and academics. After watching the presentations, the assembled group at each university broke into small groups to discuss the cases and what could be learned from them.

The projects prioritized social and environmental values over profits, mobilized the untapped and undervalued resources of the community, and built partnerships across a variety of differences. For example, an organizer of Home Paddock, a co-operative association of independent farm-based food and home crafts producers, explained how, by collectivizing their marketing efforts and occupational health and safety training and certification, a group of self-employed rural women were able to generate extra-farm income to enable their families to stay on the land. A self-named "jack-of-all-trades" told the story of WoodWorx, highlighting the growing interdependence between the local logging and paper manufacturing multinational and a group of retrenched electricity workers and unemployed youth who have gained access to the unwanted timber on company land. With a portable saw mill, they process the timber on site and then make beautiful (and marketable) outdoor furniture in a public access woodworking shop. An executive from a regionally dominant capitalist enterprise that was downsizing as a prelude to closure discussed the financial assistance and training the company was providing to its soon-to-be-retrenched workers, allowing them to retrain in occupations in which they might become self-employed in the noncapitalist sector. A community worker spoke about the new connections being forged between those serving out community service orders, elderly and disabled people, kindergarten kids, and interested local residents at the Fig Tree Community Garden, where previously "marginalized" people volunteer their labor and have created such a productive environment that they are now starting to market their garden produce.[23]

What emerged from this event was ample evidence of the extent and variety of noncapitalist economic practices that are being enacted in communities and regions. A conversation was begun between regions that are often pitted against each other in the race for new opportunities for "mainstream" economic development. What was patently evident was that understandings of economic difference and even of noncapitalist enterprise *do* exist, but they are likely to be voiced in terms of community building and environmental sustainability – that is, as "non-economic" and therefore marginal to the "mainstream economy." The video conference created a space where a conversation about economic revaluation could take place and where community members could see themselves as economically innovative and politically powerful.

Speaking a language of economic difference

In our projects we have actively encouraged ourselves and others to begin speaking a language of economic difference and thereby to cultivate an unconscious in which dreams, fantasies, and desires for noncapitalist forms of economic organization might take shape and circulate. In the Pioneer Valley we trained community researchers (CRs) to conduct interviews with friends and acquaintances who participated in the noncapitalist sectors of the diverse economy. The academic members of the research team were well acquainted with economic diversity and well versed in the class language briefly explicated above. But we wanted to listen to how other people made sense of their economic worlds and to engage in an inclusive, as well as an interactive, conversation.

Rather than introduce a language that was already developed, we created a set of one-page narratives (mini-case studies) drawn from the Valley that illustrated the range of economic practices (including transactions, labor, and organizational forms – see figure 1.1) in a diverse economy. At the training we asked the community researchers to break into small groups to classify the narratives. What emerged when we reconvened, not surprisingly, were multiple and incomplete typologies. Ken Byrne (2000), who designed the exercise, notes that

> these narratives were open to many different and possibly contradictory categorizations, opinions, judgments. For example, we included in the mix a firm that we saw as capitalist, but which had "green" or environmental concerns and for that reason might be attractive to some people. Consumer and producer co-operatives that were clearly part of a market economy were included. There was a communal enterprise (or worker collective). And we had stories of family and church-related activities which we ourselves had no consensus categorization for.

But it was the activity of categorization itself that "trained" the community researchers – trained them to see themselves as already active theorists of economic activity, conversant in one among many languages of economy (their own).

During the training a drawing of an iceberg was used to portray the economy, with the capitalist economy above the water line and the diverse, largely noncapitalist, community economy forming the huge submerged bulk below. We invited the CRs to collaborate with us in coming to know (and speak about) the dimly-lit economic realms below the surface of the water. And here the possibility that together we could construct a language and vision of economic difference in the Pioneer Valley became a motivating force. In their affirmative responses to our invitation, the CRs experienced and expressed desire, and we received a dose of energy and affirmation. It seemed that our language project was taking hold.

When the community researchers came back from interviewing their friends and other contacts about their daily activities, we held a debriefing retreat over a weekend. As one way to represent their findings we asked them to situate an activity from each of their interviews on a matrix taped to the wall (see figure 1.2). Predictably, the more than 50 examples were scattered around the matrix, and people were impressed by the diversity captured in this distribution. But then we gave them a set of red stickers and asked them to affix one to each activity they considered capitalist. To the amazement of everyone, only 4 of the 50 examples received stickers. This prompted a lively exploration of definitions of capitalism, as people began to distinguish capitalist from other market-oriented business activity. Over the course of the weekend, these types of exercises immersed us in a language of economic diversity, and began to elicit desires and fantasies about developing the noncapitalist sectors of the economy.[24]

An opportunity for more sustained practice in speaking a novel but shared economic language arose when a group comprising community and academic researchers, activists, and local NGO workers traveled from Massachusetts to Cape Breton, Nova Scotia to attend the Festival of Community Economics, which was a conference on worker co-operatives. Over the seven-day journey, including an 11–hour ferry ride, the group exchanged ideas, fears, hopes, and experiences of alternative economic practices. At the conference, we were immersed in the language of economic difference night and day – talking to co-operators from Quebec, other parts of North America, Mondragon and Valencia in Spain. On the way home, after four days of total immersion, the group began to fantasize about forming co-ops, dreaming up wild mixtures of activities that might be combined in a co-operative venture. We also talked about what alternatives to co-operatives there might be as ways of organizing activities in the community economy. After this experience the academic research team renamed itself the Community Economies Collective and invited our Australian colleagues, Kathie Gibson and Jenny Cameron, to join (Community Economies Collective 2001).

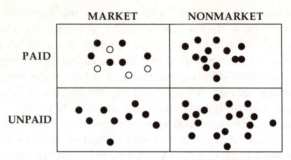

Figure 1.2 Distribution of examples from the community researchers' interview (blank dots represent capitalism)

Inhabiting new economic identities

One of our projects has been located in a resource region – the Latrobe Valley – that has experienced massive downsizing of the workforce as part of a process of privatization and restructuring (Gibson 2001). The formerly protected regional economy was opened up to international forces via the sale to global energy corporations of state-owned power stations and mines. In the absence of employment by the State Electricity Commission (SEC), many men have lost the sense of mastery they gained through involvement in a heavy industry producing the state's primary energy source, along with the accompanying sense of submission to their one-time employer – a paternalist monopoly Statutory Authority. The subject position of "worker" has been replaced by that of "unemployed person," and the repetitive practice of turning up to work has been replaced by the forced fortnightly call at Centrelink, the government unemployment office.

While the cessation of subjection to the SEC has created a potential opportunity for subjects to find alternative economic identities, many ongoing ritual practices recall the lost identity of worker: football matches on the weekend; attendance at football club or other working-men's clubs for regular social interaction; other sporting activities; union meetings; drinking with mates; and the daily performance of manhood – driving, dressing, acting, speaking a certain way, hanging out at home, mowing the lawn, and doing the car maintenance and other outdoor jobs. These activities are seen as "non-economic" and the subject positions they establish (as sports team supporters, drinking mates, club members, husbands, tinkerers) are seen as cultural, social, and domestic adjuncts to the ghost "worker" subject position.

In the Community Partnering Project we attempted to shift this representation and to see the existing activities in which many people are involved as occupying a position of value within the diverse economy. The football club, the pub, the household, and the yard are all sites in which noncapitalist (and sometimes alternative capitalist) activities are practiced. Our challenge was to assist people to recognize alternative economic subject positions and to identify with them, to help create rituals, practices, and communities that could hail men and women into these alternative identities and unleash the powers of subjection that they might then assume.

After a number of community conferences and "how-to" workshops, some working groups were formed to foster the development of new economic and social initiatives – a community garden, a community tool shed, a youth circus skills training enterprise, and a creative reuse center (Santa's Workshop). These working groups involve a wide range of Valley residents, including retrenched SEC workers, unemployed young people, housewives, high school dropouts, people on disability pensions, single mothers, and people from non-English speaking backgrounds. Recruitment to these groups has not been through the intellectual project of re-presenting the regional economy but through face-to-face individual conversations with community researchers and through attending food-based events and community workshops. In many cases, the attractions of pleasure, fun, and working with others in an environment of value have drawn people to projects they were previously uninterested in or unaware of.

Take the story of Ken, who was retrenched at the age of 54 after 30 years as an electricity worker in the Valley:

Kathie: It must have been a big thing to stop formal work.
Ken: It was a big step.
Kathie: So did you look for work?
Ken: Oh yeah, I used to go round and go down to CES (Commonwealth Employment Service) and all that sort of stuff. I thought I was flogging a dead horse, in all honesty, 'cause nobody wants you at that age. And I don't have a trade. I was never an electrician or fitter or plumber or painter or anything like that – I didn't have a trade.

Just as he might have done in an interview at the CES, Ken reiterates his lack of qualifications and seeming unsuitability for employment. Ken, however, has many skills that he has taught himself. He is a concreter, furniture restorer, cabinetmaker, gardener, and builder. In addition, he is an avid model steam-train builder and a member of two local railway clubs for which he regularly performs voluntary work as a concreter and model train driver.

Since leaving the SEC Ken has become well known for his house decorations at Christmas-time – large painted wooden pictures lit up and mounted all over the roof. His example has inspired other neighbors to decorate their houses, producing the largest concentration of decorations in the Valley. As one of the working group projects, it was suggested that a community access "Santa's workshop" be set up in a disused pre-school as a site where people could create their own Christmas decorations using materials (sheets of plywood, paint, tools) donated from local businesses under the tutelage of Ken and a community researcher attached to the project (another ex-SEC worker):

Ken: They wanted somebody to show people, to sort of guide them on – those that were interested in decorating their house as such – in the right direction.... So we got started on it and had one woman the first day...and then it gradually came until we had seventeen one day....So [for] four weeks, two days [a week]. See, it wasn't bad. And we produced quite a bit of stuff, plus we did those decorations for Advance Morwell [the town's local business association] for their Christmas trees...

Kathie: What sorts of things did you observe?

Ken: The help they gave each other was very good. Everyone seemed to get on fairly well...everyone got on well. The kids that were there were not a problem....I suppose the biggest thing...was that nobody would clean up after themselves, not everybody, but there were some that didn't, they wouldn't clean the brushes properly and this sort of stuff. But overall it was great. And the core of people that came all the time and ended up on the last day to clean up and everything...they got on well.

Kathie: So had you ever seen yourself in the role of a teacher?

Ken: No. Not really.

Kathie: Did you enjoy it?

Ken: Oh yeah, it was quite good.

After the first year of operation, a core group of participants came forward to volunteer to run the workshop again in 2000. This time the workshop assisted local people to make their own decorations and also undertook to make decorations for local businesses and community organizations, in return for donations of timber and materials that could be put back into the pool for community use. Thus far, the enterprise operates outside of formal market relations, drawing upon voluntary labor, barter exchange with local business, payments in kind, and donations.

Through the experience with Santa's Workshop, Ken has gained a new economic identity within the community economy. His work has been recognized as suitable for the "work for the dole" payment from the state and he is now able to get a higher unemployment benefit. The group has been so successful that in 2001 they started nine months before Christmas in order to be able to cover the orders they had received, while a subset of the workshop group is looking into setting up a permanent Creative Reuse Center on the site. This would collect together industry wastes that can be recycled for craft and educational projects to be sold to schools, organizations, and individuals at low cost.

Santa's Workshop has been more than a place to learn to make Christmas decorations. It has been a site where new relations of community and communality have been engendered. Ken has found himself faced with difficult challenges – people copying his designs, others not cleaning up, the difficulty of accepting strangers, and of working mainly with women who lack skills as well as confidence. He and others have risen to the challenge of accepting and working with difference, creating in the process new ways of "being together" and cultivating forms of community that are not based upon narrow town parochialism but broader Valley identification.[25]

Kathie: So did you see people you wouldn't normally see working together? Were you surprised by the connections?
Ken: Yeah, probably. There was one woman there who [had a case of] insanity bordering on genius . . . and she had a few whinges . . . but she got on quite well with everyone.
Kathie: Did you go and look at each other's decorations?
Ken: Oh yeah, the local ones. Chris and Diane's were up till a week ago. [The interview was conducted mid-year.]
Kathie: Did you know these people before?
Ken: No. Didn't know any of them.
Kathie: So now you know more people?
Ken: Yeah. Well, that's what I thought the whole thing was for – Morwell East people, that's the impression I got from [the councilor who first approached him] . . . and then it extended. But you couldn't just have an area, you've got to go to the whole Valley.

Conclusion: Multiplying Visions of Power, Community, and Politics

It might appear that we have adopted a strange and misguided strategy in this chapter on economic politics outside the binary frame. Having recognized the forceful critiques of a localist political orientation, and having been sufficiently affected by our detractors to ruminate upon their comments here, we proceed to offer up more of the same – examples from our own research projects of small and local interventions. It is as though we were into homeopathy as a political strategy: if globalization discourse has produced weak and sickly locals, we will treat these symptoms by creating small, barely profitable enterprises, offering visions of communities that survive on gifts and voluntary labor, and telling stories of depressed regions where people cluster to make artifacts in community workshops. How can such activities provide an antidote to capitalist globalization?

There are many sets of answers to that question. One set focuses upon *power*, how it is conceptualized and worked with and against. Another set focuses upon *community*, and how we enact difference and belonging. Both these sets of answers bring us back to *politics*, what it is or might become.

But first to *power*. Theorists such as Hardt and Negri, or Harvey, Smith, and Swyngedouw, are not alone in seeing globally marshaled power as the only way to challenge globalization. Here they are influenced by a long tradition of modernist political thinking, and specifically that developed in the socialist tradition. Oppositional strength is gained through convening the masses – breaking down spatial barriers, overcoming single-issue fragmentation, creating identification with one liberatory cause, meeting might with might.[26] Separateness, disarray, ambivalence, personalized actions, limited horizons, and local loyalties all signal a diminution of power in the face of the enemy. In the light of this vision, local initiatives such as those we have outlined are embarrassingly inadequate and definitely uncompelling.

Our response is to see this traditional left vision of power as but one among many. In its association with mass, domination, expansiveness, conflict, and singularity of identity, it can be seen as a masculinist and objectivist conception. The theorist seems immune to power – he can remain separate enough to analyze and strategize against it, even to counter it by mastering its tools. Alongside this conception we are eager to allow for other forms of power to be recognized and fostered.[27] We are taken, for example, with the *constitutive* power of small and local processes that are found the world over – photosynthesis, for example, or household provisioning. These processes that inhabit the entire natural and social landscape are powerfully involved in constituting creatures and subjects. In feminism we see a political project (and process of power) that covers the globe in a similarly constitutive way.

When globalization is consolidated into an all-encompassing, dominant formation against which opposition must be globally arrayed, it is consolidated in the name of the capitalist economy. The conduits of global capitalist power take the form of "the" market, the global finance sector, and transnational corporations. What happens when we begin to doubt the identity of the economy as singularly capitalist? The frame in which globalization makes sense as a single economic process disappears. The concept of a diverse economy calls forth a vision of an immensely variegated noncapitalist economic landscape which is no less global in extent than is capitalism. Its conduits of global power are many different market and nonmarket exchanges, forms of enterprise, and livelihoods. But this global power is not consolidated, concentrated, distilled, mobilized, and conflictual: it is diffuse, partial, constitutive, and sustaining.

The constitutive nature of power brings us to the power of subjection and its role in our thinking beyond the global/local binary. The judgment that size and extensiveness are coincident with power is not simply a rational calculation in our view but also a discursive choice and emotional commitment. We are interested in interrogating the investment we might have as researchers in seeing our bodies taken over by the "power" of globalization, submitting to its superior sway, and relishing our privileged insight into its workings. No such thrill immediately follows from telling stories of local becoming. Yet new emotions do get produced. In the practice of local engagements "nonrational" states can be fostered, ones that create receptivity to alternative discourses of power and economy. Our strategy for confronting globalization is thus not merely representational. It also involves novel practices, differently subjected bodies, and techniques for cultivating the capacities of local subjects – as agents rather than victims in a diverse economy (Gibson-Graham 2003).

A second worrying aspect of our work, for some, is our willingness to use a language of *community*. How can we invoke community in the light of contemporary repressive and defensive connotations and practices of communities (whether we think of the cloying cheeriness of community development or the ruthless violence of ethnic cleansing)? Hardt and Negri's recent attack upon place-based

movements voices the deep suspicion of community that many pro-
gressives harbor. Are we not just falling into the same sticky set of
associations by working with people in place on a project called
"Community Economies"? Will not these attempts at (re)vitalizing
local economic visions simply participate in constructing communities of sameness whose potential successes will be gained at the
expense of others, both without and within?[28]

Again our response is that this vision contains but one model of
community. Communities can be constituted around difference,
across places, with openness to otherness as a central ethic (Lingis
1994). Surely the project of constituting communities of tolerance and
peaceful diversity cannot be shunned at this conjuncture. And the
locality is one place to begin such a project. New forms of community are to be constructed through cultivating the communal capacities of individuals and groups and, even more importantly,
cultivating the self as a communal subject. We have attempted to do
this in our action research projects, as well as in our own social
locations in the academy. Alongside community researchers we are
speaking a new language of economy, listening to others, articulating
and amplifying each other's thoughts, creating and sharing novel
desires and fantasies. Our micropolitical cultivations involve food,
parties, pleasurable outings, and just hanging out – we have come to
see how important these are to the creation of new receptivities and
to untying the knots of fear that stand in the way of self-transform-
ation. For us, then, the process of constructing communities of difference feels like an unfamiliar and radically fresh form of politics,
rather than a recourse to parochialism and small-scale manageability
(with all the inconsequence and marginality that implies).

Finally, what can we say about an economic *politics* outside the
binary frame? In the face of the programs and plans of antiglobalization theorists and political analysts, our micropolitical experiments
can easily be dismissed. Most analysts, like Hardt and Negri (2000:
411), offer a vision of an appropriate political response to globalization that is very distant from the one we are pursuing:

> Imperial corruption is already undermined by the productivity of
> bodies, by co-operation, and by the multitude's designs on productiv-
> ity. The only event that we are still awaiting is the construction, or
> rather the insurgence, of a powerful organization. The genetic chain is
> formed and established in ontology, the scaffolding is continuously
> constructed and renewed by the new co-operative productivity, and
> thus we await only the maturation of the political development of the
> posse. We do not have any models to offer this event. Only the

multitude through its practical experimentation will offer models and determine when and how the possible becomes real.

We are no longer capable of waiting for the multitude to construct a powerful organization (Gibson-Graham 1996). Instead, we continue to be inspired by feminism as a global force, one that started small and personal and largely stayed that way, that worked on cultivating new ways of being, that created new languages, discourses, and representations, that built organizations, and that quickly (albeit unevenly) encompassed the globe.

Globalization appears to call for one form of politics – mobilization and resistance on the global scale. But we believe there are other ways of practicing transformative politics – involving an opening to the local as a place of political creativity and innovation. To advocate local enactments is in no way to suggest that other avenues should close down. We would hope for the acceptance of multiple powers and forms of politics, with an eye to increasing freedoms and not limiting options. Rather than equivocating, with paradoxical certainty, about when and how a challenge to globalization will arise (the Hardt and Negri position), we have engaged in a here-and-now political experiment – working on ourselves and in our backyards.[29] This is not because we think that we have found the only way forward, but because we have become unable to wait for an effective politics to be convened on some future terrain.

The form of politics we are pursuing is not transmitted via a mass organization, but through a language and a set of practices. A language can become universal without being universalist. It can share the space of power with other languages, without having to eradicate or "overthrow" them.[30] Academic, NGO, and internet networks can become part of a system of transmission, translation, amplification. In our (admittedly hopeful) vision, the language of the diverse economy and accompanying practices of noncapitalist development may have global purchase one day.

Speak now and hasten the future.

ACKNOWLEDGMENTS

We would like to thank Andy Herod, Paul Plummer, and Melissa Wright for inviting us to present an early version of this paper as the keynote to their conference on "Theorizing Space and Time at the End of the Millennium," which was held at the University of Georgia in April of 1999. Andy and

Melissa have since been extraordinarily patient with us as we nearly end-lessly deferred completion of the final draft. In addition, all the research and much of the thinking for the paper took place in the context of a larger collectivity – the Community Economies Collective involving Brian Bannon, Carole Biewener, Jeff Boulet, Ken Byrne, Jenny Cameron, Gabriela Delga-dillo, Rebecca Forest, Stephen Healy, Greg Horvath, Beth Rennekamp, Anna-Marie Russo, Sarah Stookey, Anasuya Weil, and ourselves.

NOTES

1 Not to all others, actually. An equally senior and well-known political theorist expressed his excitement about the presentation and then, turning to the audience, asked benignly but forcefully: "What's the matter with you people?" This did our hearts good, as you might imagine.

2 Dirlik (1999: 5) puts it thus: "While the local derives its meaning from the global, the spatial itself derives its meaning from a parallel with globality, and stands in the same oppositional relationship to the place-based as the global does to the local." It must be noted that others resist the associ-ation of space with the global alone. Massey (1999: 280), for example, prefers to imagine the spatial as much more than the abstracted spread and differentiation of "stories of progress, of development, of moderniza-tion." Her theory of space/spatiality opens up the possibility of "the existence of multiplicity," "disruption," and "the potential openness of the future" (279–85), and represents an alternative political and epistemo-logical framing of the binary (one with which we are very much in sym-pathy).

3 It is helpful to interrogate what exactly is meant by "power" in this context. John Allen (1999) has provided a useful summary of the theories of power currently being drawn upon by geographers and others. Of interest in the context of this chapter is his focus upon the different "spatial vocabularies of power" associated with each conception. He dis-tinguishes between (1) the Weberian and Marxian view that sees power as centered, as an already distributed capability that is "owned" by cer-tain individuals, groups, or institutions; (2) the view of power associated with Giddens and Mann that sees it as a medium, something that is generated as individuals, groups, or organizations "mobilize" social interactions and transmit their power through networks that are more or less "stretched" over space; and (3) the Foucauldian view of power as site-specific practices that are constitutive of subjects. He further distin-guishes between instrumental modes of power that enforce power "over others" from associational modes of power that work with others to "em-power." Throughout this chapter we will refer to Allen's summary as a way of exploring how different conceptions of power inflect views about the global/local binary.

4   Here they are drawing upon a vision of power as the capability of mo-
    bilizing resources over space through distanciated networks. Allen
    (1999: 199–200) associates this view with the work of Giddens and
    Mann.
5   Unless it can form the base from which to mobilize capabilities and
    upscale to the degree of spatial reach and scope possessed by global
    organizations.
6   Michael Watts's (1999: 90–2) criticism of the hopeful emphasis placed by
    post-development theorists and activists upon social movements, the
    "local community," and "grassroots initiatives" foreshadows, and to
    some extent mirrors, the views of Hardt and Negri. Watts is uncomfort-
    able with the "constant uncritical appeal to the local, to place and to the
    cultural (where cultural is synonymous with a self-consciously local
    sense of community)" by proponents of "poststructural approaches to
    development." Pointing to the violent localism of Hindu fascism, rather
    than the more benign localism of Andean Indian co-operatives, Watts
    warns of the "potentially deeply conservative, and occasionally reaction-
    ary, aspects of such local particularisms." What is fascinating about the
    similarities between the arguments of Watts and Hardt and Negri is
    the extent to which a heightened "sensitivity" to the conservatism of the
    local appears to be directly correlated with an emboldened faith in
    the progressiveness of the global.
7   Massey's (1999: 284) restatement of what the spatial imaginary might be
    "outside" of the place (local)/space (global) binary also emphasizes
    openness to unknown futures.
8   Though we want to be clear that we see ourselves as working within/
    alongside his project, rather than against it.
9   This is a curious comment, given that "development" is now widely
    recognized as a "local" project of particular Western economies and
    regions that very successfully became globalized (Gibson-Graham 2003).
    Think of the ways that models of development have been generalized
    from the specific industrial pathways that arose in certain places (the
    north of England in the nineteenth century or the Third Italy in the late
    twentieth century). These local stories have been transformed into gen-
    eric models that have been imposed worldwide (for a comparison with
    models of urban development and "global" cities, see McCann, this
    volume). Can Dirlik be blind to this history? Unlikely. What force is at
    large, then, that produces such analytical occlusion?
10 Activist Kevin Danaher (2001: 12) writes:

> Grassroots globalisation comprises many large and growing move-
> ments: the fair trade movement, micro-enterprise lending networks,
> the movement for social and ecological labelling, sister cities and
> sister schools, citizen diplomacy, trade union solidarity across
> borders, worker-owned co-ops, international family farm networks,
> and many others. While these constituents of grassroots globalisa-
> tion lack the money and government influence possessed by the

corporations, they showed at the WTO protests in Seattle that they are able to mobilise enough people to halt the corporate agenda in its tracks, at least temporarily.

11 Indeed, in his criticisms of the potentially regressive function of "non-confrontational" kinds of resistance advocated by postcolonial writers, Dirlik (1999: 43n, insert ours) echoes the line that Hardt and Negri take against theorists of hybridity: "One might suggest, in the present context, that nonconfrontational resistance, which may in fact be quite functional to systemic [capitalist/Empire] health, is about the most logical kind of resistance permitted under conditions of 'hybridity.'"

12 We cannot assume that because something is local and unique it is not globally consequential. Indeed, it may be extremely powerful, given the impossibility of restricting its meaning or emotional resonance to any particular location.

13 Indeed, the experience of being a woman is still being transformed, although "feminism" seems to many to have waned.

14 Capitalocentrism is the propensity to understand noncapitalist economic activities as either the same as, a complement to, the opposite of, or contained within, capitalism.

15 Clearly, in Allen's terms we are taking off from Foucault's conception of power, by first turning to look at the subjects already created by globalization discourse (including ourselves) and then beginning to think about constituting subjects empowered by different discourses. Allen (1999: 204) highlights the "microlevel" focus of Foucault's theory, seeing this as a restriction that prevents analysis of "power as a form of distanciated 'government.'" We, like Foucault, are not concerned to dispute the existence of "distanciated government" but, rather, to highlight the (concomitant and potentially counter) power of local practices of subject formation.

16 Though they may be viable and sustainable.

17 Social capital theory, which is currently enjoying a surge of interest among policy makers looking for a "third way," recognizes the importance of these social relations, networks, and non-market economic transactions, but only as preconditions (or co-conditions) for a healthy capitalism. We are interested in foregrounding many of the activities included as "social capital" but within a diverse economy of non-essentialized identities and nondeterministic dynamics.

18 The Mondragon Co-operative Corporation is a particularly inspirational example of a local experiment that operates on a global imaginative and emotional scale. The co-operative enterprises that comprise the MCC have been a catalyst of optimism and action around the world, and the co-operators who are at its heart are involved in a form of economic politics beyond the global/local binary frame. In the surplus produced through the communal class processes of the Mondragon intentional economy, co-operators have marshaled a huge potentiating force – the ability through surplus distribution to create more co-ops and a sustainable community

in the Basque region. Their high-tech commodities are sold on global markets and they have upscaled into supermarket retailing. However, rather than installing and signifying capitalism, these practices have allowed noncapitalist class processes to develop and thrive. Many visitors interested in co-operatives and worker self-management have visited Mondragon on study tours and the corporation is committed to publicizing its successes throughout the world.

19   For example, students at the local university finance their studies by working in the co-operative electronics component factory that is part of the university. Along with their formal studies, students gain experience in co-operative work practices and principles.

20   Hasana Sharp's discussion of the Althusserian concepts of overdetermination and underdetermination has helped us situate our "action research" methodology closer to the post-structuralist project of "becoming," dissociating it somewhat from its origins in the more traditional modernist project of "emancipation" (Laclau 1993). Articulating the notion of underdetermination, Sharp (2000: 32–3) writes:

> In emphasizing the unevenness of contradiction in social formations, and the way in which one social force can never be reduced to the hollow effect of another, there remains not only the various positive forces acting upon relations, subjectivities, and institutions, but the undeveloped and unforeseeable determinations which inevitably characterize material encounters. As opaque as this may sound, this opacity is precisely what Althusser, in his few somewhat cryptic remarks about underdetermination, challenges us to think: the unanticipated nature of beginnings, the possible, what will become, the unpredictable effects of encounters.

21   Here we have been inspired by William Connolly's (1999) work on micropolitics (see Gibson-Graham 2003).

22   All of the examples discussed in the remainder of this chapter emerge from a number of funded research projects. The US material was generated as part of National Science Foundation Grant no. BCS-9819138 by co-researchers Brian Bannon, Carole Biewener, Jeff Boulet, Ken Byrne, Gabriela Delgadillo, Rebecca Forest, Julie Graham, Stephen Healy, Greg Horvath, Beth Rennekamp, AnnaMarie Russo, Sarah Stookey, and Anasuya Weil. A narrative of the US project can be found in Community Economies Collective (2001). The Australian material emerged from the Australian Research Council Large Grant "Economic citizenship and regional futures" and the Australian Research Council/Strategic Partnerships with Industry and Training Grant "Building sustainable regions: Testing new models of community and council partnership" conducted by Jenny Cameron and Katherine Gibson.

23   A selection of the projects showcased has been written up as entries on the Community Economies website (www.communityeconomies.org/stories), another product of our action research projects.

24   AnnaMarie, a planner and academic member of the research team, began imagining how people involved in household economic activities, networks of mutual care, and volunteer labor might be engaged in formal conversations with economic development planners about directing resources toward enhancing neighborhood support systems that already sustain the community, rather than toward businesses that might not benefit local residents or might contribute to their displacement.

25   The old preschool site that housed Santa's Workshop has become a new kind of public space where organizational, ethical, and identity issues are negotiated by people working alongside each other in a communal environment. In Allen's (1999: 209–12) terms we could see this process as involving the practice of "associational power, or power with others," an enabling rather than dominating form of power.

26   As we noted above, this view of power is to some extent shared by theorists like Dirlik and Escobar, who look to a wide range of social movements and forms of grassroots globalization to produce resistance on a global scale. It is important to note that we fully support these movements and forms of mobilization. At the same time we are interested in making a space for additional forms of politics.

27   And here we agree with Allen's (1999: 213) concluding comments:

> There are many possibilities for exercising power with rather than over others, not all of which entail different sets of relations from those routinely described in terms of instrumental power. As yet, however, the language of power over others has a stronger hold on our spatial imaginations than that of empowerment and enablement or the entanglement of its many different forms.

28   Other critiques take a different tack and insinuate that our project initiatives, by shoring up communities that capital and the state have abandoned, are conspiring with the reactionary trend toward divestiture of public resources and abrogation of public rights, treating families and communities as newly responsible for their own welfare.

29   At another conference where we gave the keynote and which the organizers had billed as an exercise in "rethinking" left approaches, we were seen quite literally as confined to the backyard. Immediately following the plenary, our presentation on the local politics of the diverse economy was excoriated by four male discussants who categorized it as "Hills hoist socialism." (The Hills hoist, a four-sided outdoor clothes line, is an icon of Australian suburbia, a local invention that until quite recently graced the backyards of almost every quarter-acre lot and spoke of domesticity, order, and the Aussie dream of homeownership.) Hills hoist socialism, it seems, was associated with the cultural left who saw the challenging of daily practices as just as revolutionary as any other form of politics. For this resolutely left (and male) audience, our local,

face-to-face politics was clearly wrong-headed and probably overly feminized.

30   Here again feminism comes to mind.

REFERENCES

Allen, J. 1999: Spatial assemblages of power: From domination to empowerment. In D. Massey, J. Allen, and P. Sarre (eds.), *Human Geography Today*. Cambridge: Polity Press, 194–218.

Altvater, E. 1993: *The Future of the Market*. London: Verso.

Butler, J. 1997: *The Psychic Life of Power*. Stanford, CA: Stanford University Press.

Byrne, K. 2000: Personal communication with Ken Byrne, Center for International Education, University of Massachusetts at Amherst.

Callon, M. 1998: Introduction: The embeddedness of economic markets in economics. In M. Callon (ed.), *The Laws of the Markets*. Oxford: Blackwell, 1–57.

Community Economies Collective 2001: Imagining and enacting noncapitalist futures, *Socialist Review*, 28 (3 and 4), 93–135.

Connolly, W. 1999: *Why I Am Not a Secularist*. Minneapolis: University of Minnesota Press.

Danaher, K. 2001: More power to the people, *Guardian Weekly*, May 3–9: 12.

Dirlik, A. 1999: Place-based imagination: Globalism and the politics of place. Unpublished manuscript, Department of History, Duke University, Durham, NC.

Escobar, A. 2001: Culture sits in places: Reflections on globalism and subaltern strategies of globalization, *Political Geography*, 20, 139–74.

Foucault, M. 1984: On the genealogy of ethics: An overview of work in progress. In P. Rabinow (ed.), *The Foucault Reader*. New York: Pantheon, 340–72.

Gibson, K. 2001: Regional subjection and becoming. *Environment and Planning D: Society and Space*, 19 (6), 639–67.

Gibson, K., Cameron, J., and Veno, A. 1999: Negotiating restructuring: A study of regional communities experiencing rapid social and economic change. Australia Housing and Urban Research Institute (AHURI), Working Paper No. 11. Melbourne: AHURI, http://www.ahuri.edu.au

Gibson-Graham, J. K. 1994: "Stuffed if I know": Reflections on postmodern feminist social research. *Gender, Place and Culture*, 1 (2), 205–24.

Gibson-Graham, J. K. 1996: *The End of Capitalism (As We Knew It): A Feminist Critique of Political Economy*. Cambridge, MA: Blackwell.

Gibson-Graham, J. K. 1999a: Beyond global versus local: Economic politics outside the binary frame. Paper presented at the conference on "Theorizing space and time at the end of the millennium," University of Georgia, Athens, April 9–11.

Gibson-Graham, J. K. 1999b: Capitalism goes the "Full Monty." *Rethinking Marxism*, 11 (2), 62–6.

Gibson-Graham, J. K. 2000: Poststructural interventions. In E. Sheppard and T. Barnes (eds.), *A Companion to Economic Geography*. Cambridge, MA: Blackwell, 95–110.

Gibson-Graham, J. K. 2003: An ethics of the local. *Rethinking Marxism*, 15 (1).

Gibson-Graham, J. K., Resnick, S., and Wolff, R. (eds.) 2001: *Re/Presenting Class: Essays in Postmodern Marxism*. Durham, NC: Duke University Press.

Gibson-Graham, J. K., Resnick, S., and Wolff, R. (eds.) 2000: *Class and Its Others*. Minneapolis: University of Minnesota Press.

Graham, J. 1992: Anti-essentialism and overdetermination – A response to Dick Peet. *Antipode*, 24 (2), 141–56.

Hardt, M. and Negri, A. 2000: *Empire*. Cambridge, MA: Harvard University Press.

Harvey, D. and Swyngedouw, E. 1993: Industrial restructuring, community disempowerment and grass roots resistance. In T. Hayter and D. Harvey (eds.), *The City and the Factory*. London: Mansell, 11–26.

Laclau, E. 1996: *Emancipation(s)*. London: Verso.

Latour, B. 1993: *We Have Never Been Modern* (trans. C. Porter). Cambridge, MA: Harvard University Press.

Lingis, A. 1994: *The Community of Those Who Have Nothing in Common*. Bloomington and Indianapolis: Indiana University Press.

Marcus, S. 1992: Fighting bodies, fighting words: A theory and politics of rape prevention. In J. Butler and J. Scott (eds.), *Feminists Theorize the Political*. London: Routledge, 385–403.

Massey, D. 1994: *Space, Place, and Gender*. Minneapolis: University of Minnesota Press.

Massey, D. 1999: Spaces of politics. In D. Massey, J. Allen, and P. Sarre (eds.), *Human Geography Today*. Cambridge: Polity Press, 279–94.

Sharp, H. 2000: Is it simple to be a feminist in philosophy?: Althusser and feminist theoretical practice. *Rethinking Marxism*, 12 (2), 18–43.

Smith, N. 1993: Homeless/global: Scaling places. In J. Bird, B. Curtis, T. Putnam, G. Robertson, and L. Tickner (eds.), *Mapping the Futures: Local Cultures, Global Change*. London: Routledge, 87–119.

Swyngedouw, E. 1997: Excluding the other: The production of scale and scaled politics. In R. Lee and J. Wills (eds.), *Geographies of Economies*. London: Edward Arnold, 167–76.

Watts, M. 1999: Collective wish images: Geographical imaginaries and the crisis of national development. In D. Massey, J. Allen, and P. Sarre (eds.), *Human Geography Today*. Cambridge: Polity Press, 85–107.

2

The Urban as an Object of Study in Global Cities Literatures: Representational Practices and Conceptions of Place and Scale

Eugene J. McCann

Academic writing often deals in extremes – the *most* significant sites, the *most* exceptional bodies, the *most* important social relation of power – yet it may well be that significant and exceptional things also happen in (y)our own backyard.

Nast and Pile (1998: 406)

The problem with paradigmatic examples is that analysis inevitably tends to generalize from very specific cities....What should be a debate on variety and specificity quickly reduces to the assumption that some degree of interurban homogeneity can be assumed, either in the nature of the sectors leading urban transformation or in the processes of urban change.

Amin and Graham (1997: 417)

In its first issue of the new millennium, the *Annals of the Association of American Geographers* published seven essays intended to examine potential research trajectories and major questions that will shape future geographical inquiry. Two of these "Millennial Essays" deal with the issue of how to understand contemporary urbanization processes in the context of global political-economic restructuring. As such, they represent a prevalent theme not only within geography, but also within urban studies. In the first essay, Beaverstock et al.

(2000) outline a "new metageography" to facilitate continued world city research (Friedmann 1986; Friedmann and Wolff 1982; Knox and Taylor 1995).[1] Specifically, they attempt to remedy the "Achilles heel" (Beaverstock et al. 2000: 124) of world city research, which they see as being both the lack of an understanding of, and an inability to measure, the connections and flows between major urban nodes in the world economy. They suggest (2000: 127) that these problems can be overcome by moving beyond the analysis of attribute data (numbers of transnational corporate headquarters in London, for instance) to an understanding of the *networked* character of the world city system by studying "the global location strategies of major, advanced producer-service firms" and "interpreting intrafirm office networks as intercity relations." In arguing for a network-oriented approach to world city research, Beaverstock et al. (2000: 126) particularly criticize recent work in urban studies which portrays Los Angeles as "the archetypal, paradigmatic, or 'celebrity city' of contemporary world city processes," for such work, they suggest, fails to set the city within a wider context of interurban networks.

The work of the "Los Angeles School" of urban studies (e.g., Dear and Flusty 1998; Scott and Soja 1996; Soja 1989, 1996, 2000) is also highlighted in the second millennial essay, by Jan Nijman (2000), though this time as a foil for an argument that Miami, Florida – rather than LA – is the quintessential global city of the new millennium. Like the work of the Los Angeles School itself, Nijman's essay has a wider set of economic, political, social, and cultural concerns and deals with a larger array of theoretical perspectives than does the majority of world city research. Thus, while world city research tends to be based in political economy, is influenced greatly by world systems theory, and is focused on the analysis of advanced producer-services (e.g., Friedmann 1986; Knox and Taylor 1995; Smith and Timberlake 1995; Taylor 1997, 2000; Yeoh 1999), the Los Angeles School's work has tended to be much more eclectic in its theoretical and methodological approaches, even to the point where some may be reluctant to group it under a single rubric. Many associated with the LA School, for example, draw heavily from poststructuralist theory while also appealing to traditional political economy to understand a host of urban processes, from the spatiality of distinctive ethnic cultures to the rise of exurban techno poles (Dear and Flusty 1998; Dear et al. 1996; Soja 1989).[2] Although, then, in some ways Nijman's approach to understanding urban dynamics is similar to that of much of the LA school, his goal is quite different. Hence, while the LA School has tended to view Los Angeles as the model for future urban development for the twenty-first century, for

Nijman empirical analysis of the sort of economic, demographic, political, and cultural trends that have been central to writings on Southern California in recent years instead has rendered "Los Angeles as the quintessential *twentieth-century* city and points to Miami as the paradigmatic city of our time" (Nijman 2000: 136, emphasis added). For Nijman, then, understanding contemporary global urbanism means understanding trends that are most vivid in South Florida, not Southern California.

Nevertheless, while Beaverstock et al. set themselves apart from the LA School, and whereas Nijman is intent on usurping Los Angeles's position as the paradigmatic example of contemporary global urbanism, I want to suggest here that there are, in fact, strong and significant connecting threads running between these bodies of work. I will refer collectively to these writings as "*global cities literatures*" and argue that their crucial commonality is the way in which they construct the urban as a particular "theoretical object" of study (Friedmann 1995: 21). Such literatures have, I suggest, developed a *new urban object*, one defined by its clear connections to the global economy, its level of "command and control" functions within that economy, its large size, the intensity of its social and cultural interactions, and the uniqueness of its landscapes.[3] While space does not permit a comprehensive survey of all aspects of global cities literatures, I will draw on certain examples of the representational practices through which the new urban object is being created. In this regard, I am interested in understanding the urban as an epistemological category that is continually being struggled over by socially embedded communities of users and interpreters, a struggle which enables some understandings of urbanism while disabling others. I will argue here that increasing prominence of this new (global) urban object in urban studies literatures has significant implications for the way in which we understand contemporary urbanism. Specifically, there is an increasingly clear and troubling bifurcation in urban studies literatures between, on the one hand, research on the world's largest cities (and attendant writing intended to show how other cities display signs of "globalness" [Nijman 2000; Warf and Erickson 1996]) and, on the other hand, research on what are implicitly deemed to be other "ordinary" or "local" cities.[4] Thus, global cities literatures tend to use the experience of cities like London, Los Angeles, and New York as a template for understanding urban processes everywhere. They also use these few cities as benchmarks against which the "globalness" of all other cities is judged.[5] As a consequence of this approach, places that do not vividly express similar processes to those seen in the "global cities" are deemed to be less affected by globalization and are less likely to be seriously studied. In turn, this leads to a problematic deficiency in our understanding of the social processes that shape these supposedly "nonglobal" or "less-global" places and the lives of those who live in them. From this argument, the chapter will proceed to a discussion of how a new language for understanding place may prove helpful to the development of an urban studies that does not privilege the global as a scale of analysis. I will conclude by outlining how the issue of defining a theoretical object for global cities research is of importance in the larger pursuit of theorizing contemporary globalization processes.

"The Urban" as an Object of Study

From the late 1960s onwards, "the urban" has become an increasingly important object of critical inquiry, especially in the context of Marxism. Urban sociologists and economic geographers have engaged in ongoing discussions of how the urban as an object of study should be treated with reference to standard Marxist categories and in the context of wider social, political, and economic changes (e.g., Katznelson 1993; Zukin 1980). Before the work of Castells (1977), Harvey (1973), and Saunders (1986), the urban was generally approached as an ahistorical container of social activity. The raising of a distinct "urban question" by Castells (1977) initiated the development, through the 1970s and 1980s, of divergent views of the urban's conceptual importance in the theorization of the capitalist mode of production. By the 1980s, this had led to Marxist research on how urban social movements related to social movements organized around the point of production, how social reproduction developed in cities, and how the urban built environment was related to production, exchange, consumption, and the division of labor. As Harvey (1983: 504) put it: "The overall conception that emerged was [one that viewed] urbanization as the contradictory unity of all these aspects of capitalism."

Since the mid-1980s, however, a new "globalized" definition of the urban has developed in which questions about cities are asked in reference to the "supraurban scalar hierarchies" of the contemporary global economy (Brenner 2000: 366). This development has led to a situation where other questions about less obviously globalized cities (or parts of cities) and about the urban political struggles running through them are less likely to be heard (Amin and Graham 1997). As I suggested above, these literatures are in the process of constructing a new object of urban study defined by varying definitions of "globalness." As Brenner (2000: 366) notes, "[while] previous conceptions of the urban [saw it] as a relatively self-evident scalar entity, contemporary urban researchers have been confronted with major transformations in the institutional and geographical organization not only of the urban scale, but also of the supraurban scalar hierarchies and interscalar networks in which cities are embedded."

One crucial example of the "rescaling" of urban studies is the literature on world cities, represented by Beaverstock et al. (2000). Indeed, Friedmann (1995: 21–6), a leader in this work, is quite explicit in setting out his "theoretical object." He outlines five "agreements" that underpin the "emerging research paradigm" on world cities: (1) World cities are "the organizing nodes of a global economic system;" (2) they articulate a network of space economies that constitute the "space of global accumulation," a space much smaller than the world as a whole; (3) they are characterized by their high levels of urbanization and intense economic and social interaction; (4) they can be arranged in a hierarchy on the basis of their ability to attract global investment; (5) they are controlled by a powerful transnational capitalist class that continually faces conflict with subaltern groups with a lesser ability to command space.

The creation of this new urban object of study since the 1980s has produced a great body of knowledge about the way certain cities act as command and control centers in the global economy, articulating local, regional, and national economies into it. The fruits of this research have recently begun to be represented in graphic as well as written form, especially under the auspices of the Globalization and World Cities Study Group (Beaverstock et al. 1999; Taylor 2000). Among other things, this group has mapped the 55 cities they see as being the world's most "global" (see figure 2.1). In so doing, I would argue, this group of global cities researchers is constructing a "new metageography" of urban life, a metageography powerfully represented visually by the roster and map that they have produced. The object of their studies, already spelled out by Friedmann, can now be easily apprehended in a graphic form that also emphasizes the scale at which this construction of the urban is articulated.

If, as Brenner (2000: 366, his emphasis) argues, the urban question is "increasingly being posed as a *scale question*" through which cities' previously taken-for-granted relations to supra-urban scales are now being reinterrogated, then Katherine Jones's (1998: 27) convincing argument that scale (the urban scale, for instance) is a *representation* (i.e., it is an epistemological category that is made persuasive through its inherent rhetorical "power of selection and simplification

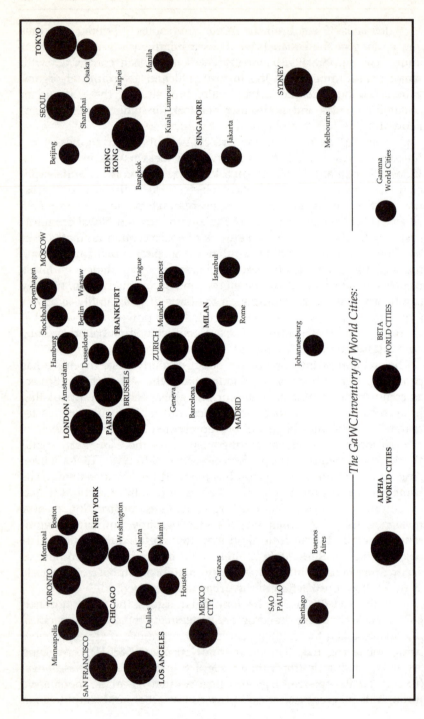

Figure 2.1 The world according to GaWC (the Globalization and World Cities Study Group).

Source: Reprinted from J. Beaverstock, R. G. Smith, and P. J. Taylor 1999: A roster of world cities. *Cities*, 16 (6), 445–58, with

– or categorization") is all the more significant. The persuasive rhetoric of the global cities literatures (including the rhetoric of its cartography [see Harley 1992]) must, then, be seen as a reframing of the urban question in a manner through which certain cities are articulated at a new scale – archetypal globalized cities – while the rest are defined (by omission) as less important to our understanding of contemporary urbanism and global restructuring.

Understanding Contemporary Urbanism: An LA Story?

The work of Beaverstock et al. represents one aspect of a larger shift in urban studies toward conceiving the urban as inherently tied to, and understandable only in reference to, supraurban networks. But, to be a workable epistemological strategy, the general principles of categorization must be bolstered by exemplary cases where manifestations of the relationships between contemporary cities and global political economic restructuring are readily apparent. While London, New York, and Tokyo have served this function for many, Los Angeles is the most celebrated case in contemporary US urban studies literatures. In this section, I will focus on some of the many "LA Stories" that have appeared in recent urban studies writings. In doing so, I will make an argument about why students of contemporary urbanism must be aware of the representations in which they engage and the categories they construct. These epistemological issues, I would suggest, are crucial to how we understand cities in the contemporary context and how we understand globalization.

While Los Angeles is not the only "Alpha World City" (Beaverstock et al. 1999) in the United States, the proliferation of writings on the place in the last 15 years has certainly elevated it to a position of significance in urban studies. It is considered by many to be the archetypal twenty-first century city. But, perhaps more interestingly, it has become an all-pervasive reference point for urban researchers in the United States. One question that needs to be answered in this regard concerns what sorts of representational practices have been employed by the LA School of urbanists in their studies of the city and why they have proven so powerful in setting the terms of debate over contemporary urbanism more generally. Furthermore, I want to ask what consequences there might be for how we understand cities in the context of how the terms of contemporary debates have been set. While I cannot elaborate on all of the LA School's work, I will identify two representational practices that I see as particularly important.

Representational practice 1: understanding the (urban) world through archetypes

A strategy that has been particularly effective in situating Los Angeles at the center of contemporary urban studies has been a representation of the city as an archetype, or paradigmatic example, of processes that are shaping all urban areas (Dear and Flusty 1998; Soja 1989; Scott and Soja 1996). This practice is composed of two seemingly contradictory impulses – to describe the city as extreme and different from most "ordinary" places while also indulging in a problematic synecdoche in which the city's experience is overgeneralized and taken to stand for the whole urban system (Amin and Graham 1997). On the one hand, as Nast and Pile (1998) note, extreme language is familiar and comforting to academic audiences, for it brings the world's complexity into sharp focus and allows us to investigate social, economic, and political processes in their strongest and clearest form. Therefore, the argument that "Los Angeles is a special place" encompassing the various processes of contemporary urban restructuring is quite appealing (Dear and Flusty 1998: 53). Equally, this language of extremes is evident in Nijman's (2000: 144) claim that "Miami feels like a lonely city because it is 'out there,' and it seems the only one in its cohort. It is a city without peers . . . But many cities in the US are likely to be affected fundamentally by trends that are found in extreme form in present-day Miami." The appeal of the extreme, then, is based on the strategic distillation of the world's complexity.[6] Yet there are important political and theoretical consequences of such an appeal. If, indeed, all the processes of contemporary urbanization are joined within one special city, whether it be Los Angeles, Miami, or another place on the "cutting edge" of urbanism, then why look anywhere else? Furthermore, the often extreme language used by skilled writers like Davis (1990) and Dear and Flusty (1998) to describe the city as both the utopic peak and dystopic nadir of postmodern urbanism has a discursive power that should not be underestimated (see Duncan 1994). Not only can we find all the important processes in Los Angeles, but reading about them can also be quite thrilling (in comparison to most other academic literature).

While the language of exemplars and archetypes indicates that these cities are extreme cases, it is also a representational strategy intended to suggest that lessons can be learned from these cases and applied elsewhere. "One can find in Los Angeles not only the high technology industrial complexes of the Silicon Valley and the erratic sunbelt economy of Houston," writes Soja (1989: 193),

but also the far-reaching industrial decline and bankrupt urban neighborhoods of rustbelt Detroit or Cleveland. There is a Boston in Los
Angeles, a Lower Manhattan and a South Bronx, a Sao Paulo and a
Singapore...Los Angeles seems to be conjugating the recent history of
capitalist urbanization in all its inflectional forms.

This recourse to synecdoche – where a part (Los Angeles) is taken for
the whole (the entire US urban system) – in the LA School's textual
strategies (Amin and Graham, 1997) is powerful in that it sets the
terms of a wider debate in which Los Angeles is always a central
reference point. On the other hand, it is simultaneously problematic
because it devalues the insights gained from concrete research conducted in urban places which are perhaps more "mundane."[7] This
point is put both succinctly and forcefully by Amin and Graham
(1997: 417) when they argue that

> [t]he problem with paradigmatic examples is that analysis inevitably
> tends to generalize from very specific cities...What should be a debate
> on variety and specificity quickly reduces to the assumption that some
> degree of interurban homogeneity can be assumed, either in the nature
> of the sectors leading urban transformation or in the processes of
> urban change. The exception, by a process of reduction or totalization,
> becomes the norm, applicable to the vast majority of what might be
> called "unexceptional" cities...If it "all comes together" in Los
> Angeles, the implication is that all cities are experiencing the trends
> identifiable in Los Angeles and that we do not really need to under-
> stand these processes.

Representational practice 2: understanding the urban through a visual metaphoric

In the same passage in which he makes a claim for the uniqueness of
Los Angeles, Soja also engages in a second representational practice
that has had a great influence on the way that the urban is currently
constructed as an object of study. He writes (1989: 193, my emphasis)
that "there may be no other comparable urban region which presents
so *vividly* such a composite assemblage and articulation of urban
restructuring processes." Notions of "vividness" and "clarity" are
often invoked in contemporary discussions of LA. They imply that
the city is a useful frame through which to understand contemporary
urbanism because manifestations of the global processes influencing
cities are so easily *seen* in the city. I would argue, however, that
whether or not the processes of global urbanism are *vivid* and easily

identified in a particular place is a problematic and singularly un-
interesting basis upon which to build an understanding of urbanization processes themselves and the spatial configurations they
produce. It would be fair to say that global cities do have greater
visible evidence of many aspects of globalization and restructuring
than smaller cities, but I would also suggest that such an accounting
of certain types of evidence has troubling consequences. What is lost
in contemporary global cities literatures is an attention to the diverse
and uneven ways in which globalization affects different places
(something to which our understanding of uneven geographical development would generally alert us). Instead, these literatures' tendency towards theorization through archetype and synecdoche leads
to the definition of a limited set of elements of contemporary urban
life – those especially "vivid" in London, New York, Tokyo, and Los
Angeles – as the benchmarks of urban globalism. If a city exhibits
these tendencies, it is "global"; if it does not, it is something other
than "global." Through this process, a binary categorization is
created and a great deal of the diversity within cities and the connections between them are lost.

Given this, it seems to me that if we are to push our understanding
of cities in global context further then there needs to be more attention paid to the representational practices through which we define
certain processes as evidence of globalism, how, by extension, we
anoint certain cities as global, and what the consequences of these
strategies might be for contemporary urban studies. The current preoccupation with the restructuring of the United States's largest cities
privileges the study of the effects of restructuring that are pronounced and easily *seen* on the urban landscape – massively
sprawling suburbs, downtown retail and residential "citadels," extensive military installations. This representational practice favors
what is *vivid and visible* on the landscape. It is characteristic of what
Gregory (1994: 340–1) identifies as a modernist "ocularcentrism," in
which our understanding of the world is shaped by privileging vision
over the other senses. The argument for the exemplary status of Los
Angeles is based, in significant part, upon exactly the type of
positivist, empirical accounting that is unconvincing as the basis for
a wider theorization of urban restructuring. Soja and others (see
Davis 1990; Dear and Flusty 1998) build a great deal of their analyses
on maps of visible landscape characteristics such as museums, closed
factories, and high technology industrial sites, as well as races and
ethnicities (based on counts of numbers of residents with Spanish
surnames, for instance [Davis 1990]). It seems to me, however, that
while on the one hand this has been a very successful epistemo-

logical strategy and has persuaded many of the merits of Los
Angeles as a "laboratory" for studying global urbanism, it is, at the
same time, a thoroughly undialectical approach which focuses on the
positive, visible features of the urban landscape (*vivid crystallizations*
easily viewed from high above) rather than on the negative, not immediately apparent processes through which it is constituted. Its
effect is to fetishize the identity of Los Angeles as a place of especially pronounced, vivid extremes, a place characterized by citadels
and slums, ganglands and gated suburbs, street warfare and spectacle.[8]

A dialectical approach, on the other hand, would entail the neg-
ation of what is immediately before our eyes. As such, "its function
is to break down the self-assurance and self-contentment of common
sense, to undermine the sinister confidence in the power and language of facts" (Marcuse 1960: ix). Thus, for Ollman (1993: 11)

> [d]ialectics restructures our thinking about reality by replacing the
> common sense notion of "thing" as something that has a history and
> has external connections with other things, with notions of "process,"
> which contains its history and possible futures, and "relation," which
> contains as part of what it is its ties with other relations.

While many of the LA School are certainly well versed in dialectical
thought, their discussions of the city tend to place an overly heavy
emphasis on understanding the world through positive "facts" on
the landscape. For instance, works that attempt to "model" the city
as the epitome of postmodern urbanism (Dear and Flusty 1998) are
characterized by a "visual metaphoric" which fails to pay attention
to the ethnographic understanding of the production of space (Gregory 1994: 295). Their cognitive maps and tentative models of the city
serve to locate the reader outside of the context of Los Angeles at
some Archimedean point high above. While there are obvious advantages to this position in terms of one's understanding of the city's
landscape as a whole, it is a viewpoint which negates the possibility
of a deep analysis of the workings of local politics and planning – the
institutional structures through which the urban is produced and
reproduced.

The effect of this ocularcentrism is to understand the space of the
city more as an abstract container than as a socially produced combination of political practices and representations. In this regard,
Dear and Flusty's (1998: 66) recent model of Los Angeles's "postmodern urbanism" reinscribes a modernist grid epistemology (characterized by their terms "keno capitalism" and "the city as gaming

board") in which certain elements of the urban landscape such as edge cities, theme parks, and gated suburbs are plugged into the grid by the abstract and all-powerful hand of capital. While claiming to be a description of a new postmodern urbanism, this model closely resembles the modernism at the heart of twentieth-century urban planning. It bears a striking resemblance, for example, to the grids developed by Patrick Geddes in the early years of this century in which he placed what he saw as the major elements of the city, its region, and life in general (Mairet 1957; Meller 1990). While Geddes expected the city to be planned by the all-knowing, benevolent planner, Dear and Flusty seem to have abdicated the planning of the postmodern city to a powerful and mobile global capitalism. There is no room, it seems, for the agency of ordinary people in local politics to shape and reshape their spaces.[9] Theirs, then, is a particular epistemological strategy that allows those who use it to answer certain questions and tell certain stories about a place while disallowing others.

An LA-centric/Globotarian Urban Studies?

So far in this discussion I have outlined two interrelated representational practices that are central to contemporary global cities literatures. I have also gone some way to identifying why these strategies have been so important, together with how they are, in some ways, problematic. Here I want to emphasize my point that the power of these global cities literatures to set the terms for *all* urban research has precipitated an increasingly clear and troubling bifurcation in urban studies literatures between, on the one hand, research on the world's largest cities and, on the other, research on other "ordinary" or "local" cities.

Nijman's (2000) millennial essay is one example of how the terms of the debate in large areas of US urban studies seem to be increasingly set by global city literatures, especially those concerned with Los Angeles. US urban studies is becoming unabashedly globotarian, leaving no room for theorization of ordinary places, and increasingly LA-centric, even when attempting to be otherwise. Thus Nijman's paper is, ostensibly, about Miami. But it is just as much about Los Angeles and the criteria that students of the city have highlighted as they have constructed their new urban object. The paper is almost entirely an argument for why Miami is more "paradigmatic" of the twenty-first century global city than is Los Angeles. As I have already suggested, the impulse to write the urban world

through archetypes is a defining characteristic of global cities literatures. In other words, from the outset (even the paper's title, "The
Paradigmatic City"), Nijman's argument about Miami is couched entirely in Los Angeles' terms. He begins by setting out four arguments
inherent to the LA School's understanding of the city: (1) LA's economic geography is emblematic of the new post-Fordist global economy, more so than New York and Chicago; (2) the city's historical
experience of a series of economic restructurings and social upheav-
als means that its built environment and social structure display an
exceptionally clear layering of social and economic experience; (3)
LA is the first truly American city and the location of a whole range
of symbolic and material practices that are not oriented toward
Europe; and (4) LA is the quintessence of the postmodern, a city
defined like no other by cultural hybridity and fragmented spatialities.

Nijman (2000: 138) then argues that in terms of mass air transportation Miami is much more internationally connected than is Los
Angeles, that Miami is less constrained by layers of economic history
than is LA, and that Miami has, instead, a much more clearly-defined
"postindustrial" economic base dominated by "trade, tourism, construction, and finance and producer services" than does LA. Furthermore, he contends that while LA might have been the first American
city to decouple itself from European urban and economic models,
"Miami finds itself one step further in this evolutionary scheme: as
the first global city" it is dominated by a majority of recent immigrants, related hypermaterialism, hyperindividualism, and exhibits
rampant corruption which contributes to a "lack of communal values
across the urban area." Finally, for Nijman, Miami, not Los Angeles,
is the quintessential postmodern city, if that term is defined in relation to degrees of cultural hybridity and spatial disorder (Dear and
Flusty 1998). He outlines a series of class and cultural disjunctures
manifested in the city's urban landscape – from the "privatopias" of
the elite island strongholds of its waterways to its various ethnic
enclaves, such as Little Havana – and argues that Miami can match
LA in terms of both the artificiality of its "themed" residential neighborhoods and public spaces, and in terms of its militarized, interdict-
ory landscapes. In all these ways, Nijman argues, Miami is at the
leading edge of global urbanism in the United States.

While Nijman's essay is not the only work in urban studies to
attempt to position a city in the ranks of world cities or to criticize
the basic tenets of contemporary writings on Los Angeles (see *Urban
Geography* 1999), it does raise questions about how contemporary
urbanists go about constructing an object for their research efforts

and underlines the point that any epistemological category is produced in, and through, communities of socially embedded users and
interpreters who continually make decisions about the most effective
way to represent and understand the world by categorization (Jones
1998). Through this social process, certain understandings are produced – about the spatial strategies of global corporations, for instance – while others – about the character of contemporary urban
community development, for example – are not. In the case of Nijman's essay, the research it presents was carried out in Miami. Yet,
epistemologically, it would not be too much of a stretch to suggest
that it is telling an LA story.

Putting the Urban in its Place: Place, Scale, and Uneven Development

So far I have outlined two prominent and interrelated strands in
contemporary urban studies research: world cities research and work
on, or in reference to, Los Angeles. Referring to them collectively as
global cities literatures, I argue that they have a commonality in the
way that they define their object of study. I suggest that through
certain choices made by various researchers – socially embedded
communities of interpreters – these literatures have reworked the
theoretical object to which their research efforts are directed. This
new urban object is a large city with high levels of connections to the
global economy, a great deal of power in shaping the contours of
supraurban economic networks, and intense, distinctive, and readily
identifiable social interactions and built environments. The new
urban object of study is, as Dear and Flusty (1998) might say, a very
special place.

Clearly, the construction of this new urban object of study has had
a great deal of positive influences on the way that cities are understood in the contemporary context of restructuring and rescaling.
This chapter is not an attack on these research efforts. Rather, it is an
attempt to contribute to discussions over the future of global studies
literatures, an attempt which stems from the conviction that a full
understanding of both urbanism and globalization processes can
only be arrived at through the ongoing theorization of cities' role in
the contemporary global political economy. What I am interested in
here are the representational practices through which this new
(global) urban object of study has been constructed. In this regard, I
suggest that these strategies have caused a problematic bifurcation in
urban studies between literatures dealing with "global" or "celeb-

rity" cities, and those focused on "local" and "ordinary" cities. Focusing on a few cities, such as New York, London, Tokyo, and Los Angeles, and generalizing from them, mistakes the part for the whole and fails to take seriously the interactions between other urban areas and supraurban political economic processes. This, in turn, produces a frequently unhelpful attention to the global as a separate sphere of activity from the local. What is at stake here, I would argue, is our understanding of place (urban and otherwise) and scale in the context of uneven development.

How might we rework our conceptual understandings of place and scale to better comprehend and intervene in the very real processes usually grouped under the rubric of globalization? This is hardly a novel question, of course, but the answer is still quite elusive. A significant issue is that, as Brenner (2000: 368) notes, "we currently lack an appropriate conceptual grammar for representing the processual dynamic and politically contested character of geographical scale." One consequence of this problem is the tendency towards exceptionalism and dualism in global cities literatures. As I have already argued, a dialectical understanding of place might provide a solution to this problem by refocusing our attention towards the multiple, contested, interconnected, and overlapping social and economic practices that constitute the spaces of cities.

This dialectical perspective starts from the premise that the world is constituted by interconnecting processes and is more than merely the sum of its parts (Merrifield 1993: 518). These individual parts are the stuff of Cartesian analyses, which hold each element – celebrity cities and ordinary cities, global cities and local cities – apart as separate objects of study and which discursively construct a world that is (at most) the sum of its parts. More specifically, and in terms of place, the understanding of the urban built environment as a moment in the circulation process of capital, as Harvey (1982, ch. 8) presents it, collapses the space/place, center/margin, and global/local dualisms often found in contemporary global city and globalization literatures. Refusing these dualisms allows us to concentrate on a relational understanding of the world – what Massey (1991) has called "a global sense of place."

Massey's (1993a: 145) conceptualization of place as produced by, and productive of, more generalized processes of uneven development allows her to argue that the

> interdependence [of *all* places] and uniqueness [of each individual place] can be understood as two sides of the same coin, in which two fundamental geographical concepts – uneven development and the

identity of place – can be held in tension with each other and can each contribute to the explanation of the other.

How, then, might we develop a "conceptual grammar" which allows us to grasp the complexities of contemporary globalization and urbanization processes without falling into the trap of theorizing through archetype and visual metaphoric? Brenner (2000), for his part, proposes the use of a set of concepts drawn from Lefebvre's work on cities. This approach sits alongside a great deal of work in geography on the social construction of scale which seeks to highlight the interconnection of supposedly separate scalar "levels," like global and local (for a useful review see Marston 2000). Here, though, I want to identify another, related convergence of thought and terminology around notions of "multiplexity" and "co-presence" which, because it is concerned with understanding the contemporary urban world as complexly interrelated, multiply layered, and unevenly developed, is relevant to my argument, namely the notion of the "multiplex city."

As Amin and Graham (1997: 417–21) have proposed it, the "multiplex city" is seen as a city wherein "the urban" is a place where diverse political, economic, and cultural networks (from the intrafirm connections of global producer services firms [Beaverstock et al. 2000] to the socio-spatial practices of the cleaners who maintain their offices [Allen and Pryke 1994]) are "co-present" with one another and interact in complex and contradictory ways. The multiplex city, then, is one in which social processes are "bundled" into intense complexes of interaction and, at the same time, "distanciated" over much larger geographical fields. All cities, whether they are "ordinary" or "exemplary," are multiplex. *Every* place is a unique "bundle" of the larger processes that constitute uneven geographical development (Massey 1993a, 1993b) and can, therefore, provide evidence of those processes. While this may seem like a rather uncontroversial assertion, it stands in marked contrast to the map of the urban world developed in the global cities literatures (figure 2.1) where only a relatively small number of places are defined as providing significant evidence of globalization.

If cities are understood as co-present "bundles" of multiple social processes and relations in a particular time-space, interacting in ways that produce unique characteristics and meanings while never being decoupled from wider networks (Amin and Graham 1997: 417–18), then it is problematic to develop an understanding of contemporary global urbanism that relies on evidence provided by only a few of these places, no matter how vivid that evidence might be. Certainly, focusing our attention on exemplary cases or on classificatory schemes which assign cities to the categories of "global," "nonglobal," or "globalizing" (Yeoh 1999) has provided a great deal of insight into the changes taking place in contemporary cities. Yet it would be unfortunate if the criteria used in these taxonomies blinded us to other evidence of globalization in cities throughout the world. After all, it is central to the concept of uneven development that *differences* from place to place are the result of the *connectedness* of all places. The notions of multiplexity and co-presence briefly outlined here, then, provide a perspective on place that emphasizes *both* the uniqueness *and* the interconnectedness of places – of all sizes and exhibiting various characteristics – as they are shaped and reshaped by global processes of uneven development.[10] The question, then, is not only one of how to understand certain cities or groups of cities, but one of how we understand globalization.

The Implications of the New Urban Object for Understanding Globalization

I will conclude by discussing how the construction of a particular theoretical object of study in global cities literatures might be related to the continued attempts to understand globalization processes more generally. Through a series of representational strategies, both textual and cartographic, global cities literatures have developed a theoretical object that not only shapes how we understand urban places but also influences the scale at which we analyze urbanization. These literatures privilege the global scale over all others as both the context for their urban-oriented research and as a primary agent in the shaping of these places. A particular understanding of globalization and global capitalism is at the heart of this new urban object (Friedmann 1995).

While it would be hard to argue with the assertion that multinational capitalist enterprises and (restructuring) state institutions play crucial roles in the production of urban space economies, the epistemological question remains: what implications spring from the decision to privilege the "global" as a scale of analysis in urban studies and to position certain urban places as the exemplars of new (global) urbanism? Drawing from the insightful work of J. K. Gibson-Graham (1996) on capitalist globalization, I would argue that the implications are profound and somewhat troubling for our understanding both of cities and of globalization. Gibson-Graham (ch. 6) makes two interrelated arguments that are relevant here. First, the dominant narrative of globalization on both the left and the right presents it as a singular and all-encompassing process that penetrates every nook and cranny of the globe in the pursuit of profit. Secondly, she argues (1996: 9) that while local places can be penetrated by global capitalist processes, according to the standard view "there is no room for the penetration of globalization/capitalism by the local. Localization, it seems, is not so much 'other' to globalization as contained within it, brought into being by it, indeed part of globalization itself." Given this, she suggests (1996: 9) that a weakness in contemporary Marxist political economy is its firm belief that

> [u]ltimately, capitalism is unfettered by local attachments, labor unions, or national-level regulation. The global (capitalist) economy is the new realm of the absolute, the non-contingent, from which social possibility is dictated or by which it is constrained. In this formulation, economic determinism is reborn and relocated, transferred from its traditional home in the "economic base" to the international space of the pure economy (the domain of the global finance sector and of the all powerful multinational corporation).

I would argue that the representational strategies of global cities literatures are central to this conception of globalization. Hence, the "new metageography" proposed by Beaverstock et al. (2000) abstracts certain cities out of their national urban systems and positions them as "command and control centers" at the heart of the "international space of the pure economy" (figure 2.1 is a perfect example of this). Similarly, the language of exemplars at the heart of LA-centric urban studies posits a similar abstraction of certain places as "global" and apart from their surrounding urban systems. In these ways, global cities literatures tell a particular story of globalization, constructing it in terms of certain producer services located in small parts of only a few of the world's cities. Furthermore, these literatures provide certain reference points around which the narrative of globalization can be organized. If, as Gibson-Graham (1996: 263) argues, "[t]he New World Order is often represented as political fragmentation founded upon economic unification...[where]...the economy appears as the last stronghold of unity and singularity in a world of diversity and plurality," then the bastions of this global economic strength are the "militarized spaces" of the global cities. In this narrative, the abstract spaces of the global economy are given concrete presence through reference to the buildings and landmarks of the City of London and New York's Financial District, for example. This tangibility only adds legitimacy to what Gibson-Graham would argue is a much less coherent system of power.

What I am suggesting, then, is that understanding the implications of these representational strategies for urban studies is also, simultaneously, about coming to terms with how we comprehend globalization. Just as Gibson-Graham problematizes the belief that there exists only a one-way penetration between global capital and local places under globalization, it is equally problematic to suggest that contemporary urbanization processes in global cities will eventually penetrate all urban places but that there is little in these other ("ordinary") cities worth studying except in reference to the new ("global") urban object. Furthermore, I am arguing that discussions of representation are, simultaneously, discussions of power – the power to define, and the power to resist, globalization. Gibson-Graham (1996: 123) notes that it was, in part, a representational strategy – one which positioned capitalist globalization as more powerful than workers' internationalism – that disempowered labor movements in the 1970s. She goes on to argue that contemporary globalization can be resisted and "redefined discursively, in a process that makes room for a host of alternative scriptings, capable of inscribing a proliferation of economic differences." A view of globalization that represents its command and control functions as existing in only a few, heavily fortified and inaccessible locations can be read as a particular discursive positioning of power with profound political implications.

The representational practices of global city literatures identified in this chapter highlight the new roles played by some of the world's large cities in the organization of the global economy. In that regard, they are valuable and worthy of further elaboration. On the other hand, the new urban object at the heart of these literatures has a tendency to obscure the linkages between global cities and their national urban systems, and to downplay the significance of research into other "local" or "ordinary" cities (Amin and Graham 1997). The same economic, political, and cultural *processes* (cycles of investment and disinvestment, exchange of knowledge and ideas, changing patterns of immigration, for instance) are co-present in all cities, although the manner in which these larger processes intersect to produce places is different. The tendency in global cities literatures to focus analysis on a few cities while also creating a dualism between the global and the local as part of the construction of a theoretical object leaves them open to criticism in terms of how they allow us to understand contemporary urbanism. Furthermore, the representational strategies at the heart of the global cities literatures also strengthen and solidify a particular and problematic understanding of globalization as a unitary and unassailable force. The abstraction of certain cities out of their urban and regional contexts, and the positioning of them in an abstract space of international capital, has the potential to reinscribe a set of problematic and power-laden Cartesian dualisms onto contemporary understandings of the global political economy. It is for these reasons that I argue that the epistemological and material power of representational strategies must continue to be a concern of those working in these urban studies literatures and on globalization more generally.

ACKNOWLEDGMENTS

Andy Herod and Melissa Wright have made very helpful comments on this chapter. The responsibility for all arguments and assertions is entirely mine.

NOTES

1   The world city hypothesis suggests that in order to understand internal change in certain cities and those cities' roles in the international division of labor, one must understand them as crucial nodes in the contemporary global economy. Recently the term "global city" has joined "world city" in characterizing certain places where the effects of globalization are seen to be most evident (Sassen 1991). These places are also said to be "command and control centers" shaping the global economy through their financial, political, and cultural institutions.
2   Soja (2000: 222–3) presents an interesting discussion of the links between the world cities researchers and the Los Angeles School, focusing on the time John Friedmann and Saskia Sassen spent in Southern California in the 1980s.
3   The literature to which Beaverstock et al. refer has seen recent questioning of what can be considered a "world" city (Simon 1995).
4   Of course, the term "ordinary" *plays along* with the notion that global cities are "extraordinary." The term is a foil to the dominant rhetoric in urban studies literature. I am more comfortable with the notion that all cities are at the same time ordinary and extraordinary – in any city, we have experiences that are both familiar and novel.
5   Of course, this is not the first time that one place has been taken as an exemplar of many in urban studies. The Chicago School of the early twentieth century developed extremely influential models of urbanization. The Los Angeles School has correctly noted that Chicago-based urban studies are increasingly difficult to reconcile with the experience of contemporary cities like Los Angeles. A new model must be developed, they argue. It is also worth noting, however, that the dominance of Chicago-based models of urbanization in the last century had a great impact

– in both useful and problematic ways – on how urbanization was understood. The temptation to shoehorn all cities into a model based on one place, whether it be Chicago or Los Angeles, or to simply disregard cities that the model cannot easily accommodate, is a dangerous one.

6   The related notion that contemporary processes of restructuring and rescaling mean that bits of Los Angeles can be found in every city (and vice versa) might resonate with a desire to shatter a positivistic notion that the city is a discrete, unproblematic entity. But that project can also create its own problems.

7   I do not want to suggest that every contemporary author writing about Los Angeles – even those who identify themselves with the "Los Angeles School" – always regard the city as exceptional. Indeed, Michael Dear and his colleagues go out of their way to admit that although they regard the city as a "special place," the processes they discuss in the context of Southern Californian urbanism are present in other US cities (Dear and Flusty 1998: 52 and n. 9; Dear et al. 1996: xi). I would contend, however, that despite these disclaimers, this criticism is still worth pursuing.

8   Each of these terms is used by at least one of the following in an attempt to characterize the special nature of Los Angeles: Davis (1990), Dear and Flusty (1998), and Soja (1989).

9   Dear's work in the realm of planning in Los Angeles and his research on the consequences of the restructuring of the welfare state on homelessness in the city makes his choice of the grid model all the more puzzling. Furthermore, his involvement with another collection of essays on contemporary Los Angeles (Dear et al. 1996) in which the voices of local activists are much more evident suggests, at best, that the "Los Angeles School" is still working through its conceptions of the contemporary US city and may, therefore, be open to other views.

10 Similar perspectives on place have been employed by others. Boden and Molotch (1994, cited in Amin and Graham 1997: 418) emphasize the "thickness of co-present interaction" in cities that develops from the opportunities for both face-to-face and electronic communication that exist in these places. Harvey (1996: 259–60) uses a similar term – "cogriedience" – to indicate "the way in which multiple processes flow together to construct a single consistent, coherent, though multifaceted time-space system." Merrifield (1993: 522), for his part, emphasizes the notion of co-presence as part of his argument for a dialectical understanding of space and place:

> Within the very moment of place . . . there lies a *copresence* of heterogeneous and conflictual processes, many of which are operative over a broader scale than the realm of place itself.

REFERENCES

Allen, J. and M. Pryke. 1994: The production of service space. *Environment and Planning D: Society and Space* 12, 453–75.

Amin, A. and Graham, S. 1997: The ordinary city. *Transactions of the Institute of British Geographers*, New Series, 22, 411–29.

Beaverstock, J., Smith, R. G., and Taylor, P. J. 1999: A roster of world cities. *Cities*, 16 (6), 445–58.

Beaverstock, J., Smith, R. G., and Taylor, P. J. 2000: A new metageography in world cities research. *Annals of the Association of American Geographers*, 90 (1), 123–34.

Brenner, N. 2000: The urban question as a scale question: Reflections on Henri Lefebvre, urban theory and the politics of scale. *International Journal of Urban and Regional Research*, 24 (2), 361–78.

Castells, M. 1977 [1972]: *The Urban Question*. Cambridge, MA: MIT Press.

Davis, M. 1990: *City of Quartz*. London: Verso.

Dear, M. J. and Flusty, S. 1998: Postmodern urbanism. *Annals of the Association of American Geographers*, 88 (1), 50–72.

Dear, M. J., Schockman, H. E., and Hise, G. (eds.) 1996: *Rethinking Los Angeles*. Thousand Oaks, CA: Sage.

Duncan, J. S. 1994: Me(trope)olis: or, Hayden White among the urbanists. In A. King (ed.), *Representing the City*. Basingstoke: Macmillan, 253–68.

Friedmann, J. 1986: The world city hypothesis. *Development and Change*, 17 (1), 69–83.

Friedmann, J. 1995: Where we stand: A decade of world city research. In P. L. Knox and P. J. Taylor (eds.), *World Cities in a World System*. Cambridge: Cambridge University Press, 21–47.

Friedmann, J. and Wolff, G. 1982: World city formation: An agenda for research and action. *International Journal of Urban and Regional Research*, 6 (3), 309–44.

Gibson-Graham, J. K. 1996: *The End of Capitalism (As We Knew it): A Feminist Critique of Political Economy*. Cambridge, MA: Blackwell.

Gregory, D. 1994: *Geographical Imaginations*. Cambridge, MA: Blackwell.

Harley, J. B. 1992. Deconstructing the map. In T. Barnes and J. Duncan (eds.), *Writing Worlds: Discourse, Text and Metaphor in the Representation of Landscape*. New York: Routledge, 231–47.

Harvey, D. 1973: *Social Justice and the City*. London: Edward Arnold.

Harvey, D. 1982: *The Limits to Capital*. Oxford: Oxford University Press.

Harvey, D. 1983: Urbanization. In T. Bottomore et al. (eds.), *A Dictionary of Marxist Thought*. Cambridge, MA: Harvard University Press, 503–4.

Harvey, D. 1996: *Justice, Nature, and the Geography of Difference*. Cambridge, MA: Blackwell.

Jones, K.T. 1998: Scale as epistemology. *Political Geography*, 17 (1), 25–8.

Katznelson, I. 1993. *Marxism and the City*. Oxford: Clarendon Press.

Knox, P. L. and Taylor, P. J. (eds.) 1995: *World Cities in a World System*. Cambridge: Cambridge University Press.

Mairet, P. 1957: *Pioneer of Sociology: The Life and Letters of Patrick Geddes*. London: Lund Humphries.

Marcuse, H. 1960 [1941]: *Reason and Revolution: Hegel and the Rise of Social Theory*. Boston: Beacon Press.

Marston, S. 2000: The social construction of scale. *Progress in Human Geography*, 24 (2), 219–42.

Massey, D. 1991: A global sense of place. *Marxism Today*, June: 24–9.

Massey, D. 1993a: Questions of locality. *Geography*, 78 (2), 142–49.

Massey, D. 1993b. Power-geometry and a progressive sense of place. In J. Bird, B. Curtis, T. Putman, G. Robertson, and L. Tickner (eds.), *Mapping the Futures: Local Cultures, Global Change*. New York: Routledge, 59–69

Meller, H. 1990: *Patrick Geddes: Social Evolutionist and City Planner*. New York: Routledge.

Merrifield, A. 1993: Place and space: A Lefebvrian reconciliation. *Transactions of the Institute of British Geographers*, New Series, 18, 516–31.

Nast, H. and Pile, S. 1998: "Everydayplacesbodies." In H. Nast and S. Pile (eds.), *Places Through the Body*. New York: Routledge, 405–16.

Nijman, J. 2000: The paradigmatic city. *Annals of the Association of American Geographers*, 90 (1), 135–45.

Ollman, B. 1993: *Dialectical Investigations*. New York: Routledge.

Sassen, S. 1991: *Global City: London, New York, Tokyo*. Princeton, NJ: Princeton University Press.

Saunders, P. 1986: *Social Theory and the Urban Question*. London: Hutchinson.

Scott, A. J. and Soja, E. (eds.) 1996: *The City: Los Angeles and Urban Theory at the End of the Twentieth Century*. Berkeley, CA: University of California Press.

Simon, D. 1995: The world city hypothesis: Reflections from the periphery. In P. L. Knox and P. J. Taylor (eds.), *World Cities in a World System*. Cambridge: Cambridge University Press, 132–55.

Smith, D. A. and Timberlake, M. 1995: Conceptualizing and mapping the structure of the world system's city system. *Urban Studies*, 32 (2), 287–302.

Soja, E. 1989: *Postmodern Geographies: The Reassertion of Space in Critical Social Theory*. New York: Verso.

Soja, E. 1996: *Thirdspace: Journeys to Los Angeles and Other Real-and-Imagined Places*. Cambridge, MA: Blackwell.

Soja, E. 2000: *Postmetropolis: Critical Studies of Cities and Regions*. Cambridge, MA: Blackwell.

Taylor, P. J. 1997: Hierarchical tendencies amongst world cities: A global research proposal. *Cities*, 14 (6), 323–32.

Taylor, P. J. 2000: World cities and territorial states under conditions of contemporary globalization. *Political Geography*, 19, 5–32.

Urban Geography. 1999: Review symposium on Dear and Flusty's (1998) "Postmodern urbanism," 20 (5), 393–416.

Warf, B. and Erickson, R. 1996: Special issue: Globalization and the US city system. *Urban Geography*, 17 (1), 1–117.

Yeoh, B. S. A. 1999: Global/globalizing cities. *Progress in Human Geography*, 23 (4), 607–16.

Zukin, S. 1980: A decade of the new urban sociology. *Theory and Society*, 9 (4), 575–601.

3

"Globalization," the "Regulation Approach," and the Politics of Scale

Kevin R. Cox

Context

Recent arguments about changes in the scales at which state activities are organized – ideas about "the hollowing out of the state" or "glocalization" – are increasingly part of the accepted wisdom in urban and regional studies. From some standpoints their acceptance is surprising. There are certainly empirical issues that might lead us to question the veracity of such arguments. But more telling, I believe, are shortcomings of a conceptual nature which stem, in turn, from the intellectual lineage upon which such arguments draw, namely what has been called "the regulation approach." Such an approach, I would argue, has fostered a belief in the separation of the political from the economic – of the state from capital – at the same time that it has entailed oversimplified views of the spatial. So, the degree to which regulation theory has found a receptive home among some human geographers, and ones of a more progressive turn at that, might raise some eyebrows.

In this chapter I want to examine critically these arguments, rooting my critique in a particular understanding of the regulation approach and how it has been "updated" in order to take account of a set of material practices which, likewise, have been subject to a questionable construction: those falling under, or traceable to, the broad heading of "globalization." The paper itself is divided into three major sections. In the first of these I try to summarize the claims that have been made and make some comments on their empirical validity. A second section turns to issues of a more conceptual character which stem, in turn, from the way in which the interventions under review have situated themselves, rather uncritically, with respect to the regulation approach. This results in a view of how one might alternatively proceed, a view whose implications for the politics of scale are drawn out in the third and final section.

New Scalar Fixes

A quick and relatively straightforward entrée into claims that a new scalar fix (henceforth the NPS or "new politics of scale") for the state is unfolding under contemporary capitalism is provided by the work of two of these claims' more cited advocates: Erik Swyngedouw and Bob Jessop. Accordingly, I want to commence this section with an outline of their respective arguments. Having remarked on the wider discursive context which has lent some credibility to these, I conclude the section with a brief outline of reasons why we should view them in their empirical applicability with a certain degree of skepticism.

Of the two people whose work is briefly reviewed here, Swyngedouw (1997a, 1997b) has been the more direct and less qualified in his assertions.[1] His key concept is what he calls "glocalization," which, he believes, has become increasingly apparent over the last quarter-century. By this he intends to signify a simultaneous shift away from the national state in the scale of what he calls "social reproduction," this being a shift upwards to supranational or global scales and downwards to the scales of the body, the local, and urban and regional configurations. These changes, he argues, have been stimulated by the globalization of the economy. This latter is by no means a top-down process, however, since Swyngedouw also assigns considerable importance to the emergence of new territorial production systems and their ability to command, and their dependence on, international markets. Accordingly, he says, corporations are simultaneously intensely local and intensely global. These economic changes correspond to what Swyngedouw calls a double rearticulation of political scales, upwards and downwards, and outwards to private capital. On the one hand, he points to the growing importance of supranational organizations like the EU, NAFTA, the WTO, and the G7. On the other, there has been a growth of new governance structures at more local levels which correspond to the needs of the new production systems. At the same time the state has retreated. The boundary between public and private has been redefined. Governance is superseding government, and there has been a retreat of the welfare state.

In terms of its implications for the scalar fixes of the state there is considerable convergence between Swyngedouw's notion of glocalization and Bob Jessop's "hollowing out of the state," which he has explored in a number of different papers.[2] More recently, Jessop has defined this as "denationalization" and has linked it to what he regards as two other trends in the reorganization of the state: destatization and internationalization. By denationalization he refers to a shift in the location of state capacities both upwards and downwards. Like Swyngedouw, he underlines the expansion of supranational state apparatuses at one pole and "the resurgence of regional and local governance" at the other. The reference to "governance" derives from his view that there are also processes of what he calls destatization under way at all levels of the state, by which he means there is occurring a shift towards state interventions that are less hierarchical, less centralized, and less top-down.

Denationalization is also connected to internationalization in a way reminiscent of Swyngedouw's observations about glocalization. Accordingly, the growth of local forms of governance and the devolution of planning responsibility for human resources and physical infrastructure reflects growing recognition of the importance of local economies to national competitiveness in an internationalized economy.[3] At the same time, however, internationalization has entailed a retreat from the welfare state in favor of what Jessop calls a Schumpeterian workfare regime, something again apparent at all levels of the state.

There would seem, therefore, to be a considerable amount of agreement between Swyngedouw and Jessop. Both argue that there has been a shift in the geographical scales of state functions, both upwards and downwards. Both link this to the related trends of the internationalization of the economy and the growing importance of what Swyngedouw terms "territorial production systems." And in both instances there is a correlative shift in the boundary between public and private, with adverse distributional consequences. These ideas, moreover, derive credibility from a broader discursive context. Indeed, to some degree their contribution is to bring various literatures together, draw out their wider implications, and demonstrate their complementarity or compatibility one with another. In this regard attention is drawn, *inter alia*, to arguments about the implications of globalization for the realization of state powers, for the redrawing of the boundary between the public and the private (which, in turn, is linked to globalization), and for the emergence of new territorial production complexes. These latter were seen as generating steering problems which would have to be resolved by the construction of respective systems of governance.[4] None of these arguments, of course, have gone without challenge. The literature on globalization and its implications has now gone through a number of different stages of critique, to the extent that the view of the emasculated state characteristic of earlier ones is now regarded with some skepticism. The data seem at best highly equivocal (Pierson 1996; see also Kenworthy 1997) and the underlying political conditions overgeneralized (Borchert 1996). A similar evolution has characterized discussion of territorial production complexes, so that for many, these are now seen to have been hopelessly overgeneralized in their occurrence (Amin and Robbins 1990; Lovering 1990).

So, in terms of the arguments upon which it has drawn, the new politics of scale should at least be in question. In addition, however, there are empirical questions. I am not arguing that there is no empirical warrant for the claims made about a new politics of scale. One can indeed point in the British case to the localization of wage bargaining (Holloway 1987), the devolution of responsibility for labor-training initiatives (Peck 1996: 221–6), or the attempt of the central government to establish something akin to US growth coalitions (Peck 1995; Peck and Tickell, 1995b). Similarly, in the United States there has indeed been an increased awareness of the challenge of internationalization and some shift of responsibility upwards to supranational organizations like NAFTA and the WTO. But, taken as a whole, the evidence is very partial and mixed. It is not so much the emergence of a level of supranational organization that concerns me here, though I think that its significance – in particular, its relation to uneven development and its role in the widening of territorial advantage – has not been entirely grasped. Rather, it is the generality and form of the changes that are claimed to be occurring at subnational levels. For example, while it might be true that in parts of Western Europe national governments are evincing more interest in the development of self-propelling growth regions than they have previously, this has by no means had as a necessary concomitant the devolution of authority – that is to say, a shift in the state's scale division of labor.[5] In Britain, for example, there is a history of projects, many of them one-off in character, orchestrated from the top down and with a minimum of local consultation: Britain's Urban Development Corporations and enterprise zones, and now the Regional Development Agencies, are cases in point.[6] The US experience is hard to compare with that in Western Europe. As Mann (1997: 484) has argued, "it is difficult to see much of a weakening of US government powers, since these were never exercised very actively." This is certainly not to say that I think an exhaustive empirical survey is what is required to arbitrate effectively the claims being made. Rather, I want to provide a conceptual critique, though one that is keyed into observable facets of the state's scalar division of labor. It is to that task that I now turn.

The Problematic Starting Point: The Regulation Approach

The starting point for those advocating a NPS – and within the context of which they draw on arguments about globalization, new territorial production complexes, and the like – is the regulation approach. This is through and through problematic, and for two reasons. The first is the way in which it assumes (along with so much of the literature on globalization that has come after it) a separation of state and capital. This results in a fetishized view of the one acting on the other, with the central state dominant at one historical moment and now, apparently, with capital in the ascendancy, or, alternatively, it suggests that the two merely co-exist in some sort of reciprocal relation. Instead, what is required – and in contrast to the altogether suspect lineage of the regulation approach – is an approach more rooted in historical materialism which sees state and capital as existing one with another in a contradictory unity. The second problem is regulation theory's aspatial character. Its concept of space boils down to a dichotomy: national vs. international, a dichotomy which is not surprising given that geographers had no part in putting it together. But, as I wish to show, this is far too crude a geography to aid in understanding the changes that have been taking place in the scale division of labor of the state.

1 The Separation of State and Capital

A major focus of the globalization debate has been the relation between capital and the state – in particular, whether or not capital has undermined state power. A common argument early on was that state power to implement macroeconomic policy had been seriously eroded by capital's enhanced international mobility. This then found its counterpoint in claims that state power should not be reduced to the macroeconomic, that its power with respect to the "supply side" remained relatively unimpaired and could be turned to mobilizing capital to the advantage of the national economy. In other words, in this debate the state and capital were characterized as doing things to each other.

Regulation theory also bears the stamp of this fundamental assumption and in this regard its debt to Keynes cannot be overstated. For Keynes, the central concern was with macroeconomic balance. For its part, regulation theory seeks, in effect, to tidy up Keynes by problematizing the issue of microeconomic balance which he thought would be solved by the market (Clarke 1988: 61). According to regulation theory, as with Keynes, the state was to be important in bringing this balance about, if not exclusively so – hence the important role assigned to an autonomous state, an autonomy that has also found its way into the literature on globalization. Globalization, however, is seen as upsetting the balance that regulation has been able to achieve: capital, it seems, strikes back. The old Keynesian strategies of fiscal and monetary policy are no longer effective as a result of the new territorial noncoincidence (Radice 1984) that has been imposed on the state.[7] In addition, globalization has upset the virtuous circle of Fordist economic growth as a result of the emergence of so-called peripheral Fordism. So, the search is now on, logically enough, for new regulatory fixes through which balance can once more be restored. A common argument here, and echoing part of the glocalization argument, is that these are likely to be found at the international level. Put another way: regulation theory lives.[8]

All this assumes, of course, that state autonomy – and now the possibility of restoring that autonomy through new regulatory fixes at an international level – should be the starting point of the analysis. But an alternative argument is that regulatory forms are themselves aspects of state structure and that this structure, which is what ultimately empowers and constrains the state in particular directions, is an object of class struggle in which the occupants of state roles themselves often participate.[9] In short, regulatory forms are a product of social compromise and not the emanation of a benevolent, far-seeing state.

So, then, how *are* we to understand the changing balance of class forces? According to the globalization literature, it has to do with the enhanced mobility of capital, the internationalization of financial markets, the creation of new international divisions of labor, and so on, which has, in turn, resulted in a reversal of the relative power of state and capital. My own view is that globalization is more product than condition and that the more fundamental condition to which globalization is one, but only one, response, is what Robert Brenner (1998) has termed "the long downturn," by which he means the period since 1970. This has been one of lower profitability, lower rates of increase in capital stock, decreased rates of increase in labor productivity and in wages in manufacturing – a sharp contrast, in other words, to the record of much of the 1950s and 1960s. Furthermore, as striking as the historical contrast has been, so, too, has been the relative uniformity with which the national economies of the West have been affected.

The general policy response to the long downturn has been an attempt to reimpose the law of value through the implementation of a neoliberal agenda. Globalization – in the senses of the establishment of branch plants in the export processing zones of less developed countries, the shift to currency convertibility, and the drive for export markets – has certainly been part of this, but only a part. If we want to talk about geography there have been restructurings *within* countries, and ones not necessarily geared to competition in international markets. But there have also been, as is far too well-known to dwell on at length, privatizations, the marketization of state functions, deregulation, an onslaught on labor through a rewriting of labor law and enhanced militancy in challenging organizing drives, and the move away from corporatist arrangements between state, labor, and business. Nor should we neglect to mention the implementation of free trade areas. Hence, while the advocates of glocalization and the hollowing out of the state might interpret these developments as exemplifying the creation of that holy grail of the regulationists – that is to say a new supranational layer of *governance* – they can also be interpreted as part of the long-term program of reasserting the law of value by widening spheres of substitutability.

However, if globalization has been only a part of this it has nevertheless been a crucial part. This is because of the essential role it has played in imposing the agenda discursively. Quite how the "globalization discourse" emerged when it did would require serious study, for it was not until sometime in the 1980s – long after the onset of the long downturn and the implementation of neoliberal policies – that it crystallized. There was an earlier literature dwelling on the fiscal crisis of the state, the need to segregate production from distribution, and the problem of governability that makes no mention of globalization.[10] Then, quite suddenly, the globalization discourse exploded on the scene. What seems to have changed in all this, though, was the recognition of the difference it could make in defusing the class tensions that neoliberalism inevitably generated. Attempts to drive down wages, which have certainly been part of the neoliberal medicine, are inevitably politically fraught unless they can be referred to some anonymous force like "international competition." So, too, is it the case with creating mass unemployment in order to reassert the disciplines of the labor market. In short, arguments about a global-ization juggernaut have provided a politically convenient cover for reimposing the disciplines of the market, and in the highly diverse forms those strategies have assumed.[11]

That states should take the initiative in the way I am proposing should not be surprising. Like capitalist firms, state agents, too, are subject to the pressure of capital as an abstract force – as value end-lessly circulating and seeking profitable outlets. The pressures are not necessarily from particular coalitions of capitalist firms, though clearly if policy initiatives fail to be endorsed after the fact and sup-ported by emergent coalitions of forces, then they will fail. And argu-ably this is the course that Thatcherism took, for it was certainly unpopular in its very early days among British business. So, when Mrs. Thatcher famously said "There is no alternative," all that she was doing was reasserting the necessary unity between state and capital in the face of contradictions subsequent to the shift in the balance of class forces brought about by the long downturn.

2 The aspatiality of regulation theory

But while we can shed doubt on the role of globalization as a mater-ial force, and one that underpins arguments about glocalization and the hollowing out of the state, there is also the point that to the extent that space *does* matter in understanding recent changes in economy and state then the regulation approach seems not the strongest point from which to begin. It is not a body of literature that was originally developed by geographers and its geography turns out to be a highly simplified one of national vs. international. Certainly, there has been interest recently on the part of geographers in moving beyond this in the direction of more complex spatializations.[12] However, these tend to have been limited, reasonably enough, by regulation theory's abid-ing interest in a process that focuses more on the state's role in achieving balanced growth than in promoting growth in the context of external challenge – failure, in other words, to escape from the state/capital separation that has been one of the hallmarks of the regulation literature. This is unfortunate, because the work of geo-graphers on the question of space has not only been fertile but espe-cially so in the context of issues of uneven development. It therefore offers attractive bases from which to launch a critical understanding of the globalization–regulation nexus, though one which will result in a discarding of the regulation approach as we know it.

More specifically, three concepts – when taken in tandem and when allied with an historical materialism that discards state-capital separation in favor of a contradictory unity – seem to offer at least steps towards a solution to the problem of the state's changing scalar fixes. Two of these ideas are a product of the spatialization of social theory led by Massey and Harvey over the last couple of decades. From Massey I take the notion of capital's geographic division of labor, and from Harvey the contradiction between fixity and mobility – a spatial form of the contradiction between use and exchange value – and its implications for capital.[13] These ideas, I believe, can be brought into a fruitful relation with one another, and even more so when combined with the idea of what I will call "the scale division of labor." Indeed, I would argue that it is changes in the scale division of labor that are at the center of arguments about globalization. Let us take each of these different ideas in turn:

i) Capital's geographic division of labor:

Both the social and technical division of labor are projected onto space, the first in the form of particular regional specializations and the second as, for example, corporate headquarter cities, branch plant towns, white collar and blue collar towns respectively, and so forth. A similar logic applies to the division of consumption and is especially apparent in the residential differentiations of metropolitan areas. This is not to say that there is a straightforward, one-to-one relation between places and positions in geographic divisions of labor or consumption: corporate headquarter cities will include branch plants, booming metropolises can, on closer examination, disclose rustbelts, just as the most upmarket suburb can include evidence of previous layers of investment corresponding to the consumption of very different housing classes. The effects, in other words, are statistical.

ii) Capital's scale division of labor:

This is a less familiar notion. The claim is that labor is divided at different geographical scales (some more locally and some at larger geographic scales) as in the categories of economic base theory. Thus, we should recall that nonbasic labor is labor that is, in effect, divided locally among those activities serving the market which is, in turn, created by firms that are involved in "export" activities. The latter, therefore, form part of a more geographically extended division of labor. This is not to say that the idea is an easy one to grasp in terms of the sorts of categories that prevail in understandings of the state's scale division of labor: thus, the "national" vs. "international" distinction is fraught with pitfalls when applied to capital. More will have to be said on that point.

iii) The movement of capital through successive stages of fixity and movement:

At the heart of David Harvey's historical-geographical materialism is the contradiction between fixity and mobility. In order for capital to be valorized it has to be embodied in relatively fixed physical and social infrastructures and resources. But once valorized, the value so realized is free to come to rest elsewhere. To the extent that this occurs, then value may no longer flow through the social relations of firms – resulting, in some places, in the threat of bankruptcy, unemployment, and fiscal crisis for state agencies. As a result, conflicts can acquire a markedly territorial form. Class struggle remains crucial but is now passed through a prism of territorial competition and conflict. As Harvey (1985: 152) says: "Global processes of class struggle appear to dissolve before our eyes into a variety of interterritorial conflicts" – which, incidentally, seems to have been one of the effects of the discourse of globalization.

But powerful as Harvey's conception has been, particularly in spatializing capital, I believe that its utility can be enhanced by bringing it into a closer relation with both the geographical and the scale divisions of labor. This is especially so if we are to use it in understanding the contemporary politics of scale. After all, Harvey's territorial coalitions are typically engaged in trying to defend an existing position or in securing an enhanced position in wider geographic divisions of labor. But as they do so through, for example, sales and investment trips overseas or the upgrading of the local physical infrastructure, and as markets expand geographically as a result of these efforts, so the scale division of labor changes and new geographic divisions of labor are created at larger geographic scales. Furthermore, as this process plays itself out relations of uneven development and of regulatory deficit bind the various geographically distinct clusters of territorialized interests together and lay the foundations for new state scalar fixes – albeit contested ones – at a variety of different scales that go far beyond those envisioned by the idea of the hollowing out of the state.

In exploring these themes I want to focus on three specific issues warranting extended scrutiny. The first of these is the tendency of the NPS to overemphasize the international. It is as if the scale division of capital has been redefined so that the international now assumes dominant weight. I alluded earlier to Radice's use of the idea of "territorial noncoincidence" as central to the problematic of the NPS. But this is a relationship that is found at other levels of the state as well and, as we will see, this calls into question some of the claims that have been made.

The second issue that is raised derives from the difficulties that have been encountered in (literally) talking about capital's scale division of labor. There is presently no satisfactory language that can extend to the full variety of production. Economic base theory and central place theory only take us so far. Beyond that point we tend to revert to the language of the scalar division of the state, in particular the national and the international. But this is highly unsatisfactory. Labor that is divided nationally in the US is divided internationally among the member states of the EU. So there is a confusion of scales that we need to consider, though this, too, can be turned to fruitful effect.

The third and final issue – and one at the heart of the matter – is the role played by territorially-based coalitions in constructing and contesting new geographic divisions of labor at new, larger, but multiple, geographic scales. As I point out below, an account of the role of relations of local dependence and the formation of coalitions to defend and enhance the flow of value through local social relations is conspicuously lacking in the NPS. Yet it is only by taking them into account that we can understand the (highly political) struggle over new scalar fixes and the meaning of those fixes for something that has also eluded the NPS, namely the role that hollowing out has played not so much in privileging capital, though that may have occurred too, but in facilitating the ability of some national growth coalitions to construct new forms of domination, new forms of imperialism, with respect to those of other countries.

Beyond Internationalization

It is empirically evident that the positions within wider divisions of labor and consumption for which localities and regions struggle through their various growth coalitions are not necessarily international ones. In fact, in some cases this is so obvious as to be hardly worth dwelling on. In US metropolitan areas forces clustering around local governments – forces variably including small retailers, developers, landlords, homeowners, and even utilities anxious about underused infrastructure – form coalitions to create new positions and to compete for existing positions within geographical divisions of consumption and production at the metropolitan scale. This is a world of upmarket and downmarket suburbs, gentrifying and red-lined neighborhoods, of warehouse and office park suburbs, and of yet others where the nonresidential tax base is more industrial in character. It is also a world of struggle between central city and periphery as the former strives to remake itself as an entertainment center for the whole metropolitan area and as a still-vibrant residential area. And it is one in which inner-suburbs strive to maintain privileged positions in the geographic division of consumption against the threat posed by outer-suburbs with their greenfield sites and ability to annex still more.

A response to this line of argument might be that those focusing on positions in geographic divisions of consumption and production within urban regions cannot afford to ignore the position of the whole region in still-wider geographic divisions of labor. Similarly, the fact that a city or suburb has a distinct role in the geographic divisions of labor and consumption of a particular urban region does not mean to say that it might not also play a role in a wider division of labor – the reconstruction of the central city as a center for higher-order office functions is a case in point. That does not entail, however, that that division of labor necessarily be international in character. In the US there is a jostling over positions in wider geographic divisions of labor similar to that within urban regions that again, seemingly, has little to do with internationalization and that likewise feeds into debates about governance in urban regions.[14] Some labor is divided almost entirely intra-nationally: insurance, banking, the convention business, the retirement industry, education, and health, for example. Other labor is divided in part intra-nationally and in part inter-nationally.[15]

Accompanying the emergence of these ever-shifting fields of contestation have been new institutions of governance designed to regulate the activities of agents at lower levels of the state's scalar division of labor and to respond to some regulatory deficit. These have included metropolitan planning boards and metropolitan transport/port/airport authorities, along with a revivified role for the county. This would suggest that metropolitan governance is by no means a simple response to the needs of a metropolitan economic base within a much more far-flung circulation of value but that it is equally, if not more so, concerned with regulating relations between constituent local governments – and, to the extent that its mission is at the local/nonlocal interface, that does not necessarily imply that the wider division of labor within which a position is sought exists at the international level.

But the emergence of, or resort to, coordinative structures of this nature should not obscure the fact that the outcomes of these struggles are highly uneven. By definition, as some succeed to higher levels in a wider division of labor others are relegated to lower ones, producing a landscape, in other words, of corporate headquarter cities and branch plant towns, new industrial spaces and rustbelts, and upmarket and downmarket suburbs.[16] In consequence, struggles around new institutional fixes, along with their various scalar expressions, cannot be divorced from the essentially unequal positions of the different, territorially-defined agents. New institutional fixes are therefore seen, variably, as a means of mitigating uneven development, as a way to protect a position of privilege, or, alternatively, as vehicles through which to widen advantages already enjoyed.

One result of this in the United States has been an ongoing and highly complex struggle around the scalar division of labor of the state, a struggle that has had several dimensions. One aspect of this has been between those states approximating to what became known as the Snowbelt and those in the so-called Sunbelt. The proximate cause for this was the displacement of employment from the old Manufacturing Belt to branch plants (particularly in small towns) in the South and Mountain West, though this was aggravated by the over-representation in the former of declining sectors like steel and consumer electronics. This led to demands from bipartisan forces in the Midwest and Northeast for what was called "a leveling of the playing field," one that was to be brought about by such measures as a federalization of the welfare state and the rescinding of the right-to-work clause of the 1947 Taft–Hartley Act.[17] Federalization would have been upwards so as to protect labor markets and businesses dependent on the health of particular local economies in what by then had become defined as the Snowbelt. In the ensuing struggle, however, the forces for decentralization prevailed under the aegis of the "New Federalism" of the Reagan and subsequent administrations. However, this had little or nothing to do with arguments about internationalization and competitiveness in a global economy.

But, superimposed on this has been a further set of conflicts between areas dependent on branches of the economy impacted by imports and those dependent on local economic bases which are highly export-oriented. The result has been a struggle between protectionist and liberalizing forces, or, in other words, conflict around the scale at which labor should be divided. This is ongoing and the outcomes represent by no means a victory for the forces of trade liberalization. It was, we should recall, the threat of protectionism that induced the Japanese automobile firms to establish branches in the United States and convert what had been expanding as part of the international division of labor into one more national in character.

Scalar Confusion

Thinking about things in this way, however, as a relation between the scale divisions of labor of capital and state respectively, mediated by the struggles of territorially-based coalitions one with another, exposes to view another problem in the NPS. This has to do with how we typically talk about geographic scale. To talk about the scalar division of labor of the state in terms of, for instance, the national, the supranational, and the subnational is one thing. But to talk about the scalar division of labor of *capital* in the same terms is quite another and risks serious confusion. The problem is that, unlike the case of the state's scale division of labor, we have no language for talking about capital's scale division of labor, apart that is from economic base theory and perhaps central place theory. This reflects many things. These include the ways in which a given capital can be part of both smaller scale and larger scale divisions of labor – there are relatively few firms which cater purely to international markets, for example. There is also the wide, seemingly impossible to categorize, variety of scales at which different capitals operate, some continental, some truly global, others quite evidently at the level of the urban region, and still others at many, many "in-between" scales. But a danger resulting from this dilemma is that we will lapse into categories like "national" and "international," as I did immediately above and as apparently is the case of the NPS. This can have serious implications for subsequent analysis, for what is a scale division of labor for capital at the national scale in one case may be international in another. To take one example, there are considerable differences in the degrees to which national economies are internationalized. Trade as a proportion of GDP is highly variant among the various OECD economies. The US economy, as is well known, is a much less open one than say that of Belgium or the Netherlands.[18] As a result, in the United States it is reasonable to assume that the markets to which urban regions have historically been oriented in trying to create for themselves new positions in a geographic division of labor have tended to be more national in scope than in less-closed economies.[19]

The rise across the United States in the twenty-year period after the Second World War (Anton and Reynolds n.d.: fig. 1) of various state departments of economic development coincides, significantly enough, with the emergence of new spatial divisions of labor on the part of firms within the United States.[20] As corporations separated off different functions in the form of branch plants, corporate head-quarters, distribution centers, and so forth, so it was possible for localities to compete for them and to start thinking of a future as a corporate headquarters city, a branch plant town, or a distribution center. This was occurring long before talk of globalization and continues to the present day.[21] In geographic terms, the United States is a very large economy, which helps account for its relatively low degree of openness. What would be international trade or tourism in Europe is often interstate (i.e., domestic) in the case of the United States. But, and importantly, the EU experience is in some ways recapitulating that of the US, for the internationalization that has occurred there has been primarily that of economic integration among the members themselves (Kleinknecht and ter Wengel 1998). This has been so much the case that by 1995 the EU economy was considerably more closed than that of the US: both exports to, and imports from, non-EU countries constituted less than 10 percent of GDP (ibid.: 641). Accordingly, Oskar Lafontaine (1998: 74), leader of the German Social Democrats, in responding to arguments about the pressures of the international, has argued that:

> Of course it is true that financial markets are international, but com-modity markets and labour markets tend to be regional. Therefore, initially, our efforts have to be concentrated on Europe. For, as in the US, in Europe, too, the percentage of foreign trade is less than ten percent. That means that the decisive switching points with regards to commodity traffic and labour markets still operate within the larger regions: in America, on the one hand, and here in Europe, on the other.

Furthermore, as the barriers to trade among EU members have come down, in the process creating the sort of internal market characteristic of the US for a very long time, the same competition for more desirable positions in a geographic division of labor that is only international to a very limited degree has taken shape. Corporations now develop their locational strategies with respect to the EU as a whole, rather than with respect to some particular member country.[22] Production facilities can be consolidated so as to achieve economies of scale, or relocated to take advantage of the lower labor costs existing in particular countries and regions.[23] There has obviously been a repositioning of cities with respect to this unified market, and this has been one source of the emergence of "border" cities like Lille or Barcelona.

In consequence, with the development of the EU, the enhanced integration of national economies one with another, and the locational strategies for which that has been the condition, debates similar to those in the United States have occurred around the scalar division of labor of the EU. As in the US case, labor and welfare standards have been to the fore and the member countries emerge once more as counterparts of the US states, competing for inward investment (Dunford 1994) – though with some restraint from the EU Commission in the form of limits to the financial incentives that can be offered. British resistance to accepting the Social Chapter is predicated in significant part on the belief that this protects its position as a relatively low-wage platform for production and export to the EU as a whole (Marquand 1994: 18).[24] There are also, however, and just as clearly, geographically localized forces in favor of something akin to the federalization of welfare standards sought in the United States by representatives of relatively high-wage areas. These have emanated primarily from Germany where the German labor movement has been a significant force and would like to extend to the rest of the EU the same sort of leveling upwards that it was able to achieve in the former East Germany.[25]

The territorialization of social relations

So far in this argument territorialization and its implications for the politics of scale have been implicit. The struggle for positions in wider divisions of labor, as well as over the restructuring of state institutions, is led by state agencies that are usually in coalition – though sometimes after the fact – with some capitalist interests and even some workers, all with stakes in particular places. But quite why these conflicts have this territorial character, and what the implications of territoriality are, have yet to be clarified.

The point of departure here is Harvey's (1985a; 1985b) path-breaking notion of historical-geographical materialism and the emphasis he placed there on the contradiction between fixity and mobility – between, as I remarked above, the need for a portion of capital to be invested in physical and social infrastructures of long life, and the need for the value subsequently produced to be free to search out the most profitable investments, regardless of their location. The implication of this is that to the extent that the value produced does not return to flow through these fixed physical and social relations then they are in imminent danger of devaluation, with all that that implies for profits, employment, wages, and the revenues of state agencies in particular places. In response, local actors often organize territorially-based coalitions which seek both to defend those fixed assets against that threat and, beyond that, to preempt the possibility altogether through the widening of markets, the modernizing of infrastructures, and through facilitating the decentralization of some activities in the form of branch plants, back offices, and so forth. My contribution has been to try to bring this conception into a closer relation with struggles around the geographical division of labor, its implications for capital's scale division of labor, and, through that, for the scalar division of labor of the state.

The struggles and conflicts that we observe in urban regions of the United States among the different local governments and their developer allies are fundamentally of the territorial sort identified by Harvey. They make no sense outside of the substantial dependence of local governments on their own tax bases or the commitments of developers to particular place-specific projects (major regional shopping centers, new upmarket developments, office and industrial parks) and the, often rearguard, struggle of smaller retailers to salvage what they can – through attempting to create new niches for the older retailing complexes of which they are a part – from a scale division of labor that is working to their disadvantage.

The integration of housing, labor, and property markets at a metropolitan level, and the resultant uneven development it spawns, have, as I remarked earlier, been the conditions for the creation of institutions of governance at the level of the urban region as a whole or, alternatively – or even as part of this – of an enhanced role for the county. But it has not been entirely bottom-up. There have also been forces at the metropolitan level which have been central to attempts to create a new layer of governance. In some instances these have come from those industries that are crucial to the economic base of the region as a whole. A case in point is Silicon Valley, where the computer industries have looked beyond the various municipalities to the county – specifically, by assuming more of the responsibility for land-use planning, the county has been seen as a means of mitigating the housing cost problem (Saxenian 1985: 88–93; Trounstine and Christensen 1982: 144–5, 170–1). A more general feature of these institutions has been the role that the utilities serving the urban region as a whole have played in organizing networks of association with chambers of commerce and local governments so as to effectively mediate the inward investment process (Cox and Wood 1997).

In some cases, and as per the NPS, the goal in establishing these institutions is to position the region in a division of labor that is international in scope. This is clearly so in the instance of Silicon Valley. But it is by no means the universal one. Moreover, one can expect the establishment of those institutions that they see as promoting their agenda, together with the rules and practices that come to govern their operation, to be highly contested by constituent local governments, their development interest allies, and the residents' associations that often line up alongside them. So, in creating new institutions of governance those struggling for positions within a division of labor or consumption that is metropolitan in scale will necessarily enter into the process of alliance construction with interests concerned about the position of the whole region in still wider geographic divisions of labor. Furthermore, these interests have a strong territorial moment. In the Silicon Valley case, what is at stake is a set of inter-firm relations, a pool of highly skilled labor that would be difficult – if not impossible – to reconstitute elsewhere. Likewise, the role that the electric and gas utilities have played in the formation of local economic development networks cannot be understood outside their own extreme levels of local dependence.[26]

One objection to this line of argument might be that it is highly context-specific, that the sorts of local dependence, the sorts of dependences on the health of particular local and regional economies that I have drawn on – those of local government, developers, the utilities – are peculiarly US in nature. There is some validity to this. For example, fiscal home rule and historic federal limits on the ability of utilities to spread their geographic risks by takeovers of utilities elsewhere are clearly important.[27] The federal structure of the state is also significant. States vary considerably in their land-use laws. This means that the knowledge that developers acquire in one is rarely portable to another in any frictionless fashion: what serves well in Denver will not necessarily serve well in Fairfax County, Virginia or in Pittsburgh, Pennsylvania.

This claim of context-specificity, therefore, might be a reasonable one, though the sheer demographic weight of the United States suggests that conditions there are an important qualifier to claims of generality about the contemporary politics of scale. But the sorts of local dependences enjoyed by the US states, both fiscal and electoral, are not that dissimilar from those of the member countries of the EU. Indeed, if anything, the latter are even more dependent on respective national economies as a result of the absence of even the most rudimentary elements of EU social and infrastructural provision within their respective jurisdictions, apart, that is, from Social Fund expend-

THE POLITICS OF SCALE   103

itures.[28] The fact of this dependence is, in turn, supported by the recent appearance of a territorial competition among member states for the investments of multinational corporations.

In contrast, in the NPS the territorial moment enjoys only the most spectral of existences. There is reference to territorial production systems but no suggestion that the demand for their own institutions of governance might, by virtue of the dependence of respective agents on particular spaces, be bottom-up rather than, or in addition to, top-down. Likewise, an emergent territorial noncoincidence as a result of globalization is a problem for central branches of the state, but quite why it would be a problem remains implicit.

An important effect of this is that even at those levels which it privileges – the national and the international – the processes that are occurring prove elusive. So, even though it might seem difficult to divorce a consideration of so-called internationalization or globalization from issues of dependent development and colonialism, that seems to have been the effect. Harvey's (2000: 13) comment with respect to that discourse of globalization, of which I believe the NPS is a particular example, is thoroughly apropos:

> The more the left adopted this discourse as a description of the state of the world (even if it was a state to be criticized and rebelled against), the more it circumscribed its own political possibilities. That so many of us took the concept [globalization] on board so uncritically in the 1980s and 1990s, allowing it to displace the far more politically charged concepts of imperialism and neocolonialism, should give us pause.

Furthermore, he suggests that adopting such a discourse "made us weak opponents of the politics of globalization particularly as these became more and more central to everything that US foreign policy was trying to achieve."

The struggle to defend and/or achieve improved positions in an international division of labor is, as I have stated earlier, a process that is unequal in its outcomes. The international institutions constructed in order to respond to regulatory dilemmas at the international level will inevitably, therefore, be the focus of a jostling for advantage. Likewise, emergent supranational institutions of governance will be seen as creating new opportunities. Martin Shaw has tried to give these institutions some coherence by defining something he calls "the western state" – something superficially congruent with both "glocalization" and "the hollowing out of the (national) state." This he sees as organized around the leadership of the United States and working through overlapping organizations like the IMF, the G7, the World Trade Organization, and NATO – that is to say "a massive, institutionally complex and messy agglomeration of state power centered on North America, Western Europe, Japan and Australasia but whose writ...has had in many senses genuinely global reach" (Shaw 1997: 501). Like other states, this one has centrality and it is Washington, DC that is the center. The role of the US administration in the various institutions constitutive of the "western state" is determined, he argues, not only by its national interests but also by the exigencies of global leadership.

But leadership has its advantages. In this regard, Panitch (2000) has written of the United States as "the new imperial state." Arguing that "the process of globalization, far from dwarfing states, has been constituted through and even by them" (Panitch 2000: 14), he goes on to suggest that, by virtue of its domination of international organizations like the IMF and the World Bank, the US has sought to bring about policy changes in the Western European states so as to reproduce US imperial dominance. In addition, the sheer size of the US economy and its attraction to transnational corporations has provided the US state with a degree of power it might not otherwise have.[29]

Likewise, there is little doubt that the East Asian crisis was seen by the United States, if not so effectively used in practice, as an opportunity. What Baghwati has called the Wall Street–Treasury–IMF Complex was clearly out to impose a complete neoliberal program on the developing economies of East Asia and, if possible, on Japan as well.[30] As Bello (1998) has argued, the US saw the crisis as an opportunity for liberalizing state-assisted economies to its advantage. Thus, a view long held in US policy circles has been that the Japanese/Asian model hinders US investment and exports (through encouraging protectionist policies in Asia) while enhancing the ability of those countries to penetrate the US market. With the winding down of the Cold War, the US has been ready to enforce its will.[31]

Conclusions

Images of a rescaling of the state, a shift of state authority both upwards to a new layer of supranational institutions and downwards to local and regional branches of the state or to decentralized forms of governance, have become common, even influential. Attempts to understand these changes have been linked to transformations in the structure of the space economy, particularly interrelated processes of localization and internationalization. An important effect has been a recomposition of class relations.

These characterizations and understandings raise empirical issues. My focus in this paper, however, has been primarily conceptual and, in particular, the problems that ensue when the chosen point of departure is regulation theory. At the heart of regulation theory is a separation of state and capital which has found resonance in recent glocalization/hollowing out the state arguments. This has assumed the specific form of an unfortunate acceptance of what has been termed by others the problem of the state's territorial noncoincidence. The economic events which the state needs to regulate in order to achieve its goals are – territorially – increasingly beyond its grasp. This is the way in which capital comes into opposition with the state and undermines its (effective) power. The result of this assumption is that the way in which the state has been involved in the construction of globalization, not just materially but also discursively, and how it has exaggerated its effects for its own purposes, is missed. Instead of examining as the starting point capital's restructuring strategies in the context of the long downturn, and as they are mediated by the state, globalization is introduced as, in effect, a *deus ex machina*.

In this regard, there is an interesting tension in the glocalization/ hollowing out literature between the regulatory framework – perhaps straitjacket – on the one hand, and a recognition that states need to look to their economic base through restructuring strategies on the other. Thus Jessop (1994: 261–2) has suggested that "almost all states have become more involved in managing the process of internationalization in the hope of minimizing its harmful domestic repercussions and/or of securing maximum benefit to its own home-based transnational firms and banks... This leads to the paradox that, as states lose control over the national economy, they are forced to enter the fray on behalf of their own MNCs... The combination of the late Fordist trend to internationalization and the post-Fordist stress on flexible production has encouraged states to focus on the supply-side problem of international competitiveness and to attempt to subordinate welfare policy to the demands of flexibility." In other words, states are being forced into doing something that they do not want to do, something that somehow goes against their regulatory agenda, and that provides growing support against the claims of redistribution. States themselves, it would seem, are participating in the globalization of respective economies, though reluctantly and as a result of forces pressing from outside.

The other problem with regulation theory from the standpoint of saying something about the state's changing scalar fixes is its geography, which is highly oversimplified and reduced to a simple national vs. international contrast. This has been a target for geographers, albeit within the terms of regulation theory. As a result of that limitation, they have yet to escape from an assumption about space also embedded in that theory's primitives: that it is about order rather than struggle.

In order to address these issues, then, I have drawn on Harvey's writings about the geopolitics of capitalism, suitably amended. From the standpoint of addressing the state's scalar fixes, Harvey's conception has many advantages: it does not fall into the trap of state-capital separation, and it is as open with respect to the diverse scalar expressions of geographically uneven development and its tensions as it is possible to be. Furthermore, the concern with its contradiction between fixity and mobility means that struggle over space is central to its concerns. I have found it useful, however, to place it in a closer relation with geographic conceptions of the division of labor. This is for two reasons.

First, it is around the achievement and defense of improved positions in the geographic division of labor that alliances of state and capital organize themselves. This is something characteristic not just of the national level but of whatever the geographic scale at which capitals and state agents find themselves dependent on localized social relations, and this covers a tremendous variety of possibilities. Second, as they so organize, as they seek to defend a quasi-monopoly position, so commodity chains are lengthened and scale divisions of labor undergo change – something which is quite central to the literature on new state scalar fixes but which I have tried to emancipate from a simple, and highly misleading, national/international distinction.

The geopolitics implied by this conception is clearly quite different from what we might extract from images of a glocalizing world. Instead of the emphasis on order, on the "local-global disorder" (Peck and Tickell 1994), the stress is on struggle. Order, to the degree that it is achieved, is a mere means to successful struggle, perhaps a tactical retreat in the face of a strengthened labor movement, as in capital's "Golden Age" or, as with the new supranational state institutions, a means of imposing a new imperialism. The question is obvious but perhaps we need a reminder: order for whom?

This is a principle that cannot be forced into a simple national–international or local–global understanding of geographic scale. Interests are constituted at many different geographic scales and contest positions in scale divisions of labor that are equally varied and equally subject to redefinition. Equally, part of the problem is the way the territorial has been marginalized. But as I hope to have shown, any attempt to understand the state's scalar fixes should examine the concrete unities of state and capital that are the vehicle through which it is constructed – and in far more varied forms than can possibly be grasped by the ideal types that have recently become influential and which betray the significance of an unfortunate encounter: when globalization met regulation theory.

ACKNOWLEDGMENTS

The author would like to express his appreciation for the helpful comments of the editors, Ray Hudson, Andy Jonas, Bae-Gyoon Park, and Andy Wood on an earlier draft of this paper.

NOTES

1 To say "less qualified" is not intended as a criticism. A problem with Jessop's work is that qualifications are made but how, and the degree to which, they might counter his major claims is not addressed.
2 His 1999 paper provides a good overview of his position, but see also Jessop (2000).
3 Neil Brenner (1998: 3), who has clearly absorbed and for the most part accepted the arguments of Jessop and Swyngedouw, provides a good example in his discussion of global cities: "As coordinates of state territorial organization, global cities are local-regional levels of governance situated within larger, reterritorialized matrices of 'glocalized' state institutions. The re-scaling of the state is a key 'accumulation strategy' through which cities throughout the world economy are being promoted by their host states as locational nodes for transnational capital investment."
4 For an early statement along these lines see Storper and Scott (1989).
5 Moreover, the record of New Towns in Britain and the various *pôles d'équilibre* in France might give pause as to the novelty of such interest.
6 The decentralization of the employment relation is another area where the evidence is very mixed. A recent survey by Kenworthy (1997: 37) notes that in most OECD countries wages are still determined at the sectoral level. There is also a danger of reading off the experience of all the advanced capitalist societies from that of Britain and the United States. A recent review of the record of works councils notes: "There is striking convergence among developed nations, with the sole exception of the United States and Great Britain, that works councils or similar institutions, intermediate between managerial discretion and collective bargaining, are part of a well-functioning labor relations system. In most of Europe, the past decade witnessed both an expansion of the collective participation rights of workers and more extensive production-related

communication and cooperation between managements and work-forces" (Rogers and Streeck 1994: 148, cited in Kenworthy 1997:38).

7 The term is actually Murray's (1971). But, as far as I know, Radice was the first to apply it to an understanding of the demise of Keynesian policies.

8 This is a more common theme in the globalization literature than it has been credited with. Both Hirst and Thompson (1997) and Drache (1996) emphasize the need for new institutions of governance at the international level.

9 This, in fact, is the essence of Jessop's strategic-relational approach to the state, an approach which curiously he does not draw on in his "hollowing out of the state" thesis (see MacLeod 1997: 545).

10 Offe's (1984) widely cited book *Contradictions of the Welfare State* was part of this, as was O'Connor's (1973) *Fiscal Crisis of the State* and Crozier et al.'s (1975) edited collection *The Crisis of Democracy*. Significantly, in his introduction to Offe's book, John Keane (who edited the English-language version) writes (p. 17): "Offe does not consider whether the present transnational migration of industrial capital to the peripheral capitalist countries is a direct response by capital to this encroachment upon its power" and cites approvingly the study of Fröbel et al., *The New International Division of Labor*, which appeared in 1980 and was to prove highly influential.

11 On the other hand, in some cases it would seem that it has also meshed with the goals of particular sectors of the economy. Webber (1998), in a paper that underlines the unity of state and capital that I am emphasizing here, shows how in the case of policy changes in Australia globalization may have resulted less from the desire to reimpose the disciplines of the market and more from the intersectoral struggle between, in that instance, manufacturing industry that had been protected and the mining and agricultural industries (and more recently retailing) which wanted those barriers lifted so as to reduce their own costs of operation. Thus, he states (p. 135): "It is possible to argue that recent changes in policy are less a matter of deregulation than an element of a process of restructuring, a change in the strategy of growth away from the import-substituting industrialization of the early post-war years and into a policy of internationalization. Economics, by this argument, is not separate from politics. As this example intimates, it is also possible to argue that globalization has been the process whereby a whole host of nations have altered their strategies of growth, that we have created global pressures as much as being their innocent victims."

12 Examples include Gertler (1999) and Peck and Tickell (1995a).

13 Massey actually uses the expression "the *spatial* division of labor." I prefer "geographic" to "spatial" since I think it is less encumbered with associations (as with the technical division of labor) and more flexible.

14 The economic bases of some urban regions (e.g., Hartford, CT; Nash-ville, TN; Fort Lauderdale, FL; Rochester, MN) are almost entirely de-

pendent on regional or national markets and relatively unaffected by international competition. To find one equally dependent on international markets, on the other hand, is not easy.

15   Consider, in this regard, the wide differences that exist between sectors in terms of trade as a proportion of total production.

16   Though, as I cautioned earlier, these effects are always statistical: not all the variance is between places.

17   The Taft–Hartley Act allows states the option of enforcing the so-called "right-to-work" (RTW) clause in labor contracts, in effect banning the union shop whereby workers hired in a unionized workplace have to join the union within a certain period. Such right-to-work legislation has been taken up primarily in Southern and Mountain West states, which have historically been hungry for inward investment (so that they might move upwards in the geographic division of labor) and which generally lack the strong representation of organized labor that could have opposed RTW legislation.

18   The average of imports and exports as a percent of GDP for select countries in 1998 was as follows: Belgium, 62%; Canada, 38.5%; France, 21.5%; Germany, 23.5%; Italy, 25.5%; Japan, 7.25%; the Netherlands, 45.5%; the United Kingdom, 31%; and the United States, 12.5%.

19   This statement clearly abstracts from competition for finance and, indeed, my whole approach has tended to abstract from the question of its internationalization. However, finance capital clearly exhibits its own characteristic circulation patterns. It is now well known, for instance, that portfolio investment exhibits a very strong national bias, as does foreign direct investment. This is despite the rapid growth in rates of internationalization for both of these forms of finance (Kenworthy 1997: 11, 13).

20   By 1970, 35 of the states had established economic development departments.

21   Neil Brenner (1998: 18) has written: "as coordinates of state territorial power, Fordist-Keynesian regional and local regulatory institutions functioned primarily as transmission belts of central state socioeconomic policies. Their goal was above all to promote growth and redistribute its effects on a national scale." But in the United States, where local economic development initiatives aimed at attracting inward investment have a much longer history, this was just not the case.

22   Thus Dunford (1994: 109) suggests that "[t]he removal of non-tariff barriers makes it easier to supply the whole of the European market from a smaller number of locations and reduces further the incentive to locate inside of national markets."

23   Lung (1992) has referred to the tendency for the auto assemblers to locate their new factories in lower-wage regions like the Iberian Peninsula or Southern Italy. The much-publicized Nissan factory in Northeastern England falls in the same category. But he also points out how this is less likely in the manufacture of skill-intensive, upmarket cars such as those produced by Mercedes and BMW.

24   Dunford has referred to the way in which differences in welfare legisla-
     tion are influencing industrial location decisions, identifying the much-
     publicized and controversial movement of a Hoover factory from Dijon
     to Cambuslang in Scotland as a case in point.

25   Quoting Oskar Lafontaine (1998: 76) once again: "It would be a mistake to
     get involved in a competition to see who delivers the lowest welfare bene-
     fits, who has the least employment rights when it comes to workplace
     dismissals, and who has the least worker participation in management.
     Some conservatives are of the opinion that we should stage such competi-
     tions in the European Community, but it would be a mistake. What has
     gone on in the building trade is a good example. We do not want to
     prohibit foreign workers taking jobs on German building sites, but we
     insist that foreign workers be employed on our building sites according
     to collective tariff agreements laid down in Germany!"

26   These include not just the utilities, though they are the ones who often
     organize the inward investment process. Other locally dependent inter-
     ests, dependent on the growth of the local economy, will also be to the
     fore in supporting the new infrastructural investments (such as an
     expanded airport or modernized dock facilities), development projects
     seen as clearing away the obstacles to the city's ability to expand its
     economic base. These will include the land development complex (the
     developers, the building supply industries, savings and loans institu-
     tions), some banks that have yet to expand beyond a particular urban
     base, and the local media empires consisting of overlapping newspaper
     and TV-station ownerships.

27   This may obviously be changing. The implications of the deregulation of
     the electricity industry for the interest of the utilities in local economic
     development are far from clear. They are now limited to the function of
     distribution and no longer have an assured rate of return on assets,
     which has made them very cautious about investing in new physical
     infrastructure. Rather, their interest in local economic development now
     seems to be confined to one of directing potential users in the direction
     of underused capacity in their system. The future of their economic
     development departments is presently in something of a limbo. The fact
     that power generation has been split off and that the generators can sell
     to whatever industrial user they wish, regardless of where they are lo-
     cated, has also altered the balance of forces.

28   Judging from the concern evinced by Britain's Labour government for
     the North–South divide, this dependence, at least in its electoral aspects,
     can extend to the geography of the national economy as well.

29   In this context Panitch (2000: 17) cites Susan Strange approvingly:
     "TNCs based in the United States, plus TNCs based elsewhere but
     having a large part of their profit making operations in the US, play a
     dominant role. Any TNC, whatever its nationality, that hopes to keep a
     substantial share of the world market now finds it indispensable to oper-
     ate in the territorial United States. The political authority, therefore, that

most TNC executives are likely to heed the most and be most anxious to avoid offending, is that based in Washington."

30 Baghwati is quoted from a December 31, 1997 interview with the *Times of India* (cited in Wade and Veneroso 1998: 19).

31 This is not to say that states may not have to be prodded before they see the possibilities opening up. As Radice (1998: 268–9) has written: "globalization in its early business-school form... can be seen as an argument about how US capitalism could resist the challenge to its hegemony. When the Johnson administration took measures to limit capital exports in 1968, there were strong echoes of earlier debates over the US's world role; although US firms were able to replace domestic funding sources with Eurodollar or local borrowings, those parts of US business with major interests abroad had to challenge this neo-isolationism. The argument that global expansion was the inevitable path of business development served two purposes. First, it signaled to US labor and to federal and state governments that capital could respond to high wages and high taxes by shifting abroad. Secondly, it encouraged the US state to promote a more liberal international regime in trade and finance, which could give US business a competitive advantage while its competitors' operations remained overwhelmingly national."

REFERENCES

Albo, G. 1994: "Competitive austerity" and the impasse of capitalist employment policy. In R. Miliband and L. Panitch (eds.), *Between Globalism and Nationalism: Socialist Register 1994*. London: Merlin Press, 144–70.

Amin, A. and Robbins, K. 1990: The re-emergence of regional economies? The mythical geography of flexible accumulation. *Environment and Planning D: Society and Space*, 8 (1), 7–34.

Anton, T. J. and Reynolds, R. (n.d.): Old federalism and new policies for state economic development. Discussion Paper, A. Alfred Taubman Center for Public Policy and American Institutions, Brown University.

Bello, W. 1998: East Asia: On the eve of the great transformation. *Review of International Political Economy*, 5 (3), 424–44.

Borchert, J. 1996: Welfare-state retrenchment: Playing the national card. *Critical Review*, 10 (1), 63–94.

Brenner, N. 1998 Global cities, glocal states: Global city formation and state territorial restructuring in contemporary Europe. *Review of International Political Economy*, 5 (1), 1–37.

Brenner, R. 1998: The economics of global turbulence. *New Left Review* 229, 1–265.

Burnham, P. 1997: Globalization: States, markets and class relations. *Historical Materialism*, 1, 150–60.

Clarke, S. 1988: Overaccumulation, class struggle and the regulation approach. *Capital and Class*, 36, 59–92.

Cox, K. R. and Wood, A. 1997: Competition and cooperation in mediating the global: The case of local economic development. *Competition and Change*, 2 (1), 65–94.

Crozier, M., Huntington, S., and Watanuki, J. (eds.) 1975: *The Crisis of Democracy: Report on the Governability of Democracies to the Trilateral Commission*. New York: New York University Press.

Drache, D. 1996: From Keynes to K-Mart: Competitiveness in a corporate age. In R. Boyer and D. Drache (eds.), *States Against Markets*. London: Routledge, 31–61.

Dunford, M. 1994: Winners and losers: The new map of economic inequality in the European Union. *European Urban and Regional Studies*, 1 (2), 95–114.

Fröbel, F., Heinrichs, J., and Kreye, O. 1980: *The New International Division of Labour: Structural Unemployment in Industrialised Countries and Industrialisation in Developing Countries*. Cambridge: Cambridge University Press.

Gertler, M. 1999: Negotiated path or "business as usual"? Ontario's transition to a continental production regime. *Space and Polity*, 3 (2), 199–216.

Harvey, D. 1985a: The geopolitics of capitalism. In D. Gregory and J. Urry (eds.), *Social Relations and Spatial Structures*. London: Macmillan, 128–63.

Harvey, D. 1985b: *The Urbanization of Capital*. Oxford: Blackwell.

Harvey, D. 2000: *Spaces of Hope*. Berkeley and Los Angeles: University of California Press.

Holloway, J. 1987: The red rose of Nissan. *Capital and Class*, 32, 142–64.

Jessop, B. 1994: Post-Fordism and the state. In A. Amin (ed.), *Post-Fordism: A Reader*. Oxford: Blackwell, 251–79.

Jessop, B. 1999: Narrating the future of the national economy and the national state? Remarks on remapping regulation and reinventing governance. In G. Steinmetz (ed.), *State/Culture*. Ithaca, NY: Cornell University Press, 378–405.

Jessop, B. 2000: The crisis of the national spatio-temporal fix and the tendential ecological dominance of globalizing capitalism. *International Journal of Urban and Regional Research*, 24 (2), 323–60.

Kenworthy, L. 1997: Globalization and economic convergence. *Competition and Change*, 2 (1), 1–64.

Kleinknecht, A. and ter Wengel, J. 1998: The myth of economic globalisation. *Cambridge Journal of Economics*, 22, 637–47.

Lafontaine, O. 1998: The future of German social democracy. *New Left Review*, 227, 72–87.

Lovering, J. 1990: Fordism's unknown successor: A comment on Scott's theory of flexible accumulation and the re-emergence of regional economies. *International Journal of Urban and Regional Research*, 14 (1), 159–74.

Lung, Y. 1992: Global competition and transregional strategy: Spatial reorganization of the European car industry. In M. Dunford and G. Kafkalas (eds.), *Cities and Regions in the New Europe: The Global–Local Interplay and Spatial Development Strategies*. London: Bellhaven Press, 68–85.

MacLeod, G. 1997: Globalizing Parisian thought-waves: Recent advances in the study of social regulation, politics, discourse and space. *Progress in Human Geography*, 21 (4), 530–53.

MacLeod, G. 1999: Place, politics and "scale dependence." *European Urban and Regional Studies*, 6 (3), 231–53.

MacLeod, G. and Goodwin, M. 1999: Space, scale and state strategy: Towards a re-interpretation of contemporary urban and regional governance. *Progress in Human Geography*, 23 (4), 503–27.

Mann, M. 1997: Has globalization ended the rise and rise of the nation-state? *Review of International Political Economy*, 4 (3), 472–96.

Marquand, D. 1994: Reinventing federalism: Europe and the left. *New Left Review*, 203, 17–26.

Murray, R. 1971: The internationalization of capital and the nation state. *New Left Review* 67, 84–109.

Notermans, T. 1997: Social democracy and external constraints. In K. R. Cox (ed.), *Spaces of Globalization*. New York: Guilford, 201–39.

O'Connor, J. 1973: *The Fiscal Crisis of the State*. New York: St. Martin's Press.

Offe, C. 1984: *Contradictions of the Welfare State*. Cambridge, MA: MIT Press.

Panitch, L. 2000: The new imperial state. *New Left Review*, 2 (New Series), 5–20.

Peck, J. 1995: Moving and shaking: Business elites, state localism and urban privatism. *Progress in Human Geography*, 19 (1), 16–46.

Peck, J. 1996: *Work-Place*. New York: Guilford.

Peck, J. and Tickell, A. 1994: Searching for a new institutional fix: The *after-Fordist* crisis and global–local disorder. In A. Amin (ed.), *Post-Fordism: A Reader*. Oxford: Blackwell, 280–315.

Peck, J. and Tickell, A. 1995a: The social regulation of uneven development: Regulatory deficit, England's South East and the collapse of Thatcherism. *Environment and Planning A*, 27, 15–40.

Peck, J. and Tickell, A. 1995b: Business goes local: Dissecting the business agenda in Manchester. *International Journal of Urban and Regional Research*, 19 (1), 55–78.

Pierson, P. 1996: The new politics of the welfare state. *World Politics*, 48, 143–79.

Radice, H. 1984: The national economy: A Keynesian myth? *Capital and Class*, 22, 111–40.

Radice, H. 1998: "Globalization" and national differences. *Competition and Change*, 3, 63–291.

Rogers, J. and Streeck, W. 1994: Workplace representation overseas: The works council story. In R. B. Freeman (ed.), *Working Under Different Rules*. New York: Russell Sage Foundation, 97–156.

Saxenian, A.-L. 1985: Silicon Valley and Route 128: Regional prototypes or historic exception? In M. Castells (ed.), *High Technology, Space and Society*. Beverly Hills: Sage, 81–105.

Scott, A. J. 1988: *New Industrial Spaces*. London: Pion.

Shaw, M. 1997: The state of globalization: Towards a theory of state transformation. *Review of International Political Economy*, 4 (3), 497–513.

Storper, M. and Scott, A. J. 1989: The geographical foundations and social regulation of flexible production complexes. In J. Wolch and M. Dear (eds.), *The Power of Geography*. London: Unwin Hyman, 21–40.

Swyngedouw, E. 1997a: Neither global nor local: "Glocalization" and the politics of scale. In K. R. Cox (ed.), *Spaces of Globalization*. New York: Guilford, 137–66.

Swyngedouw, E. 1997b: Excluding the other: The production of scale and scaled politics. In R. Lee and J. Wills (eds.), *Geographies of Economies*. London: Arnold, 167–76.

Trounstine, P. J. and Christensen, T. 1982: *Movers and Shakers*. New York: St. Martin's Press.

Wade, R. and Veneroso, F. 1998: The Asian crisis: The high debt model versus the Wall Street–Treasury–IMF Complex. *New Left Review*, 228, 2–23.

Webber, M. 1998: Producing globalization: Apparel and the Australian state. In A. Herod, G. Ó Tuathail, and S. Roberts (eds.), *An Unruly World? Globalization, Governance and Geography*. London: Routledge, 135–61.

4

Retheorizing the Scale of Globalization: Topologies, Actor-networks, and Cosmopolitanism

Alan Latham

Introduction

> World is crazier and more of it than we think,
> Incorrigibly plural. I peel and portion
> A tangerine and spit the pips and feel
> The drunkenness of things being various.

Louis MacNeice in McCormack (1999)

The past decade has seen a flourishing of interest in the problematics of geographical scale. This concern with scale is closely related to a wider preoccupation throughout the social and economic sciences with the process of globalization. Whereas early theorists of globalization stressed homogenization and destratification, scale theorists have pointed out how we are currently witnessing what Zygmunt Bauman (1998: 70) describes as "a world-wide *restratification*, in the course of which a new socio-cultural hierarchy ... is put together." This restratification is constructed through a complex bricolage of objects, ideas, images, and people, a bricolage which has created an existence for many – rich as well as poor – in which movement between the worlds of the local and global is an everyday, taken-for-granted event. Nevertheless, while pioneering scale theorists like Neil Smith (1987, 1992, 1993) and Erik Swyngedouw (1992a, 1992b, 1996), and related theorists of globalization such as Doreen Massey (1993, 1999b) or Manuel

Castells (1989, 1996a), have provided valuable leverage into this new global world, they have generally failed to develop, I would argue, an adequate analytical language for exploring the ways in which everyday life practices are intertwined between the local and the global. Indeed, there is an irony in the contrast between the dexterity many individuals, entrepreneurs, and organizations show in negotiating the scaling of the global to the local, and the clumsiness of the dominant contemporary academic descriptions of this scaling. In this chapter I want to examine the limitations of these dominant analytics of globalization and scale and argue for the usefulness of retheorizing globalization in terms of what Michel Serres (1982; Serres and Latour 1995) has called topologies.

To talk of topologies is to draw on the recent work of geographers and sociologists such as Nigel Thrift (1995, 1996a, 1999a, 1999b), Jon Murdoch (1995, 1997a, 1997b, 1998, 1999), and Kevin Hetherington (1997a, 1997b, 1998) who, along with Serres, have been trying to rethink the traditional analytical tools with which time and space have been theorized in the human sciences. Developing the notion of a topological analysis of globalization, I want to examine how such an analysis helps us productively articulate a sense of the ways in which specific places are simultaneously made as both local and global, without necessarily being wholly either. I want to argue that, through looking closely at the collection of actor-networks (cf. Callon 1986, 1991; Latour 1987, 1991, 1992, 1993, 1996; Law 1994) involved in the construction of actual places – that is to say, the skein(s) of relationships between bodies, materials, and information through which society is built and unbuilt – it is possible to gain a better understanding of the diverse and discontinuous agglomeration of relationships through which the "global" is, in fact, made. In arguing this, I do not wish to claim that the world lacks structure or hierarchy. Bauman is right to assert that globalization involves a process of restratification. Rather, my aim in stressing that the world is made up of complex intertwinings of actor-networks, that it is "fibrous, threadlike, wiry, stringy, ropy, capillary" (Latour in Thrift 1999a: 302), is to further our understanding of how social structure and hierarchy are built and maintained through more complex and heterogeneous assemblages than is usually realized.

There are, of course, many possible ways to advance this argument. However, one of the strategic advantages that the actor-network focused, topological approach that I am advocating here has is that it allows us to see how very ordinary objects and relations are implicated in holding together quite extraordinary "imbroglios" (Latour 1993: 3) of time-space. Given this, I want to begin by introducing a place quite obviously organized by a range of global-(izing) relationships – Ponsonby Road, Auckland, New Zealand. This road is a place theorists of globalization should be able to make sense of with relative ease. Yet, as we will witness, Ponsonby Road's uncanny familiarity has more surprises and complexity within it than conventional accounts will allow.

Tuatara

> It's perfect as it is: two
> beaded glasses on the bar,
> our faces eager with stories,
> the lovely pause before
> the next headlong rush,
> & still such pleasure in it.
>
> Anne French (1998: 13)

Ponsonby Road is a sprawling, charming, mess of a street skirting the margins of Auckland's downtown office district (see figure 4.1).[1] Originally a retail and service strip for the Victorian and Edwardian weather-board bungalows which crouch on the slopes to its left and right, the fortunes of the road have see-sawed enormously throughout its 120–year history. From a state of relative prosperity, the Road slid into dereliction in the 1950s and 1960s. Isolated by the construction of motorways to its north and west, and weakened by the slow but steady suburban exodus of the professional and tradesman families which had been the traditional core of the Ponsonby community, Ponsonby Road came to be defined by the tatty corner stores, rag-tag second-hand furniture dealers, and the camphor-ball smell of the charity clothing shops struggling for survival along it. In 1992, when three Auckland filmmakers banded together to take out the lease of the former Salvation Army store, not an awful lot had changed. The area around the Road *had* experienced a gradual economic revival as a new generation of Pakeha professionals rediscovered the tightly bound charms of colonial architecture and property speculation. On the Road itself, a cheerful hodgepodge of slightly tatty ethnic restaurants had made themselves a home. Yet these somehow added to Ponsonby Road's languid, hung-over feel. Sensing a business opportunity, Richard Riddiford, Jonathan Dowling, and Michele Fantl set about changing Ponsonby Road for good. Ripping out the original art deco shop frontage and trading the peeling white paint for spangley silver, they transformed one of these tatty old buildings into Tuatara,

Figure 4.1   Ponsonby Road: cafés, bars, and restaurants

a bar cum café cum restaurant which opened in February 1993 oozing confidence, style, and money.

Riddiford, Dowling, and Fantl conceived Tuatara as a meeting place for people working in the new media industries – advertising, television production, and print enterprises – to which they belonged and for which Ponsonby, and Ponsonby Road, was becoming increasingly central. Its aesthetic, polished wooden floors, white walls, crisp black leather snugs, and subdued lighting whispered a cosmopolitan knowingness which broke with New Zealand's traditional masculine drinking culture, while also nodding to the international orientation of its target clientele. As Riddiford (1998) put it in a statement to the Liquor Licensing Authority, Tuatara was "a move away from the old style booze barns and all they stood for" in favor of a more urbane environment where "people comfortably socialise and dine,... a place where women could come alone or meet with friends without feeling threatened."

The prosperity of Tuatara and fellow innovators like SPQR, famed for its gorgeously flamboyant wait-staff and pre-raphaelite concrete and steel interior, attracted a multiple of imitators and competitors, including The Garage Bar, Woody's, Chill Bar, Atlas Power Café, GPK, Masala, Crush, The Oval, Yum Yum Noodles, Sushi and Barfly, Summer Street Café, One Red Dog, Estasi, Angelsea Bar and Grill, Bella, Bistro Bambina, The Safari Lounge, Stella, Surrender Dorothy, The Red Tomato, Decadenza, Melanzane, and Blitz. Many of these establishments introduced their own distinctive aesthetic and culinary innovations but, most importantly, they all shared Tuatara's cosmopolitan, anti-provincial outlook. Indeed, visiting Auckland recently, an American university professor and expert on globalization remarked on the uncanniness he felt walking down Ponsonby Road: there were the same stylish restaurants and cafés with the same athletic-looking, tanned professionals dressed in carefully tailored casual wear dining within them that he had encountered during his travels elsewhere around the Pacific Rim.

The American professor's comment is suggestive. The Ponsonby Road of today *does* have a feel similar to many gentrified inner-city streets throughout the world. It is no longer marked by its former dilapidation and its rehabilitation is defined in some way by its globalness. But, while Ponsonby Road and the people who populate its restaurants and bars clearly do bear the marks of the kind of globalized middle-class consumption culture described by writers like David Harvey (1989a, 1989b), Saskia Sassen (1991, 1998), or Helmut Häußermann and Walter Siebel (1987), there are also other things in play. For one, implicit within the work of writers like Harvey et al. is the idea that global trends originate within specific "ordering and control centres" (Amin 1997: 130), first-order world cities like New York, London, Paris, Los Angeles, Hong Kong, or Tokyo. Incubated in these cities of innovation, cultural trends cascade downwards, passing through ever more marginal and insignificant cities and regions. Yet, to take an example, the style of casual dining combined with casual drinking which is central to Tuatara's image has only emerged as a significant trend within the London hospitality scene in the late 1990s, and it has no obvious equivalents in many so-called world cities. More centrally, the many vernacular elements within Ponsonby Road point to something beyond the merely global. Tuatara itself is named after the mosaic of a Tuatara lizard by the New Zealand artist Warren Tippet which greets customers as they enter. Equally, Riddiford's stress on the need to work against and remould local customs and habits suggests that what is unfolding along Ponsonby Road is no simple copy of a metropolitan original. How, then, are we to interpret the threading together of the local and the global that is taking place in spaces like Tuatara?

In asking this question, I want to put forward three central criteria through which we can judge the efficacy of any attempt to make sense of this fundamental local–global dialectic:

1)   Any account must view the world as constituted by a multitude of spatialities and temporalities, and it should be capable of narrating the connections, disconnections, and interdependencies that either link these spatialities and temporalities together or that keep them apart.
2)   It must be able to make sense of the small actors and small transformations remaking the world, *as well as* the large ones. Following from this, it should not assume *a priori* that what is large is more important or more global than what is small.
3)   Last, it must be able to tell clear and relevant stories about the world. To do this requires not only a capacity to tell concrete stories about how relationships are bound together (Giddens 1984: 17) through time and space. It additionally demands that we can make some kind of judgement about the importance and hierarchy of these relationships.

In the section that follows I want to examine how two figures central to the debate on the spatial-temporal dimensions of globalization – Manuel Castells and Doreen Massey – have framed the global/ local problematic. My purpose in doing this is, in part, to show what is at stake in the argument about the nature of the time-space of globalization. My other aim is to highlight some limitations within the accounts of even highly sophisticated thinkers like Castells and Massey, and to begin to show how a greater attention to the three criteria set out above can aid in developing more insightful accounts of our global/local world.

Theorizing the Global I: Manuel Castells and Doreen Massey

Castells – space of flows

Manuel Castells is perhaps the social sciences' most audacious theorist of globalization. Starting out with the aim of writing a general theory of capitalist urbanization (Castells 1976), Castells moved on to nothing less than an examination of the techno-social bases of contemporary industrial society (Castells 1985, 1989, 1996a, 1997, 1998; Castells and Hall 1994). Such a broad-scale examination was necessary for, as he wrote in *The Informational City* (1989: 1), "[a] technological revolution of historic proportions is transforming the fundamental dimensions of human life: time and space." This transformation is structured around three key trends:

Information Technology. Through the past 30 years or so, the development and dissemination of a range of information technologies have transformed the world economy (Castells 1989, 1994, 1996a, 1996b). Technologies like the integrated circuit, the microprocessor, digitalization, genetics, and the Internet have created a whole new range of products and production possibilities. Thus, this period has seen the introduction of a vast array of new consumer products which are dependent on microelectronics – personal computers, VCRs, mobile phones, video games, CDs, and so forth – as well as the reinvigoration of established consumer goods markets. It has also seen the development of new modes of development in which knowledge *qua* knowledge has become *the* central economic driving force (Castells 1996a: 17).

Network Organizations. Central to this new "informational" mode of development is a new, emergent organizational form: "the network enterprise" (Castells 1996a, 1996b). The defining organizational form of the industrial mode of development was the vertically integrated firm. In contrast, in the informational mode of development production is structured through complex networks of linkages and alliances between companies. These organizational networks are constructed in response to specific projects and, as such, are much more fluid and nonhierarchical than was the case with the vertically integrated firm. What is more, as new communications technologies allow for the real-time coordination of materials and information across space, these network organizations are much less bound together by spatial propinquity than ever before.

Real Virtuality. Just as information technology is changing the logic and trajectory of production, so too is it altering the way in which culture is produced and understood. In place of a culture structured through the mass media, media are increasingly organized through more personalized and specialized channels. Thus, the new media continue the earlier trajectory of saturating society in a sea of visual and aural communication. But the experience of this communication is structured through very specific communities and associational networks, not through rigid, nationally organized ones, as was previously the case. The end result of this, Castells (1996a: 373, 1997) argues, is the generation of a "culture of real virtuality ... a system in which reality itself ... is entirely captured, fully immersed in a virtual image setting."

The product of these three trends is the development of what Castells has famously called "the space of flows" (Castells 1989, 1996a, 1997). This space of flows is the dominant spatial-temporal logic of the emergent informational society. It is defined by a profound lack of spatial *and* temporal depth.

In stressing the centrality of the space of flows, Castells is not arguing that the world is becoming more homogeneous. In fact, his argument goes some way in the opposite direction. It suggests that the logic of the informational age is precisely to generate and recycle local difference. The space of flows uses difference as a resource both for producing cultural innovation and as a way for maintaining an exit strategy from places where it is currently committed. However, this difference is generated and sustained within an intensely asymmetrical relationship between local and global forces. As a cultural resource within the space of flows "[l]ocalities become disembodied from their cultural, historical, geographical meaning, and reintegrated into functional networks, or into image collages, inducing a space of flow that substitutes for a space of places" (Castells 1996a: 375). Equally, localities are economically dependent on the decisions of a global elite owing no allegiance to any particular place or nationality. Thus, Castells argues that the articulation of an ever more pervasive and powerful space of flows generates a profound disjuncture between people's everyday experience and the structural logic of the global economy.

Castells's argument deserves to be taken seriously. Nevertheless, his conceptualization of globalization suffers from a number of important limitations.

A critique of the space of flows

From its very beginning, one of the key tropes of critical globalization theory has been that of local disempowerment in the face of global forces (Frank 1969; Wallerstein 1979). Zygmunt Bauman demonstrates this tradition's ongoing vitality in his critically acclaimed *Globalization: The Human Consequences* (1998: 2), where he writes "[b]eing local in a globalized world is a sign of social deprivation and degradation." And Bauman is by no means alone. David Harvey (1989, 1996, 2000) frames globalization as local disenfranchisement, as do Neil Smith (1993, 1996, 1997) and Erik Swyngedouw (1992a, 1996), while the single most significant claim of the global cities literature – itself inspired by John Friedmann (1986) and carried forward by the prodigious scholarship of Saskia Sassen (1991, 1994, 1998) – is that cities like London, New York, and Tokyo have become key staging points in global economic networks which float over and beyond the control of any individual community or nation-state [see McCann, this volume, for a critique of the representational practices concerning scale often employed in the global cities literature].

Castells's account of the space of flows fits neatly into this tradition of globalization writing. But, while a sense of disempowerment and disenfranchisement may be one of the central phenomenological dimensions of contemporary globalization, and while it may well provide an important justification for studying globalization, analytically it is a poor place from which to begin. This is for three reasons.

First, such accounts immediately assume *a priori* that global processes are indeed strong and possess some kind of systematic logic. Not only does this produce a unidirectional narrative – the global, the space of flows, produces events to which the local is obliged to respond – but it refuses to ask the question of how actors who appear powerful came to be so, and how this power is maintained. Second, and in a related manner, Castells's account does not engage with the inherent "stickiness" of the world (Callon 1986). Dominant actors within the global economy might like to portray the world as a smooth communicative surface over which they have mastery. Yet, the reality is that it takes a Herculean effort to make and maintain any communicative network (cf. Thrift 1995, 1996b). The networks of computers, software, fibre optic cables, exchanges, telephones, modems, and satellites which play a central role in the production of

Castells's space of flows require a huge amount of work to keep going, and their actual reach is much more limited and moody than Castells's flow metaphor suggests – as anyone who has used a mobile phone will testify. Moreover, this is to say nothing of the difficulties of moving actual materials from place to place, or the complexity generated through the soft confusions of culture and language. Finally, by viewing the global as something that is abstracted from and beyond ordinary senses of time and place, Castells's theorization is built – with varying degrees of covertness – on a view of the local as inherently autarchic, stable, and culturally authentic (Amin and Thrift 1994; Amin 1997).

Massey – geometries of power

In making these criticisms I do not intend to deny the significance of the trends highlighted in Castells's work. What the criticisms point to, rather, is the need for a more differentiated notion of the time-space of globalization. It is just such a differentiated approach that Doreen Massey has been seeking to articulate over the past couple of decades. Beginning with an interest in industrial restructuring and regional inequalities in the United Kingdom during the late 1970s and early 1980s, Massey has been evolving a complex and subtle account of the interconnections between local, regional, national, and global processes (Massey 1979, 1984, 1991, 1994, 1999a, 1999b; Massey and Meegan 1978, 1982; Allen et al. 1998).

The originality of Massey is her refusal to see these differing scalings of time-space as a simple hierarchy.[2] This is quite beautifully expressed in the short article "A Place Called Home?" (in Massey 1994, originally published in 1992). Massey begins "A Place Called Home?" by outlining the economic and cultural trends that have given rise to a general sense that the world *is* becoming more global. She is in agreement with Castells that indeed something important is afoot. But she cautions her readers not to get too excited. Most people live in quite ordinary places. Most of their concerns are resolutely ordinary. And much of the supposed newness of globalization actually represents shifts in the shape and trajectory of well-established relationships. The much-touted fact, for example, that globalization is bringing First and Third World populations into close contact in cities like New York and London is only novel when viewed from a First World perspective. Most so-called Third World populations have been daily confronted by the presence of Western colonization cum globalization for generations. Much of the confusion about globalization springs from this lack of perspective. In fact, almost all places (or should we just say ALL places?) are a hybrid mixture of local and more widely stretched relationships. All places are constituted through what Massey calls a "power geometry" in which it is not a simple case of the "global" being something above, or determinate of, the local (Massey 1994: 164, 1993, 1999b).

It is precisely this blurring of the distinction between the local and the global (and indeed the regional and national for that matter) which makes the idea of a power geometry so productive. It frames the global as something realized through the articulation of a complex interconnection of variously local relationships, not as something that is above, or simply predatory of, the local. Thus, the question posed by globalization in all its various guises is not how it is stripping the local of its authenticity – how, in Castells's (1996a: 375) words, "[l]ocalities become disembodied from their cultural, historical, geographical meaning." Rather, the question is the ways in which the stretching, articulation, and intersection (Massey 1995: 2) of different social relations across time-space have changed, and how this reorganization of social relationships in time-space is altering people's concrete experience of their world.

Massey's argument leads to the conclusion that understanding the global/local requires tracing out the actual relationships through which places are made as "articulated moments in networks of social relations and understandings" (Massey 1994: 154). It also stresses the multiplicity of much that we like to refer to as "the global." This is not simply to celebrate the processes of cultural fragmentation and bricolage which Castells views as central to the space of flows's colonization of the local. As Massey points out, "[t]oday's global world is not just some glorious hybrid, complex, mixity; it is also systematically riven" (1999b: 43). Nevertheless, it is to say that the ways in which different individuals or communities relate to, and are able to shape, that which is global depends crucially on their social position and on the particular form of globalness in question.

Massey's conceptualization of time-space as a complex weaving together of relationships of varying spatial-temporal stretch provides a strong platform from which to study processes of globalization. But a careful reading of Massey's work does raise three important questions, namely:

What kind of geometry? One of the great strengths of Massey's theorization of time-space is its strong sense of multiplicity. The contemporary world is not governed by one or two spatialities and temporalities, it is home to many over-lapping ones (Massey 1992, 1999a). It follows that we must learn to think beyond the familiar categories of absolute, Euclidean, and relative space. Yet Massey's language, as well as the examples she uses to illustrate her argument, is strangely wedded to these familiar terms. She talks of social relations being "stretched" across time-space, of people being physically fixed in space, of privileged elites being hypermobile. Not only does this suggest (even if inadvertently) a kind of planar notion of time-space, but it also fails to recognize the peculiar geometries of the more metaphorical and imageric elements of the time-space(s) of globalization. There is a need, not adequately addressed in Massey's writing, to develop a more sophisticated geometric language for framing the time-space of globalization.

How do we trace a power geometry? A second strength of Massey is her recognition that we cannot *a priori* say what is local and what is global (Massey 1994: 130). Rather, we must make the effort to trace out the interaction of actual relationships in particular time and places. But Massey does not provide a robust enough analytical language nor a sufficiently sophisticated methodological instruction on how to do this. What relationships should we be tracing? In how much detail? And from what materials are these relationships fashioned? The physical? The material? The discursive? All three? Here Castells, with his interest in different forms of networks, media flows, and virtuality, is potentially more useful than Massey. But we also need other guides to help us avoid reproducing the more exaggerated elements of Castells's analysis.

What kinds of stories? Perhaps the most attractive characteristic of Massey's thought is her clarity. Articles like those collected together in *Space, Place, and Gender* (1994) offer a subtle yet powerful sense of what the time-space of our local/global world is like. But the generality of these pieces also raises the question of how we should go about narrating *in detail* the time-space of the "networks of social relations and understandings" through which actual places are made. How do we convey a sense of the complexity, the multiplicity (of materials, of subjectivities, of spatialities and temporalities), the determinacy and serendipity?[3]

In the remainder of this chapter I want to argue that a useful way to begin to address the questions outlined above is to remap the notion of a power geometry onto topological space. I want further to suggest that in so doing it is productive to ally ourselves closely with the work of actor-network theory (ANT).[4] First, however, I want to return to Ponsonby Road and the question of what kind of globality a restaurant inhabits.

Theorizing the Global II: Topologies and Networks

GPK is a large restaurant/bar occupying nearly half a block of street frontage at the northern end of Ponsonby Road. It opened in November 1995 at the peak of a boom in restaurant, café, and bar openings along the Road and has been hugely successful. Even now, several years after its opening, customers often have to wait up to an hour for a table on Friday and Saturday nights, and this despite a significant expansion into the neighboring building undertaken in 1998. Its interior is stylish and expensive, although not ostentatiously so. It has the compulsory polished wooden floors, neat whitewashed walls, and tidy bi-folding doors opening up onto the street. Large pot plants give the restaurant a sense of relaxed orderliness. When asked, Dominique Parat and Peter Howard, founders and co-owners of GPK, describe its aesthetic as a contemporary reworking of the idea of a Parisian brasserie – the wooden indoor chairs and tables, sourced from a local distributor, are originally French (see figure 4.2).

GPK is known for the quality of the gourmet wood-oven pizzas (after which it is named, GPK stands for Gourmet Pizza Konnection) topped with a range of exotic and unlikely combinations – roasted baby potatoes with Italian farmhouse bacon, for example. It also serves an interesting *à la carte* menu based loosely on Mediterranean cuisine with an Asian-Pacific Rim inflection. The general ambience – the smart casualness, the contemporariness, the stylishness – and character of GPK reprises that of early 1990s innovators like Tuatara and SPQR but without their chutzpah (SPQR) or glamour (Tuatara). But unlike Tuatara or SPQR, it has very little that distinguishes it as a unique, let alone a uniquely Auckland, space – even its name was lifted from a Californian restaurant. Indeed, perhaps the only thing that really distinguishes GPK as being of Auckland is its bland cosmopolitanism. Like the Sky Tower and the mirror glass clad offices in central Auckland, it has the knowing feel of a wider international design aesthetic without any feeling of genuine originality. Strolling past the diners leisurely sipping their chilled glasses of Sauvignon Blanc at the tables outside GPK, I suspect that the feeling of uncanniness felt by the visiting American professor might have been particularly acute.

Figure 4.2 GPK (Gourmet Pizza Konnection). Owned by Peter Howard and Dominique Parat, GPK opened in November 1995 after taking over the lease of two pre-existing restaurants. Its mix of gourmet pizzas and a simple Mediterranean-inspired *à la carte* menu has been hugely successful.

Actor-network theory

This brief encounter with GPK is – for the mainstream analyst of globalization – reassuringly familiar. The Parisian brasserieness, the Mediterraneanness, the gourmet pizzaness (so very Californian and so very trans-cultural) seem to underline Castells's (1996: 375) portrait of places being "disembodied from their cultural, historical, geographic meaning, and reintegrated into . . . image collages, inducing a space of flow that substitutes for a space of places." We are, then, back with the comforting notion of Ponsonby Road as a globalizing/ homogenizing space. But this Baudrillardian (1981, 1988) view of GPK as a space of simulacra, emptied of authenticity and meaning, contradicts two important realities, these being the longevity of GPK and the internal stability of GPK. Thus, GPK has managed to survive in what is a very competitive and precarious industry. During the 1990s one in six of the licensed restaurants, cafés, and bars that opened along Ponsonby Road ceased trading within twelve months of opening. After two years the figure is over one-third of businesses. GPK, however, has managed to embed itself successfully within the social consciousness of a significant portion of the Auckland restaurant-going public and, through this embedding, it has come to have meanings and significances which go beyond those planned by Howard and Parat. Equally, GPK – along with other enduring establishments like SPQR and Tuatara – has managed to stabilize itself within the social landscape of Ponsonby Road, not through radical change but through convincing people of its constancy and through people integrating this constancy positively into their restaurant and drinking habits. Thus, Howard and Parat, when talking about GPK, stress the importance of a kind of fidelity to the idea of GPK, as they do to the care and attention that is necessary to make GPK the kind of restaurant/bar that it is. Certainly, GPK has changed over the seven years it has been in business but these changes have been gradual and subtle and they have concentrated on enhancing the *existing* characteristics of the restaurant/bar, not on radical overhauls.

Now, I do not want to discount the issue of authenticity nor the question of the spatial tropes through which spaces like restaurants are structured (and perhaps globalized) that Castells's approach raises. But we clearly need a more nuanced analytic. Perhaps, then, we should take Massey's advice and try to follow some of the networks through which GPK has been made and maintained. This immediately begs the twin questions voiced at the end of the last section – what is a network and how do we follow them (cf. Thrift and Olds 1996)? In pursuing these questions below, I want to suggest that the work of actor-network theorists like Bruno Latour (1986, 1987, 1988, 1990, 1991, 1992, 1993, 1999), Michel Callon (1986, 1991; and Latour 1981), John Law (1994, 1999, 2000), and others offers useful advice on both these questions. I do so for four reasons:

The actor-network: The first strength of ANT is its underlying premise of a world made up of complex "imbroglios" (Latour 1993: 3) of human and nonhuman actors, that is to say a world made up of complex intertwinings of *actor-networks*. For Latour and Callon the concept of an actor-network has a very specific meaning (and serves a very specific purpose). Specifically, it refers to the way in which people *and things* work to create the world BUT only through operating in combination with other actants who define the field of possible movement. Or, put another way, the study of actor-networks is the study of the "associations" between different materials and relations through which orders and hierarchies are made (and unmade) and through which "society is...held together [and] made durable" (Latour 1986: 276, 1991). This is a notion of network which is quite different from the popular idea of the network as "transport without deformation," the world of the World Wide Web and "double-click information" (Latour 1999: 15). Instead it is meant to refer to something "like Deleuze and Guattari's term rhizome...a series of *transformations* – translations, transductions – which could not be captured by any of the traditional terms of social theory."

The stories of translation: This notion of actor-networks as spaces of "translation" and "transductions" leads neatly to the second attraction of ANT. The space of a restaurant/bar like GPK is all about translation, movement, and displacement. The translation of ideas/inspirations/visions of people like Parat and Howard into the wood, paint, bricks, chrome, glass, cloth, wine, food, light, and so forth that make up the space of an *actual* restaurant is a remarkably complex process. This process is even more complex when we bring in the role of the diners, or ask explicitly what imperatives the nonhuman objects enlisted in the restaurant's production and maintenance bring with them. ANT offers a language and a set of tools to talk about all these things. In short, it helps bring into view the way "the world is made up of billions of happy or unhappy encounters, encounters which describe a 'mindful connected physicalism' consisting of multiple paths which intersect" (Thrift 1999a: 302, the phrase in quotation marks is from Brenner 1993).

The symmetry: Saying that there is a need to take into account the action of the nonhuman *as well as the human* implicated within the actor-networks of a space like GPK implies a notion of symmetry –

that is to say it implies that we need to analyze the nonhuman in the same "register" that we examine the human (Callon 1986: 200; Latour 1987, 1993). The world is made up of complex mixtures of humans and nonhumans, both of which have the capacity to "act." The idea of symmetry demands that we cannot assume *a priori* that it is the human part of any actor-network that is the key element in drawing any given actor-network together. Only by tracing out the web of relationships between the various actants that make up an actor-network can this balance be established. In a similar manner, we cannot assume that we know how long an actor-network is, or at what scale it operates, before we have actually studied the relations through which it is made. We must make the effort to follow the path of the network and see where that takes us.

The spatiality of ANT: The final strength of ANT is its spatiality. As Jonathan Murdoch (1997: 332) has highlighted, Latour's "portrayal of social life as necessarily dependent upon nonhuman resources makes space and time central to the theory of actor-networks." But the way that ANT views this spatiality is radically different from mainstream notions of time-space. Instead, it sees time-space in terms of the association of different *actor-networks topologies* (Murdoch 1997, 1998; Law 1999). Topology is a branch of geometry concerned not with distance *per se* but with ways in which relations are stretched and folded while maintaining certain essential properties as a space (see Peterson 1988; Hetherington 1997a, 1997b). Topology is, as Michel Serres – the "godfather" of topological analysis as employed by ANT – puts it (quoted in Murdoch 1998: 358), the "science of nearness and rifts" which studies "the attributes of the spatial which secure continuity for objects as they are displaced through space" (Law 1999: 6).[5] Viewed topologically, time-space consists of multiple pleats of relations stitched together, such that nearness and distance as measured in absolute space are not in themselves important. Rather, what is important are the "ways that spaces emerge as socio-material relations...arranged into orders and hierarchies" (Murdoch 1998: 359). Nearness and farness are not the product of distance (though that is in all sorts of ways built into relationships) but the articulation and disarticulation of diverse foldings of actor-networks (see Latour 1997; Thrift 1999a, 2000).

Drawing on these four elements of ANT – and remembering the three criteria set out above to judge the efficacy of any theorization of the global/local – we can outline some principles to guide us in our pursuit of the networks through which GPK is made: (1) we are not interested in networks but in actor-networks; (2) actor-networks are defined by their heterogeneity; (3) we must be alert to this hetero-geneity, for we cannot assume *a priori* that it is the human part of actor-network that is central to any event; (4) we must carefully trace out relations between different human and nonhuman actants to see what it is that is "acting"; (5) we cannot assume we know the scale (global or local) or size (small or large) of an actor-network but must attempt to trace out its various patterns of association through which it obtains certain effects of size or scale.

Thus armed, let us return to Ponsonby Road.

Following the Heterogeneous Actor-networks of GPK

Walk into GPK early on a weekday morning and you will likely as not find Dominique Parat seated at his desk in a large office upstairs from the dining and kitchen areas of the restaurant. From his office, and that of his restaurant manager opposite, Parat coordinates the working of the diverse networks of suppliers, cooks, waiters, dish-washers, and cleaners that make GPK work. I will come back to these networks, but here I want ask another question: how did Parat get here, that is to say how did he get to be in this office where he so confidently discusses orders with his suppliers, plans the next month's menu, and, very occasionally, meets nervous researchers keen to know about how he made it all happen?

A straightforward story: Parat arrives at GPK

Dominique Parat is French. On leaving school he trained as a chef in a Michelin starred restaurant in Annecy, a small town 10 miles south of Geneva. This was a formal, traditional French chef's apprentice-ship. Upon completing his training Parat "drifted" around France, working in a range of restaurants as he went. In 1981 after travelling through Australia for a number of months, Parat arrived in Auck-land. He liked New Zealand so he stayed, cheffing for five years in Orleans, a French restaurant in Parnell, a fashionable Auckland inner-city suburb. In 1986 he helped set up Zira, another French restaurant, and in the late 1980s the restaurant Kalarney. In 1992 he became part-owner of Isobar, a bar cum restaurant in downtown Takapuna, the commercial heart of the prosperous, solidly suburban, middle-class North Shore of Auckland (see figure 4.3). Here he first experimented with the idea of gourmet pizzas and nurtured his plans for a larger, more substantial gourmet pizza restaurant/bar that would include a quality *à la* carte menu, a plan that, with the help of Peter Howard, eventually developed into GPK.

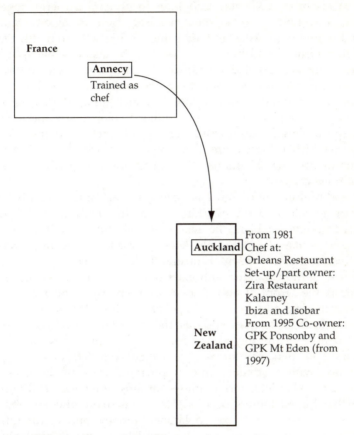

Figure 4.3   Dominique Parat travels toward GPK

A more heterogeneous story

The above vignette is a very straightforward story. It is neat and tidy but it does not tell us much. This is partly because it leaves out a lot of seemingly extraneous, but nevertheless important, detail. There is not anything about the work which went into setting up and running Zira, Kalarney, or Isobar. Of course, it would be impossible to retrace in detail Parat's movements through these spaces, but we can discern a number of more general patterns. Thus, as Parat moves from school, to apprenticeship, to Auckland, and finally the GPK on

Ponsonby Road we can see him doing at least two things. First, he starts acquiring a range of formal and codifiable techniques, rules, and recipes. He learns how to cook, but also how to order produce, how to organize a kitchen, and how to prepare a menu, together with a whole range of other skills necessary for running a restaurant. Second, coming to Auckland he removes himself from the tightly defined traditions and hierarchies of French cuisine while simultaneously using the knowledge embedded within it to navigate through Auckland. It is tempting to see this from the start as a kind of "going global." But, initially, Parat is doing no such thing. Rather, he rides on the back of previous French culinary colonialism and goes to work (for a New Zealand employer!) in a French Restaurant (called Orleans, which is pretty French!) – and a French chef in a French restaurant cooking traditional French cuisine can hardly be called global now, can it?

Instead of thinking of Parat as "going global," it is, arguably, more accurate to talk of Parat working to localize himself. Thus, as he moves through Auckland he works at collecting together potential allies and contacts – including Peter Howard, his future partner in GPK (as he earlier was in Zira and Kalarney, see figure 4.4) and himself a New Zealander with extensive experience working in and managing the "front of house" restaurant environment. He also sets about gathering and knitting together a whole lot of other, more individualized, resources such as the knowledge tied-up with the ebb and flow of the day-to-day routine of running a New Zealand restaurant kitchen, the knowledge which comes from an ongoing interaction with customers and suppliers, a sense of the taste and palate of Aucklanders, and an understanding of the *habitus* (Bourdieu 1984) that his customers occupy. More concretely and tangibly, he gathers together things like cookbooks, money, and credit ratings. Thus, as Parat moves through Auckland he begins to bind himself into a plurality of actor-networks – those of banks and suppliers (or more precisely their software and computer systems), other restaurateurs, and the restaurant-going public. In short, and in the more familiar language of economic geography, he "embeds" himself within a web of social/material relationships (cf. Granovetter 1985; Amin and Thrift 1992; Grabher 1993; French 2000).

Parat and Howard as mutable mobiles

Now, within this "localization" something very interesting starts to happen. Parat begins to appear much less French or, to be more

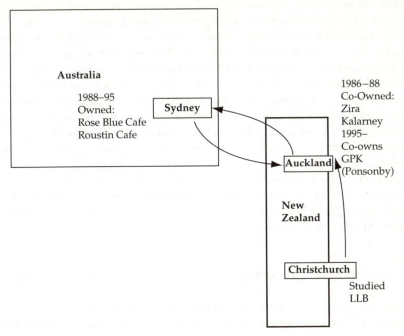

Figure 4.4 Peter Howard travels toward GPK

accurate, the restaurants that he owns and works in do. Instead, they start to take on strange and novel forms. They gain pizzas, "bouquet" New Zealand wines and beers, rows of TV screens showing endless loops of rugby players and golfers, weekend breakfast menus of American pancakes and eggs benedict, and they fill up with (expensively) underdressed Aucklanders rather than the exclusively well-dressed ones that populated Orleans. So what has Parat (ably partnered by Howard) done? Or, perhaps it would be better to ask, what has happened to Parat? Well, he has become what I would term, borrowing from Latour (1987), a kind of "mutable mobile."

In Bruno Latour's (1987, 1988, 1990) terminology, immutable mobiles are objects capable of fixing pieces of knowledge and allowing that knowledge to move and be used well beyond its place of origin. Immutable mobiles in the form of things like textbooks, maps, and certain kinds of machines and tools allow actor-networks to travel and establish relationships of the same form and type as at the point from which they came. An immutable mobile is a quite fantastic entity, but for it to perform its work of translation it needs to stabilize a whole world of relationships around it – and while this sometimes works, sometimes it does not (cf. Mol and Law 1994; Latour 1996). Parat, as a *mutable* mobile, travels much more fluidly than that. He uses his skills to work at recombining elements in new patterns, to introduce new actants, to alter established relationships. He wants to run a restaurant (or restaurant/bar) – that is what he knows about and this is why, within the context of restaurants, we can sensibly talk of him as a kind of mobile. But he adjusts and alters (as they do him) the elements arranged within his various businesses – the food on the menu, the style of dining, the location, the furniture, the ambience, his business partners – to try and create a place which works within the particular field of circumstances (actor-networks) in which he finds himself. With GPK he translates a series of elements into a space immediately recognizable as a restaurant, but one quite different to that which he left in Annecy as a freshly trained chef some 20 years before.

Becoming French, becoming Kiwi?: topologies of cosmopolitanism

So, has Parat, our mutable mobile (ably abetted by Howard, of course), now gone global? If we just trace the material stretch of the most obvious actor-networks that center on GPK, clearly he has not. The ingredients sourced from local suppliers are nearly all produced in New Zealand, as is most of the wine and beer. There are exceptions, but they are bought from local importers, not directly from overseas. The wait-staff are, by and large, "locals" while the simply designed menu means GPK does not need rigorously trained French chefs – inexperienced Aucklanders trained in the GPK kitchen will do perfectly nicely. Of course, we could trace all these actor-networks a bit further and we would find they reach out to the rest of globe. But GPK's interaction with these longer networks is *mediated* by "local" elements of these longer actor-networks. Indeed, what is striking about the economic evolution of the hospitality industry along places like Ponsonby Road is the degree of their integration into what are remarkably dynamic endogenous local/national growth nodes.

But if we examine the materiality of GPK from a topological perspective, its globality multiplies. Parat and Howard – or, rather, the various elements of the actor-networks that they have assembled and established around GPK – perform an intensive set of translations that fold a series of semiotically encoded narratives into the space of the GPK, narratives which embody a profound sense of globalness (cf. Hetherington 1987a, 1987b). Through these enfoldings GPK stops being simply a slightly rickety two-storey Edwardian building and becomes a restaurant. We could begin to name and decode these plural – but intermixed – enfoldings. Indeed, we have already encountered some of the more obvious ones, the Parisian Bistroness, the Californianess. Others have only been hinted at – the urbane New Zealand cosmopolitanness (the knowing list of New Zealand wines, the relaxed casualness of the wait-staff, and so forth), the urban middle classness (the expense of the décor, the orderliness, the Europeanness). But what is perhaps most striking about the space of these enfoldings is the routes through which they come to GPK.

To think about the ways ideas, styles, fashions, and images move and are translated through time-space we have to move away from the notion of actor-networks and think more in terms of fluidity. This is to follow the lead of Arjun Appadurai (1996, although see also Mol and Law 1994), who has suggested that we should view the world as enveloped in a complex and disjunctive set of what he calls "-scapes." These -scapes (Appadurai talks of ethno-, media-, techno-, finance-, and ideo-scapes) are patterns of thought, practices, and so forth that are no longer tightly tied to a single territory but are on the move, circulating through the world, separating and combining in complex and highly fluid ways. Indeed, we might also think about the mobility of these -scapes as viral like, often receiving passage on the back of more structured networks such as international transportation routes, telephone networks, the Internet, and so forth. The trick that Parat and Howard have performed in creating GPK is the translation of a set of vague yet globally/universally recognizable notions of restaurants, bistros, cosmopolitanism, and urbanity into a spatial narrative (a spatial semiotics) that resonates with the social imaginaries of Auckland restaurant-goers. Indeed, the materiality of GPK has become a site for the very enactment and embodiment (and hence realization) of those imaginaries. That is why it is so popular, and that is why it makes so much money.

Conclusion: Topologies, Scale, and the Local/Global

[W]hat we need [in order to] to produce geographies of global change is less exaggeration and more moderation. (Nigel Thrift 1995)

This chapter began with the suggestion that the dominant social scientific approaches to globalization and scale lacked an adequate language for exploring the way in which everyday life practices are intertwined between the local and the global. I have tried to highlight some of the key reasons for this weakness and to argue that a possible way of addressing this flaw is to draw on the ideas of Actor-Network Theory and topology. Nevertheless, the way a topologically oriented ANT analysis makes sense of the world's spatiality raises profound questions about how we understand scale. It is on these questions of scale – the question that is, after all, the key focus of this book – that I want to conclude this chapter.

For ANT (as indeed for Michel Serres), scale is not something of great interest in and of itself. Both Latour and Law have argued that size and scale are "relational effects" (Law 2000: 133; Latour 1993) – a sentiment echoed clearly by Nigel Thrift (1995: 33), who has gone so far as to write: "[t]here is no such thing as a scale. Rather, size is an uncertain effect generated by a network and its modes of inter-action." Now, in certain respects this is an argument compatible with the conceptualization of scale offered by the likes of Smith (1992, 1993, 1997) and Swyngedouw (1992b, 1996) mentioned in the intro-duction. Smith (1993: 95–101), for example, sees scale as produced through, and constitutive of, social relationships and social conflict (see also Brenner 1997, 1998a, 1998b, 1999). Where the conceptualiza-tion of scale offered by Smith and others loses purchase is in the conviction that scale is somehow central to how space and time are ordered. Certainly, sometimes networks of people and objects do work together to generate discrete scales, a particular ordering of time-space that allows certain kinds of activities to take place – the huge amount of work that has gone into creating the nation-state system is one very prominent example of this. But many other places operate through much more promiscuous orderings that escape the idea of scale. By seeing scale as one of *the* central elements of spatial differentiation – a central dynamic in the generation of "difference," as Smith writes (1993: 95) – scale theorists, in fact, blunt our sense of how spatial difference is produced and maintained.

The spaces of Parat and Howard's GPK or Richard Riddiford et al.'s Tuatara are of a type that escapes the grasp of scale. They are local, they are global, just as they are also profoundly national. Equally, they are in certain senses profoundly cosmopolitan, as they are in many ways deeply parochial. This is not simply a case of mixing up scales – what Swyngedouw (1992b) has called "glocaliza-tion." The kinds of globality that GPK, Tuatara, and similar establish-ments on Ponsonby Road embody are not built around any conventional notion of scale at all. What a topologically oriented approach offers is a way of making sense of these kinds of nonscalar spatialities, as well as an avenue through which to break down apparent divisions between scales into more analytically useful accounts. Drawing on the geometric language of topology allows us to disassemble the global – to see it in its particularity, to see that it is provisional and not some monolith over which we can have no influence. This is not to throw away the concept of scale. We do, after all, still live in a world of places, regions, nations, and so forth. It is simply to be more sceptical of its importance and analytical purchase. Indeed, Thrift's suggestion that there is no such thing as a scale – along with the arguments advanced in this chapter – should perhaps be interpreted less as a repudiation of a concern with scale *per se*, and more as call not to take conventional notions of scale for granted.

NOTES

1   The discussion of Ponsonby Road and its restaurants, cafés, and bars is based on research undertaken by the author between February 1998 and September 1999 as part of a New Zealand Foundation for Science, Technology, and Research Post-Doctoral Fellowship. The research into the entrepreneurial networks involved in the development of Ponsonby Road as a hospitality strip included analysis of Auckland City Council files, Auckland Liquor Licensing Authority files, semi-structured interviews with owners and other key people involved in the hospitality industry, as well as use of local newspapers and magazines. Two other smaller sites were also studied, Jervois Road (immediately to the west of Ponsonby Road) and Devonport (on Auckland's North Shore). I would like to thank all those people who aided in my research, and NZFoRST for funding it.

2   Certainly this is more the case for her most recent writings. Earlier work, most notably *Spatial Divisions of Labour* (1984), articulates a more rigid hierarchy of the local, regional, national, and global.

3   Massey has addressed some of these questions directly in her work with John Allen and Allan Cochrane on the southeast of England in *Rethinking the Region* (Allen et al. 1998; see also Massey 1995).

4   The affinity between ANT and the arguments developed by Massey has been highlighted by Murdoch (1998).

5   The profoundly nonlinear and non-Euclidean view of space-time of topological analysis is perhaps best summarised by the following analogy proffered by Serres. Imagine a handkerchief, Serres (Serres and Latour 1995: 360) suggests:

> If you take a handkerchief and spread it out in order to iron it, you can see in it certain fixed distances and proximities. If you sketch a circle in one area, you can mark out nearby points and measure far-off distances. Then take the same handkerchief and crumple it, by putting it in your pocket. Two distant points suddenly are close,

even superimposed. If further, you tear it in certain places, two points that were very close become very distant. This science of nearness and rifts is called topology, while the science of stable and well-defined distances is called metrical geometry.

REFERENCES

Allen, J., Massey, M., and Cochrane, A. 1998: *Rethinking the Region*. London: Routledge.

Amin, A. 1997: Placing globalization. *Theory, Culture and Society*, 14 (2), 123–37.

Amin, A. and Thrift, N. 1992: Neo-Marshallian nodes in global networks. *International Journal of Urban and Regional Research*, 16, 571–87.

Appadurai, A. 1996: *Modernity at Large: Cultural Dimensions of Globalization*. Minneapolis: University of Minnesota.

Baudrillard, J. 1981: *For a Critique of the Political Economy of the Sign*. St. Louis: Telos Press.

Baudrillard, J. 1986: *America*. London: Verso.

Bauman, Z. 1998: *Globalization: The Human Consequences*. New York: Columbia University Press.

Boudieu, P. 1984: *Distinction: A Social Critique of the Judgement of Taste*. London: Routledge and Keagan Paul.

Brenner, L. 1993: *History After Lacan*. London: Routledge.

Brenner, N. 1997: Global, fragmented, hierarchical: Henri Lefebvre's geographies of globalization. *Public Culture*, 10, 135–67.

Brenner, N. 1998a: Between fixity and motion: Accumulation, territorial organization and the historical geography of spatial scales. *Environment and Planning D: Society and Space*, 16, 459–81.

Brenner, N. 1998b: Global cities, glocal states: Global city formation and state territorial restructuring in contemporary Europe. *Review of International Political Economy*, 5 (1), 1–37.

Brenner, N. 1999: Globalization as reterritorialisation: The re-scaling of urban governance in the European Union. *Urban Studies*, 36 (3), 431–51.

Callon, M. 1986: Some elements of a sociology of translation: Domestication of the scallops and the fishermen of St Brieuc Bay. In J. Laws (ed.), *Power, Action and Belief: A New Sociology of Knowledge?* London: Routledge, 196–233.

Callon, M. 1991: Techno-economic networks and irreversibility. In J. Laws (ed.), *A Sociology of Monsters: Essays in Power, Technology and Domination*. London: Routledge, 133–161.

Callon, M. and Latour, B. 1981: Unscrewing the big leviathan: How actors macro-structure reality and how sociologists help them do so. In K. Knorr-Cetina and A. V. Cicourel, (eds.), *Advances in Social Theory and Methodology: Towards an integration of Micro- and Macro-Sociologies*. Boston: Routledge, 277–303.

Castells, M. 1976: *The Urban Question*. London: Edward Arnold.

Castells, M. 1985: High technology, economic restructuring, and the urban-regional process in the United States. In M. Castells (ed.), *High Technology, Space and Society*, London: Sage, 11–40.

Castells, M. 1989: *The Informational City: Information Technology, Economic Restructuring, and the Urban-Regional Process*. Oxford: Blackwell.

Castells, M. 1994: European cities, the informational society, and the global economy. *New Left Review*, 204, 18–32.

Castells, M. 1996a: *The Rise of the Network Society*. Oxford: Blackwell.

Castells, M. 1996b: The net and the self: Working notes for a critical theory of informational society. *Critique of Anthropology*, 16 (1), 9–38.

Castells, M. 1997: *The Power of Identity*. Oxford: Blackwell.

Castells, M. 1998: *End of Millennium*. Oxford: Blackwell.

Castells, M. and Hall, P. 1994: *Technopoles of the World: The Making of the 21st Century Industrial Complexes*. London: Routledge.

Frank, A. 1969: *Latin America: Underdevelopment or Revolution*. New York: Monthly Review.

French, S. 1998: *Boys' Night Out*. Auckland: Auckland University Press.

French, S. 2000: Rescaling the economic: Geography of knowledge and information: Constructing life assurance markets. *Geoforum*, 31, 101–19.

Friedmann, J. 1986: The world city hypothesis. *Development and Change*, 17, 69–84.

Giddens, A. 1984: *The Constitution of Society: Outline of the Theory of Structuration*. Berkeley: University of California Press.

Grabher, G. (ed.) 1993: *The Embedded Firm: On the Socioeconomics of Industrial Networks*. London: Routledge.

Granovetter, M. 1985: Economic action and the social structure: The problem of embeddedness. *American Journal of Sociology*, 91 (3), 481–510.

Harvey, D. 1989a: *The Urban Experience*. Oxford: Blackwell.

Harvey, D. 1989b: *The Condition of Postmodernity: An Enquiry into the Origins of Cultural Change*. Oxford: Blackwell.

Harvey, D. 1996: *Justice, Nature and the Geography of Difference*. Oxford: Blackwell.

Harvey, D. 2000: *Spaces of Hope*. Edinburgh: Edinburgh University Press.

Häußermann, H. and Siebel, W. 1987: *Neue Urbanität*. Frankfurt: Suhrkamp Verlag.

Hetherington, K. 1997a: Museum topology and the will to connect. *Journal of Material Culture*, 2 (2), 199–218.

Hetherington, K. 1997b: In place of geometry: The materiality of place. In K. Hetherington and R. Munro (eds.), *Ideas of Difference*. Oxford: Blackwell, 181–99.

Hetherington, K. 1998: *Expressions of Identity: Space, Performance, Politics*. London: Sage.

Latour, B. 1986: The powers of association. In J. Laws (ed.), *Power, Action and Belief: A New Sociology of Knowledge?* London: Routledge, 264–80.

Latour, B. 1987: *Science in Action: How to Follow Scientists and Engineers Through Society*. Cambridge, MA: Harvard University Press.

Latour, B. 1988: *The Pasteurization of France*. Cambridge, MA: Harvard University Press.

Latour, B. 1990: Drawing things together. In S. Woolgar and M. Lynch (eds.), *Representations in Science*. Cambridge, MA: MIT Press, 18–60.

Latour, B. 1991: Technology is society made durable. In John Laws (ed.), *A Sociology of Monsters: Essays on Power, Technology and Domination*, London: Routledge, 103–31.

Latour, B. 1992: Where are the missing masses? The sociology of a few mundane artifacts. In B. Wiebe and J. Laws (eds.), *Shaping Technology/Building Society: Studies in Societal Change*. Cambridge, MA: MIT Press, 225–48.

Latour, B. 1993: *We Have Never Been Modern*. Hemel Hempstead: Harvester Wheatsheaf.

Latour, B. 1996: *Aramis or the Love of Technology*. Cambridge, MA: Harvard University Press.

Latour, B. 1997: Trains of thought: Piaget, formalism and the fifth dimension. *Common Knowledge*, 6, 170–91.

Latour, B. 1999: On recalling ANT. In J. Law and J. Hassard (eds.), *Actor Network Theory and After*. Oxford: Blackwell, 15–25.

Law, J. 1994: *Organizing Modernity*. Oxford: Blackwell.

Law, J. 1999: After ANT: Complexity, naming and topology. In J. Law and J. Hassard (eds.), *Actor Network Theory and After*. Oxford: Blackwell, 1–14.

Law, J. 2000: Transitivities. *Environment and Planning D: Society and Space*, 18, 133–48.

Massey, D. 1979: In what sense a regional problem? *Regional Studies*, 13, 233–43.

Massey, D. 1984: *Spatial Divisions of Labour: Social Structures and the Geography of Production*. Basingstoke: Macmillan.

Massey, D. 1991: The political place of locality studies. *Environment and Planning A*, 23, 267–81.

Massey, D. 1992: Politics and space/time. *New Left Review*, 196, 65–84.

Massey, D. 1993: Power-geometry and a progressive sense of place. In J. Bird, B. Curtis, T. Putnam, G. Robertson, and L. Tickner (eds.), *Mapping the Futures: Local Cultures, Global Change*. London, Routledge, 59–69.

Massey, D. 1994: *Space, Place, and Gender*. Minneapolis: University of Minnesota Press.

Massey, D. 1995: *Spatial Divisions of Labour: Social Structures and the Geography of Production*, 2nd ed. Basingstoke: Macmillan.

Massey, D. 1999a: Spaces of politics. In D. Massey, J. Allen, and P. Sarre (eds.), *Human Geography Today*. Cambridge: Polity, 279–94.

Massey, D. 1999b: Imagining globalization: Power-geometries of time space. In A. Brah, M. Hickman, and M. Mac an Ghail (eds.), *Global Futures: Migration, Environment and Globalization*. Basingstoke: Macmillan, 27–44.

Massey, D. and Meegan, R. 1978: Industrial restructuring verses the cities. *Urban Studies*, 15, 273–88.

Massey, D. and Meegan, R. 1982: *The Anatomy of Job Loss: The How, Why and Where of Employment Decline*. London: Methuen.

McCormack, D. 1999. The drunkenness of things becoming various: Towards a geography under the influence. Paper presented at the RGS-IBG annual conference Leicester, Jan. 1999. Paper available from author, c/o Dept. of Geography, University of Southampton, Southampton SO17 1BJ, UK.

Mol, A. and Law, J. 1994: Regions, networks and fluids: Anaemia and social topology. *Social Studies in Science*, 24, 641–71.

Murdoch, J. 1995: Actor-networks and the evolution of economic forms: Combining description and explanation in theories of regulation, flexible specialisation, and networks. *Environment and Planning A*, 27, 731–57.

Murdoch, J. 1997a: Towards a geography of heterogeneous associations. *Progress in Human Geography*, 21 (3), 321–37.

Murdoch, J. 1997b: Inhuman/nonhuman/human: Actor-network theory and the potential for a non-dualistic and symmetrical perspective on nature and society. *Environment and Planning D: Society and Space*, 15, 731–56.

Murdoch, J. 1998: The spaces of actor-network theory. *Geoforum*, 29 (4), 357–74.

Murdoch, J. 1999: Accommodating complexity? Some thoughts on standardisation and the stratification of space. Paper presented at the ESRC one day seminar Complexity and Space, Open University.

Peterson, I. 1988: *The Mathematical Tourist: Snapshots of Modern Mathematics*. New York: Freeman and Company.

Riddiford, R. 1998: Statement of Evidence to the Liquor Licensing Authority, Tuatara Liquor Licensing File, Auckland City Environments, Aug.

Sassen, S. 1991: *The Global City: New York, London, Paris*. Princeton: Princeton University Press.

Sassen, S. 1994: *Cities in a World Economy*. London: Pine Forge Press.

Sassen, S. 1998: *Globalization and its Discontents: Essays on the New Mobility of People and Money*. New York: New Press.

Serres, M. 1982: *Hermes: Literature, Science, Philosophy*. Baltimore: John Hopkins University Press.

Serres, M. and Latour, B. 1995: *Conversations on Science, Culture and Time*. Ann Arbor: Michigan University Press.

Smith, N. 1987: Dangers of the empirical turn: Some comments on the CURS initiative. *Antipode*, 19, 59–68.

Smith, N. 1992: Geography, difference and the politics of scale. In J. Doherty, E. Graham and M. Mallek (eds.), *Postmodernism and the Social Sciences*. Basingstoke: Macmillan, 57–79.

Smith, N. 1993: Homeless/global: Scaling places. In J. Bird, B. Curtis, T. Putnam, G. Robertson, and L. Tickner (eds.), *Mapping the Futures: Local Cultures, Global Change*. London: Routledge, 87–119.

Smith, N. 1996: *The New Urban Frontier: Gentrification and the Revanchist City*. London: Routledge.

Smith, N. 1997: The satanic geographies of globalization. *Public Culture*, 10 (1), 169–89.

Swyngedouw, E. 1992a: Territorial organization and the space/technology nexus. *Transactions of the Institute of British Geography*, New Series, 17, 417–33.

Swyngedouw, E. 1992b: The mammon quest: "Glocalization", interspatial competition and the monetary order: The construction of new scales. In M. Dunford and G. Kafalas (eds.), *Cities and Regions in the New Europe*. London: Belhaven, 39–67.

Swyngedouw, E. 1996: Restructuring citizenship, the re-scaling of the state and the new authoritarianism: Closing the Belgian mines. *Urban Studies*, 33 (8), 1499–1521.

Thrift, N. 1995: A hyperactive world. In R. Johnston, P. Taylor, and M. Watts (eds.), *Geographies of Global Change*. Oxford: Blackwell, 18–35.

Thrift, N. 1996a: *Spatial Formations*. London: Sage.

Thrift, N. 1996b: Shut up and dance, or, is the world economy knowable? In P. Daniels and W. Lever (eds.), *The Global Economy in Transition*. London: Longman, 11–23.

Thrift, N. 1999a: Steps to an ecology of space. In D. Massey, J. Allen, and P. Sarre (eds.), *Human Geography Today*. Cambridge: Polity, 295–322.

Thrift, N. 1999b: The place of complexity. *Theory, Culture and Society*, 16 (3), 31–69.

Thrift, N. 2000: Afterwords. *Environment and Planning D: Society and Space*, 18, 213–55.

Thrift, N. and Olds, K. 1996: Refiguring the economic in economic geography. *Progress in Human Geography*, 20 (3), 311–37.

Wallerstein, I. 1979: *The Capitalist World Economy*. Cambridge: Cambridge University Press.

Part II

Rhetorics of Scale

Introduction: Rhetorics of Scale

Andrew Herod and Melissa W. Wright

The poststructuralist interventions across disciplines have turned critical attention to how discourse and language represent powerful arenas of dynamic political struggle. As a result, it is no longer sufficient to describe reality as a steadfast phenomenon that presents itself readily for observation, description, and analysis. Instead, we must interrogate how the very terms by which we define and categorize reality are themselves political tools that contribute to the consolidations and/or subversions of the various power regimes that constitute our material and social worlds. Hence, in much of the debate over "globalization" the issue has shifted from inquiring into whether or not the world is actually becoming more globalized to how globalist terminology is deployed (and what is at stake in its deployment) across the diverse cultural landscapes around the world. This focus on discourse and language forces recognition of how the terms by which we define and describe globalization are themselves powerful tools that can be used in myriad ways across the spectrum of local responses to events recognized as intrinsically "global." How discourses of globalization take shape and are used toward different purposes, clearly, holds significant material implications for political praxis. Thus, it seems that almost daily we hear that a particular government policy or program must be reformulated so that "we" may respond to the growing challenges of "globalization," or that employers claim they must undercut workers' wages and conditions of employment because "globalization is forcing us to do so." Perhaps somewhat paradoxically, this is a discourse which the political left has also frequently accepted rather uncritically, particularly with regard to the beliefs either that opponents of neoliberal globalization are condemned to operate at the sub-global level (i.e., that the global is the domain of capital) – we can see this in the popular "think globally, act locally" slogan, for example – or that local actions are inherently parochial and doomed to failure (for more on this argument, see Herod 2001 and Gibson-Graham 1996). The discourse of globalization, then, appears to be a powerful disciplining force into which both the political right and the political left have often bought.

In similar fashion, discourses of "the local" and "localization" can also be powerful discipliners of social praxis. For example, rhetorics of localism are often used as a means of exclusion, such that being presented as "not local" can undermine the legitimacy of particular political actors. Thus, Bridge (1998) shows how mining interests in the western United States have used a rhetoric of localism to undermine environmentalist opposition to the industry. Likewise, Mitchell (1998) shows how California agribusiness interests constructed a rhetoric of localness during the 1930s to try to limit the influence of union organizers among migratory workers. Conversely, in an analysis of a dispute in Britain concerning the desires of a mining company to extract gravel deposits from a location close to a national historic site, Murdoch and Marsden (1995) have shown how environmental activists themselves organized successfully to pit the "local" concerns of the mining company against the "national" cultural heritage interests of the British public. Similar examples could be found with regard to how the rhetorical construction of scale and identities at other spatial resolutions is used to define legitimacy and attachments to place, and so to discipline people's social behavior – cultural regionalism and various forms of nationalism are obvious examples of this.

Bearing in mind that the way in which rhetorics of scale are constructed and deployed can be significant determinants of material practices, we have gathered together in this section three chapters which, in different ways, explore the construction and use of rhetorical practices concerning scale. In the first of these Ken Hillis, Michael Petit, and Altha Cravey examine how a belief in the necessity of neoliberal globalization is being inculcated into the minds of school children in the United States through a well-financed and slick educational cum media campaign sponsored by the Virtual Trade Mission (VTM). Established in 1996 under the auspices of private business and the President's Export Council (itself a presidential advisory board on matters of international trade), the VTM has as its goal to get students to think of neoliberal globalization as an inevitable and unquestioned process. Central to the VTM's strategy, Hillis et al. suggest, is the promotion of a shift in student self-identity away from place-based concepts of citizenship and towards a globalized sense of entrepreneurship. By providing educational packages of videos, literature, websites, and simulation games to US high schools, the developers and sponsors of the VTM encourage students to think of themselves as "global entrepreneurs" who must identify with US corporate interests so that in the new globalizing economy the United States is not "left behind" and "Team America" can maintain its economic and political hegemony.

The activities of the VTM raise interesting questions with regard to issues of geographical scale. In particular, they show how the ways in which identity is constructed may be deeply scaled, together with how struggles over such scales of identity can have significant political ramifications. Whether one thinks of oneself as, for instance, an Angelino, a Californian, a Westerner, an American, or a citizen of the world really does mean something and can have very significant material consequences. Thus, in the United States recent anti-federal government rhetoric espoused by many land-owners in western states such as Colorado and Wyoming has portrayed federal policies towards land management as a "War on the West" in which "Westerners" need to organize against the interference of "pesky Easterners" and "federal government bureaucrats," many of whom themselves are actually from Western states. The construction of an identity of "the Westerner" is central to this political and economic struggle over land. Likewise, the recent conflicts in the Balkans have seen many people "down-scale" their identities from that of Yugoslavian to that of Serb, Croat, Macedonian, and the like. In the case of the VTM, then, corporate America is attempting to meet its long-term goals, Hillis et al. maintain, through a conscious rescaling of the cultural identities of the next generation of workers about to enter the labor force. Yet this is a complex scalar strategy, for in the process of emphasizing the importance of getting the students to see themselves as postnational global entrepreneurs and consumers the VTM also promotes an "American" cultural identity – the goal is, after all, to ensure that US-based corporations will win out in the brave new world of twenty-first-century global capitalism. The rhetoric promoted by the VTM thus positions the idea of globalization in highly selective ways.

Following from this, Andrew Kirby looks at how the discourses of scale which have been central to academic debates during the past two decades or so with regard to globalization have largely been incongruous with the discourses of scale which have dominated much popular culture, at least in the United States. Thus, he suggests, much of the academic language relating to scale with which the academic community has engaged – the global, the local, the global-local dialectic, glocalization – are not ways in which most ordinary people usually think about the spatial relationships between places, at least if popular culture is anything to go by. Hence, although thanks to the 1999 protests in Seattle the word "globalization" is now more widely recognized in the media and popular culture, concepts such as glocalization would probably draw blank stares from the average person in the street.[1] Even the concept of the "global economy" is relatively new, for until fairly recently "world economy" would have been the preferred term.[2] Instead, Kirby submits, popular culture in the United States – which, given the international dominance of US cultural production, is increasingly a globalized popular culture – has more frequently concerned itself with what he calls the "extraglobal" scale, by which he means that movies, television programs, popular music, youth magazines, and fiction have more typically explored how humans position themselves in relation to the broader cosmos, rather than how they interrelate in a global setting. Through examining the genre of science fiction, Kirby explores how the popular imagination has often diminished the significance of the global in favor of concerns about the Earth's relation to other worlds and galaxies, a diminution which seems almost heretical to academics concerned with the new forces of the global political economy such as the World Trade Organization.

Much as popular culture and academic discourse have often been disconnected when it comes to issues like globalization and the extra-global, so too, Kirby argues, are the technological transformations which have facilitated what has come to be called globalization themselves bringing about a transformation in many people's everyday conceptions of scale. Hence, the absorption into our everyday consciousness and language of terms and concepts such as "cyberspace" and "virtual reality," he maintains, are having an impact upon scalar discourses. Indeed, what does it mean to talk about "geographic scale" when referring to cyberspace? What are the implications for how we think about scale of increasingly coming to see our contemporary world as a world of flows (Castells 2000), rather than as a world of territorially defined spaces? For Kirby, then, the growing pervasiveness within popular culture of terms such as "front regions" and "back regions" – terms closely associated with the spread of computer technologies – are challenging academic (and even popular) conceptions of scale as hierarchical, conceptions which have traditionally thought of "regions" as meso-level structures of spatial resolution which sit somewhere between the local and the global. The point, then, is not simply that the language of the academy and of popular culture are different – after all, it is not unreasonable that the specialized language of intellectuals would not mirror that of everyday life – but that the very ways in which scale is represented and thought of in popular culture appear to be quite different from how scale is often theorized in academic circles.

Continuing the theme of the discursive construction of scale, the final chapter in this section by Susan Mains examines the politics of the policing practices engaged in by the United States Border Patrol along the US–Mexico border. Through an analysis of the Border Patrol's "Operation Gatekeeper" (which was launched in 1994 along the San Diego–Tijuana border as a means of better enforcing US immigration law), Mains shows how Border Patrol agents have attempted to reinforce and reproduce a "national" scale of (US) cultural identity in the face of an increasingly vigorous hybrid "border" culture which is being fed by growing immigration from Mexico and other Central American countries – immigration which is itself driven by processes of globalization and economic retrenchment south of the border. Through its practices, the Patrol effectively protects and reinforces the construct of a national community in the face of migrant transgressions which challenge this construct and which threaten to replace it with a *mestizo* community that stretches across the territorial divide between the United States and Mexico. In imposing on the borderland the disciplining practices of the US nation-state, Mains argues, the Border Patrol is effectively recreating on a daily basis a national scale which differentiates between the territorial spaces of the United States and those of Mexico. In turn, through such an assertion of the national scale at the border those within the federal government who are opposed to large-scale immigration from Mexico are able to divide the border area into spaces which are considered "safe" and "ordered" (i.e., the United States) and those which are considered "dangerous" or "chaotic" (i.e., Mexico), a discursive division of the landmass of the North American continent which serves to discipline the citizens of both countries in powerful ways.

An important aspect of these disciplinary and scalar practices, however, is the fact that they are saturated with gendered tropes. Typically, in much Border Patrol literature and media resources such as videos about the Patrol's day-to-day work the border itself is characterized as being under siege from drug smugglers and undocumented aliens. In response an authoritative presence is needed to maintain order and to protect the nation, which itself is seen as vulnerable and in danger of being violated by the penetration of these foreign bodies. The need for such an authoritative presence protecting an increasingly violated national territory, Mains argues, reproduces a heterosexist discourse of male and female binaries in which masculinist practices must police the entrances to the body of the (US) nation. Furthermore, such a discourse of immigrants as criminals and dangerous to the national body politic allows particular social characteristics to be mapped onto vast abstract images of "outsiders." Discipline and masculinity, then, become the representational and material modes through which scale, identity, and power are reinforced. Consequently, Mains avers, scale, at least in this case, should be seen not as a universal concept but, rather, as a discursive construction of space that is constantly being negotiated and contested on a daily basis by the actions both of the Border Patrol (through its attempts to reinforce a notion of what agents and policymakers see as a distinct "American" identity) and by those of the undocumented Mexican migrants who, by crossing the border and attempting to evade the Patrol, effectively seek to undermine such an identity and so to transgress the national scale which US immigration policy is seeking to defend.

NOTES

1 According to www.Wordorigins.org, the term *Globalized quota* first appears in 1959 in *The Economist* in reference to quotas on car imports to Italy, while the word *globalization* itself first appears in Merriam-Webster's *New International Dictionary* in 1961. However, we would aver that the term "globalization" was not really widely adopted within public discourse (at least in the United States) until sometime in the past decade or so.

2 If one were to accept a materialist argument concerning the adoption of language and terminology, it would be reasonable to infer that the shift in discursive terrain from talk of the "world economy" or the "international economy" to talk of the "global economy" would not have been expected to occur until the various nationally defined economies which served as the basis for the international trading economy that lasted until roughly the end of the Bretton Woods era were more completely interconnected by the foreign direct investment activities of transnational corporations. This transformation in the material organization of the planet's economic relationships is captured nicely in Neil Smith's (1990: 139) observation that "Capitalism inherits the global scale in the form of the world market...[but] as ever, what capital inherits in one form it proceeds to reproduce in another [such that the] world market based on exchange is transformed into a world economy based on production and the universality of wage labour."

REFERENCES

Bridge, G. 1998: Excavating nature: Environmental narratives and discursive regulation in the mining industry. In A. Herod, G. Ó Tuathail, and S. Roberts (eds.), *An Unruly World? Globalization, Governance and Geography*. London and New York: Routledge, 219–43.

Castells, M. 2000: *The Rise of the Network Society* (2nd ed.). Oxford: Blackwell.

Gibson-Graham, J. K. 1996: *The End of Capitalism (As We Knew it): A Feminist Critique of Political Economy*. Cambridge, MA: Blackwell.

Herod, A. 2001: *Labor Geographies: Workers and the Landscapes of Capitalism*. Guilford: New York.

Mitchell, D. 1998: The scales of justice: Localist ideology, large-scale production, and agricultural labor's geography of resistance in 1930s California. In A. Herod (ed.), *Organizing the Landscape: Geographical Perspectives on Labor Unionism*. Minneapolis: University of Minnesota Press, 159–94.

Murdoch, J. and Marsden, T. 1995: The spatialization of politics: Local and national actor-spaces in environmental conflict. *Transactions of the Institute of British Geographers*, New Series, 20, 368–80.

Smith, N. 1990: *Uneven Development: Nature, Capital and the Production of Space* (2nd ed.). Oxford: Blackwell.

5

"Adventure Travel for the Mind®": Analyzing the United States Virtual Trade Mission's Promotion of Globalization through Discourse and Corporate Media Strategies

Ken Hillis, Michael Petit, and Altha J. Cravey

At first I felt very out of place.... Business, money, global trade, that's not me.... But now I see that...I was walking in a very small world.

Raquel Coran, Junior Class President, W. H. Adamson High School, Dallas, Texas

This chapter analyzes the United States Virtual Trade Mission (VTM), a public/private media strategy developed to indoctrinate US students in the values of globalization as defined by US multinational companies such as General Electric, Boeing, Hughes Electronics, TRW, Raytheon, and General Motors. An important aspect of the VTM is its classroom project, one that depends heavily on slick corporate videos and an increasingly sophisticated array of websites extolling a virtual future. The VTM's strategy, we argue, seeks to promote student acceptance of a shift in identity formation away from place-based or regionally inflected concepts of citizenship and towards a more privatized and global sense of "entrepreneurship" – an identity more amenable to corporate agendas within the so-called "new global economy." Central to this project is the issue of geographic scale, for the promotion of an identity shift from citizen to entrepreneur also encourages students to shift their focus from the local and national to the global, even as they are also encouraged to identify with a jingoistic "America first" ideology. Hence, the VTM continually reminds students that not ponying up to corporate global strategies flirts with being "left behind" in the new global economy, while the VTM web pages and classroom materials rely on registered slogans such as "It's School to Work to the World® with the VTM!" and "Click on to become a World Wise and World Ready Winner®!" to cajole students into thinking of themselves as global "entrepreneurs."[1] Despite, or per-haps because of, the highly capitalized social relations under which communications technologies and globalization are being developed and deployed, the VTM discursively places globalization as a neces-sary and inevitable component of future progress (particularly so for the high school audience that the VTM targets), while, in the process, the VTM's organizers participate in, and draw from, a heavily medi-ated culture in which communication technologies are naturalized as ideologically neutral "tools."

It is significant, then, that in its "educational" materials the VTM trades in many of the discourses behind the hegemonic logic of glob-alization and its dynamics reverberate with the assessments found in such treatises as Thomas Friedman's (1999) *The Lexus and the Olive Tree* and in the work of the "new economy" digerati such as Kevin Kelly of *Wired* magazine in which communication technologies are positioned as mere conduits to satisfying identity needs and personal desires, thereby deflecting critical attention from the implications such technologies may have for social relations. Indeed, it is as if the organizers of the VTM have taken a page from a text such as Farid Elashmawi and Philip Harris's (1998) *Multicultural Management 2000: Essential Cultural Insights for Global Business Success* wherein the authors adapt insights generated by cultural studies and apply them to corporate agendas, suggesting (p. 1, emphasis added) that "[b]ecause of the significant social and political changes that are cur-rently underway, there is real opportunity for traders and entrepre-neurs, *free of ideology*, to engage in peaceful commerce for the benefit of humankind. The globalization of the mass media has shown many people the possibilities available within modern society, and has made them desire improvements in their quality of life. Such market needs can only be met on a global scale when a new class of managers and professionals come [sic] equipped with multicultural skills. Such commercial competencies are critical as we transition into the 21st century." In ostensibly seeking to teach students about the world, the VTM's materials strive to "educate" them within the context of multinational agendas that have appropriated formerly alternative images of cultural hipness and environmental progressiveness. In so doing, we suggest, the VTM may be seen as being part of what Crystal Bartolovich (1995: 119–20) refers to as "corporate cultural studies" in which many contemporary corporations have "emphasized their 'cultural' educative function to an unprecedented degree. So deeply have these ideas pervaded the corporate workplace that professors of corporate cultural studies do not rely on traditional schools alone as ideological apparatuses, but often form their own schools, such as Motorola University[,]...to train managers to shoulder the burden of globalizing capital. For these corporations, all the world has become not only (ideally) a single marketplace, but also a school."

Our analysis of the VTM, then, is a grounded case study of how rhetorics of globalization operate within broad institutional contexts in which a hybrid state–corporate sponsorship of new information technologies and media strategies positioned as pedagogical tools is being introduced into public educational institutions. In conducting this analysis, we extend Sally Marston's (2000) argument that an adequate theorization of spatial scale must articulate relations of production with those of consumption and social reproduction. We suggest that the classroom, where reality is both produced and consumed, is a meaningful place to explore how contemporary corporate strategies concerning rhetorics of globalization work to bridge one's local identity, one's identity as a US national, and the possibility that one might become a corporate global entrepreneur. Further, the VTM's focus on the classroom indicates that its organizers also grasp the significance of particular social spaces or sites, and theirs is a clever strategy for seducing learners to the VTM's corporate agendas. Thus, drawing on Kevin Cox's (1998) argument that local places can be distinguished as both a space of dependence *and* a space of engagement, we suggest that the VTM can be seen to operate as the locus where dependency and engagement come together – students, *dependent* on learning processes to "get ahead" in the world (and doing so in the embedded local context of the classroom), *engage* with opportunities such a setting opens to them. So, too, do underfunded public schools which, dependent on stagnant or decreasing public funding, engage with the VTM as an alternative source of classroom materials. Such "politics of space" operate on the various identity formations noted above, potentially conflating (or "glocalizing") distinctions among them. A corporate venture with the imprimatur of the federal state, the VTM's strategy suggests an easy, if not seamless, linkage of a student's experience of herself as a US citizen articulated to identification with private capital accumulation and its global reach and flow.

The assessment that follows divides into three areas of analysis: (i) examining the objectives and membership of the Virtual Trade Mission; (ii) discussing techniques by which the VTM, as a disciplining media strategy, promotes corporate ideologies and identity formations; and (iii) examining how the VTM's rhetoric of globalization positions the rest of the world as one "big emerging market" awaiting US entrepreneurial "harvesting" – a view that deflects consideration of issues of geopolitics, ethical relationships between individuals, scales of economic exploitation, and regional, national, and identity differences.

The Virtual Trade Mission: Objectives and Members

The US Virtual Trade Mission commenced in September 1996 under the auspices of private business and the President's Export Council – a US presidential advisory committee on international trade, itself established in 1973 during the Nixon administration. A key component of the VTM's stated mission is to "provide participating students a multimedia introduction to the big emerging markets and the opportunity they present for America's businesses and entrepreneurs to develop export sales and, thereby, to support America's economic growth."[2] Using educational packages designed by companies such as UPS, MCI WorldCom, the international engineering and construction company Fluor Daniel, and the international agriculture and food processing giant Cargill, high school students assume the role of business strategists assigned the task of expanding US global markets. United Airlines, for example, asks students to complete an "Export Challenge Workbook," part of which requires them to develop an ad campaign to entice 16- to 20-year-olds to visit Hong Kong.[3] MCI's video depicts a family bicycle company "going global" courtesy of Internet technology, thereby presenting *globalized US entrepreneurs* as a newly emergent and technicized class. AT&T, a company that seeks to be at the forefront of providing Internet access and technology, provides a "home" for the VTM website. Not surprisingly, the site includes a prominent link to AT&T Business Services.

A look at the various constituent "members" of the VTM offers a sense of the competing, even contradictory, interests that are both included and occluded by the VTM's strategies. Thus, "stakeholders" include:

The President's Export Council;
US multinational corporations;
  US educators and their high school students;
Several Newly Industrializing Countries (NICs) such as China, Korea,
  Malaysia, Singapore, Thailand, and Indonesia, along with Argentina,
  Poland, and Hungary, whose governments participate in the project;
Two labor unions, the International Brotherhood of Electrical Workers
  (IBEW) and the United Steelworkers of America (USWA), which operate
  in both the United States and Canada.

These groups have different interests and agendas – Poland may
compete directly with Korea, Argentina's unions may differ with the
IBEW on workers' needs in a global economy, and so forth. Cash-
strapped US public high schools and their frequently overburdened
teachers are encouraged to affiliate with the program to bring new
teaching opportunities into the classroom at little to no cost. However, students are provided almost no information about the corporate agendas such "opportunities" carry with them. Corporate
sponsors, on the other hand, benefit from the legitimation and resources provided by the co-sponsoring President's Export Council –
factors which assist entry of private agendas into public sites of
learning and ideological formation. Indeed, a close reading of the
VTM's literature and public stance highlights the Mission's strong
effort to insinuate into a still public educational curricula the perceived need by business elites for a unified "corporate vision sufficient to motivate associates and employees" (Barry 1997: 90). In the
case of the VTM, the message promotes one overarching goal: "Team
America" must win.

How the VTM Promotes Corporate Ideologies

Part of the VTM's appeal to students lies in its use of media celeb-
rities. Olympic athletes are introduced as favorable models for international competition whereby each nation-state's representatives
cooperate to create the event, even as nationals cheer their own
teams. Yet the Olympic model, with its "winners" and "losers,"
cannot explain the complexities of a world economy. Indeed, the
homology depicted between the Olympics and the global economy
borders on the immoral. It is one thing for a developed country such
as Canada to win a bronze medal in Track and Field. It is arguably
not homologous that between 1989 – when the Free Trade Agreement (the predecessor of NAFTA) came into effect – and 1994 that a

minimum of 42,000 high-wage Canadian manufacturing jobs were lost to US parent plants.[4] These were precisely the kinds of jobs performed by workers represented by the USWA's and IBEW's "branch plant" Canadian locals, and a reading of these unions' VTM literature strongly suggests their participation in the VTM flows from hopes of stemming similar job exportation from the US to so-called Third World or Newly Industrializing Countries.[5]

Although use of the Olympic motif may, then, seem an innocent way of introducing students to issues of international competition, we would suggest that the VTM's Olympic metaphor, made concrete by the use of Olympic athletes as embodiments of global trade in videos shot in classroom settings, actually deflects meaningful consideration of the complexities involved in the United States' winning in the global marketplace. Thus the use of 1996 gold medallist Rochelle Stevens, an African-American, speaking to W. H. Adamson High School students in Dallas, Texas suggests that disenfranchised US minorities can improve their lot simply by harmonizing their personal goals with corporate strategies. Furthermore, the VTM's use of such celebrity performances forecloses the kind of educational experience that might flow from examining the difference or gap between individual (US) bodies as winners and, for example, "winners" such as a deforested Thailand or "losers" such as a deforested Madagascar. Rochelle Stevens's highly disciplined body operates as a synecdoche that signifies not only the Olympian but also the Olympics and, by extension, the new global entrepreneur who will be made spiritually better and economically victorious through the kinds of self-discipline and engagement in the competitive spirit envisaged by the International Olympic Committee. Hence, while the VTM makes use of the theme of the "Olympic spirit" – which might be considered by some to be part of a progressive politics of internationalism, given that the reestablishment of the Games in 1896 by Baron Pierre de Coubertin was originally seen as an expression of international fraternity among the world's amateur athletes – the focus on Stevens as an *individual*, *personal* winner uses a regressive politics of scale to deflect considering the broader politics of the Olympic enterprise, its ongoing commodification and related bribery scandals included. This collapse of distinctions between the performative body's scale and that of the Olympic enterprise also deflects the problematics of globalization by focusing on the Olympics as a cooperative competition among modern nation-states. Hence, while Olympic competition may resonate with an Argentina competing against a Poland for access to US markets or even a South Carolina competing against an Ohio for a BMW plant, it is scarcely applicable to the rarefied corporate environments of large multi-nationals such as Fluor Daniel, which compete worldwide against a select number of corporate competitors, which owe little allegiance to "home" nation-states or minority bodies, and which often get to write their own rules of the game, given that many of the biggest "winners" of globalization are multinationals which themselves have annual revenues larger than the GNPs of many developing nations.

By the same token, while the spirit of the Olympics suggests that all countries are equal on the sports field, the erasure of considerations about how neoliberal globalization is reinscribing colonial relationships (which, by definition, are about *un*equal relationships between nations) is quite evident in MCI-WorldCom's VTM video "In Gear" in which Mexico becomes a "pure zone" of "ecotourism" for affluent US youth, a fantasy in which the broader reality of Mexican industrialization goes unconsidered. Significantly, MCI-WorldCom's video operates on several levels. Primarily, it depicts an emancipatory and optimistic scenario of the possibilities for middle-class Mexican women to exercise "entrepreneurial" talent, suggesting that Mexican and US middle-class realities are nowadays pretty much equivalent. At the same time, the video's promotion of information technology as the solution to personal aspirations in the new corporate "global village" avoids calling the attention of a more environmentally-aware generation of US teens to the exportation of the dirty side of information technology to the maquiladora zones, those places "on the other side of the tracks" where disposal of the toxic chemicals involved in the manufacture of the computer components necessary for such information technology is easier than under US environmental regulations. The video, therefore, neither speaks about how the maquiladoras exemplify the exportation to Mexico of the social costs of producing many of the goods which US consumers desire to purchase, nor how their rise required Mexico's dismantling of its successful nationalist industrial project linked to good wages, benefits, and unionization. Further, MCI-WorldCom's video participates in a metaphysical view of technology in which technology (in particular, information technology) is, by definition, equated with progress. The video shows a "gee-whiz," as-of-yet unperfected web-based instant English–Spanish translation technology as fully operational and suggests that the solution of intransigent social and political issues through the application of high technology articulated to corporate goals is "just around the corner." Such suggestions not only feed into the contemporary cultural push toward all things digital as a social panacea but also, through linking technology to globalization, reinforce the belief that both are inevitable and unalloyed goods, and should not be resisted. Indeed, "technology equals progress" is an important mantra in contemporary global trade, just as the politics of protectionism once were to individual nation-states.

The Rhetoric of Globalization

An analysis of the rhetoric of globalization as reflected in the Virtual Trade Mission suggests that multinational corporations construct and position the idea of globalization in highly selective ways. For example, Thomas McNab, spokesperson for VTM participant Aquatics Unlimited, writes that "recognizing the world as a vast economic and social community of *increasing interdependence and opportunity* cannot be overstated...[T]oday's students...are the newest recruits for TEAM AMERICA....They will need to be shown...that vision and specific educational skills are needed to garner the international business opportunities that await them" (italics ours).[6] Clearly, McNab's comments implicitly refute that aspect of US national identity – exemplified by the "America first" rhetoric of right-wing populists like Patrick Buchanan – which trades in isolationism and xenophobia. He is not, however, refusing the opportunities available to corporations seeking global capitalist hegemonies from mining more imperialistic aspects of US national identity, and his comments reveal the VTM as a strategy to harness such imperialist aspects of US national identity to corporate global strategies in order that US national interest may prevail over time under the rubric of "globalization."

Indeed, McNab's ambitious vision encapsulates well a key aspect of the VTM's implicit agenda: global "entrepreneurs" or "wealth builders" are the new form of individual cultural identity, and US students need to adopt this attitude to ensure the United States continues to be "on top." Thus, within the VTM the national scale of cultural identity, encapsulated in the "Team America" rhetoric, elides into the global scale of identity and US national hegemony is inscribed worldwide. The VTM, trading in an amalgamated "picture language" of the American Dream, imperialist discourse, and the new enterprise culture, instructs students to "go global" under the sign of a utopian future in which "entrepreneurs" supersede mere "citizens" and their now supposedly provincial local perspectives.

Certainly, then, the VTM agenda makes use of US national identity concepts, for the VTM's principal goal is, after all, to interpolate US youth more fully into the new global economy. However, the ways in which the VTM constructs *personal* identity, we would suggest, smoothly elides the tension between being both "American" and a "global entrepreneur," and in so doing it also valorizes the kinds of post-modern multiple and "spatially distributed" identities that we see as leading to, among other things, a kind of "colluding" schizophrenia. Workers are asked to embrace "globalization" and its attendant "global village" worldview, yet they are made keenly aware that US competitive interests are paramount within this global environment. Furthermore, the VTM produces this awareness even as students are asked to align themselves with multinational corporations whose interests are centered on the bottom line, market share, and competitiveness, rather than any particular nation-state's interest or those of its various constituent citizens. This conflation can be seen in a young white female student's comment at a VTM Student Forum held in Chattanooga, Tennessee in 1998: "We have to make the Chinese people feel good about the American people, and we have to make the American people feel good that we're going to the Chinese market because we have to show them that it's going to give us more jobs, and we have to show the Chinese people that it's going to give them more jobs if Boeing goes over there and gets that contract."[7] The student's ambiguous use of an undefined "we" and "us" indicates the kinds of conflations of personal identity to corporate interests encouraged by the VTM. Does "we" refer to a cohort group of high school students, Chattanooga residents, Tennesseeans, Southerners, Americans, global entrepreneurs, or future Boeing workers? Moreover, "people," whether Chinese or American, are collapsed into "jobs" and "markets," thereby conflating citizenship, consumption, and entrepreneurship. In the process of such a reconfiguration of identity the VTM inculcates in students the belief that globalization is always a win-win situation. Individual workers are no longer only laboring bodies but are now encouraged to identify as part of a world economy in which entrepreneurship and the exchange of goods become the privileged source of personal identity and meaning, no matter what position one has within the hierarchy of jobs that results from a global contract. Thus any focus on class position is absent, as shown in the VTM's relentless boosterism of this new identity formation: "The VTM provides you with a compass, connections and, if you really work at it, more than a few career choices and civic values as you realize your potential as a worldwide customer, worker, investor and citizen."[8] In this quotation, then, the VTM lays bare the hierarchy of identity formations required to most fully realize corporate agendas: one is first a customer and only incidentally a citizen.

Clearly, the VTM is about mediating compliance and disciplining personal expectations in the next generation of US workers who will enter labor markets made more fiercely competitive by the very procedures the VTM promotes. Its pilot educational/ideological media strategy works to produce a complicity of intention between the separate interests of working Americans and the multinationals that increasingly understand and position their corporate interests as surpassing US national interests. "Globalization" as an idea is discursively constructed as both class-free and a process in which "America [must be] first," and this calls into question the geographic scales at which – and the geographic spaces within which – identity is constructed, for within the VTM identity is simultaneously based both on narrower geopolitical considerations such as nation-state affiliation and on a wider global scale in which specific geographical considerations are either unimportant or are narrowly defined. For example, Newly Industrializing Countries participating in the VTM are represented in limited, even stereotypical, ways, a representation reflective of both the contributions of US multinationals but also of the very nation-states that have affiliated with the VTM in hopes of increasing market-share for their goods in the US. For example, Malaysia, while encouraging US students to consider that country's needs in the global arena, describes itself foremost as "a tropical wonderland."[9] Although this hardly seems the first thing an industrializing country might seek to project about its self-image, the image of paradise that the Malaysian government projects via its participation in the VTM concords with US cultural tropes of the "exotic orient," thereby appealing to comfortable "America first" stereotypes while disarming resistance within US markets (will Americans really think a tropical wonderland capable of out-competing them in the manufacture of, say, computer components?). This shallow view of globalization suggests how the VTM promotes established and shop-worn cultural discourses and ideologies of development and "otherness."

The VTM also demonstrates how mainstream US trade unions increasingly align themselves with an "America first" discourse, one that trades on the disaffection toward multinational corporations on the part of mostly white, male employees whose job security is threatened by corporate global strategies. Thus, while the IBEW's website instructional materials help US student-entrepreneurs learn that the interests of US multinationals often include the loss of existing US jobs, and the IBEW student workbook directs attention to issues of social advocacy, noting that "'harmonizing' downward is not an acceptable alternative for workers," this union's same material for students aligns itself with US corporate interests by opposing "hidden national subsidies" made by foreign governments that place "our" US companies at a competitive disadvantage in an international market.[10] Of course, these unions have different goals from those of a multinational corporation or a Singapore (although, at the same time, they themselves increasingly are large-scale enterprises, as evidenced in the 1999 absorption of the United Rubber Workers by the United Steelworkers of America). It is significant, though, that union arguments on VTM-sponsored websites do dovetail to a great degree with the corporatist mantra of "free trade" which opposes foreign governments subsidizing "their" multinationals (but which invariably turns a blind eye to the "corporate welfare" received by nominally "US" multinationals, both in the United States and abroad). We should remember, however, that free trade and the "level playing field" that is its discursive terrain of operations are most often promoted by imperial powers – such as late Victorian England and the US today – who are in the position to dictate what constitutes this "level playing field." Hence, the unions' educational packages for US high schools participating in the VTM echo, and even rationalize, the reactionary assault against the Clinton administration's first-term efforts to implement rudimentary national health insurance in which US Health Maintenance Organizations (HMOs) and other corporate interests reduced the complexity of Canada's federal Medicare system to a "hidden subsidy" to Canadian corporations because it relocated the financial onus of paying for workers' healthcare from those corporations to the tax system. Consequently, in its VTM materials, rather than seeing Canada's healthcare system as providing a more comprehensive social safety net than is available in the United States, the IBEW buys into a rhetoric in which Canadian-based firms, including branch-plant operations of such giants as Ford and GM, are said to benefit from an unfair subsidy and consequently are not operating on the US-defined "level playing field." The end result is that the unions involved in the VTM play into a privatizing corporate agenda in which the US must dominate, no matter how disingenuous the logic of rationalization and avoidance required. Significantly, by participating in the discourse of the so-called level playing field – the dimensions and scale of which are discursively positioned in advance by the powerful, including the corporate players who comprise the VTM – the unions introduce a *moral* argument which suggests that regional and national differences, where inimical to US labor interests, should be eliminated.

As a *privatized* corporate hybrid of website and video-based education, celebrity classroom visits, propaganda, and advertising, then, the VTM works to reconceptualize what we mean by "public education" toward something that might more succinctly be termed "corporate indoctrination." Students are no longer students but are now "consumers" of the branded reality produced through corporate agendas. In entering an educational arena increasingly reconceptualized as one which must above all foster the growth of the "new economy," the VTM seeks to inculcate in future US workers the ahistorical and decontextualized belief that corporate agendas have the common good at heart, even if this means the loss of these workers' own jobs. Such internal or personal incoherency articulates to the VTM's wider disjointed message to students wherein, for example, Singapore is part of the big emerging market the US seeks to penetrate and conquer, yet is also a fierce competitor – an Intelligent Island whose aggressively competitive business and labor practices serve both as a warning to, and a model for, US students encouraged to minimize a sense of identity based on citizenship and place in favor of entrepreneurship, technology, and the mythic neocosmopolitan potential to be part of the "big picture" of global information and capital flows.

Clearly, the executives of a UPS or a Fluor Daniel grasp the importance of "economic and geographic literacy" for US workers, but the VTM seeks to produce this "literacy" in highly cynical ways. For example, the VTM website course "Globalization 101" directs students to a number of sites where they can learn about relevant issues. These sites include, among others:

The Business Round Table, an association of leading US corporate CEOs whose sole purpose is to "promote policies that will lead to sustainable, non-inflationary, long-term growth in the US economy";
GoTrade, a network of business lobbyists organized to pressure Congress to extend to China the status of Permanent Normal Trade Relations (PNTR);
The Trade and Development Centre, a joint venture of the World Bank and World Trade Organization;
The CATO Institute (a right-wing economic think-tank);
The Organization of American States, whose stated goal is to establish by 2005 the Free Trade Area of the Americas (FTAA).[11]

Yet the underlying goal of the geographic literacy produced by the use of VTM videos, websites, and high-profile encounters between students and Olympians is to produce affinities between students and global processes that dovetail with the purposes of the corporations funding the VTM. Implicitly, students are encouraged to view as inevitable and even desirable the decline of publicly funded higher education and the critical thinking it at least ideally promotes, and to embrace the processes of globalization which frequently force governments, in a race to the bottom, to cut social expenditures – such as those for education – so that they may remain low-tax (and thus attractive) destinations for freely circulating global capital. Indeed, the VTM website informs students "life long learning has replaced a college diploma as the dance ticket to success."[12] Students are thus encouraged to accept as inevitable the nexus of big global corporations and big emerging markets that sounds the death-knell for the kind of job security and social welfare earlier enjoyed by many workers in the older Fordist economy. In its place they are offered up the dubious consolation that the big emerging markets will provide compensatory opportunities for those in the US who are subject to the social dislocations that globalization augurs because neoliberal globalization will facilitate consumption overseas of what "we" (i.e., the United States) produce – a consolation which conveniently ignores, however, the fact that neoliberal policies and structural adjustment programs are, in fact, reducing the living standards and the very purchasing power of millions of workers in developing countries who will thus be unable to afford many of the goods produced in the United States.[13]

Conclusion

The importance of the relationship between ethics and geographic scale subtends this paper, and we would argue that a sense of scale is important in achieving ethical relationships between and among individuals and groups and other objects, subjects, and peoples. However, the VTM suggests – exemplified in its exhortation "Welcome to...citizenship in the New Global Economy" – that consideration of, and identification with, locality is increasingly out-moded.[14] Students are told that the only scale that really matters is the global one and that interrelationships and money all flow down from the global to the local in a fashion that precludes making connections across or between localities, except as such connections facilitate the flow of capital and the emergence of "postnational" commodity identities. Trading on a variation of the American Dream to further a corporatist agenda cloaked in the technophillic rhetoric of globalization and instrumental personal opportunity, the VTM teaches students that a too-parochial focus on only the places around them will keep them from getting ahead while, by inference, VTM materials also propose that too-focused a concern for other geographically distant localities such as polluted, gendered, and transient maquila zones is counterproductive to achieving the enhanced economic success and concomitant "big-picture" and entrepreneurial subjectivity promoted by the VTM agenda. Rather, economic success will be obtained by decoupling one's sense of self from particular localities – near or far – in favor of a top-down hierarchical sense of world scale. The resulting distributed sense of self promoted both by the VTM and the networked communication technologies upon which it relies will then be available for rearticulation to the interests of US multinationals positioned by the VTM as the essence of globalization and all that is now hyped as culturally desirable. Such a strategy, we suggest, conflates the global and the personal, replaces politics with economics and technology, and thereby works to devalue the relationships that people have to the material places within which they live. This has important implications for the politics of scale, for organizing against such a strategy increasingly requires appeals to the various components of individual and group identities distributed unevenly yet cotemporally along an array of ideas of the personal, the local, the regional, the national, and the global.

We have discussed, then, the VTM student audience and note that all the VTM multinationals are US-based. This is arguably not surprising. Large US companies operate globally, and they believe that to do so successfully the US labor force needs to have a greater instrumental awareness of the broader world. Yet this quasi-official promotion of a culture of entrepreneurship avoids the gritty reality behind the "American Dream" – not everyone can be a successful entrepreneur. If there are winners there are likely to be still more losers, as the early material produced by the VTM-affiliated unions that support "free" trade at least partially acknowledged. We acknowledge, though, that an argument can be made, along the lines of Michel de Certeau's (1984: xiii–xix), that the VTM helps students in "making do," that it might assist them in optimizing "opportunities that must be seized 'on the wing'" within a "system they [have] no choice but to accept." Such ironic accommodation, however, forecloses the educational potential of the kind of critique we make here. The VTM is a propaganda tool and we see no reason why it, and the visual and verbal metaphors and synecdoches it trades in, should not be critiqued. Indeed, a key understanding underpinning our argument is that the modern concept of ideology, far from being a useless concept or a "thing" or signifier floating free of referents, is alive to the degree that it is always operationalized "within" dominant forms of cultural ritual (Sloterdijk 1987). This is how any one ideology achieves its cultural point of purchase and this, then, is why the actor Jeremy Jackson, who plays the character Hobie on the television series *Baywatch*, is employed in the Fluor Daniel VTM video to promote corporate strategies to a culture and generation increasingly appreciative of the value of celebrity status. This is why we can note that the VTM seeks the collusion of students in its goals, rather than claiming it promotes a "false consciousness."

In an increasingly mediatized culture, the consumption of visual images and spectatorship, viewing and watching, coupled with "edu-tain me," has become a dominant ritual, a factor implicitly embedded in the VTM's MTV-style approach depicted in the videos many member corporations produce. Websites and media strategies are the contemporary rituals through which the corporate strategies and ideologies of the VTM are visualized, hypertextualized, fetishized, lived, and diffused.[15] And while it is perhaps no accident that the VTM does not address how a society organized according to consumption of images might also rework itself into a network of individuated entrepreneurs, we note that it is precisely the interpolation of information technology and other media strategies with classroom locales, wherein reality is explicitly produced and consumed, that is central to any "success" to which the VTM strategy may lead as part of "the work of producing and reproducing the organization and management of a global production system" (Sassen 1998: 203).

These issues overlap, and the continual evolution of the VTM website raises new questions about the relationships among them. How does, for example, the IBEW's current agenda to protect US jobs dovetail with the VTM's utopian emphasis on technology, websites, videos, celebrity status, and Olympian achievement? Each seems a subset of a broader discursive strategy that positions the United States first in a "go for gold" mindset that scuppers meaningful assessments of the widespread cultural and economic differences both within the US and between different parts of the increasingly naturalized "global village." With the partial exception of its affiliated US unions, the VTM advertises not only an unconsidered acceptance of multinational global activities but also promotes the ambiguous interplay of job exportation, worker exploitation, and the reification of US imperial dominance. In sum, the strategy by which the VTM is operationalized confirms that visual representation, icons, and "an economy of signs" are key tools in structuring the increased scales of operations, geographic diffusion, and profits sought by multinationals and those who seek their favor. We close, then, with the words of media theorist Lynn Spigel (1992: 217), who notes in her assessment of television culture that "the global village, after all, is the fantasy of the colonizer, not the colonized."

NOTES

(NB: With regard to URLs for the *Virtual Trade Mission*, dates listed are those when the site was last accessed. As can be imagined, this site is an evolving resource and so some of these links no longer work. However, we have included them here to give a historical picture of what was on the website at different times).

1 *Virtual Trade Mission*, June 13, 2000 (www.virtualtrademission.org/home.htm) and *Virtual Trade Mission*, Sept. 1, 2001 (www.virtualtrademission.org/Beta/home.html).
2 *Virtual Trade Mission*, Feb. 23, 1999 (www.virtualtrademission.org/vtm_mission.htm).
3 *Virtual Trade Mission*, Feb. 23, 1999 (www.virtualtrademission.org/workbook/work1.htm).
4 Thanks to Chris Merrett for information on relationships between high-wage Canadian manufacturing jobs lost and the Free Trade Agreement between the US and Canada. Applying the US Department of Labor's unemployment multiplier of 2.7 to the 42,000 lost Canadian jobs suggests that at least 112,000 jobs were lost to free trade during the five-year period following FTA implementation. *Statistics Canada* confirms that trade has increased dramatically since 1989. However, real wages are lower and poverty rates higher than before this date.
5 *Virtual Trade Mission*, Feb. 23, 1999 (www.virtualtrademission.org/sponsors/uswa.htm).
6 *Virtual Trade Mission*, Feb. 23, 1999 (www.virtualtrademission.org/sponsors/au.htm).
7 *Virtual Trade Mission: Program Highlights* (undated VTM video).
8 *Virtual Trade Mission*, Dec. 9, 2000 (www.virtualtrademission.org/home.htm).
9 *Virtual Trade Mission*, Feb. 23, 1999 (www.virtualtrademission.org/quick_facts.htm).
10 *Virtual Trade Mission*, Feb. 23, 1999 (www.virtualtrademission.org/workbook/wkbk_ibew.htm).
11 Only one site which speaks to the problems of globalization is included: the International Forum on Globalization (www.ifg.org). However, the arguments against globalization presented on this site (March 26, 2000) are countered by the "Investing in the Global Economy" page (www.virtualtrademission.org/financialtools.htm), which feeds into students' entrepreneurial spirit by listing a number of sites that enable one to "be an international investor," sites which include those of Charles Schwab, Fidelity Investments, Fortune Investor, Morgan Stanley/Dean Whitter, Paine Webber, and Salomon Smith Barney.
12 *Virtual Trade Mission*, March 26, 2000 (www.virtualtrademission.org/home.htm).

13 For instance, one of the problems Coca-Cola faces in "opening up" markets in Africa is that over half of the continent's population earns less than a dollar a day.
14 *Virtual Trade Mission*, Sept. 1, 2001 (www.virtualtrademission.org/Beta/home.html).
15 We recognize that all imperial powers seek suzerainty over the social reproduction of reality both within and beyond their territorial limits. As such, a partial antecedent for the VTM is arguably present in Sir Halford Mackinder's early twentieth-century efforts to foster "imperial vision" among British schoolchildren through the use of textbooks and slides (see Ryan 1997).

REFERENCES

Barry, A. M. 1997: *Visual Intelligence: Perception, Image and Manipulation in Visual Communication*. Albany: SUNY Press.
Bartolovich, C. 1995: The work of cultural studies in the age of transnational production. *Minnesota Review*, 45–6 (Fall), 117–46.
Cox, K. 1998: Representations and power in the politics of scale. *Political Geography*, 17, 41–4.
de Certeau, M. 1984: *The Practice of Everyday Life* (trans. Steven Rendall). Berkeley: University of California Press.
Elashmawi, F. and Harris, P. R. 1998: *Multicultural Management 2000: Essential Cultural Insights for Global Business Success*. Houston, TX: Gulf Publishing Company.
Friedman, T. L. 1999: *The Lexus and the Olive Tree*. New York: Farrar, Straus, Giroux.
Marston, S. 2000: The social construction of scale. *Progress in Human Geography*, 24 (2), 219–42.
Ryan, J. R. 1997: *Picturing Empire: Photography and the Visualization of the British Empire*. Chicago: University of Chicago Press.
Sassen, S. 1998: *Globalization and Its Discontents*. New York: New Press.
Sloterdijk, P. 1987: *Critique of Cynical Reason* (trans. Michael Eldred). Minneapolis: University of Minnesota Press.
Spigel, L. 1992: The suburban home companion: Television and the neighborhood ideal in postwar America. In B. Colomina (ed.), *Sexuality and Space*. New York: Princeton Architectural Press, 185–218.

6

Popular Culture, Academic Discourse, and the Incongruities of Scale

Andrew Kirby

In this chapter I want to propose that there is a significant and important incongruity between the ways in which scale is often thought about and represented in academic circles, and the ways in which it is often thought about and represented in the realm of popular culture. Specifically, I argue that comfortable heuristics around which much academic discourse has recently revolved – "the global," "the local," and, even, "the glocal" – do not represent ways in which most people outside the academy think of scale, even though what we can term "scalar thinking" is, in fact, quite usual. Indeed, scalar discourses beyond the academy often seem to be at odds with our own intellectual constructs – the global and the local, I would maintain, are simply not self-evident terms of everyday reference for most people, regardless of how much it appears that they just "seem to present themselves" to many academics (Taylor and Flint 2000: 43). Thus, much academic theorizing about scale and its construction has represented it as linear and predictable, a way of organizing social processes and forms into a hierarchical taxonomy. Part of the attraction of world-systems theory, for instance, is its promise to integrate what is small with what is large, connecting the household, the territorial state, and the global capitalist economy (Taylor 1981; Wallerstein 1974). In turn, the scalar progressions of world-systems theory are in many ways not so far removed from the repetitive spatial taxonomies employed by physical scientists. Hence, astronomers and other physical scientists have tended to organize the components of the universe (ranging from particles through to planets) using a simple geometric progression such as $meter^{-1}$, $meter^1$, $meter^{10}$, and so forth. On the other hand, non-academic constructions of scale, I would argue, are typically quite different, insofar as they usually have less to do with taxonomy and much more to do with ways of thinking about, living in, and seeing the world.

Elaborating upon this argument, then, in this chapter I will discuss two examples of how scalar discourses in popular culture appear to be at odds with those of the academy. The first of these non-academic constructions of scale is what I shall term here an "extraglobal" scale, by which I mean it is an understanding of scale through which humans position themselves not within a global setting but, rather, within the broader canvas of the cosmos.[1] The second is very different, and can be thought of as the way in which people position themselves as individuals against that which remains hidden, unseen, and, often, unknown. Central to my argument is the recognition that popular culture very much represents an arena within which relevant social constructions, including those of scale, are created and refined. Consequently, the incongruity between academic and popular discourses is something that is important to interrogate as we attempt to theorize "scale" as a social construct and as we think about how political practices are scaled. If academics are to engage in progressive political praxis, then it is necessary to have some conception of how the public understanding of, and sensitivity to, scale may be quite different from ours as academics, for it is within popular culture that we see the ways in which individuals structure their world and it is there, consequently, that we see interesting developments with respect to space and scale (e.g. Frith 1996; Neale and Smith 1998).

The chapter itself is organized as follows. First, I discuss how much Western popular culture has tended to focus less on what has become a contemporary object of fascination among academics – namely, globalization and the local–global dialectic – and more on the relationship between the Earth and the extraglobal. Second, I examine how technology is auguring transformations among public perceptions of time and space – here we can think of how "real time," "virtual reality," "the shrinking globe," and "cyberspace" have caught the popular imagination, for example. This is being reflected, I propose, in a popular discourse in which many people are coming to think about the spaces of everyday life less in terms of clearly defined hierarchical spatial resolutions such as "the local" and "the global," and increasingly in terms of flows and "front regions" and "back regions." Thus the current fascination in the United States and elsewhere with "reality-based TV" and with internet "voyeurism" – here I am thinking particularly of the plethora of

webcasts showing everything from live sex shows to surgical operations to women giving birth – in which we can watch other people
live their lives in the most intimate of detail without having to be
physically close to them is, I suggest, breaking down distinctions of
what it means to talk about "inside" and "outside," "here" and
"there," and "up" and "down," a breakdown which has obvious
implications for how we think about scale. The chapter ends with a
brief set of synoptic comments.

Diminishing the Global

Globalization and the discourse of the academy

The steady emergence during the past two decades or so of a discourse within the academy around issues of "globalization" has dramatically transformed the nature of social science inquiry. From book
and journal titles to conference themes to calls for university curricula
to be updated and "globalized" so that we may better prepare students to work in a global economy, a discourse of globalization has
insinuated itself, it appears, everywhere. This is an important development, for such a discourse is transforming, Midas-like, virtually
every idea with which it comes into contact. In the process, a whole
new lexicon involving "globality" has emerged (see Taylor 1999).
    Typically, the emergence of such a discourse is seen to reside in a
number of contemporary social developments. Often, globalization
(as a set of economic, political, and cultural processes and outcomes)
is viewed as dependent on technological and social changes which
have led to the space-time compression (Harvey 1989) of contemporary everyday life. In such approaches, globalization has usually been
seen as the logical outcome of capital's expansionary nature, while
the development of computer and telecommunications technologies
is held as having allowed capital to coordinate its activities globally
so that, for instance, real-time transactions can now take place in the
currency markets operating across the planet. Like the relatively new
technologies (fax machines, email, the internet) which are implicated
in appearing to shrink the planet, so, too, is globalization itself often
taken to be a novel development in the human condition – and, as
experience has shown us, novel developments usually receive much
ink from academics. Moreover, such notions of novelty have been
reinforced, I think, by a belief among many that globalization somehow constitutes an end of history (at least as it has been viewed until
now), a belief that is tied up arguably both with an end-of-millennium

sentiment that we are now entering a new age which is qualitatively different from what has gone before, and with Fukuyama's (1992) proclamation that the collapse of Communism in the USSR has marked the end of great ideological conflicts around which future histories (and geographies) might be inscribed.

Of course, the way in which globalization appears itself to have readily become a globalizing discourse has not gone without critique. Janet Abu-Lughod (1991), for instance, has famously suggested that much discourse about globalization is little more than "global babble," while others have made convincing arguments that globalization is not so new and not so different from the situation extant in 1913, before the outbreak of the Great War (see Sutcliffe and Glyn 1999; Hirst and Thompson 1996). Nevertheless, despite the criticism leveled at the concept of globalization, the insinuation of such a discourse into the academy has had a number of significant impacts, two of which are perhaps particularly pertinent. First, as Harvey (2000: 13) has suggested, "many of us took the concept on board so uncritically in the 1980s and 1990s, allowing it to displace the far more politically charged concepts of imperialism and neocolonialism." The global turn is, in other words, a neologism that both reflects the more conservative times in which we live, and serves to crowd out other tropes. Second, the rise of a focus on the global has tended to diminish the importance of other scales – much less attention appears to be paid now to what were once characterized as regional problems, for example (Holland 1976; see also Brenner 1997). As meaningful academic discourse has become globally oriented, so have traditional issues become recast and disparate local issues been transformed into unified global questions. Hence, urban growth and transport problems are increasingly viewed as policy issues linked to urban air quality, which in turn has become subsumed within the larger rubric of global warming. Relatedly, seemingly all analysis of climate change is now rendered as "global climate change," even though in reality there may be one process (however murkily understood) but very many outcomes. Studies that are not driven by simple political agendas recognize that there are as many climate changes taking place as there are climate regions – in some there is warming, in some there is actually cooling. Nevertheless, the tyranny of the global scale drives out the possibility of understanding reality at other scales (for a recent assessment of the policy dilemma, see Sarewitz and Pielke 2000), such that individuals and groups have increasingly shifted from small-scale environmental problem solving to the largest scale of environmental analysis (for a discussion, see Castells 1997).

Despite the fascination in the academy with the notion of global-ization, it (and its associated discourses such as globalism, the local–global dialectic, and the glocal) have barely begun to enter the sphere of popular culture and the public's imagination, though this has started to change after the events in Seattle, when demonstrators opposed to the World Trade Organization brought the notion sharply into public focus.[2] Certainly, within the realms of music, filmmaking, art, and literature, globalization as a scale of reference for popular culture appears to be much less significant, and to have a much shorter heritage, than does popular culture's fascination with what we might think of as extraglobal scales of reference. Indeed, while few social scientists have paid much attention to the relationship of the Earth to the broader cosmos (though see Steinberg 1999 for an innovative discussion of how it has been proposed to extend the principles of territorial sovereignty and international law), within popular culture the extraglobal has long been a source of fascination and intrigue – although given that conceptions of scale are historic-ally shaped, presumably at some future point social scientists will indeed have to theorize the relationship between the global and the extraglobal, once humans begin to populate worlds other than our own.[3] It is, then, to a discussion of popular culture's fascination with the Earth's relationship to the broader cosmos that I now turn.

The extraglobal scale and the anxieties of popular culture

The heavens, of course, have preoccupied humans for millennia. For the ancient Egyptians, Greeks, Romans, and others, the heavens were central referents in people's religious lives. In more recent times, the Enlightenment became cast as a struggle between the Church and science over the place of the Earth at the center of the solar system and, at least in part, the Copernican revolution was a metaphysical struggle over the relationship between Man (*sic*) and God, a struggle which the Church did not concede until Galileo's book *Dialogue on the Great World Systems* was removed from the Vatican Index in the nineteenth century. Given the great metaphysical ambit of the En-lightenment – transforming society from a theocratic-centered know-ledge base to a science-centered one – it is not coincidental that as successful telescopes were developed in the sixteenth century they were turned on the planets and that astronomy was the first practical science undertaken in the West. It is, of course, completely consistent with my argument here that in the sixteenth century analysis of "world systems" automatically meant the study of the planets, rather than the material world envisaged by Braudel and, later, Wallerstein. The heavens, then, were both a source of mystery but also the embodiment of the complex setting in which humans found themselves. The passage of the Sun and the Moon represented the basis of the rhythms of existence and their analysis informed mathematics, while in subsequent years the stars constituted the maps that allowed terrestrial cartography to be created (Whitfield 2000).

What has arisen in the last century, however, is a rather different scientific and popular emphasis, focused upon the possibility of life elsewhere within the universe and the ways in which it might manifest itself. We are now firmly in a second phase of planetary discovery, which has surpassed the earlier efforts to reach the Moon – the goal is now to explore the cosmos for evidence of life (Goldsmith 1997). NASA's ability to transmit digital feeds from Mars has proven to be enormously popular, with sometimes millions of people logging on to its website daily, while the possibility that either remote vehicles (such as Global Surveyor) or even meteorites will give proof of some form of life remains popular, albeit improbable (see Kelly 1995). Although this interest in the possibility of life elsewhere is the focus of serious scientific exploration, it is perhaps in the realm of science fiction that it has most caught the popular imagination. Certainly, there appear to be deep-seated and complex psychological motives at play here which stretch back well beyond the late nineteenth century when the fascination with, for example, attack by beings from other worlds, long a staple of the genre, became widespread. In this regard, H. G. Wells's classic *The War of the Worlds* is perhaps the most famous prototype, encapsulating a wide set of human concerns, fears, and expectations which revolve around a belief that otherworldly creatures will be more intelligent, more powerful, and more belligerent than ourselves – nor should we forget the pandemonium which followed Orson Welles's 1938 radio broadcast of *The War of the Worlds* where hundreds of listeners needed no persuading that the United States was under attack by Martians.[4] Thus, Jung (1959) argued that there were clear archetypes to be witnessed in the stories of spaceships that are not so different from earlier myths about the chariots of the gods. Likewise, if Freud were correct that the world-as-other is dangerous, then we may be permitted to extend that logic to argue that other worlds may be even more threatening (Sampson 1993: 49). Beginning in the 1950s, tales of abductions by aliens began to be heard more frequently, tales that appear related to basic psychoanalytic fears concerning invasion, submission, and conspiracy (Parker 1995: 369) and which became prevalent in the broader context of the emerging Cold War and the threat of nuclear annihilation. Indeed, there are so many recurrent anecdotes beginning at about this time and suggesting this danger that, daring to mix scales, we might term them urban myths.

Whatever the reason, then, popular culture in the United States has shown a particular fascination with alien forms.[5] A list of the movies released in Hollywood in recent years would include *Mars Attacks!*, *Red Planet*, *Mission to Mars*, *Galaxy Quest*, *Stargate*, and *Contact*, and this is not to mention the internationally popular *X-Files*. Yet this is the tip of an iceberg that has been growing for decades. The *Alien* trilogy, *Brother from Another Planet*, *ET – the Extra Terrestrial*, *Close Encounters of the Third Kind*, and *Star Wars* were created in the 1970s and 1980s, while *Star Trek* was first produced in the 1960s. Before that was the classic period of science fiction, including *The Invasion of the Body Snatchers* and *Plan 9 from Outer Space*, and prior to that there were the TV shows and matinée movies featuring heroes such as Flash Gordon. We can go back even further to landmark novels such as Wells's *The War of the Worlds* – first published in 1898 at a time when Percival Lowell's purported observations of "canals" led to speculations that there could be life on Mars – and his *The First Men on the Moon* (1901), and even earlier to Jules Vernes's *From the Earth to the Moon* (*De la Terre à la Lune*), which was first published in 1865.

This is not, of course, a seamless genre. In each period, these were also allegorical vehicles for discussing contemporary issues and, as such, the emphasis differs widely. In the *Flash Gordon* matinée movies, for example, we see simplistic sagas of good and evil that sought to define the times in which they were made. In the 1950s and 1960s, it was very easy to see an extension of American hegemony recreated in space. In the 1970s, we see questions of technological hesitancy often contrasted with superiority and wisdom exhibited by the aliens. Equally, the writers of *Star Trek*, reflecting the earliest hints in the 1960s of what we would today call multiculturalism, created a multi-ethnic, multispecies crew of males and females who were obliged to follow the "prime directive," which was a "look, don't touch" rule for their protagonists who were thus allowed to observe, but not to meddle in, others' affairs – although, of course, in practice they did much more than meddle, rather like their real-life US military contemporaries, who acted as "advisers" in countries like South Vietnam. Despite their varied contexts, though, one common theme that does reappear time and again is that of conquest (usually of the Earth by aliens) and exploration, which, drawing on psychoanalysis, we might interpret as reflecting fears of subjugation and of encountering the unknown. Much US science fiction of the 1950s, for example, can be read as allegorical concerning fears of Soviet invasion, while *Star Trek*, to take but one example, presents its central character Captain James T. Kirk almost as a futuristic Christopher Columbus. Significantly, both conquest and exploration are about the mastering of territory and invoke spatial imaginations and their associated fears.

During the 1990s, we saw a number of movies which dealt with the implications of encountering aliens in the United States (e.g., *Star Trek: First Contact*) and the need for planetary defense (*Independence Day, Mars Attacks!*), undertaken by immigration officials no less (*Men in Black*). Such themes seem to reflect contemporary anxieties on the part of many about how undocumented immigration from Latin America and elsewhere may be undermining the territorial integrity of the US and are themes which have found political voice in the presidential ambitions of Patrick Buchanan, with his anti-immigrant "America First" slogan, and in such measures as California's anti-immigrant Proposition 187 (for more on these issues, see Smith and Tarallo 1995; also, see Mains, ch. 7 this volume). These cultural expressions are clearly both repetitive enough and complex enough to attract analytical attention.

Though spatial anxieties appear to have found expression in much science fiction, time travel, on the other hand, according to Constance Penley (1989), appears a much less significant element in science fiction, at least with regard to the US film industry. Certainly, there are movies and novels which deal with the theme: from *Terminator* to the *Back to the Future* trilogy to *Galaxy Quest*, it has become customary to travel back in time in order to change the past and, consequently, the future too. However, although Penley herself discusses time travel at some length in her book *The Future of an Illusion*, with the intent of demonstrating not Jungian archetypes but Freudian obsessions with the self as a sexual subject (themes explored in both the *Terminator* and *La Jetée/Twelve Monkeys*), and although she confounds the question at one point by writing about the spatialization of time, she concludes that "Hollywood has always been more drawn to conquering space and fighting off alien invaders than thinking through the heady paradoxes of voyaging through time" (Penley 1989: 126; also p. 136).

While it is not my intention here, then, to try to synthesize the genre of science fiction, by touching even briefly on a number of themes it is possible to suggest that whereas during the past two decades social science writers across a number of disciplines have focused a great deal of energy on thinking about processes of globalization and the political economy of the local–global dialectic, popular culture appears to have revolved much more around issues of the extraglobal. The result is that, for the most part, academic anxieties and the discourses that they generate about scale appear not to be synchronized with public anxieties and the discourses that they generate about scale. Moreover, popular culture's fascination with the extraglobal does not appear to have had any real impact on social scientists' efforts to think about the spatial scales which structure people's lives. Indeed, what is significant about considering the public's fascination with science fiction and its focus on other(world)ness is that such sentiments of popular culture appear to be totally out of step with much intellectual practice. Thus, it would be hard to find a serious social science writer, for example, who is concerned with extraglobal matters; it is hard to find a filmmaker, it seems, who is not. In fact, the academic concern for globalization seems almost passé when compared with this much bigger canvas.[6]

Of Front and Back Regions

Whereas above I suggested that there is an incongruity in scalar thinking between much academic writing, which focuses on the global, and much popular culture discourse, which focuses on the extraglobal, in this second section of the chapter I examine another aspect of popular cultural discourse which appears to be out of line with much academic theorizing about scale. Specifically, while academic notions of scale have typically conceived of "regions" as intermediary levels in a hierarchical taxonomy of space which links the local with the global, the widespread use of surveillance technologies for public entertainment, especially when they are harnessed to penetrate the mysteries of how people around us live their lives, are bringing with them an alternate discourse, one which implicitly conceives of the division of space not so much in hierarchical terms as in the horizontal terms of "front" and "back." Certainly, the notion of front and back regions is not unknown to social science, for fifty years ago sociologist Erving Goffman used the terms to describe how people maintain different forms of behavior in different settings.[7] Yet it is the rise of computer technologies associated with virtual reality and cyberspace which have both popularized these terms in the contemporary period and which are having, I argue, a significant impact upon the ways in which many people are thinking about the spatial relationships between places.

In this regard, then, it is clear that the development of technologies of surveillance and penetration have allowed us to see into places which until fairly recently were invisible to us. Although this is not a

completely new phenomenon – X-rays have enabled the interior of
the body to be viewed for over a century – the pace of technological
change and the widespread use that is being made of such technologies within society do appear to be molding, to a much greater extent
than before, the ways in which people now think about space and
time. Thus, technologies associated with magnetic resonance imaging
(MRIs) have allowed doctors to produce interactive computer generated models of the human body on which to practice before ever
getting into the Operating Room. Likewise, surveillance technology
is allowing the remote monitoring of everyday spaces, a development which has raised interesting legal questions concerning the
right to privacy in public and/or private spaces.[8] In terms of popular
culture, such technologies have facilitated the emergence recently of
a whole slew of "reality based" (i.e., supposedly nonscripted) television programs which allow us to peek from afar into other people's
lives, whether it is in the form of simple edited videotape of the
police bursting into people's apartments (*Cops*), of relative strangers
living in communal settings (*Real World*, *Big Brother*), or of maintaining a home refurbished to Victorian standards (*The 1900 House*). Of
course, to maintain novelty, this trend towards hi-tech eavesdrop-
ping has increasingly moved into more exotic situations, such as the
Australian Outback or a desert island (*Survivors*). While it is obvious
that these programs are edited, they do function in an important
manner in that they contribute to our understanding of our collective
experience, or what Harré (1984) terms our "common sense."

In response to the emergence of such technologies and the
common sense amongst the public which has accompanied them,
social commentator Paul Virilio (1997: 55) has argued that "inside
and outside are gradually losing their importance" as dualisms
around which everyday life is organized, for the boundaries between
the two are becoming increasingly difficult to determine. This is important for the way in which we think about the scaling of our
world, for frequently scale has been thought of by academics as a
way of delineating between easily-differentiated spaces (for example,
the national scale delineates between different territorial units,
thereby determining who is inside or outside a particular country).
Hence, in the case of a computer-generated "virtual reality" game, is
the player "inside" or "outside" of the "location" in which the game
is actually taking place? Although Virilio's point may be debated as
far as material life goes – the penchant in contemporary America for
the entombing of the family in larger and larger homes, set in more
elaborately guarded and differentiated communities, is undoubtedly
reemphasizing the boundaries between "inside" and "outside" (see

Putnam 2000) – in terms of the use of surveillance technologies and their influence on popular culture, Virilio appears to be correct. This seems to be nowhere more clear than in the phenomenon of "webcasting," to which I now turn.

All the lonely people: the world of webcasting

One technological development which has caught the popular imagination in recent years is webcasting, that is to say the transmission of digital information via the internet. It can be thought of as a new medium of communication, primarily because it allows the viewing of situations in perpetual real time with little or no editorial oversight. In their most minimal form, webcasts consist of a single-shot digital camera attached to a computer server on which, every few minutes, a new photo is uploaded and relayed to the visitor. Some of these cameras have a certain whimsy attached to them, such as the one in Iowa that points, in season, to nothing more compelling than a field of growing corn. Others have more of a surveillance function, showing street intersections or places where traffic jams are common. Yet others are commercial pornography sites. Webcasting is interesting, though, because it draws implicitly on notions of front and back regions, inside and outside, and connects these to questions of what reality is and how we can identify it. To explore such ideas I want to use briefly the example of one of the first webcasts to gain public notoriety, namely that of the JenniCAM (www.jenni-cam.org).

The JenniCAM is distinguished by its longevity and its relative complexity. The camera has been placed successively in the dorm room, then an apartment and, subsequently, the house of a young woman (Jennifer Ringley) who, at the time of writing, lives and works in her home in Sacramento and who carries on her daily existence under the gaze of the camera. As can be imagined, logging on can reveal a photo of the living space, a photo of the bed, a photo of the resident asleep, or something more active. This produces some very troubling and yet interesting notions about the relations between individuals, the individual and the collective, about voyeurism and display, about pornographic images, and about privacy. The complexity of the site is a result of its varied facets, which include streamed video "programs," still photograph galleries, links to other sites (including interviews with the subject), and extensive written diaries. There are also links for e-mail and a FAQ section that provides a rationale for the project.

The author/performance artist rationalizes her life/work as follows:

What can I expect to see on the JenniCAM?

Anything I may be doing in my apartment. Reading email, sleeping, working, goofing off, entertaining guests, whatever.

Do you censor the JenniCAM?

Nope – I never know when the camera is going to take the picture so I have no time to prepare, and I never feel a need to hide anything going on anyway. The only time the image isn't spontaneous is when I have guests. Though I encourage all my visitors to be at ease with the camera and to ignore it as I do, there are and always will be a certain number of camera-shy people in the world. When this happens, the standard is to follow whatever they're most comfortable with. If this means turning the camera away or some other compromise, so be it. Other than this, though, the camera shoots pictures spontaneously and naturally.

Do you ever stage what we see?

No. The concept of the cam is to show whatever is going on naturally. Essentially, the cam has been there long enough that now I ignore it. So whatever you're seeing isn't staged or faked, and while I don't claim to be the most interesting person in the world, there's something compelling about real life that staging it wouldn't bring to the medium. You may notice in the scattered archives that there are sequences which are clearly staged. These are all old sequences from a different stage in my conception of the cam. There are no longer any of these "shows," nor will there be at any point in the future. I hope you can appreciate how this lends itself to the integrity of the camera and what it shows.

Where did you get the idea to do this?

Initially I bought the camera to update portions of my webpage with pictures of myself. A friend joked that it could be used to do a FishBowl cam, but of a person. The idea fascinated me, and I took off with it. Initially the JenniCAM had an audience of half a dozen of my close friends, and it spread like wildfire from there.

Why are you giving up your privacy like this?

Because I don't feel I'm giving up my privacy. Just because people can see me doesn't mean it affects me – I'm still alone in my room, no matter what.

You're naked sometimes, is this pornography?

This site is not pornography. Yes, it contains nudity from time to time. Real life contains nudity. Yes, it contains sexual material from time to time. Real life contains sexual material. However, this is not a site about nudity and sexual material. It is a site about real life.

How should we go about making sense of this phenomenon? On one level, it reveals a very common dimension of the internet, insofar as the visitor is encouraged to sign up for a subscription to the site. This is rationalized on the grounds that the hundreds of thousands of hits that the site receives daily can tie up a small server and so some form of economic rationing is necessary. More important, though, are the meanings that can be attached to this display.

Simplistically, this is about voyeurism, of course, a psychological drive which owes little to contemporary technologies. Thus, 50 years ago James Stewart's character in Hitchcock's *Rear Window* spent his summer successfully observing his neighbors with binoculars, and his physical therapist observed that he was part of "a race of peeping toms." But what the digital feed camera lens does, however, is to problematize the dualism between front and back regions, between the world of the observer and the previously hidden and private world of the viewed. With the JenniCAM, we are allowed to transgress at will, and without repercussion, into an extensive and perpetual back region which would normally be hidden from us by the walls of this person's house. Thus, to the extent that we are allowed to do so by the owner of the webcam, we can see how someone else behaves when they sit in front of a computer all day, how often they stop work, how often they scratch themselves, and how often they take a bathroom break.[9] We can see how someone else behaves with their pets, with their friends, and with their lovers.

Of course, such notions of front and back regions, of spaces usually open and usually hidden from view, are not new. It appears to have been a constant of human belief that there is always yet another dimension of reality that is concealed from us. Before Judeo-Christian religion, it was customary to think of an underworld in which the power of the gods was located. This hidden dimension has maintained its imaginary power: think of Lewis Carroll's *Alice through the Looking Glass*, for instance (a story replete with images of presence and absence, not to mention the associated psychoanalytical concerns), plus its many analogues such as *The Chronicles of Narnia*. As we come closer to the present, though, it seems that fascination with the relationship of that which is visible to that which is hidden has become more, rather than less, common. The twentieth century can be measured as the period in which science became ever more mysterious and ever more concerned with what cannot be seen. It is marked by photographs of the trajectories of atomic particles, by MRI scans and multidimensional theoretical physics. It is reified by the permanent shadow of an individual cast on a wall in Hiroshima, the transfiguration of a human being, from presence to absence, by an atomic explosion.

Although they are not new, then, I would argue that notions of front and back regions have been given a vigorous reworking in the last twenty years as the computer has become a crucial adjunct to our imaginations. Over that period, computer games, in which it is customary to think about endless hidden spaces, parallel worlds, virtual rooms, and dungeons have become commonplace, and entire generations have grown up thinking about the computer in this recursive manner, as a tiny, alternate universe in which we can (re)-locate ourselves. This has spilled over into other technologies, the best example of which is the new generation of DVDs that take a standard Hollywood movie and then turn it into an interactive product. Although they are never advertised and thus depend on word-of-mouth for their popularity, many DVDs contain what are popularly known as "Easter eggs," namely hidden features that can only be found by inside knowledge or trial and error – much like the standard computer game. For example, in the millennial edition of *Terminator 2*, which is advertised to contain two different versions of the movie, the savvy viewer can, at an appropriate point in the main menu, dial in an eight-digit code (the date of the Judgment Day of the movie's subtitle). When done successfully, this releases a *third* version of the story that results in an ending not seen before in any of the previous incarnations of the film. Again, the existence of this version is not advertised or discussed anywhere in the copious materials that accompany the release. But as the geeks who create these little surprises know so well, that would provide no great challenge to the many aficionados of such things.[10]

For sure, such implicit conceptions of front and back regions appear in other realms of popular culture.[11] Thus, while the world of Harry Potter has received some criticism from religious fundamentalists because of its focus upon witchcraft, no one has objected to the basic premise of the series, namely that there is a hidden world (i.e., a back region) of magical entities such as Platform $9\frac{3}{4}$ on a London railway station that can only been accessed by those with corresponding magical abilities. So, while these constructs are hardly unique to the digital world (see Harbison 1994), it is nonetheless this digital universe that represents the clearest examples of the nonhier-archical thinking about front and back regions and spaces which have insinuated themselves into the discourses of popular culture. This is manifested most clearly in the global success of *The Matrix*, a movie whose entire premise is that there is an inverted world of reality that is hidden beneath the surfaces of the vast computer pro-gram that is our sorry reality.

Concluding Comments

One of the problems of trying to analyze popular culture is that it is inherently disposable. Accordingly, efforts to scrutinize movies and hit records (distinct from "film" and "music") can seem trite. Yet, it would be the elitist mistake made by the Frankfurt School to assume that because something has mass appeal, it must also be lacking in substance and/or merit. More importantly, we should remember that mass culture has potential to accomplish social change, and is often treated by the state with exactly that in mind. The Hayes Code, for instance, was introduced in order to reduce the number of Holly-wood movies that portrayed issues of sexuality and drug use, some-thing that was accomplished for an extended period (Neale and Smith 1998). The labeling of television programs and compact disks, based on "graphic content," has also become commonplace in the US, and many other countries have comparable advisories.

Bearing this in mind, in this chapter I have attempted to contrast the manner in which concepts of space and scale are created in the academic and in the popular realm, and to show, via two brief examples, that these are often disconnected. In the first part of the chapter, the emphasis was upon the way in which popular culture has focused much more upon an extraglobal scale – the place of the Earth within the universe – than it has upon a mondial or global scale so in vogue within economic and political discourse. In con-trasting these two scales (the extraglobal and the global), we can see that there are clear differences of emphasis and inference. Much recent academic discourse in political economy has focused upon the elevation in importance of global organizations created in order to deal with global crises. Thus, for many academics a diminution of the global scale seems almost heretical at present, as political activists focus upon the World Trade Organization and both scientists and environmentalists debate global warming. By taking globalization as something new, as something compelling, something threatening, policy-makers (many of whom are informed by academic discourse) stand ready to make social and political choices that will define the twenty-first century.

In the realm of popular culture, on the other hand, while global forces have sometimes been depicted on television (*The Man from U.N.C.L.E.*) and in movies (*The Art of War*), what is interesting is that there has been much more of a focus upon the extraglobal and the relationship between the Earth and the rest of the cosmos. Moreover, much of the recent consideration of issues of the global in popular culture have been tied to religious fundamentalist end-times rhetoric (Tabor 1995). Hence, the *Left Behind* series by Tim LaHaye and Jerry Jenkins, for example, has sold tens of millions of copies in a progression of novels that tells what happens once the Christian faithful are taken to heaven.[12] A pivotal event occurs as evil becomes manifested in a global political entity, as the publisher's summary indicates (www.leftbehind.com):

> After a stunning turn of events, world leader Nicolae Carpathia officially takes his place as the Antichrist and begins his three-and-a-half year reign of terror over the earth. The Tribulation Force scrambles to survive as the Antichrist decrees that every human being must have the mark of loyalty or die.

Indeed, much Christian fundamentalist rhetoric has explicitly opposed entities like the United Nations and the World Trade Organization precisely because it sees in such developments the emergence of a "one-world government" which, according to scriptures, will signal the imminent arrival of Satan. Thus, while this fundamentalist thought has its roots in a distant past, it clearly resonates with, and responds to, the contemporary world and an explicit dread of secular global forces. For many American readers, this juxtaposition of scripture and geopolitics seems to constitute a seamless lens of interpretation which goes some way, I would assert, toward explaining why US voters are so mistrustful of any manifestation of global policy such as the Kyoto protocol on global warming, which has been accepted enthusiastically in Europe but never embraced in the United States.

The second example developed here has deliberately gone in a contrasting direction, by thinking about smaller and smaller spaces that constitute hidden or back regions, and their relationship to exposed front regions. This is a perspective that has emerged during recent decades among individuals who are used to electronic games and the internet and who have increasingly come to see a world of information flows rather than a world of clearly defined and hierarchical Euclidean spaces. The fact that discourses concerning front and back regions have entered popular consciousness so widely in recent years with regard to computer technologies is significant for two reasons. First, it has taken those involved in computer technology (especially computer games and technologies of surveillance), rather than those in the academy, to popularize such discourses – most people beyond the academy have undoubtedly never even heard of Goffman, let alone read his thoughts on front and back regions. Second, as with popular culture's fascination with the extra-global, such discourses also represent a way of thinking about spatiality and the scaling of everyday life which is incongruous to much academic theorizing about geographic scale. In examining the issue of webcasting and how surveillance technologies, virtual realities, and the concept of cyberspace are leading people to think about space and spatial relations in new and different ways, what I have tried to do here is to elaborate upon the ways in which the global–local metric appears to be of marginal importance in understanding how many people scale their own thoughts and their own corner of the world. While "the region" may be an important spatial resolution for academics, one which bounds clearly delineated spaces and which links in hierarchical fashion the local with the global, for many computer-using Generation X-ers and Generation Y-ers the concept of "regions" relates much more to the horizontal connections between the front and back parts of cyberspace, a conceptualization which incorporates neither hierarchy nor clearly delineated Euclidean spaces. Thus, they may look up, they may look within; they more rarely, it seems, turn their gaze to the global or the local.

ACKNOWLEDGMENTS

Numerous individuals have contributed to this chapter. Parts of it were presented to the department of geography at Arizona State University and as the Norma Wilkinson Annual Lecture to the faculty of urban and regional studies at Reading University in England in 1997. Carla Bluhm read part of the material and made valuable comments, as did participants in the Space/Time conference in Athens, GA in 1999, including, to an unusual extent, the editors themselves. Thanks to all, with the usual disclaimers.

NOTES

1 I have chosen to use the word "extraglobal" to describe the spatial scale
   that includes this world in the cosmos, rather than the term "extraterres-
   trial," which carries a lot of cultural baggage because of its almost exclusive association with science fiction.
2 It is interesting to note that, as so often happens, a spatial abbreviation
   such as "Seattle" serves to diminish the instance (cf. "Waco," "Oklahoma
   City"); in this case, a protest about the complexities of globalization is
   reduced to the accident of its location in the state of Washington.
3 Lefebvre does make use of the term "planetary," although that is actually
   analogous to the mondial or global scale (Lefebvre 1973; Shields 1998: 94).
4 Interestingly, despite the fact that in *The War of the Worlds* Wells writes
   about the Martians' technological superiority relative to late nineteenth
   century human technology – a "reality" which Wells clearly used to play
   upon fears of invasion and conquest – the Martians' plan to conquer the
   Earth ultimately fails because they die as a result of having no immunity
   to the local bacteria, very much a low-tech solution.
5 A longer analysis would necessitate interrogation of the extent to which
   popular culture is itself fragmented. Thus, comedian Richard Pryor suggests that a preoccupation with demons or aliens is a solely Anglo phenomenon. On the other hand, we don't have far to turn to find a funk
   band like Parliament descending from a spaceship in their 1980s stage
   show. (For more on the complexities of identifying a single culture, high
   or low, see Frith [1996].)
6 Is this simply a function of chronology – has popular culture just had
   more time to process extraglobal rather than global themes? This is not
   convincing. If we interpret globalization to be about domination on the
   one hand (Americanization) and integration on the other (leading, like
   NAFTA, to immigration), then we know that this has been going on for a
   good while. And we know because these phenomena have been marked
   by cultural artifacts, if not always by academics. Hence, complaints about
   "Ellis Island Art" dominated the first decade of the twentieth century, as
   did Chaplin's "immigrant movies" (Hughes 1997). Themes of defending
   the liminal frontier against otherness are implicit in two of Orson Welles's
   movies from the 1940s and 1950s (*The Third Man* and *Touch of Evil*). More
   recently, mainstream Hollywood vehicles dealt with the collapse of the
   textile industry due to foreign competition in *Norma Rae* (1979) and the
   movement of jobs to Mexico in *Roger and Me* (1989).
7 The usual example derived from his work is the manner in which professionals in the food industry behave when they are in the public settings
   of the restaurant and the ways they behave when they are in the closed
   settings of the kitchen. Goffman wrote about this for his dissertation,
   some 50 years ago, but went on to study other forms of dramaturgical
   behavior in settings such as psychiatric hospitals (1969, 1981). The front of

the restaurant, then, is designed for the benefit of the individual dining while the rear, in which there occur all kinds of behaviors that speed up the production of the food but which might shock the diner into fleeing the establishment, is designed for the benefit of the management and the employees. Certainly, anyone who has read George Orwell's *Down and Out in London and Paris* will remember his gleeful descriptions of how the kitchen staff bent all the rules of hygiene for their own purposes, including the furthering of the class war.

8   A recent drug conviction upheld by the US Supreme Court involved the use of thermal imaging technologies (to detect excessive heat escaping through the roof of a house) without a warrant. The plaintiff's attorneys claimed this represented an invasion of privacy and a dangerous attack on civil liberties because it enabled police to single out anyone whose house may generate excessive heat plumes (whether the result of grow-ing marijuana or simply of having poor roof insulation) on suspicion of engaging in drug trafficking, without any additional probable cause (see the article by the appropriately named Greenhouse 2001; see also Graham 2001).

9   One question we might ask ourselves is whether this voyeuristic gaze differs in any way from pornography, especially if we are unpersuaded by Ms. Ringley's response that what she is presenting is simply "real life." Thus, one aspect of the JenniCAM which is significant in this regard, I think, is the reversal of the usual power relations in the sex industry, where the link between actor and camera is fixed and in which the camera is decidedly not controlled by the individual upon whom it is focused. In the case of the JenniCAM, however, we find that the individual upon whom the camera is fixed is very much in control of the technology (see e.g. Chancer 1998, ch. 5). Ms. Ringley surrenders what she chooses and is quite able to manufacture the image that we see. As such, she becomes not simply the object but the subject. For example, she can provide enough lighting so that an image is visible during the night, the moment, arguably, when the voyeur is most likely to penetrate the darkness.

10 Like the subversive insertions in some feature-length cartoons, these additions can remain hidden for long periods of time (profanities inserted into *The Lion King* were undetected until high-quality digital versions were sold for home use). Programmers, like those who inserted so-called "Transient Witticisms" into the splash screen of the Photoshop software (option-click above the word Adobe below the main graphic), know that word of mouth will eventually reveal what is hidden.

11 Again, in a longer treatment of this topic it would clearly be necessary to focus on the centrality of this logic to the framing of the gay experience in the second half of the twentieth century (Duberman 1991). The use of the closet is one of the best known expressions of a spatial metaphor that we possess, so that it is not at all coincidental that so much gay male literature of the pre-Stonewall generation can be linked to what Thom

Gunn terms the "inside-outside game": think of *The Picture of Dorian Gray*, *My Beautiful Room is Empty*, and *Giovanni's Room*.

12   According to the publisher: "The best-selling end-of-time fiction series tells the riveting stories of people who, after the rapture of the church, are left behind to experience the tribulation and other events prior to Christ's return to Earth. With the prophetic teachings of the Bible as the background, this dynamic apocalyptic fiction has captured the imaginations of millions" (www.leftbehind.com).

REFERENCES

Abu-Lughod, J. 1991: Going beyond global babble. In A. King (ed.), *Culture, Globalization and the World-System*. Binghampton: SUNY Press, 131–8.

Brenner, N. 1997: Global, fragmented, hierarchical: Henri Lefebvre's geographies of globalization. *Public Culture*, 10 (1), 135–67.

Castells, M. 1997: *The Information Age*. Oxford: Blackwell.

Chancer, L. S. 1998: *Reconcileable Differences: Confronting Beauty, Pornography, and the Future of Feminism*. Berkeley: University of California Press.

Duberman, M. 1991: *Cures*. New York: Dutton.

Frith, S. 1996: *Performing Rites: On the Value of Popular Music*. Cambridge, MA: Harvard University Press.

Fröbel, F., Heinrichs, J., and Kreye, O. 1980. *The New International Division of Labour: Structural Unemployment in Industrialised Countries and Industrialisation in Developing Countries*. Cambridge: Cambridge University Press.

Fukuyama, F. 1992: *The End of History and the Last Man*. New York: Free Press.

Goffman, E. 1961: *Asylums: Essays on the Social Situation of Mental Patients and Other Inmates*. New York: Doubleday.

Goffman, E. 1981: *Forms of Talk*. Oxford: Blackwell.

Goldsmith, D. 1997: *The Hunt for Life on Mars*. New York: Dutton.

Graham, S. 2001: "Guest editorial: The spectre of the splintering metropolis." *Cities*, 18 (6), 365–8.

Greenhouse, L. 2001: Heat-seeker's ability to pierce the home comes under Supreme Court's scrutiny. *New York Times*, Feb. 21.

Harbison, R. 1994: *Eccentric Spaces: A Voyage Through Real and Imaginary Worlds*. Hopewell, MA: Ecco Press.

Harré, R. 1984: *Personal Being*. Cambridge, MA: Harvard University Press.

Harvey, D. 1989: *The Condition of Postmodernity: An Enquiry into the Origins of Cultural Change*. Oxford: Blackwell.

Harvey, D. 2000: *Spaces of Hope*. Berkeley: University of California Press.

Holland, S. 1976: *The Regional Problem*. London: Macmillan.

Hughes, R. 1997: *American Visions*. New York: Knopf.

Jung, C. G. 1959: *Flying Saucers: A Modern Myth of Things Seen in the Skies*. New York: Harcourt, Brace, Jovanovich.

Hirst, P. and Thompson, G. 1996: *Globalization in Question.* Cambridge: Polity Press.

Kelly, K. 1995: *Out of Control: The New Biology of Machines, Social Systems and the Economic World.* Reading, MA: Perseus.

Lefebvre, H. 1973: Le mondial et le planétaire. *Espace et Société*, 8, 15–22.

Neale, S. and Smith, N. (eds.) 1998: *Contemporary Hollywood Cinema.* London: Routledge.

Parker, I. 1995: Communion and invasion: Outer space and inner space. *Free Associations*, 5 (3), 357–76.

Penley, C. 1989: *The Future of an Illusion: Film, Feminism and Psychoanalysis.* Minneapolis: University of Minnesota Press.

Putnam, R. D. 2000: *Bowling Alone: The Collapse and Revival of American Community.* New York: Simon and Schuster.

Sampson, E. 1993: *Celebrating the Other.* Boulder, CO: Westview.

Sarewitz, D. and Pielke, R. 2000: Breaking the global warming gridlock. *Atlantic Monthly*, 286 (1) 54–64.

Shields, R. 1998: *Lefebvre, Love and Struggle: Spatial Dialectics.* London: Routledge.

Smith, M. P. and Tarallo, B. 1995: Proposition 187: Global trend or local narrative? Explaining anti-immigrant politics in California, Arizona, and Texas. *International Journal of Urban and Regional Research*, 19 (4), 664–76.

Steinberg, P. 1999: Navigating to multiple horizons: Toward a geography of ocean-space. *Professional Geographer*, 51 (3), 366–75.

Sutcliffe, B. and Glyn, A. 1999: Still underwhelmed: Indicators of globalization and their misinterpretation. *Review of Radical Political Economy*, 31 (1), 111–32.

Tabor, J. 1995: *Why Waco?* Berkeley: University of California Press.

Taylor, P. 1981: Geographical scales within the world-economy approach. *Review*, 5, 3–11.

Taylor, P. 1999: Places, spaces and Macy's. *Progress in Human Geography*, 23 (1), 7–26.

Taylor, P. and Flint, C. 2000: *Political Geography: World-Economy, Nation-State and Locality.* New York: Prentice-Hall.

Virilio, P. 1997: *Open Sky.* London: Verso.

Wallerstein, I. 1974: *The Modern World-System.* New York: Academic Press.

Whitfield, P. 2000: *Mapping the World: A History of Exploration.* London: Folio.

7

Maintaining National Identity at the Border: Scale, Masculinity, and the Policing of Immigration in Southern California

Susan P. Mains

> The San Ysidro port of entry records more than 40 million legal cross-ings a year, mostly by law-abiding, middle-class Mexicans like the families that go to Big Boy. While hundreds of thousands of Mexicans risk their lives sneaking across the line, hundreds of thousands of others cross legally and casually. They either meet the modest financial criteria required for a border-crossing card, which permits trips in the immediate area, or they have US resident status because they were born or have lived north of the line. They go to San Diego to work, shop, see a movie (the proximity to San Diego multiplexes has all but wiped out movie theaters in Tijuana), visit Sea World, meet friends and relatives.
>
> Rotella (1998: 21–2)

The US–Mexico border is most frequently crossed at its westernmost section. Consequently, the US government has invested a consider-able amount of attention and resources in the surveillance and po-licing of this part of its national territory. The key federal institution for actually monitoring this border landscape is the United States Border Patrol. Over the last ten years the profile of the Border Patrol, particularly in the vicinity of the San Ysidro, California port of entry, has grown substantially in conjunction with the development of "Operation Gatekeeper," a program designed to limit undocumented immigration into the United States from Mexico. This increase in federal law enforcement activities has raised significant questions for Mexican and US residents over how policies and discussions about immigration are addressed, and what should be the role of community organizations in shaping and/or challenging these changes in immigration control. The control of undocumented immigrants has become a central issue in a number of political questions, not least of which is the impact that widespread migration from Latin America may have upon "American" (that is to say, US) culture and national identity.

In this chapter I explore the policing of borders and identities through an investigation of the material and discursive practices of the United States Immigration and Naturalization Service (INS) and, in particular, the Border Patrol (which is the uniformed branch of the INS responsible for control of undocumented immigration into the US). In undertaking this exploration I will interrogate the ways in which social and spatial constructs of the border have been utilized at different moments, and the complimentary and contradictory ways in which these government entities have approached immigration. By doing so I will seek to unearth the spatial and social assumptions embedded in discourses of immigration, wherein dominant cultural values are reinforced and reinscribed onto specific places and bodies through the deployment of specific scalar imaginaries.

At first glance, the INS appears to be a relatively straightforward object of analysis: its structure and goals are framed around fairly narrowly defined notions of right and wrong, justice and crime, and safety and threat. Under closer scrutiny, however, the fractures in these discourses become increasingly apparent, while understandings of the sociospatial power which this federal agency exercises become more complex. I argue that discourses of immigration control are not only limited to physical restrictions (e.g., separations controlled by a border fence) but are thoroughly intertwined with narratives of nationalism, scale, and masculinity. Before turning to this analysis, however, I begin by briefly outlining the historical context of immigration policy, followed by the structure and goals of the Border Patrol in the United States and within southern San Diego County. This will be followed by a discussion of discourses of representation, nationalism, masculinity, and scale, a discussion based on an examination of Border Patrol public information materials, interviews, and ride-alongs. The concluding section will make links between discourses of immigration policy and policing, and multiscalar conceptions of immigration and nationality.

The Institutional Framework and Historical Context for Immigration Monitoring

For most of the United States's history, the enforcement of immigration laws was largely undertaken by state boards or commissions, with direction from US Treasury Department officials. Likewise, although the US Constitution had assigned to Congress the duty of naturalizing immigrants, in practice this had been carried out by any "court of record." However, with the massive increase in immigration in the latter part of the nineteenth century, it soon became obvious that there was little uniformity among the nation's more than 5,000 naturalization courts. Consequently, in 1906 Congress passed the Basic Naturalization Act in an attempt to standardize naturalization procedures and documentation (Smith 1998). The Act also expanded the US Bureau of Immigration into the Bureau of Immigration and Naturalization (BIN). Although the 1913 division of the Department of Commerce and Labor into two separate Cabinet departments subsequently split the BIN into the Bureau of Immigration and the Bureau of Naturalization, in 1933 the two bureaus were reestablished as a single entity, the INS. The INS was made responsible for establishing consistent record-keeping systems and for intensifying deportations of undocumented migrants through the growing presence of the Border Patrol, which had been established in 1924 as a division within the Immigration Service. Currently, the agency has more than 30,000 employees in 36 INS districts at home and abroad (INS and Smith 1999: 4).

Of course, the US immigration policy which the INS and Border Patrol are expected to enforce has frequently reflected nativist sentiment or concerns about the availability of jobs for US-born residents. Although the 1882 Chinese Exclusion Act may have been one of the most extreme examples of such legislation, concerns about national security, economic decline, and racial and cultural purity have all shaped immigration policy at various times. During the past 20 years, three pieces of legislation in particular have been the subject of much political debate. The first of these is the Immigration and Reform Act of 1986 (IRCA). The IRCA addressed several components of immigration processing procedures, particularly related to "aliens" who had been residing illegally in the US.[1] It also charged the INS with disciplining employers who illegally hire undocumented workers. Although hailed by some as being immigrant-friendly due to the amnesty provisions it offered many undocumented immigrants residing in the US, the IRCA has been criticized by others for facilitating an atmosphere of hostility and suspicion towards migrants, particularly in the workplace. In California, for example, many Latino residents have complained of discrimination, despite residing in the US legally (Guttierez 1995). Thus, while the IRCA appeared to provide the opportunity to achieve legitimate residency in the US, it has been suggested that "the primary impulse behind it was restriction [of future immigration, a policy which] reflected the xenophobia of the 1970s and the 1980s" (Hondagneu-Sotelo 1994: xiv).

The second piece of legislation was the 1996 Personal Responsibility and Work Opportunity Reconciliation Act. This Act reflected an important change of focus from undocumented immigrants to residents who were legally residing in the US, for under its auspices both documented and undocumented (i.e., "legal" and "illegal") immigrants were excluded from a range of social services, while sponsors were also subject to closer scrutiny.[2] In a legal sense, the Act became a means through which other government agencies, in addition to the INS, could be used to monitor and report immigrants who were suspected of having inappropriate papers or using services for which they were not eligible. The third piece of legislation was the 1996 Illegal Immigration Reform and Immigrant Responsibility Act, which reflected an intensified and ongoing effort to curb undocumented immigration. Continued efforts to monitor the activities and mobility of undocumented workers and to increase the penalties for accepting fake identification materials can also be noted in more recent immigration policies, both those merely proposed and those actually enacted.

Operation Gatekeeper

Shifting our focus from the US more generally to California specifically, we can see several parallels in approaches towards immigration policy and enforcement through "Operation Gatekeeper," a program launched by the Border Patrol in October 1994 to intensify surveillance and deportation along the San Diego–Tijuana border. As part of a "multi-year strategy" to create an overarching framework for policing the border (INS 1999: 1), Operation Gatekeeper was developed in conjunction with similar projects in El Paso, Texas (Operation Hold the Line), McAllen, Texas (Operation Rio Grande), and Tucson, Arizona (Operation Safeguard). At the outset of the program, Operation Gatekeeper's activities were focused on the westernmost section of the border at San Diego's Imperial Beach, an area where the majority of undocumented immigrants were believed to cross. As a "vulnerable" region (INS 1999: 1), the western border area saw a substantial increase in the number of agents on patrol and the deployment of newly-developed surveillance equipment. As the number of migrants passing through the Imperial Beach section of the border declined, the area included in Operation Gatekeeper was expanded eastwards to include the 66-mile stretch of border that came under the San Diego sector's jurisdiction. These moves led to a dramatic reduction in the volume of undocumented crossers in San Diego and led to the further expansion of the program in 1998 to include California's Imperial Valley. According to the INS, this new operation "targets alien smuggling rings that moved to the El Centro area in response to the increased Border Patrol presence in San Diego" (INS 1999: 2). In addition, the number of patrol agents in El Centro grew substantially during the late 1990s in order to deal with this movement of people eastward.

Operation Gatekeeper is not the first effort that has been made by the INS to curb undocumented immigration from Mexico. In the mid-1950s the tellingly-named "Operation Wetback" was established to intensify surveillance and deportation proceedings. Ironically, Operation Wetback, which involved sweeping raids of barrios, stores, and community centers, was instituted while the guest-worker "Bracero Program" (also known as the Emergency Farm Labor Act of 1942) was in operation. Thus, although the Bracero Program enabled US employers to legally hire farm workers from Mexico after a minimum wage and maximum work hours had been set with the Mexican government, expulsions of workers under Operation Wetback could be used to discourage local organizing by immigrant workers. Furthermore, despite assurances concerning working conditions, workers were vulnerable to abuses by employers. Ultimately, however, Operation Wetback was halted amidst growing complaints by immigrant advocacy groups about the excessive and frequently discriminatory and *ad hoc* nature of deportation actions, several of which resulted in the deportation of legal residents who were thought to be "Mexican" (Rylander 2000: 4).

Operation Gatekeeper has not been without its own share of controversy. Although the effectiveness and impacts of the program have been given variable reviews, depending upon one's political perspective, without doubt most would agree that it has substantially reduced the visibility of people who cross "on the fence" at the Imperial Beach section of the border.[3] However, many analysts (including those in state and federal government) have pointed out the difficulty of measuring the frequency of undocumented migrants with any level of accuracy. One independent bi-national research unit at the University of California, San Diego, which has been attempting to undertake such a project using extensive random interviews at border crossings states that: "The 5 to 6 million monthly northbound border crossings are made by approximately 521,000 individuals. The largest groups are frequent crossers or people who cross the border between 4 and 19 times per month" (San Diego Dialogue 1994: 3). In addition, this research group notes (1994: 7) that: "The primary purpose stated for crossing the border to visit the US is shopping [42 percent of trips]." In relation to illegal crossings, the UCSD group argues (San Diego Dialogue 1994: 36) that:

> The Border Patrol's estimate of successful crossings "on the fence" is the highest such estimate available. Social service workers familiar with undocumented crossers suggest that as many as 8 to 10 apprehensions may happen before a person successfully crosses "on the fence" for the first time. If all apprehensions were of persons who were apprehended even 5 times before making one successful crossing, then the number of successful crossers would be 9,676 (rather than [the Border Patrol] estimate of 48,381), or approximately the same number as those denied admissions or arrested in the legal ports of entry.

From this study alone the variability in estimates of undocumented immigration appears substantial and highlights the fact that, despite the (often alarmist) tone that pervades much policy and immigration control literature, these numbers are far from certain (Mains 2000).

Policing Contemporary Border Landscapes and their Representations

An introduction: border stories

To move beyond an examination of current immigration policy towards understanding the complexities and disciplining practices that are embedded in the contemporary border landscape, it is helpful to examine specific examples of this physical and social terrain and the ways in which they are interwoven with constructions of scale. To explore these relationships, in this section I will examine contemporary policing practices utilized by the Border Patrol, particularly in the San Diego sector of the border. To begin with, I will outline two case studies of the border landscape drawn from fieldwork conducted during 1996–8 in Tijuana, San Diego, and Los Angeles, fieldwork which included a series of in-depth interviews with a range of community organizations addressing immigration (including the Border Patrol).

Vignette 1

When I first arrived at the Imperial Beach Border Patrol Station, I was welcomed into a small office while being greeted by local Border Patrol agents. After a brief introduction to the department, a selection of videos was shown (a common practice for most visitors). The first video is a short documentary made by the INS, which shows the dangers to undocumented migrants coming from Mexico and crossing the border while stumbling through ditches, railway lines, and embankments. Another video shows the dangers faced by police officers who inadvertently pull over undocumented migrants under the suspicion of transporting illegal drugs. Shown from the perspective of a security camera – which is fitted to the dashboard of the patrol car – this film shows a police officer being shot and left to die at the side of the road, during the process of investigating the occupants of a car.

The third film presented by Border Patrol illustrates their efforts to overcome "common" dangers by showcasing the advantages of the new surveillance technology being introduced along the US–Mexico border. Much of this film was shot using infrared, night-vision cameras, which are controlled by Border Patrol agents. This short documentary is effectively a direct cut of footage from an arrest of approximately thirty people who are navigating through the hills and scrubland at night, having just crossed into the US. The cameras used by the Border Patrol are heat-sensitive and show the shapes of the people crossing through the hills. The information from these cameras is then relayed to mounted Patrol agents who, fairly rapidly, round up the "trespassers," arrest them, and send them back over the border. After watching these films I was taken on a tour/ride-along with a Border Patrol agent along a five-mile stretch of the border fence, from the coast at Imperial Beach to a few miles east. On a more recent visit to the new San Diego Headquarters I was again shown similar films before accompanying an agent on a border tour of the same area.

Vignette 2

After meeting with US Border Patrol agent Gloria Chavez of the Public Affairs Office, I traveled with her along the western stretch of the border fence from Imperial Beach to the San Ysidro port of entry. Along the way we conversed about the role of the Border Patrol, stopped and observed several points of the border landscape, and conversed with agents who were currently on patrol. As dusk was setting towards the end of the tour, we stopped at part of the fence that overlooks the dry Tijuana River channels separating the US and Mexico and talked with some Patrol agents who were watching a truck that was illegally dumping something into the riverbed. The agents opened a door in the fence so that I could take a photograph of the scene. I then asked the two agents about how they ended up doing this kind of work and where they grew up: one was from Los Angeles, and the other from Tijuana. The latter agent, Raoul Villar-eal, had been working with the agency for three years. When I asked where he was from he laughed and said he grew up in Tijuana, 15 minutes from where we were standing. Raoul explained that he came to the US in 1984 and was "naturalized" in 1989. He also stated that he still knew people and had family in Tijuana, and that they were pleased he had come over and had "done well" by managing to obtain a job with the Border Patrol. Both Gloria and Raoul said that family and relatives were proud of people who had successfully been employed in an agency like the Border Patrol.

I asked Raoul if the fact that he was originally from Tijuana made him feel awkward when he first started patrolling and he responded that "no, it was a job," the same as being in the police force, plus there was a "certain amount of respect," that other people seemed to know where to draw the line and they "know you're doing a job." He explained that sometimes people would see him and go "hey, aren't you...? Now you're on the other side?" He laughed again and said that because of his accent when he spoke in Spanish other people knew he was from Tijuana.

After this discussion Gloria and I were driving back to the Border Patrol Office and she explained further that agents' families were proud because it was a tough academy to go through. Additionally, she stated that Raoul and the US Border Patrol challenged the notion that "if you're Mexican you're going to help illegals cross," because he was enforcing the law (fieldnotes 7/15/98).

The above vignettes serve as a useful introduction to the ways in which patrolling the contemporary border landscape involves different methods for constructing identities and scale, for they present a means by which a particular "story" of the border is told. Specifically, they represent moments where stories of the border are produced and negotiated through the mutual construction of scale and identity – through the Border Patrol agent and the nation – in order to navigate and narrate the borders of what "America" means. For example, the vignettes provide moments where the identity of the Border Patrol and individual agents are intimately interwoven with the local context and the larger notion of maintaining a distinct US national identity, safe from "foreign" incursions. Likewise, the videos shown to me provided an important means of framing the border before experiencing the physical context of the area. Equally, although Gloria (the agent in vignette 2) gave up her time to answer questions during our border tour and to stop her patrol car at different places, the tour provided a very selective and disciplined view of agents at work.[4] My ability to explore how Border Patrol agents would represent their individual and local activities within the context of their national (and international) implications, together with how I would perhaps represent them, was, therefore, patrolled through the way the border tour was itself constructed. The tour became a key process through which individual and local activities were explained in light of their national (and international) implications.

Significantly, during border tours the localized practice of patrolling was very much situated within nationalist discourses about safety and control, but they were not entirely exempt from personal stories. The conversation with Raoul provided an unusual opportunity to discuss the ways in which personal and professional borders are negotiated, in addition to larger attempts to define Latinos and Mexican-Americans as behaving in a single way towards undocumented immigrants. Ironically, as Raoul now policed new immigrants, his position within this border context was one which, while critiqued as "la Migra," was also recognized as an individual achievement because he was employed in a stable job. This story represents the ways in which identity is multiscalar and how scale is reconfigured through identity: Raoul is a local resident who has succeeded in his career, is a disciplining presence at an international border, and is also representative of a national institution and federal immigration policy. It can also be noted that individual uniformed agents are an important means by which the concept of national territory and legal jurisdiction is reinforced. In setting the scene for what follows, it should further be pointed out that this is a very "male" landscape – women are vastly underrepresented in the patrol units, while male agents signify a particular form of national authority and monitoring that is associated with patriarchy and physical strength. At the same time, the notion of an "American" (i.e., US) identity and territory is multiple: it exists in narratives justifying the presence of the Border Patrol at a regional scale, it is discussed in individual homes in Tijuana and San Diego, and Raoul's body is itself a multiscalar manifestation of various practices (of a journey of immigration, of a Latino male authority figure, and of a national government institution). This locale, therefore, is continually recreated through stories of identity and scale. Identity does not exist only as an individual, regional, or national phenomenon, and neither are these scalar identities firmly fixed. Simultaneously, the notion that identities exist in different forms in relation to different places, both physical (e.g., the actual border fence) and imaginary (e.g., a "Free America"), at various times reproduces scale in an ongoing process.

Setting the scene: re-presenting scale

In a commentary addressing conceptions of scale in geography, Jones (1998) notes that the concept can be viewed as a category that is epistemological – that is, it provides a mode for understanding the world – rather than simply functioning as an ontological category or as a fundamental structure of the way we experience place. As she (1998: 26) explains:

> Once we accept that participants in political disputes deploy arguments about scale discursively, alternately representing their position as global or local to enhance their standing, we must also accept that scale itself is a representational trope, a way of framing political-spatiality that in turn has material effects. And, if scale is a trope, then we can no longer see it as neutral or transparent in *how* it represents.

This understanding of scale is particularly relevant if we examine the means by which the Border Patrol utilizes specific meanings of scale and space in order to address concerns related to borders and immigration. As Jones (1998: 25) comments, there can be a range of ways in which scale can be utilized, produced, and read:

> One may look at these examples as evidence that the construction of scale proceeds through representational practices – scale may thus be understood as situated relationally within a community of producers and readers who give the practice of scale meaning . . . Scale is therefore both historically specific and subject to change, not simply in terms of concepts such as "globalization" and the technologies and material practices that produce it, but rather in terms of the very concept of scale itself.

Scale, therefore, is not a universal concept but is a discursive construction of space that is constantly being negotiated and contested at different moments and in various ways. Thus, for organizations attempting to control immigration, discursively reproducing scale as fixed, ontological, and vulnerable enables a representation that prioritizes and demarcates borders that "require" protection. In a similar vein, for immigrant advocates discursively re-presenting scale offers an opportunity to challenge attempts to "fix" borders and identities, and provides a system of policing dialogue that strategically encourages fluidity and openness. As Jones (1998: 26) continues: "It is the power of selection and simplification – or categorization – that gives representations their persuasive power." Hence, while immigrant advocacy groups have attempted to *locate* the global, that is to say they have attempted to expose the ways in which discourses of globalization have manifested themselves at a national, city, and individual level, the INS and Border Patrol have attempted to naturalize discourses of globalization in ways that largely erase individual migrants at a local scale and recreate them into an abstract national (and international) presence (e.g., "the Mexican problem"). At the same time, as will be discussed below, discourses of the border and immigration produced by the Border Patrol represent ongoing negotiations and tensions between national identity and masculinity.

Bounding Identity: The Nation, Scale, and Masculinity

The INS and Border Patrol's efforts to present their activities through tightly controlled representations reflects a desire to discursively discipline their and others' identities. In this regard, Foucault's (1979: 215–16) analysis is particularly helpful:

> "Discipline" may be identified neither with an institution nor with an apparatus; it is a type of power, a modality for its exercise, comprising a whole set of instruments, techniques, procedure, levels of application, targets; it is a "physics" or an "anatomy" of power, a technology. And it may be taken over either by "specialized" institutions (the penitentiaries or "houses of correction" of the nineteenth century), or by institutions that use it as an essential instrument for a particular end (schools, hospitals), or by pre-existing authorities that find in it a means of reinforcing or reorganizing their internal mechanisms of power...; or by apparatuses that have made discipline their principle of internal functioning; or finally by state apparatuses whose major, if not exclusive, function is to assure that discipline reigns over society as a whole (the police).

For Foucault, then, discipline is not in a single institution, object, or practice, but is embedded in a series of discursive practices that are utilized to control and limit the activities of citizens. For example, the Border Patrol reproduces discursive practices that discipline immigrants representationally (e.g., through videos and television announcements about dangerous immigrants) and materially (e.g., through surveillance equipment, detention centers, and patrols). These disciplinary practices are undertaken in conjunction with laws, media coverage, and immigration procedures, which also construct the image of an "immigrant" within a particular discursive field. In turn, these disciplinary procedures are frequently internalized through self-disciplinary procedures that lead immigrants to circumscribe their own practices in order to avoid punitive action by other social groups, including federal government agencies such as the INS. Tied to these efforts to bound identities, disciplinary practices also regulate space in that specific locations or people are represented as "safe," "dangerous," and/or "criminal," and are therefore constructed as being a part of, or separate from, the dominant culture (both socially and physically) – for example, particular behaviors may be decried as "un-American" (and so, by implication, "foreign") even if conducted by US citizens within the spatial boundaries of the United States.

Significantly, such disciplinary discursive formations are shot through with gendered tropes. Hence, recent critiques of national identity, for instance, have illustrated the ways in which "the nation" has been marked as feminine – as vulnerable and morally susceptible to corruption – and, therefore, in need of a guardian (Kandiyoti 1994; Nash 1994). With regard to immigration politics, the US – which is often represented by the gendered symbol of "Lady Liberty" (i.e., the Statue of Liberty) – is viewed by many of its citizens as a space that requires protection through institutions that systematically police and reinforce dominant cultural values and limit economic resources to "deserving" citizens.[5] To maintain and preserve a distinct US identity with a specific sociodemographic make-up, an authoritative and visible monitoring presence is required at the nation's borders. This requirement is fulfilled through the policing actions of the Border Patrol agents whose "efforts to deter illegal immigration," though localized in the sense that they work particular stretches of the border, "present benefits not only for San Diego [in the case of Operation Gatekeeper], but for the Nation" as a whole (INS 1995: 22). The corporeal practices undertaken at the border, then, protect and reinforce the construct of a national community – which, by definition, relies on excluding others. Through their daily practices,

Border Patrol agents reproduce notions of the national and of maintaining the integrity of the nation's borders in an era of increasing flows of population from the Global South to the Global North, and reinforce ideas touched on in a speech by former President Clinton (Department of State 1993): "The simple fact is that we must not – and we will not – surrender our borders to those who wish to exploit our history of compassion and justice. We cannot tolerate those who traffic in human cargo, nor can we allow our people to be endangered by those who would enter our country to terrorize Americans."

Just as space, representation, and identity are interrelated and bound together through an ongoing process of discipline and negotiation, so too is scale. Scale is part of a discursive process that situates identities, people, and places as part of an overarching framework within which scale itself is also reconfigured. Scale is represented through the practices of individuals (a Border Patrol agent) and institutions (the INS), and is relational – it changes meaning in different contexts.[6] Hence, an exploration of the ways in which codes of gender, sexuality, and race are depicted and contested in relation to immigration illustrates the ways in which identity, representation, and scale are intricately interlinked. Thus, the nation and its protection are frequently situated within a patriarchal and heterosexual discourse of scale – opposites working to reproduce unequal relations of power and community – in which the imagined national community and its territory are feminized in popular representations and are represented as being in need of protection and guidance through masculinist institutions such as the federal government, the courts, and the Border Patrol. Such discourses of national identity throw up significant dichotomies around scale in that attention is often shifted towards monitoring individual female bodies – many anti-immigrant and white supremacist groups, for instance, have expressed concern that nonwhite immigrant women's higher fertility rates may lead them to out-reproduce the US-born European-American population – while masculinity becomes naturalized as an institutional and national norm. Masculinity exists at a general scale and at the same time reproduces scale as a gendered trope. Discipline and masculinity become the representational and material modes through which scale, identity, and power are reinforced.

The significance of the Border Patrol, then, is not simply that it is a visible presence at the border (and beyond) but that the process of defending and securing at the national scale "America" is interwoven with concepts of masculinity. Hence, concerns about US sovereignty and Mexican immigration commonly draw upon notions of masculinity by making links between strong male agents on patrol, enforcing boundaries and national sovereignty, and the protection of a robust community (and underneath this a *virile* US political economy). The Border Patrol agent, therefore, is not only representative of the INS but is also a key gauge through which the strength, achievements, and vigilance of an "American" identity can be measured. Border Patrol agents attempt to protect US territory and morality from Mexican incursions, and rely on their individual efforts to negotiate constructions of masculinity. The Border Patrol is seen as being an active symbol both of the US government and of potential local and international threats to US territorial integrity and, hence, identity. Through this mode of scalar representation, masculinity is a nodal signifier for strength and the clear delineation and maintenance of borders.

Equally, recruitment materials for the Border Patrol highlight masculinist concepts of rigor, opportunity, and physical challenge. One brochure, for instance, states: "It's the kind of job that will challenge you on every level – physically as well as mentally. It's not a career for everybody." Indeed, as Patrol Agent Gloria Chavez stated during an interview, this image of a physically and mentally strong individual, which relies upon traditional gender roles, means that for her and many other women "[i]t has been a challenge, being female, [which is the case] in general, in law enforcement. It requires a bit of extra effort. The agency has accepted women and we're being treated equally as men [because] it's the federal law and county law [but] a lot of male agents don't feel secure enough with you assisting them" (fieldnotes, San Diego, July 1998). Likewise, the endurance and dynamism of potential agents are constantly emphasized in INS literature: "One of the most important activities of a Border Patrol Agent is line watch. This involves patrolling the areas along the US border, particularly between the US and Mexico. This is rigorous outdoor work, often in isolated areas and under extreme weather conditions" (US Border Patrol 1997). Similar to practices in mainstream Hollywood cinema examined by Mulvey (1989), the border, then, is depicted in a system of representation wherein the agents' gaze is a male active one hunting the feminized immigrants who await apprehension. Agents are part of the spectacle – and sport – of masculinity, but at the same time are given leeway to control the direction of the action.

Significantly, the reproduction of national identities (i.e., maintaining the United States's "American-ness") through individual agents' everyday practices and discipline is represented as part of a "team effort" for the greater good. This representation runs parallel to discourses of masculinity and nationalism found in mainstream media representations of sport in which concerns about national unity, the family, and heroism – concerns which function on a variety of scales – are, quite literally, played out on the sports field (and the border fence). As Kibby (1998: 24) explains in relation to the film *Field of Dreams*:

> While the film can be read in specifically American terms, for international audiences it dealt with global concerns of failed fathering and declining patriarchal power. *Field of Dreams*, like the other revisionist sports films of the period, worked in tandem with Robert Bly's men's movement and vague projects of recapturing an archetypal masculinity through a recuperation of father-son relationships. [Thus, the] first two words spoken in *Field of Dreams* are "My father." Baseball is a metaphor for traditional masculine values, for a time when sons conformed to the practices of their fathers, and one man's personal vision can restore the father in various symbolic representations. The willingness of Ray Kinsella to pursue his personal vision enables an erasure of eighties conflicts in lived masculinities, conflicts arising out of urbanization, immigration, feminism, civil rights, and economic downturn.

I would argue that the team spirit suggested in Border Patrol recruitment materials suggests a similar nostalgia for a form of identity, nation, and geography that is simplified (i.e., where there are clearly identifiable divisions between the national space of the United States and the national space of Mexico, rather than a hybridized mestizo "border region" which overlaps these spaces) and based on a representation of an imagined "American" past, for, as Kibby (1998: 23) points out, "nostalgia . . . is a response to a fear of change, either actual or impending, it represents concern over, or denial of, the future."

Such a past landscape of authority and policing enables the maintenance of hegemonic gender codes and facilitates continuation of existing systems of privilege. To call such codes into question necessarily requires an interrogation of the system through which individual, national, and international identities and borders are reproduced. As I have noted elsewhere (see Mains 2000), such a desire to reinforce the Border Patrol as guardians of the nation encourages a greater intensity of policing and aggressive surveillance that may also be seen as a response to the increasing visibility of immigrants in the US. Thus, as Andreas (2000: 142) notes in relation to immigration policy:

> The narrative that dominates much of the official policy debate in the United States, for example, characterizes borders as under siege by clandestine transnational activities, with the smuggling of drugs and

migrants drawing most of the attention. It is a nostalgic narrative: it assumes that borders once constituted effective shelter. For those who consider them now "out of control," the narrative provides a rallying cry to "regain control."

Hints at this sense of nostalgia for a past where identity and space could be more easily navigated and demarcated can be seen in some agents' growing concerns about the nature of their work. While conducting interviews with Border Patrol agents during ride-alongs, several people stated that the job was not what they had expected it to be, but was, to some extent, much "safer" and more passive (agents often sit in their patrol cars for several hours observing a stretch of the border). The new technologies that have been hailed as "freeing up" agents from tedious work and bringing the border into a modernized high-tech age (e.g., through the increased reliance on surveillance technology, as opposed to foot patrols) have led to a certain disillusionment because there is a decreased need for a heroic masculinity to contain threats in this western "wilderness." As one recent report (CNN 2000) notes: "[N]ow, here in California's San Diego sector, [Border Patrol agents] find relatively few immigrants coming across the border – and some agents may be suffering from border boredom...In recent years up to 13 percent of the 8,000 Border Patrol agents nationwide have left for new jobs in law enforcement." Ironically, the master gaze and panoptic high-tech surveillance of the border have distanced many of the border agents from the landscape and, to a certain degree, have changed the nature of the job. This change in the Border Patrol's activities is significant, in that contemporary popular media images illustrate the ongoing popularity of the agency as pioneering and adventurous (perhaps again reflecting a nostalgia for a lost masculinity in the home and as part of a national sociospatial imaginary). Yet, in keeping with the sports analogy raised above, many agents fear that they may simply become the minor league players in the competition for control (symbolically and physically) of the border.

The speed of surveillance technology has also altered representations and negotiations of agents' bodies, the border landscape, and immigration.[7] The ability to move technologically and physically at a rapid speed, and to have a significant degree of mobility, has historically been associated with white masculinity and the active control of space. Mobility has also been a key component of a mythical western landscape where discourses of "open" space and movement – for certain social groups – have been popular spatial tropes. This mobility and "freedom" have reinforced a policing presence that is apparently unbounded and exciting – one Border Patrol slogan suggests this is "a career with borders, but no boundaries" – while at the same time it encourages the reinforcement of legal borders. Paradoxically, while agents' mobility is viewed as important for expelling unwanted bodies from the US's national space, the mobility of immigrants is regarded as individually and nationally threatening. Within this discourse, these latter movements are described as not only challenging the integrity of US laws and territory, but they also call into question the abilities and authority (and masculinities) of individual agents.

Such anxieties about changing technologies and the scale of their impacts on human morals and the body have run through large portions of twentieth century representations of law and order. In his study of bodies and machines, for instance, Seltzer (1992: 156) notes that there has been a recurring theme of technology enabling humans to overcome the impeding forces of the natural world – of "technological 'transcendence' of the natural body." Yet, this transcendence or expansion of personal space beyond the scope of the physical body through the use of technology has been accompanied by an increasing anxiety about the significance of the individual. While surveillance equipment may have enabled increased mobility for the Border Patrol as an institution, it appears to have been unable to overcome the specific emotional and career concerns of its employees. Although technology has been hailed as enabling a modern identity and a "collective" body (Seltzer 1992) – one which has been important in forging an "imagined" national community (Anderson 1994) – in the case of the Border Patrol agents discussed here this collectivizing process is one which has been viewed by many as an emasculating experience. These recent changes may, however, be important for rethinking future forms of policing that need not necessarily rely on traditional gendered notions of authority and control.

Conclusion: Scale as Representation and Practice

Fiscal Year 2000 proved to be another remarkably dynamic year for the INS Office of International Affairs. Not only are we extending our reach abroad, but we are also building relationships with INS Regions and Districts in support of strategic priorities. Whether working on enforcement or benefit issues, the responsibilities we bear and the challenges we face are extraordinary. (INS 2000: 1)

Immigration policy is significant in that, while being commonly associated with a rigorous and impartial system of examination, it is thoroughly embedded in shifting societal conceptions of "outsiders," migrant workers, and fragile race relations. Although described as a national (and international) phenomenon, immigration policy is also thoroughly intertwined with (and reinforced by) local and individual practices (Andreas 2000). In a parallel vein, although referred to as neutral monitors, the practice of policing employed by the Border Patrol necessarily relies on specific kinds of practices and representations which deploy scalar constructs and value particular forms of interaction that are heavily dependent on gendered and sexualized connotations.

In examining both the changes in immigration policy outlined above and the contemporary approaches toward monitoring undocumented immigrants, it is significant to note that the "movement" of immigrants from a nation "outside" the US is invariably represented as a movement at a national scale which apparently would inhibit the economic advancement of the US at an individual, national, and international level – anti-immigrant discourses such as that of Patrick Buchanan, for example, often implicitly suggest that the entire Mexican nation would relocate to the United States if the border were unpoliced.[8] The movement of immigrants, therefore, is one that is associated with the (feminized) "natural flows" that can too easily become out of control. A discourse of "immigrants as criminals" also collapses the representational scales of immigration control narratives, allowing individual characteristics (such as those associated with crime) to be mapped onto vast abstract images of outsiders (Cornelius 1982; Wolf 1988). Representation and scale, therefore, are as much about depicting and communicating identity as they are about a process of reinforcing, challenging, and producing new identities (Jones and Natter 1999). In conjunction with this, identity and representation do not exist "out there," but are thoroughly spatial and embedded in discourses of policing and the US–Mexico border.

It seems strange, perhaps, that in a period where discourses of globalization and increased mobility are commonplace concerted efforts are being made to reinforce the physical and imaginary borders of the United States as a nation. However, the increasing localized mechanization – or militarization – of the Border Patrol in San Diego County and a reliance on traditional notions of masculinity in popular discourses are not limited to this locale, but operate on a variety of levels. These discourses emphasize the disjuncture between economic, social, and physical scales of mobility and globalization (Mains 1999). Thus, in a commentary addressing "Masculinity as a foreign policy issue," Enloe (2000: 2) points out that adopting a "tough" stance on military policy and international relations is also embedded in US foreign policy:

> A feminist analysis turns the political spotlight on the conventional notion of manliness as a major factor shaping US foreign policy choices. It demonstrates that popular gender presumptions are not just the stuff of sociology texts. Every official who has tried not to appear "soft" knows this. For example, early in his administration, Bill Clinton made known his abhorrence of landmines and his determination to ban them. But by 1998, he had caved in to military pressure and stated, instead, that the US would not sign the widely endorsed international landmines treaty until the Defense Department came up with an "alternative."

Similar to discourses outlined above, in these discussions of foreign policy the "hard" stance on military intervention and images of the tough male body become symbolic of the nation and (inter)-national integrity. Indeed, the INS deploys policing programs not only within US territory but in a vast array of locations throughout the world (for a review of these activities, see INS 2000). In terms of the construction of scale and identity, I would argue that although there is an effort to construct the image of an interlocking and inte-grated system of international relations, this is combined with on-going practices that privilege masculinity, reinforce borders between "us" and "them," and bind the notion of international governance to a construct of an abstract (white) male body. The practices at the US–Mexico border, therefore, do not challenge the notion of globalization but actually fit snugly within its inherent contradictions.

In closing, it is important to note linkages made between dis-courses of globalization and the introduction of surveillance technol-ogy. Ironically, technologies that have been used to increase international communication and information are also being used to reinforce borders at a national scale. In conjunction with this increase in the use of technology, the outdoor landscape that was once viewed as representative of escape and healthy activities is, in fact, permeated by surveillance equipment that relies on passive observa-tion. However, as Andreas (2000: 143) notes, this contradiction sug-gests that policing the border is not so much about protecting the local landscape from individual Mexican "transgressors" as it is about "image crafting." Countries throughout the world have at-tempted to curb immigration, either in an attempt to bolster their political identity and to appease their wealthy neighbors (e.g., in the case of Spain) or to reassure their increasingly vocal domestic population that they will not be outnumbered by new immigrants who are frequently represented as less desirable (e.g., as can be seen in mainstream news in the United States). While immigration concerns are made more concrete by focusing on physical sites of border crossing, these sites are frequently signifiers for much broader, wide-ranging, and punitive efforts to police national identity. Despite popular claims of improved international mobility and calls for intensified globalization, borders are being reconstructed rather than "retired" and the global social and economic conditions – racism, sexism, nationalism, downsizing, restructuring, poverty, etc. – that facilitate their use as a political rallying cry for increased immigration controls continue.

NOTES

1   Among other things, the Act (8 U.S.C. § 1324B):
    a) Authorized legalization (i.e., temporary and then permanent resident status) for aliens who had resided in the United States in an unlawful status since January 1, 1982 (entering illegally or as temporary visitors with authorized stay expiring before that date or with the government's knowledge of their unlawful status before that date) and who are not excludable.
    b) Created sanctions prohibiting employers from knowingly hiring, recruiting, or referring for a fee aliens not authorized to work in the United States.
    c) Increased enforcement at US borders.
    d) Created a new classification of seasonal agricultural worker and provisions for the legalization of certain such workers.
    e) Extended the registry date (i.e., the date from which an alien has resided illegally and continuously in the United States and thus qualifies for adjustment to permanent resident status) from June 30, 1948 to January 1, 1972.
    f) Authorized adjustment to permanent resident status for Cubans and Haitians who entered the United States without inspection and had continuously resided in country since January 1, 1982.
    g) Increased the numerical limitation for immigrants admitted under the preference system for dependent areas from 600 to 5,000 beginning in fiscal year 1988.
    h) Created a new special immigrant category for certain retired employees of international organizations and their families and a new non-immigrant status for parents and children of such immigrants.
    i) Created a non-immigrant Visa Waiver Pilot program allowing certain aliens to visit the United States without applying for a non-immigrant visa.

j) Allocated 5,000 non-preference visas in each of fiscal years 1987 and 1988 for aliens born in countries from which immigration was adversely affected by the 1965 Act.

2 Among other things, the Act (Public Law 104–193)

a) Barred legal immigrants (with certain exceptions) from obtaining food stamps and Supplemental Security Income (SSI) and established screening procedures for current recipients of these programs.

b) Barred legal immigrants (with certain exceptions) from entering the US after the date of enactment from most federal means-tested programs for 5 years.

c) Provided states with broad flexibility in setting public benefit eligibility rules for legal immigrants by allowing states to bar current legal immigrants from both major federal programs and state programs.

d) Increased the responsibility of the immigrants' sponsors by: making the affidavit of support legally enforceable, imposing new requirements on sponsors, and expanding sponsor-deeming requirements to more programs and lengthening the deeming period.

e) Barred undocumented, or "not qualified aliens," from most federal, state, and local public benefits.

f) Required the INS to verify immigration status in order for aliens to receive most federal public benefits.

3 The phrase "on the fence" refers to those persons who do not cross in the ports of entry.

4 For example, my asking "in what ways is this job different from how you imagined it?" prompted one agent to respond that the job was not what he thought it would be but that it was "more political" and resulted in me being ushered back into the patrol car.

5 Obviously, the image of Uncle Sam is also used to represent the United States. However, I would argue that this white, male image is usually used to represent the nation in times of war or other periods of national concern through a different process of association. Representations of Uncle Sam only indirectly relate to immigration in a round-about way through appeals to an assumed homogeneous patriotic populace that largely exclude notions of racial, gender, and cultural diversity.

6 For instance, to say "I live at the border" – by definition, at the boundary of two nationally-defined political spaces – can mean "I live in Imperial Beach and between the US and Mexico," or "I am part of a transnational region and an international world of immigration and commerce," or "I live on the other side of the fence from my husband, because I can get work in National City as a nanny."

7 For a more detailed discussion of new technologies at the border, see Mains (1999).

8 Mexico is often described as being outside the United States, even though it is very much inside an American spatial imaginary – existing as its "constitutive outside." This term refers to a co-constitutive process of categorization, an understanding that requires Mexico to be constructed

as both present in, and in opposition to, the US (Dixon and Jones 1998; Natter and Jones 1997). Naming a center, therefore, involves simultaneously naming a periphery, the latter of which enables the definition of the center. Identity, therefore, does not ensue from a center, but is always dependent on an excluded periphery, as there are always traces of the latter in the former.

REFERENCES

Anderson, B. 1993: *Imagined Communities*. London: Verso.

Andreas, P. 2000: *Border Games: Policing the US–Mexico Divide*. London: Cornell University Press.

CNN 2000: Border Patrol Suffers From Boredom in San Diego Sector. www.CNN.com (Jan. 20).

Cornelius, W. A. 1982: *America in the Era of Limits: Nativist Reactions to the "New" Immigration*. San Diego, CA: Center for US–Mexican Studies, University of California, San Diego.

Department of State. 1993: Protecting US Borders Against Illegal Immigration. *Dispatch Magazine*. [Available at http://dosfan.lib.uic.edu/ERC/briefing/dispatch/1993/html/Dispatchv4no32.html.]

Dixon, D. and Jones, J. P. 1998: My dinner with Derrida, or spatial analysis and poststructuralism do lunch. *Environment and Planning A*, 30 (2), 247–60.

Enloe, C. 2000: Masculinity as a foreign policy issue. *Foreign Policy*, 5, 36: 1–4. [Available at www.foreignpolicy-infocus.org/pdf/vol5/36ifmasculinity.pdf.]

Foucault, M. 1979: *Discipline and Punish: The Birth of the Prison* (translated by A. M. Sheridan Smith). New York: Pantheon

Guttierez, D. G. 1995: *Walls and Mirrors: Mexican Americans, Mexican Immigrants, and the Politics of Ethnicity*. Berkeley: University of California Press.

Hondagneu-Sotelo, P. 1994: *Gendered Transitions: Mexican Experiences of Immigration*. Los Angeles: University of California Press.

INS (Immigration and Naturalization Service). 1995: *Operation Gatekeeper: Landmark Progress*. Washington, DC: Office of International Affairs, Immigration and Naturalization Service.

INS (Immigration and Naturalization Service) 2000: *Building a Global Community: Fiscal Year 2000 Report*. Washington, DC: Office of International Affairs, Immigration and Naturalization Service.

INS (Immigration and Naturalization Service) and Smith, M. L. 1999: *Overview of INS History*. Washington, DC: Office of International Affairs, Immigration and Naturalization Service.

Jones, J. P. and Natter, W. 1999: Space "and" representation. In A. Buttimer, S. Brunn, and U. Wardenga (eds.), *Text and Image: Social Construction of Regional Knowledges*. Leipzig: Selbstverlag Institut fur Landerkunde, 239–47.

Jones, K. T. 1998: Scale as epistemology. *Political Geography*, 17 (1): 25–8.

Kandiyoti, D. 1994: Identity and its discontents: Women and the nation. In P. Williams and L. Chrisman (eds.), *Colonial Discourse and Post-Colonial Theory: A Reader*. New York: Columbia University Press, 376–91.

Kibby, M. D. 1998: Nostalgia for the masculine: Onward to the past in the sports films of the eighties. *Canadian Journal of Film Studies*, 7 (1): 16–28.

Mains, S. 1999: Statutes of liberty: Migration and urbanism in the borderlands. *APCG Yearbook*, 61, 42–66.

Mains, S. 2000: An anatomy of race and immigration politics in California. *International Journal of Social and Cultural Geography*, 1 (2), 143–54.

Mulvey, L. 1989: *The Visual and Other Pleasures*. Basingstoke: Macmillan.

Nash, C. 1994: Remapping the body/land: New cartographies of identity, gender and landscape in Ireland. In A. Blunt and G. Rose (eds.), *Writing Women and Space: Colonial and Postcolonial Geographies*. New York: Guilford, 227–50.

Natter, W. and Jones, J. P. 1997: Identity, space, and other uncertainties. In G. Benko and U. Strohmayer (eds.), *Space and Social Theory: Geographical Interpretations of Postmodernity*. Oxford: Blackwell, 141–61.

Rotella, S. 1998: *Twilight on the Line: Underworlds and Politics at the US–Mexico Border*. New York: W. W. Norton.

Rylander, C. K. 2000: The economy: Growth without prosperity. *Bordering the Future* (March issue, available at: www.window.state.tx.us/border/ch02/ch02.html) (last accessed Nov. 27, 2001).

San Diego Dialogue. 1994: *Who Crosses the Border?: A View of the San Diego/Tijuana Metropolitan Region*. San Diego: University of California, San Diego Extension Service.

Seltzer, M. 1992: *Bodies and Machines*. New York: Routledge.

Smith, M. L. 1998: *Overview of INS History*. [www.ins.usdoj.gov/graphics/aboutins/history/articles/OVIEW.htm (last accessed November 27, 2001).]

US Border Patrol. 1997: *A Career Without Borders* (recruitment pamphlet issued by the US Immigration and Naturalization Service).

Wolf, D. 1988: *Undocumented Aliens and Crime: The Case of San Diego County*. San Diego, CA: Center for US–Mexican Studies, University of California, San Diego.

Part III

Scales of Praxis

Introduction: Scales of Praxis

Andrew Herod and Melissa W. Wright

As anyone who has been involved in political activism will probably acknowledge, political success or failure frequently turns upon the geographical scale at which actors can organize themselves. In the case of labor unions, for instance, successfully developing national collective bargaining agreements which equalize wage rates within an industry can be crucial in limiting employers' abilities to play groups of workers in different regions of the country against each other on the basis of variations in wage rates – a practice referred to as "whipsawing" (see Herod 2001 for examples). Likewise, the politics of abortion in the United States have frequently revolved around issues of the geographic scale at which rights should or should not be protected. Thus, although the right to abortion is protected nationally by the US Supreme Court's 1973 *Roe v. Wade* decision, many antiabortion activists and their supporters have attempted to undermine this right by encouraging various state legislatures to pass laws which place such significant burdens on women that their abilities to exercise these rights are often undercut – for example, in the years since 1973 numerous states have required waiting periods or other hindrances before an abortion can be carried out. Furthermore, struggles over the scale at which political praxis is conducted may be crucial determinants of the resources actors can secure for their cause – expanding the geographical scale of a dispute may allow one side to draw upon a much wider set of social resources than if the dispute remains local (see McCarthy and Mayer 1977). Likewise, control of the scale of a dispute may restrict the resources to which an opponent can gain access – keeping a dispute local may limit the influx of money, information, and other forms of support from outside groups. Thus, the ability to define something as a "local," "national," or "global" issue can shape in important ways the subsequent evolution of any particular political struggle.

Within political struggles, concepts such as "up-scaling" and scalar "jumping" have emerged as being important to strategies for translating local concerns into larger political movements. For example, in his work on the politics of antigentrification struggles in New York City, Neil Smith (1989, 1990, 1993) has shown how homeless activists and advocates adopted the strategy of expanding their struggle from Tompkins Square Park – site of a 1988 police riot against homeless people – to encompass the whole Lower East Side. In so doing, they were able to make important links between the homeless people who had been living in the Park and other tenant and squatter groups in Lower Manhattan. Similar sentiments about the importance of such upscaling of political struggles are to be found in the admonition by many on the political left that labor unions need to "go global" so that they may match the global organization of capital. However, it should not simply be assumed that organizing at a larger scale than one's political opponents is always either a necessary or even the most efficacious strategy to obtain one's goals. Indeed, such an assumption often privileges the global scale over all others, since it assumes that whoever "goes global" first always has the edge (at least, perhaps, until humans establish themselves on other planets!). Instead, we must also recognize that sometimes the ability to articulate struggles at smaller scales than one's opponents – "going local" or "regional" or even "national," as it were – can be the key to success. For example, local branches of national labor unions may prefer to negotiate contracts on a local basis rather than as part of a national "master" agreement. Such decisions reflect their relative strength at the local level and, usually, the membership's faith in the local leadership's ability to negotiate more successfully than can the national leadership. In the United States, for instance, many unions in southern states have begun to opt out of high-wage national agreements because not to do so means that they may lose work to cheaper, nonunion operations (see Herod 2001, ch. 5, for examples from the longshoring industry). From another angle, efforts to organize in new environments, such as in a cross-border context, often require that more attention be given to the specific issues expressed at the local, rather than national, level in order to build a constituency across an array of differences, including national, cultural, and class divisions, among others (see Wright 2001; Wills 2001; Hensman 2001). Indeed, the integration of local differences into broad-based organizations or coalitions oftentimes reveals a more dynamic approach to leaping across scales. Furthermore, the jump is not always unidirectional, as groups move back and forth through a constant negotiation of the scales of vision, action, and solidarity.

Bearing some of these considerations in mind, the three papers in this section all deal, in different ways, with the issues of the scale at which political praxis is organized. The first of these, by Jeff Crump, examines scalar struggles that took place during the course of a labor organizing campaign conducted in the Midwestern United States during the 1940s and 1950s. This period in US labor history was one of intense rivalry between the two main competing national labor bodies – the American Federation of Labor, a craft-oriented body established in 1886, and the Congress of Industrial Organizations, which had been established in the 1930s and believed in industrial unionism.[1] It was also a period of "Red-baiting" as the Cold War played itself out in the US labor movement. In his chapter, then, Crump considers how, in this context, issues of geographic scale were crucial in a four-way struggle waged between the federal government, the International Harvester company, and two rival labor unions which were seeking to represent workers in the farm implements industry, these being the Communist-oriented Farm Equipment and Metal Workers' Union (the FE) and the non-Communist United Auto Workers union (the UAW). As Crump shows, geographical scales of organization were significant in these struggles in several ways.

First, the FE and the UAW had very different political philosophies with regard to where union power should lie. For the FE, power was seen to reside at the level of the shopfloor. Consequently, the union emphasized worker control of the spaces of production and a great deal of local autonomy among its constituent branch unions. For the UAW, however, it was the ability to cut deals with the employers at the national level that was seen as key to providing good wages and benefits to its members. Consequently, the union's national leadership attempted to squash local autonomy amongst its constituent member unions, for too much local autonomy might disrupt carefully orchestrated national goals. Second, although the FE believed in the importance of local autonomy, it did also recognize that strength in the face of employer and federal government opposition would be gained by developing networks across the industrial landscape which would link the various FE local unions together. Such "scale-stretching" networks helped define an emergent regional scale of union activism. Third, in its opposition to the FE, the UAW, the International Harvester company, and the federal government all attempted to undermine the legitimacy of FE organizers by manipulating the scalar discourse surrounding their identity. Thus, FE leaders who had Communist sympathies, even if born in the local community, were accused of not being "legitimate locals" but, instead, were said to be "outsiders" and "Soviet stooges," a strategy designed to weaken their hold over the loyalties of their members at a time of growing Cold War tensions. For its part, the federal government, in the form of the Federal Bureau of Investigation, also attempted to divide spatially FE local unions by arresting some of their officials as they traveled between the cities in which such local unions were located – a recognition that the FBI understood the significance of the scale-stretching networks which the FE had managed to establish and that it would do its damnedest to disrupt such networks, so as to isolate each of the local union branches (see Blomley 1994 for a discussion of how the Thatcher government likewise used arrest powers to disrupt the movement of sympathy pickets during the 1984–5 British coal miners' strike). The resolution of such scalar struggles, Crump suggests, had significance not only for the ultimate demise of the FE but also continues to have an impact upon the labor politics of the Midwest half a century later.

The second chapter, by Hilda Kurtz, examines racial politics and issues of environmental justice in a campaign waged during the mid-1990s over the proposed siting of a new petrochemical plant in rural St. James Parish, Louisiana. Located along the Mississippi River, St. James Parish is predominantly African-American in its demographic make-up and, at the time of the dispute, was already home to some eight of the river corridor's 137 petrochemical facilities. In 1996 Shintech Inc., a US subsidiary of a Japanese transnational corporation, applied for a permit to build a polyvinyl chloride (PVC) plant in the parish. Although such a plan was supported by economic development officials in the state capital of Baton Rouge, local residents who would actually have to live close to the proposed plant and its potentially health-threatening pollution organized to oppose the granting by the state of permission for the facility's construction. In particular, they argued that the efforts of state economic development officials and of the corporation to locate the plant in the parish community of Convent was an instance of environmental racism and violated Title VI of the 1964 Civil Rights Act, which mandates that no entity receiving federal funds (such as the Louisiana Department of Environmental Quality, which would have to approve the site) shall engage in practices which disparately affect groups identified by race, color, or national origin. Given that the Shintech plant would likely exacerbate the impacts of pollution upon the largely African-American population in the parish, protestors argued that the LDEQ's issuance of a permit to build the plant violated the residents' civil rights. As Kurtz examines, however, determinations of civil rights' violations would turn on the spatial scale at which practices of environmental racism were seen to occur.

For Shintech's opponents, the key to arguing that their civil rights would be violated by the building of the plant lay in determining which residents would be disproportionately affected by the new facility. This was vital, for federal civil rights law only recognizes environmental discrimination on the basis of race and not on the basis of socioeconomic status. Thus, it was not enough to show that the plant posed a disproportionate risk to poor people. Instead, pro-testors had to show that it would place a disproportionate burden of pollution on the parish's African-American residents. However, proving such a claim would rest very clearly upon defining the exact area of impact around the plant – using different sized buffers around the plant would result in very different configurations of the affected populations, such that a buffer of one size might result in an affected population which was more heavily African-American than would use of a buffer of a different size. In addition to the spatial politics surrounding just how large an impact area was con-sidered to be appropriate for evaluating claims of environmental racism, Kurtz shows how the way in which the dispute was repre-sented in scalar terms was also central to how it unfolded over time. Specifically, she introduces the concept of "scale and counter-scale frames," by which she means the ways in which disputes are discur-sively framed as part of a broader politics of scale.

Drawing upon this concept of scale and counter-scale frames, Kurtz shows how activists and state economic development planners attempted to frame the dispute in divergent ways to suit their respective purposes – economic development officials argued that *state-level* policy dictated that this was the most appropriate location for the plant and that its construction would have benefits for the state as a whole, whereas St. James Parish opponents of the plant argued that their *local* experiences of pollution needed to be con-sidered. Likewise, the efforts of the office of Governor Mike Foster to divide the racially diverse coalition which had formed to oppose Shintech relied upon framing the dispute spatially in such a way as to try to make distinctions between the interests of the parish's white and black citizens. In turn, opponents of the plant sought to frame the dispute in such a manner as to emphasize the unity of the par-ish's residents. As Kurtz highlights, struggles over the scale at which environmental racism was seen to operate, together with efforts to frame in radically different ways the spatial implications of the dis-pute (state-level implications versus implications within the parish, for example), were central to the political praxis of both proponents and opponents of the plant.

In the final chapter of this section, Helga Leitner, Claire Pavlik, and Eric Sheppard contend that debates over contemporary processes of globalization have spawned two distinct sets of literatures, these being literatures which discuss globalization and the emergence of economic and political networks, and literatures which discuss globalization and the reconstruction of scales of governance. Somewhat curiously, they maintain, these two literatures have largely tended to develop separately. Yet, they argue, there is much to be gained through a more thorough engagement between the two. In particular, they suggest that geographic scale is a relevant aspect of how networks function and that the distinctive geography of networks poses challenges to current conceptualizations of the politics of scale. Furthermore, they ask whether network modes of governance can be considered an alternative to hierarchies or whether they need to be understood in relation to hierarchies. As a means of addressing some of these issues – and thus of stimulating a fruitful interchange between these two sets of literatures – Leitner et al. examine the growth of a number of inter-urban networks which have been created in the European Union for the purpose of linking together cities and regions that share certain characteristics or social and economic problems.

While the creation of transnational networks between cities and regions is not necessarily a new phenomenon in and of itself, during the past two decades the European Commission has encouraged the formation of such networks as a means for cities and regions to discuss matters of common interest. Some such networks are thematic in nature – for example, there are networks for cities which are dealing with problems such as high levels of homelessness and unemployment or the closure of military bases and the restructuring of defense-related industries after the end of the Cold War – whereas others are territorial in nature, such as the Arc Atlantique which links together cities from Spain, Portugal, France, Ireland, and the United Kingdom that lie along the Atlantic coast. Still others have both thematic and geographic criteria for membership. All, however, have significant implications for the nature of spatial praxis across the European Union as they link places near and far in nexuses of economic, political, and social relationships. In particular, such networks provide a means for "horizontal" collective action among cities and regions that may allow actors to challenge hierarchical relations between different scales of political governance. Through an analysis of how a number of such transnational networks operate,

Leitner et al. investigate how, through these networks, cities and regions may strengthen their power and authority in relation to national governments and also, possibly, with regard to the policy-making practices of the European Commission.

In different ways, then, all three of these chapters highlight the importance of geographic scale in the structuring and practice of political struggle. Although they each address very different empirical issues, all consider how the scale at which political praxis is organized can shape the outcomes of particular disputes and thus how struggles over scale have implications for the ways in which the economic and political landscape is made.

NOTES

1 Craft unionism is a form of unionism in which unions are organized along craft lines – plumbers, carpenters, and so forth – whereas industrial unionism is a form of organization wherein all workers in a particular industry or sector belong to the same union, regardless of the actual job they hold in that industry.

REFERENCES

Blomley, N. 1994: *Law, Space and the Geographies of Power*. New York, Guilford Press.

Hensman, R. 2001: World trade and workers' rights: In search of an internationalist position. *Antipode*, 33 (3), 427–50.

Herod, A. 2001: *Labor Geographies: Workers and the Landscapes of Capitalism*. Guilford: New York.

McCarthy, J. D. and N. Z. Mayer. 1977: Resource mobilization and social movements: A partial theory. *American Journal of Sociology*, 82, 1212–41.

Smith, N. 1989: Rents, riots and redskins. *Portable Lower East Side*, 6, 1–36.

Smith, N. 1990: *Uneven Development: Nature, Capital and the Production of Space* (2nd ed.). Oxford: Blackwell.

Smith, N. 1993: Homeless/global: Scaling places. In J. Bird, B. Curtis, T. Putnam, G. Robertson, and L. Tickner (eds.), *Mapping the Futures: Local Cultures, Global Change*. London: Routledge, 87–119.

Wills, J. 2001: Uneven geographies of capital and labour: The lessons of European works councils. *Antipode*, 33 (3), 484–509.

Wright, M. W. 2001: A manifesto against femicide. *Antipode*, 33 (3), 550–66.

8

Contested Landscapes of Labor: Rival Unionism in the Farm Implements Industry

Jeff R. Crump

There is only one side for business – its side – and it operates on the principle of getting as much as it can; it can be deterred in its exploitation only by applying economic and political power 365 days a year.

United Farm Equipment and Metal Workers' Union leaflet, quoted in Gilpin
(1992: 613)

On February 10, 1949, a pitched battle between members of Local 104 of the Farm Equipment and Metal Workers' Union (FE) and recruiters of the rival United Auto Workers (UAW) broke out at the gates of the International Harvester (IH) Works in East Moline, Illinois. As UAW organizers challenged the legitimacy of FE members coming off shift with cries of "Reds," "Commies," and "Go back to Moscow!", some 200 loyal FE workers organized themselves into a powerful phalanx and engaged the UAW organizers in a wild mêlée (*Chicago Daily Tribune* 1949). As the battle between the two sides escalated, the verbal jousts turned into brutal fistfights and, by the end of the day, one FE member and twelve UAW organizers were in local hospitals with a variety of injuries (Gilpin 1992: 241). Although such a brawl was perhaps the most extreme manifestation of the rival unionism which gripped the farm implements industry in the late 1940s, the efforts of the larger and nationally-influential UAW to depose the FE by raiding its membership and by calling representation elections in plants organized by the FE meant that in the coming years farm implements workers throughout the Midwest would be forced to choose between two radically different philosophies of trade unionism. Furthermore, at the same time that the FE and the UAW were fighting over the right to represent workers in the farm implements industry, International Harvester and the FE were engaged in a brutal struggle over who would control the shopfloor: the company or the union. Workers in the industry, then, were not only faced with a contest between two rival unions, but they were also confronted by a global corporation determined to roll back the gains of organized labor.

The purpose of this chapter is to examine the spatial and scalar strategies of the FE, the UAW, the International Harvester Corporation, and the US government in the struggle over who would represent workers in the farm implements industry. Although it was often disguised in the material and rhetorical battles between the participants, the critical issue in the contest was whether workers or management would exert control over decisions at the scale of the shopfloor. According to the FE, ideology dictated that union power should reside at the level of the shopfloor, where production could be controlled. From the perspective of the UAW, IH, and the federal government, however, control of the shopfloor was the prerogative of management and any union challenging this power structure was overstepping its bounds. Whereas, then, the FE saw power emerging from control of the local spaces of the shopfloor, for the UAW and its business unionist leaders reliance on national-scale clout and institutions, and a restriction on local actions (particularly wildcat strikes which might disrupt delicate negotiations over national union objectives), were key to achieving their goals through careful bargaining with employers. As Brody (1980: 197) points out, for the UAW – influenced as it was by an emerging philosophy of "business unionism" – "[t]he entire thrust of the union–management relationship aimed at containing [local rank-and-file militancy]."[1]

In highlighting this fundamental difference between the philosophies of the FE and of the UAW, my intention here is to show that geographic scale is a contested material and ideological construction and that political power rests not only on the material control over particular places, but on the legitimacy that accrues to those actors who are able to control the discursive construction of scale (Herod 1991, 1997; Smith 1993; Swyngedouw 1997, 2000). To a large extent my argument is derived from Mitchell's (1998) insightful analysis of how scalar narratives based on localism were deployed by California agricultural capital to control the local spaces needed for the national and global capitalist system to function. As Mitchell points out, the ability to depict labor unions as "outside (i.e., nonlocal) agitators" is a prominent scalar strategy often deployed by capital – both local and extra-local – to undercut their local legitimacy. In this chapter, however, I plan to take Mitchell's argument one step further by demonstrating that such discursive strategies have also been used within the labor movement itself.

In this chapter I will also draw attention to the role of the state in shaping the discursive and material terrain of the struggle between the FE, UAW, and IH. In particular, I want to argue that local politics are not just the province of local political actors. As the following case study amply illustrates, agents of the national state can and do actively intervene in what are usually viewed simply as "local" politics (Cox 1998). The ability of the national state thus to extend its reach into all scales simultaneously suggests that, rather than depicting scalar struggles mechanistically as a set of interactions between actors residing at separate scales, a more appropriate metaphor is that of a network of intertwined actors (see Cox 1998 and Latham's chapter 4 in this volume).

My narrative proceeds in chronological order and covers the period from the founding of the FE in 1937 as a division of the Congress of Industrial Organizations' Steelworkers' Organizing Committee (CIO SWOC) to its ultimate merger in 1955 with the UAW (also a CIO affiliate). I begin by explaining the strategies used by the FE to organize workers in the farm implements industry and to bring improved working conditions, higher wages, and better benefits to those employed by IH. Next, I outline the struggle between the FE and UAW and describe how both the UAW and IH attempted to undermine the local legitimacy of the FE by convincing its members that their union was controlled by leaders following the instructions of foreign masters deep in Communist Russia – that is to say, that FE leaders' actions reflected not the concerns of local workers but the desires of the far-away Kremlin. Here, I also illustrate the important role played by the Federal Bureau of Investigation and the House Un-American Activities Committee in disrupting the spatial organization of the FE, which ultimately led to its demise. In my conclusion, I will attempt to distill the lessons of the FE story and how the labor movement of today can use them in its efforts to confront global capital.

Building a Radical Union: Strategic Scalar Constructions

In the mid-1930s, IH workers were "represented" by unions organized by the company itself. In each plant the company organized works councils whose main purpose was to communicate the company's demands to its workers. The leadership of the works councils was comprised of hand-picked, anti-union workers who displayed an "almost feudal obsequiousness toward management" (Ozanne 1967: 196). IH claimed that with the company unions in place, there was no need for employees to affiliate with outside unions and terminated any employee seeking to organize workers outside of the company framework.

All of this changed with the passage in 1935 of the National Labor Relations ("Wagner") Act, which recognized the right of employees to unionize and gave union organizers a legal avenue to challenge IH's company unions. In 1936, the Congress of Industrial Organizations (CIO) filed a complaint with the National Labor Relations Board (NLRB) alleging that because the works councils were organized by the company itself, they could not possibly represent the interests of IH workers. The subsequent NLRB ruling supported the CIO's arguments and IH was ordered to disband the company unions and allow open representation elections. The adamantly anti-union IH, however, refused to abide by the NLRB decision and appealed the case to the US Supreme Court, although without success (Ozanne 1967). Nevertheless, even in the face of this loss in the highest court in the land, IH continued to keep union organizers out of its plants by organizing "plant unions" led by the heads of the now disbanded works councils. Despite having the law on its side, then, for the FE organizing the IH plants would prove to be a difficult task and the shopfloor of IH was certainly not a safe place to "talk union." Workers identified as union organizers were immediately fired and anti-union workers reported any suspected union activity to management. The only secure locations for union organizers to meet were in the nearby taverns beyond the earshot of foremen and workers whose allegiance was suspect. As one FE organizer has commented: "We would never sign anybody up in the shop. If there was anybody who looked to me like he was pretty good material for the union, I would say, well Sam, or Joe, how about a beer on the way home? Just about everyone would say, sure, why not? And then we'd stop at the tavern, have a drink, and then of course we would talk union. And sign up new members. Now that was a slow process" (interview with Hank Graber, quoted in Gilpin 1992: 76).

Although it was national-level legislation such as the Wagner Act that provided the judicial basis for CIO organizing drives at IH, union leaders believed that the key to bringing union representation to the farm implements industry was to organize workers via a strategy which would be sensitive to the local geographies of the Midwest's industrial and labor structure. Initially, FE organizers focused their attention on the large IH plants located in Chicago, plants which together employed approximately 14,000 workers (Foley 1965; Gilpin 1989). IH had three main Chicago operations: the McCormick Works (which produced harvesters), the Tractor Works, and the Chicago Twine Mill, in which a predominantly female labor force spun fiber (grown on IH plantations in Honduras) into the twine used in harvesting machinery (Gilpin 1989). Outside of Chicago, IH operated the Farmall tractor plant (the largest tractor factory outside of the USSR) in Rock Island, IL and the harvester works in East Moline, IL. IH also produced plows and other implements at Canton and Rock Falls, IL. However, at several of these plants what were essentially still company unions claimed to represent workers and company pressure made it hard to sign up enough potential members to force a union vote. Consequently, the FE filed a second complaint with the NLRB alleging that the plants' unions remained illegally under the company's control. While it took nearly three years before the NLRB issued a final judgment, in February 1941 the Board ruled in the FE's favor and ordered representation elections at six IH plants, including the McCormick Works and the East Moline (the Harvester Works) and Rock Island (the Farmall Works) plants (Ozanne, 1967: 197–8). Significantly, although the NLRB ruling cleared the way for local union elections by forcing IH to disband its company unions, the ruling also set in motion a bitterly fought contest between the FE (affiliated with the CIO) and a union of the rival American Federation of Labor (AFL), which was organizing in the industry and which covetously eyed these plants. In the elections to represent farm implements workers across the Midwest that followed, the FE was victorious at the all-important McCormick Works, the lynchpin in the IH chain. However, while this victory secured for the FE a territorial base in Chicago, its strength outside the city remained limited – at the Harvester Works in East Moline the FE won by a vote of 815 to 630, but at the nearby Rock Island Farmall plant the union lost by a vote of 1,692 to 1,383 (Gilpin 1992: 102).

While the foothold of the FE remained tenuous, the union's efforts to broaden its geographic scale of influence began to gain momentum. Part of the success was undoubtedly due to the dogged recruiting efforts of FE organizers, but the growing working-class movement evident throughout the Midwest provided important "demonstration effects" as well (Lipsitz 1994).[2] By the late 1930s, a sense of working-class consciousness based on militant unionism had spread throughout the cities – large, medium, and small – of the Midwest. The emerging regional scale of union activism encouraged a growing sense of confidence and militancy among IH workers.

Particularly important were the examples of union activity in the meat packing and steel industries (Page 1998). As Gilpin (1992: 103) recounts, within Illinois "Harvester employees could come into contact with organized steelworkers, packinghouse workers, miners and electrical workers...Harvester workers came late to industrial unionism, but they could not have been unaffected by the movement they witnessed around them." Potent union strongholds soon developed among the farm implements workers of the Quad Cities (Davenport and Bettendorf, Iowa, and Rock Island and Moline, Illinois), where the FE built strongly rooted, local scale support in each plant and in the nearby working-class neighborhoods. Fostering the growth of unionism in the Quad Cities were the labor schools led by a local Catholic priest, W. T. O'Connor (Melcher 1964). A militant (but staunchly anti-Communist) labor organizer, O'Connor worked to raise the consciousness of farm implements workers throughout the region. The impact of the labor schools was reinforced by virtue of the fact that farm implements workers were exposed to the success of the United Packinghouse Workers of America (UPWA) in organizing meatpacking plants in cities such as Waterloo and Ottumwa, Iowa, which were also centers of farm implements production (Warren 1995).

As the FE constructed local bases of strength, it also developed scale-stretching networks that linked union strongholds together into a bulwark of militant unionism. Based in Chicago, FE organizers constantly circulated between union headquarters and the union locals scattered throughout Illinois and Iowa. Many FE members also attended regional labor schools and annual FE conventions, thus providing them with the opportunity to meet fellow workers from throughout the Midwest. These activities were important, for as Wills (1996) points out, solidarity – based on a belief in the efficacy of direct action and union organization – is developed by workers themselves on a very personal basis as they "talk union." Such gatherings, then, helped to bolster the emerging sense of power among the rank-and-file and fostered a growing sense of working-class identity. This sense of FE power and working-class identity was further augmented by the union's deep commitment to issues of social justice, a commitment which impacted working people more broadly throughout the region.

The union's campaign against racism is perhaps the most notable example of its broad political agenda that combined shopfloor power with broader issues of social justice. In the evolving multiracial environment of Midwestern industrial cities, the FE's all-out attack on racism was an important element in its success. FE organizers constantly preached (and practiced) racial unity and fought for racial equality on the shopfloor and in the working-class communities surrounding the plants. A number of African-Americans held important leadership positions in the union, especially in the Chicago locals (Gilpin 1989). Such efforts earned the FE the loyalty of the many African-American workers in the IH chain. The involvement of left-wing unions in such community-building activities was in great contrast to the practices of the UAW, which at this time focused primarily on workplace issues such as wages and benefits (Holmes and Rusonik 1991).

Piecework and power on the shopfloor

While activities such as organizing labor schools and its antiracism campaign were important for developing the FE as a regional organization, FE leaders fervently believed that the key to power was constant shopfloor struggle against the dictates of management. In particular, IH's reliance upon a complex system of piecework pay scales provided a major arena of confrontation between workers, union stewards, and management. According to IH management, piecework was essential to achieve the worker efficiency necessary for profitable production. For the leaders of the FE, however, piecework was the means by which IH management held down wages and controlled the shopfloor. FE leaders complained that "Sometimes you think you get a pretty good price on a job. You work along, devising short cuts, a little more efficiency and make some more money. You can't relax too long. Any day now the time study man may come along and tell you the job is being changed...What's the purpose? An excuse for re-timing the job to take advantage of all your well-earned experience" (quoted in Gilpin 1992: 113).

Although disputes over piecework standards originated at the level of the shopfloor, the FE used to its full advantage the framework devised by the federal government to regulate labor relations. A key FE strategy was to "jump scales" (Smith 1993) from its locus of power on the shopfloor to the federal level by using judicial remedies for shopfloor problems. Thus, the union filed suits first with the NLRB and then, during the course of the Second World War, with the War Labor Board (WLB) to force the company to address workers' demands.[3] In so doing, the FE effectively constructed a spatial strategy that attempted to "box in" IH by simultaneously agitating on the shopfloor and campaigning at the national scale. Using such a dual-pronged scalar strategy, however, was not the only example of the FE thinking strategically about the scale at which decisions concerning labor relations should be made. Once the union was ensconced in each IH plant, its next goal was to force the company to equalize wage rates across the company chain, a strategy designed to limit IH's ability to play workers in different communities across the region against each other in an endless downward concessionary spiral (a practice known colloquially as "whipsawing"). With this aim in mind, in 1943 the FE asked the WLB to set piecework rates equally in all IH plants. The FE also fought for gender equality on the shopfloor and requested that the WLB order IH to eliminate the lower piecework rates paid to female workers. Although the WLB ultimately did not agree to the setting of national piecework rates, it did order the substantial increases necessary to bring women workers up to par with their male counterparts.

Building on this victory, the union now set its sights on forcing IH to develop a system of piecework rates that took into account the actual production conditions under which workers toiled. Given that the company used its system of piecework to set the pace of production and control the wages earned, wresting away from the company this power was the key to giving workers command over the shopfloor. To achieve its aims, the union once again turned to the national-scale labor regulation system. The FE argued that piecework standards were set assuming unrealistic conditions which were rarely (if ever) experienced on the shopfloor. Thus, the union asked the WLB to order IH to negotiate a more realistic piecework pay system. In a ruling that significantly shifted the balance of power on the shopfloor, the WLB found in favor of the FE and directed the company and union to renegotiate how the piecework pay system worked across all of its plants. The resulting agreement gave union stewards the right to protest any piecework pay rates they thought were unfair and provided the legal basis for union members to shut down production and otherwise contest the authority of management to set piecework pay rates.

Drawing upon a cadre of militant union stewards who were well-known for their willingness to halt production over seemingly minor disputes between a single worker and foreman, the well-organized FE was able to use a skillful combination of direct shopfloor action and judicial remedies to wrest a significant degree of worker control over conditions on the shopfloor, greatly increasing union power at that scale. Moreover, because their philosophy of unionism was based on the idea that power resided on the shopfloor, the FE's national leaders respected the right of local branch unions to initiate wildcat strikes. The union's aggressiveness promoted loyalty and solidarity among its members and encouraged workers to affiliate with it, such that by the end of the Second World War the FE had organized approximately 30,000 workers at ten IH plants in Chicago, the Quad Cities, and other locations throughout the Midwest (Melcher 1964). In the Quad Cities alone, there were over 10,000 FE members at two major IH plants and the union had established itself at several John Deere facilities (Foley 1965). The union had also successfully brought the 12,000 workers at the giant Caterpillar Works in Peoria, IL into the FE fold (Melcher 1964).

By the time the 1946 contract negotiations opened, then, the FE had achieved a remarkable degree of power which it fully intended to exercise to achieve a number of goals concerning piecework rates, the rights of workers to receive the full piecework pay even under adverse conditions such as power outages or lack of materials, and full pay for union stewards. Taking the workers out on strike, the solidarity of the union forced IH to make a number of concessions and the FE achieved a clear victory. As Gilpin (1992: 165–6) notes: "power on the shopfloor was the essence of the contest and when the union prevailed...FE members were ensured a good deal more control over the pace of production, the rates of compensation and the quality of their working lives. Harvester had been stripped of the ability to freely and unilaterally manipulate its piecework system to extract the maximum profit per employee."

The growing power of the FE, though, was not a singular event. Rather, it was part of a rising tide of worker militancy that was shaking the very foundations of US capitalism in the late-1940s as workers defied union leaders and directly confronted management through wildcat strikes, shopfloor showdowns with foremen, and street demonstrations. Concerned that this show of rank-and-file worker power threatened to undermine their own power, however, business leaders and conservative union leaders sought to restrain such militancy. As Lipsitz (1994: 91) comments, "[n]o plans for the postwar world could afford to ignore the power, consciousness and activism workers displayed...as leaders of unions and corporations both understood" and the radical actions of the FE and other unions soon provoked a strong counterattack by an alliance of business, conservative union leaders, and the federal government. Increasing tensions between the United States and the Soviet Union fueled a growing anti-Communist campaign which provided an important justification for attacks on the left-wing elements of the labor movement, whose legitimacy was challenged on the basis that Communist leaders, supposedly controlled by a foreign power, did not represent the wishes of *local* American workers.

The role of the federal government in providing legitimacy to the claims of Communist subversion was crucial. Indeed, Schrecher (1992: 139) has suggested that while "[c]orporations, other unions [and] the Catholic Church all joined forces to drive the Communists out of the labor movement...it was the federal government that guaranteed the success of these endeavors [and] legitimated the[ir] efforts." Thus, in 1947 a coalition of Republicans and conservative Democrats passed the Taft–Hartley Act, a major piece of labor law legislation intended to restrict the power of unions by limiting the right of workers to strike and by outlawing one of labor's major weapons, that of the secondary boycott. This provision of the new law was an explicit recognition that one way to rein in the power of workers was to limit their abilities to develop solidarity across space – rather than allowing workers to stretch their scale of support to confederates in other plants in other communities, outlawing secondary boycotts would isolate workers by helping to limit industrial disputes to individual workplaces. Taking direct aim at radical labor leaders, Taft–Hartley also required union officers to sign an affidavit declaring that they were not members of the Communist Party. Any union with officers refusing to sign the affidavit was prohibited from appearing on the ballot in the representational elections upon which union growth hinged. Left-wing unions such as the FE were particular targets of the legislation and its leaders joined a nationwide protest against this requirement by refusing to sign the affidavits – an action that made them (and the union they represented) ineligible to appear on the ballot in representational elections. In addition to the pressure applied at the scale of the national state, the major national labor organization (the CIO) singled out left-wing unions and pressured them to replace leaders with ties (alleged or real) to the Communist Party (Rosswurm 1992).

Ultimately, the refusal to sign the affidavits would cost the FE a great deal, for it opened the way for the rival UAW to challenge the FE.[4] As the FE and other left-wing unions came under attack, the UAW announced its intention to bring the workers in the farm implements industry under its aegis. To do so, though, the UAW would have to attack the very foundations of the FE and force representation elections at each FE-controlled plant. One of its first opportunities to do so came shortly after the passage of Taft–Hartley, when the 12,000 member FE local at the Caterpillar Tractor Works in Peoria, IL went on strike. Without a signed contract, Caterpillar, sensing an opportunity to rid itself of the difficult FE, filed a request with the NLRB for a new representation election. Because its leaders refused to comply with the Taft–Hartley requirements, the FE could not appear on the ballot and Caterpillar workers received a ballot that had only two choices: the UAW or no union. With their FE local effectively eliminated from consideration, workers chose the UAW, costing the FE one-quarter of its membership in a single uncontested election. Although this represented a significant setback for the FE, the union did nevertheless still retain its power base in the plants of IH.

To summarize, then, in the face of entrenched opposition by International Harvester and challenges by a rival union, the FE had successfully organized a number of plants throughout the Midwest by thinking strategically about space and scale. The union had focused its organizing efforts on several large plants in Chicago – a city with a long history of union support – but had subsequently expanded out of those local bases of strength by using traveling organizers to link plants throughout the region. Equally, although the FE believed strength came from controlling the local spaces of the individual shopfloors in plants across the Midwest, the union was not averse to using federal labor law to pursue its goals. Furthermore, the union recognized that if it were to be successful, it would have to expand its interests beyond the scale merely of the shopfloor to organize throughout the communities in which IH and other employers' plants were located, a strategy achieved by focusing not just on issues arising out of the workplace but by focusing on issues of social justice which stretched beyond the shopfloor. Based upon their ideological convictions, the national FE leadership also allowed individual local unions to retain a great deal of autonomy to conduct wildcat strikes and other industrial actions within the very decentralized system of union power which characterized the FE's operational structure. Indeed, as we shall now see, the struggles between the FE and the rival UAW to represent workers in the farm implements industry would revolve around, among other things, crucial questions concerning the appropriate geographical scale – locally or nationally – at which worker power should be expressed.

Scale and Strategy: Shopfloor Militancy versus National Business Unionism

Significantly, the conflicting philosophies concerning trade unionism expressed by the FE and the UAW were reflected in the contrasting spatial strategies adopted by the rival unions. Although the differences between the FE and UAW were quite numerous, three main contrasts can be identified.

First and foremost, the unions differed greatly in their ideological orientation. Although the extent of the connections between the FE leadership and the Communist Party are unknown, it is likely that at least some FE leaders were members. Many others, while not card-carrying Communists, certainly shared the leftist orientation of the leaders. Accordingly, the FE leadership took the position that the interests of capital and labor were fundamentally opposed and that workers could only gain power through a constant contest against capital. In their view, there was no room for compromise between capital and labor. As FE President Milt Burns once stated: "The philosophy of our union was that management had no right to exist" (quoted in Gilpin 1992: 179).

On the other hand, the UAW, led by Walter Reuther, rejected such radical views and thought that the key to labor power was to reach an accommodation with capital which provided workers with certain rights, wages, and benefits, yet did not challenge the basic prerogatives of capital. Reuther believed that to achieve the national stature needed to negotiate with top business leaders, the radical impulses of rank-and-file workers and local union leaders had to be restrained. Reuther's philosophy of "business unionism" was made quite evident in the 1950 "Treaty of Detroit" contract between the UAW and General Motors (GM). Although the UAW did win significant wage increases, cost-of-living clauses, and pension benefits, it also effectively conceded command of the shop-floor to management, undercutting the attempts of rank-and-file workers to gain a measure of control over their day-to-day working lives (Stromquist 1994: 168–9). These differences in ideological orientation, then, meant that while the FE largely focused upon shopfloor actions, the UAW was more nationally oriented in its concerns.

The second critical difference between the FE and the UAW was the level of autonomy that the national leadership allowed local branch unions to exercise. Reflecting its commitment to a national-scale strategy, the national leadership of the UAW maintained strict control over its branch unions. After the settlement between the UAW and GM in 1946, for instance, the UAW replaced shop stewards drawn from the rank-and-file with union-appointed committeemen, effectively quelling localized militancy and restoring management's control over the shopfloor. Such actions also bolstered the authority of the national UAW leadership by sending the message to union members that localized rebelliousness would not be tolerated (Davis 1986: 81). As a further aid in controlling militancy at the local scale, the UAW concentrated authority at the regional and national scales and punished any branch union that defied the dictates of the national leadership.

In contrast, power on the shopfloor and in the local community was the key spatial strategy of the FE. Unlike the UAW, the FE depended on a cadre of locally-elected union stewards to build localized strength. When a dispute arose, union stewards would roam the shopfloor, ordering workers to halt production and walk out. Workers respected the leadership of their shop stewards and participated in frequent wildcat strikes – in 1947 there were 83 wildcat strikes at the IH East Moline Harvester works alone (Gilpin 1992: 297). In their support for spontaneous wildcat strikes, which by their nature occurred without prior permission, the FE leadership demonstrated its faith in the efficacy of direct local shopfloor action. Unlike UAW leaders, the national FE leadership strongly supported militancy at the local scale and much of the strength of the FE resided in the excellent organizational skills of its leaders and their willingness to grant autonomy to local union activists. Although the FE's strategy certainly relied upon utilization of federal labor law, it was the national leadership's willingness to allow local branch unions a great deal of latitude in their dealings with management which was the hallmark of the FE.

A third key difference was in the negotiating stances taken by the rivals. The UAW favored long-term contracts and signed a five-year agreement with IH in 1950. In contrast, FE leadership believed that any lapse in the pressure on management would result in rapid erosion of the gains made by workers and preferred short-term contracts which allowed them to keep constant pressure on the company. Reflecting this strategy, the FE signed only a two-year agreement in 1950. Not only did the two unions have different strategies when it came to the spatial scales at which they operated, but they also appeared to have quite different strategies when it came to the temporal scales (long- versus short-term contracts) within which they operated.

In sum, the FE followed a very different philosophy regarding labor's relationship with capital, exercised a different internal scalar distribution of responsibility and power, and engaged in quite different strategies to those of the UAW when it came to contract negotiations. These differences translated into very distinct spatial and scalar strategies deployed by the rival unions, not only in their contest with management but in their struggle with each other over who would represent farm implements workers. For example, in its initial efforts to eliminate the FE, the UAW worked at the national scale to isolate the FE from the broader labor movement. To accomplish this goal, the UAW mounted a campaign to have the FE and other left-wing unions kicked out of the CIO. Under the prodding of CIO board member and UAW President Walter Reuther, the CIO passed a resolution ordering the FE to merge immediately with the UAW. Since one of the conditions for the merger required that the left-wing FE leaders resign from the union, the UAW's demand for merger was refused. As a consequence, the FE was expelled from the CIO at its national convention in November 1949. At the same time, other left-wing unions were disaffiliated from the CIO, including the United Electrical Workers (UE), then the CIO's single largest union. The basis for these expulsions relied upon an anti-Communist campaign which sought to undermine the legitimacy of left-wing unions by "invok[ing] the language of national security and charg[ing] the left-wing unions with failing to support American foreign policy" (Schrecher 1992: 146).

Removing the FE from the CIO effectively isolated the union from the mainstream of the national labor movement. However, in order to gain control of the farm implements industry, the UAW still needed to win representation elections at each of the plants represented by the FE. To do this, it had to convince FE members to shift their allegiance to the UAW. While on the surface it might appear as if the nationally-powerful UAW, with its huge financial resources and the backing of the CIO, would have little trouble convincing FE members that their interests would be better served by affiliating with the UAW, in practice the Autoworkers found it nearly impossible to dislodge the FE from its strongholds in the factories of IH. Given the excellent contracts negotiated on behalf of its members by the FE, the UAW could hardly claim to provide workers with higher pay or better benefits. Instead, the UAW's campaign attempted to undermine the local legitimacy of the FE leaders by convincing union members that their union was actually under the control of Communists with direct links to Moscow and that, implicitly, their leaders' actions did not reflect the local or regional needs of workers in the industry but, rather, were dictated by the whims of paymasters across the Atlantic on the other side of the Iron Curtain. In this sense, part of the UAW's strategy was to intimate that FE leaders – even if born in the local community – were not "legitimate locals" but were really outsiders unconnected to the goals and aspirations of the "true" American Midwestern worker and that these leaders were attempting to transplant "foreign" ideologies to the Great Plains, a region that epitomized what it was to be "American." Such efforts can be readily seen, for example, in a 1949 UAW leaflet that referred to the FE leadership this way: "Commissar Gerald Fielde runs the

FE. He could not sign Non-Communist Affidavits last year – and 'resigned.'...DeWitt Gilpin, writer for the *Daily Worker* and *New Masses*, puts out FE poison propaganda" (quoted in Gilpin 1992: 167).

As the UAW actively engaged in red-baiting FE members, their efforts were met with direct opposition by angry FE workers, and street battles occurred in front of many plants. Moreover, despite the UAW's pervasive attempts to undermine the FE's local legitimacy, the FE won representation elections in Chicago, the Quad Cities, Charles City, Iowa, and in South Bend, Indiana (Foley 1965). Even though the UAW managed to force eleven different representation elections in various IH plants between 1949 and 1953, in every case workers voted to remain in the beleaguered FE (Gilpin 1992: 249). Although it is doubtful that most FE members were in support of Communism, the claim that FE leaders only represented the interests of international Communism was at odds with the daily experience of FE members. Every day, FE members witnessed the strong commitment of their union stewards and other FE officials to giving workers a voice in the day-to-day operations on the shopfloor itself. The votes of FE members indicated a broad agreement with the FE's philosophy of trade unionism, which emphasized the importance of shopfloor power led by the rank-and-file. While many FE leaders did have ties to the Communist Party, it is apparent that they also did an excellent job of negotiating strong contracts and worked hard (and successfully) to protect workers' rights on the job.

The reliance on a philosophy which emphasized shopfloor actions was in direct conflict with the UAW's brand of business unionism which relied on strict control of local militancy and emphasized the contractual obligations of unions to management. It was also directly in opposition to the stance favored by IH management. Consequently, as the 1952 contract negotiations opened, it became clear that IH intended to get rid of the militant FE.

The 1952 IH strike

By the time the 1952 contract negotiations got underway, the FE was under attack at several different geographical scales. The union had been isolated nationally from the rest of the labor movement and its leadership was besieged by the requirements of Taft–Hartley. Furthermore, at the local scale it was also fending off the vigorous decertification efforts of the UAW. It was not surprising, therefore, that as the contract negotiations between the FE and IH began in 1952, the company felt that the time was ripe to break the union. Taking a page from the UAW's playbook, IH's fight to destroy the FE started with an attempt to undermine its local legitimacy by attacking FE leaders as "outside agitators" and "Joe Stalin's friends." IH launched its media offensive by taking out numerous ads in the *Chicago Daily Tribune* and newspapers throughout the region, denouncing the "Commies" leading the FE and suggesting "that the most influential leaders of the FE are either Communists or Communist sympathizers and fellow-travelers. It is also our belief that many of the FE's actions are dictated by Communist purposes rather than genuine trade union purposes" (quoted in Gilpin 1992: 396).

The union responded to IH's attack with numerous leaflets, hand-bills, and strike bulletins of its own. For their part, FE leaders contended that IH's charges were mainly intended to facilitate the domination of labor by capital. As they noted, "The smoke screen used by the Harvester company and its agents is the well-known antilabor practice of calling individuals and organizations Communists. The real issue is this: Will Harvester succeed in slashing rates and forcing yellow dog contracts on workers, or will Harvester employees win the present battle for badly needed gains?" (quoted in Foley 1965: 43).

At the national scale, the federal government's state security apparatus also intervened on behalf of IH as agents of the Federal Bureau of Investigation (FBI) attempted to delegitimate FE union leaders locally. In February 1952, FBI officials detained some Quad Cities FE members for questioning about the political background of their fellow members. Refusing to answer the FBI's questions, FE officials maintained that they had spotted "the face of the employer behind the mask of the FBI" (quoted in Foley 1964: 37). FBI agents maintained close surveillance of union members and were particularly interested in the patterns of spatial interaction of the various FE locals, an interest which indicates that the FBI's strategy was clearly designed to disrupt the material spatial organization constructed by the union to link its local strongholds together into a regional network of union activism. Evidently, the FBI's actions were intended to attack the local legitimacy of the union by undermining both its ideological and its geographical basis.

When contract negotiations finally began, IH refused to use the existing contract as a basis for negotiation. Instead, the company presented the FE bargaining committee with a completely new contract, one intended to destroy the union's shopfloor power base. Given its reliance on shopfloor struggle, from the FE's point of view the most objectionable clause was the proposed elimination of pay for shop stewards and new work rules – such as the company's reserving for itself the right to fire any shop steward who called a work stoppage – that drastically reduced the union's power on the shopfloor. Clearly, IH intended to rein in the strength of the FE's activist union stewards and thereby undercut the shopfloor influence won earlier by the FE (Gilpin 1992: 390–1).

Unwilling to accept such a contract, on August 21, 1952, the FE went on strike. Determined to break the strike, IH management and its supporters engaged the FE on a number of scales. First, at the local scale, despite numerous and determined pickets, the company did not close any of its plants. Rather, it kept them open and began an aggressive campaign to convince local workers to cross the picket lines. As part of this strategy, IH management invaded the local territorial bases of the union, sending foremen and other management representatives into the working-class taverns and other establishments frequented by workers. Foremen also visited the homes of striking workers and urged them to cross the picket lines and return to work. This strategy was intended to challenge directly the local micro-geography of union power and to undermine the territorial control of FE members.

For their part, FE members vigorously contested the company's invasion of local union territory. Mass picketing was undertaken at plant gates and union members kept track of strike-breaking scabs. At the contested plant entrances and in the surrounding neighborhoods violence occurred on a daily basis. Automobiles containing scabs were surrounded by angry workers and marked with yellow paint. The names of "scab-herding" foremen were published in local editions of FE strike bulletins and the homes of strike breakers were also attacked. Angry union members demanded that IH stay out of their taverns, neighborhoods, and homes. As one union leaflet stated: "We don't want you in our homes, or calling us on the phone. You stay out of our affairs altogether and we'll all be O.K." (Gilpin 1992: 399).

As the localized struggles in front of plant gates and in working-class neighborhoods continued, right-wing Congressmen operating at the national scale intervened in the struggle. Acting to undercut the local legitimacy of FE leaders, in September 1952 the House Un-American Activities Committee (HUAC) held hearings in Chicago to examine the influence of Communists in the labor movement. Although HUAC's visit was welcomed by IH, labor leaders had a different opinion of HUAC's mission. Recognizing the spatial strategy being employed by HUAC – namely, attacking the FE's geographic core of support – the union charged that "Chicago is soon to have an unwelcome visit from the House Un-American Activities Committee.

It has been moving from city to city, at the invitation of employers and reactionary politicians, to smear and disrupt unions engaged in fights for better conditions. Chicago's turn is next" (Foley 1964: 41).

In an effort to discredit the leaders of the FE and thereby to convince workers to cross the picket lines, then, pressure at both the national and local scale was being applied. Local newspapers trumpeted HUAC's charges of Communist influence in the IH strike. The three main negotiators representing the FE (President Grant Oakes, Gerald Fielde, and DeWitt Gilpin) were subpoenaed to testify. In their testimony before the HUAC committee, though, each refused to affirm or deny whether they had been, or were, members of the Communist Party (Edwards 1952). Their testimony (or lack thereof) was widely publicized across Illinois and their left-wing connections were used in an effort to undercut support for the IH strike at a time when US troops were fighting in Korea and an anti-Communist climate had flowered in the isolationist soil of the Midwest.

Following the HUAC hearings in Chicago, the FBI directly intervened into the local labor struggle by arresting an FE official, William Sentner, in Rock Island, Illinois. Under FBI surveillance, Sentner, an admitted member of the Communist Party, was coordinating strike activity in Iowa, Illinois, and Missouri. Because he crossed state lines in his activities, he was charged with conspiring to overthrow the US government (Foley 1964: 44). This intervention of the national state security apparatus not only disrupted the spatial organization of the union in a material sense (in that it prohibited Sentner from traveling between IH plants), but it also facilitated the ideological attack on the FE by again casting doubt on the legitimacy of the union's leadership. In fact, the ability of anti-FE forces to limit the movement of organizers between plants was a key element in their strategy to isolate geographically each plant's workforce and to break up any structures of interaction between plants out of which regional-scale solidarity may have emerged, and is a strategy which has striking parallels with the efforts by the Conservative government of Britain to limit the mobility of pickets during the 1984–5 coal miners' strike. Indeed, the ability to traverse space to make links between workers in different locations – or, alternatively, to impede such traversal – can be a crucial element in industrial disputes, a fact recognized by Blomley (1994: 152) who suggests that in the British miners' strike "space, or more specifically, movement through space, became an essential tactical concern for both the union and antistrike forces."

The FE was also attacked at the scale of the shopfloor, which had previously served as its base of power. Indeed, the company's contract proposal was a blatant effort to eradicate a whole scale of control exercised by the FE. At the same time, federal government subpoenas pulled FE negotiators from the bargaining table to HUAC meetings, thereby hampering the union's abilities to negotiate strong contracts for its members. The result of such actions was that the FE's local-scale territorial bases of support, scale-bridging networks, and the material and ideological basis of its power were all directly challenged. Simultaneously, the FE was not able to draw upon the resources of the wider national labor movement, since it had been expelled from the CIO and was unlikely to receive support from the CIO's even more conservative rival, the American Federation of Labor. Moreover, not only did the UAW not help the FE but, because they had a signed contract that was not to expire until 1955, UAW members continued to work while the FE was on strike. Furthermore, during the strike the UAW itself sought to undermine the FE by calling for a representational vote at the IH plant in Canton, Illinois. While this effort failed, union organizers and resources had to be diverted to Canton in the midst of the hard-fought strike.

By November 1952, it was clear that the FE had lost the strike. The union's finances were largely exhausted and many workers had heeded IH's call to return to work. Furthermore, as long as the FE was without a contract with IH, it was exposed to decertification elections. Therefore, national FE leaders and the leaders of the allied UE, convinced that to save the union a contract had to be signed, urged local union officers to accept the contract offered by IH (Foley 1965: 44). From the standpoint of the national leadership, fighting off the raiding tactics of the UAW required that a contract settlement, even a bad one, be reached as soon as possible. However, many local leaders, especially those in the Quad Cities area, remained adamantly opposed to the settlement. With the strike's loss and the FE's acceptance of IH's contract came bitter dissension between local and national leaders. Although the workers reentered the plants with the fighting spirit that typified the FE, the contract that the FE was forced to sign strictly limited the efficacy of shopfloor militancy. The most immediate impact of the new contract was the provision which allowed the company to dismiss any workers initiating shopfloor actions such as wildcat strikes. The full impact of the new contract was felt in the months following the strike as many union leaders, especially shop stewards, were fired. It was not long before IH had successfully decimated the strong shopfloor leadership that had been the hallmark of the FE.

As a result of the 1952 strike's loss, the FE's leadership had been split, contract provisions had succeeded in eliminating many of the most aggressive shopfloor leaders, and the workers' will to fight had been sapped. Furthermore, the ever-present UAW was beginning to score victories in core locals. Under these conditions, FE leaders faced a new round of contract negotiations with IH in 1955 and the leadership recognized that its members would be forced to sign an even worse contract in the upcoming talks. Even though the majority of workers stayed loyal to the union, the remaining leaders knew that farm implements workers would have to present a united front in 1955. With this in mind, they reluctantly entered into merger talks with the UAW. Reaching an agreement between the two bitter foes was difficult. In the end, the FE agreed to lead its remaining locals into the UAW and the UAW agreed to retain the leaders of the FE.

Discussion

As the example of union struggles within the farm implements industry illustrates, the social production of scale is a powerful and fluid element in labor geography. The power of the FE was built through a combination of militant action at the local level and skillful use of national-scale state-sponsored support for labor organization. In addition, many of the leaders of the FE, via their membership in the Communist Party, were guided by a broad framework of ideology and tactics that sought to build an international labor movement. Although the FE was very strong at the local scale, it could not, however, have achieved its power without its ability to articulate local militancy with national-scale strategy. As a result of their capacity to exert pressure on IH at a multiplicity of scales and through various strategies, workers in the FE were able to secure significant gains from one of the most powerful and anti-union companies in the United States. Direct shopfloor action, legal challenges, and regional coordination of activity all played a role in the FE's strategy. The strength of local militancy lay in its ability to consistently challenge management's prerogatives on the shopfloor. The frequent use of wildcat strikes to enforce the union's power on the shopfloor provided workers with a powerful sense of solidarity. Yet, this strategy had its limitations. The constant struggle and chaos on the shopfloor became tiresome to maturing workers faced with growing families and a desire to enjoy the fruits of their labors (Gilpin 1992). Even in the union strongholds of Chicago and the Quad Cities, IH was able gradually to wear down the workers.

There are, though, several important lessons to be learned from the FE story. First, the importance of establishing a strong local-scale territorial basis is obvious. By developing a core of dedicated union members on the shopfloor, the union was able to gain local legitimacy by demonstrating its dedication to changing the working conditions experienced everyday by workers. Shopfloor struggle also meant that workers were convinced of the direct relevance of the labor movement in their daily lives. This sense of direct relevance was quickly lost as the business unionism of the UAW took the power out of the hands of local workers. To many workers, unions became just another special interest group, while the "business-unionist" orientation of many US union leaderships and bureaucracies has meant that "the U.S. labor movement has no alternative social and political...vision [but] merely seeks higher wages and improved benefits for its membership" (Holmes and Rusonik 1991: 11). Although recent attempts by labor unions to address a broader spectrum of issues are certainly encouraging, much was lost with the demise of unions such as the FE.

Second, the FE's commitment to issues that affected the community outside of the factory was a critical element in their approach. The antiracism of the FE and the actions of its members to break down racial barriers mirrored the efforts of other left-wing unions such as the UPWA (Page 1998). By dedicating itself to social justice both for union and nonunion workers alike, the FE gained the support of the broader community. Such support is critical to the success of unions, and the damaging effects of a lack of community support were certainly evident in the defeats suffered by unions in more recent strikes such as those against the Caterpillar Corporation in Peoria, Illinois and in the 1985–6 strike against the Hormel meat-packing company in Austin, Minnesota (Crump and Merrett 1998; Schleuning 1994).

Third, without the intervention of the federal government, the FE could never have achieved the strength it did. In providing state support for union organization, the passage of the 1935 Wagner Act clearly signaled that the national state supported the organizing efforts of labor unions. In addition, it provided a national-scale legal apparatus to adjudicate conflicts between capital and labor. It is important to recognize, however, that even though the state played a pivotal role in facilitating the growth of unions, state power was also used to limit labor power. When grassroots labor militancy threatened the postwar stability of the capitalist system, the state acted to restrict union influence. Thus, the enactment of the 1947 Taft–Hartley Act constrained the ability of labor to organize strike support across space. In addition, the broad reach of the state apparatus (i.e., the FBI and HUAC) was strategically deployed against the FE and other radical unions. Indeed, without the use of federal government power to undermine the local legitimacy of FE leaders and to disrupt physically the scale-bridging networks set up by the union to coordinate strike activity across space, it is unlikely that the UAW and IH would have been able to dislodge the FE. Such interventions, then, were a key factor in setting the conditions for the much vaunted postwar "bargain" between capital and labor, which was not possible until anticapitalist left-wing unions such as the FE had been destroyed.

Fourth, from a theoretical point of view, in this chapter I have tried to highlight the role of the state in the politics of scale. In both the discursive and material realms, the state actively shapes the outcome of scalar struggles. As the FE–UAW–IH battle indicates, struggles over scale are not simply a two-way contest between capital and labor. The ideological stance of the state can either undermine or promote the local legitimacy of the labor movement. Furthermore, by controlling patterns of movement across space, the state also exerts command over the material construction of scales of union struggle (Wills 1996). Therefore, the challenge for labor geography is not just to analyze contests between capital and labor, but to also theorize the role of the state. This is important, because within the nascent field of labor geography, the role of the state has often been viewed rather mechanically. Local politics are assumed to be the exclusive province of local political institutions and national-scale political activity is viewed as the purview of the national state. In contrast to these rather rigid views of the scales of state activity, I would argue that there is a great deal of scalar interpenetration by various state actors. As the FE–UAW–IH case indicates, the national state actively intervenes in local politics, particularly when national security interests appear threatened. Likewise, gaining local legitimacy and community support is not simply a matter of having a strong local-scale base of power. Thus, local power is partly the result of influence at broader scales while, conversely, political power at scales beyond the local is difficult to achieve without a local basis.

Consequently, I would argue that, as Cox (1998:2) suggests, rather than adopting an "excessively areal approach to the problem" of scale and struggle – one which sees local and national arenas of labor politics as relatively distinct spatial resolutions at which and within which workers and their institutions act – it may be more fruitful to conceptualize the geography of labor–capital–state relations as an *intertwined network*. By utilizing the more flexible metaphor of the network, I would aver, we can move away from overly simplified, mechanistic perspectives which conceive of local and national scales of labor politics as operating on what are viewed as quite separate, easily distinguishable, and largely unconnected spatial levels, and can instead view workers and their institutions as constituted simultaneously as local and national (and regional and global) actors.

Finally, it would be a mistake to conclude that the influence of the FE does not live on. In the Congressional elections of 1998, the support of union members at the former FE stronghold at the IH (now Case-IH) Harvester works in East Moline provided the organizational support that led to the reelection of a pro-labor Democrat, Lane Evans, over a well-financed Republican challenger. The sons and daughters of the FE both remember and reflect the militancy and solidarity that is the legacy of that union.

NOTES

1　Business unionism is a philosophy which suggests that workers will gain most through careful negotiation with their employers, rather than by massed action. It also typically assumes that the focus of union action should be the workplace rather than broader social and political struggles. Hence, it is also sometimes referred to as "bread and butter unionism," in contrast to the "social movement unionism" which seeks to organize workers around issues beyond simply those of the shopfloor. In the case of the UAW, this philosophy was solidified by its 1950 negotiation with General Motors of what has come to be known as the "Treaty of Detroit," a contract agreement which, among other things, linked real wages to productivity growth, provided for automatic cost of living adjustment to compensate for the effects of inflation on real wages, and resulted in the union recognizing the ultimate authority of management to organize production and make investment decisions.

2　The term "demonstration effects" refers to the ways in which union success (or failure) in one place may spur (or discourage) union efforts elsewhere (see Wills 1996).

3　The War Labor Board was the wartime incarnation of the National Labor Relations Board which had been established by the National Labor Relations Act.

4　Although the UAW is usually associated by most people with the automobile industry, we should not forget that the union's full name is the United Automobile, Aerospace and *Agricultural Implement* Workers of America.

REFERENCES

Blomley, N. 1994: *Law, Space and Geographies of Power.* New York: Guilford Press.

Brody, D. 1980: *Workers in Industrial America.* New York: Oxford University Press.

Chicago Daily Tribune 1949: 2 CIO factions in battle, score hurt in riot at East Moline. Feb. 11, p. 1.

Cox, K. R. 1998: Spaces of dependence, spaces of engagement and the politics of scale, or: looking for local politics. *Political Geography*, 17 (1), 1–23.

Crump, J. R. and Merrett, C. D. 1998: Scales of struggle: Economic restructuring in the US Midwest. *Annals of the Association of American Geographers*, 88 (1), 496–515.

Davis, M. 1986: *Prisoners of the American Dream: Politics and Economy in the History of the United States.* New York: Verso.

Edwards, W. 1952: Five unions' chiefs defy US, refuse to say whether they are Commies. *Chicago Daily Tribune*, Sept. 4, p. 1.

Foley, J. E. 1965: *Labor Union Jurisdictional Disputes in the Quad-Cities Farm Equipment Industry, 1949–55.* Unpublished Master's thesis, Department of History, University of Iowa, Iowa City, IA.

Gilpin, T. 1989: Labor's last stand. *Chicago Labor History*, 18 (1), 42–57.

Gilpin, T. 1992: *Left by Themselves: A History of the United Farm Equipment and Metal Workers Unions, 1938–1955.* Unpublished Ph.D. dissertation, Dept. of History, Yale University, New Haven, CT.

Holmes, J. and Rusonik, A. 1991: The break-up of an international labour union: Uneven development in the North American auto industry and the schism in the United Auto Workers. *Environment and Planning A*, 23, 9–35.

Herod, A. 1991: The production of scale in United States labour relations. *Area*, 23, 82–8.

Herod, A. 1997: From a geography of labor to a labor geography: Labor's spatial fix and the geography of capitalism. *Antipode*, 29 (1), 1–31.

Lipsitz, G. 1994: *Rainbow at Midnight: Labor and Culture in the 1940s.* Urbana, IL: University of Illinois Press.

Melcher, A. J. 1964: *Collective Bargaining in the Agricultural Implement Industry: The Impact of Company and Union Structure in Three Firms.* Unpublished Ph.D. dissertation, Dept. of Business, University of Chicago, Chicago, IL.

Mitchell, D. 1998: The scales of justice: Localist ideology, large-scale production, and agricultural labor's geography of resistance in 1930s California. In A. Herod (ed.), *Organizing the Landscape: Geographical Perspectives on Labor Unionism*. Minneapolis, MN: University of Minnesota Press, 159–94.

Ozanne, R. 1967: *A Century of Labor–Management Relations at McCormick and International Harvester.* Madison, WI: University of Wisconsin Press.

Page, B. 1998: Rival unionism and the geography of the meatpacking industry. In A. Herod (ed.), *Organizing the Landscape: Geographical Perspectives on Labor Unionism*. Minneapolis, MN: University of Minnesota Press, 263–96.

Rosswurm, S. 1992: Introduction: An overview and preliminary assessment of the CIO's expelled unions. In S. Rosswurm (ed.), *The CIO's Left-led Unions*. New Brunswick, NJ: Rutgers University Press, 1–17.

Schleuning, N. 1994: *Women, Community, and the Hormel Strike of 1985–86*. Westport, CT: Greenwood Press.

Schrecher, E. W. 1992: McCarthyism and the labor movement: The role of the state. In S. Rosswurm (ed.), *The CIO's Left-led Unions*. New Brunswick, NJ: Rutgers University Press, 39–57.

Smith, N. 1993: Homeless/global: Scaling places. In J. Bird, B. Curtis, T. Putnam, G. Robertson, and L. Tickner (eds.), *Mapping the Futures: Local Cultures, Global Change*. London: Routledge, 87–119.

Stromquist, S. 1993: *Solidarity and Survival: An Oral History of Iowa Labor in the Twentieth Century*. Iowa City, IA: University of Iowa Press.

Swyngedouw, E. 1997: Neither global nor local: "Glocalization" and the politics of scale. In K. R. Cox (ed.), *Spaces of Globalization*. New York: Guilford, 137–66.

Swyngedouw, E. 2000: Authoritarian governance, power, and the politics of rescaling. *Environment and Planning D: Society and Space*, 18, 63–76.

Warren, W. J. 1995: When "Ottumwa went to the dogs": The erosion of Morell–Ottumwa's militant unionism, 1954–1973. *The Annals of Iowa*, 54 (3), 217–43.

Wills, J. 1996: Geographies of trade unionism: Translating tradition across space and time. *Antipode*, 28 (4), 352–78.

9

The Politics of Environmental Justice as the Politics of Scale: St. James Parish, Louisiana, and the Shintech Siting Controversy

Hilda E. Kurtz

> In recent years, the problem of scale has become increasingly import-
> ant, both academically and politically, as the contemporary whirlpool
> of social and cultural change and economic transformation is accom-
> panied by a transgression of scale boundaries, the production of new
> scales, and the restructuring of others.
>
> Swyngedouw (1997: 167)

Between July 1996 and September 1998, residents of St. James Parish, Louisiana – a parish which is home to a significant African-American population already heavily impacted by industrial pollution and challenged by low educational attainment and high rates of un-employment – engaged in a sharp political contest over whether Shintech Inc., a manufacturer of plastics, should be permitted to build an integrated polyvinyl chloride (PVC) production facility in the parish town of Convent. The Shintech case soon brought to the fore important questions about environmental racism and environ-mental (in)justice in Louisiana specifically, and in the United States more generally. One of the most momentous of these questions con-cerned the geographic scale at which environmental racism and (in)-justice were seen to operate. Indeed, during the course of the siting dispute the Shintech protesters purposely framed their social griev-ances at successively larger geographic scales, emphasizing different aspects of social inequality as they went. The shifting discursive strategies of protesters and proponents alike underscored the fact that the concepts of environmental justice and injustice encompass different social processes, and can mean quite different things, at different geographic scales. Such scale-inflected ambiguity, I wish to argue here, poses considerable challenges for environmental justice activists and theorists working to address social disparities which may be experienced locally but which may originate at larger scales of political and economic activity. In examining the scalar strategies employed by opposing parties in the Shintech dispute, then, in this chapter I analyze some of the ways in which agents in grassroots struggle actively engage with, and make strategic use of, what I am here calling the "politics of geographic scale."

During the past decade, geographers and others have explored several facets of the politics of scale. Leitner (1997), for instance, has highlighted the centrality of territorial frameworks of power (tiers of government) in debates over immigration policies within the European Union. Herod (1991, 1997), in contrast, has shown how scale can be used as a means of legitimating inclusion and exclusion in social conflicts, and has illustrated this political use of scale with reference to shifting scales of contract bargaining among longshoremen's and other unions in the United States. Miller (1997, 1994) has drawn attention to the different political opportunity structures within local and national scales of government which are targeted by peace activists with both local and national plans of action. For his part, Jonas (1994: 258) has described the dynamics of "scale politics" in a succinct and suggestive formulation which has been widely cited in subsequent explorations of scale and political struggle, noting that:

> On the one hand, domineering organizations attempt to control the dominated by confining the latter and their activities to a manageable scale. On the other hand, subordinated groups attempt to liberate themselves from the imposed scale constraints by harnessing powers and instrumentalities at other scales. In this process, scale is actively produced.

One of the central questions suggested by the notion that scale can be strategically leveraged in a spatial politics of domination and liberation is, of course, *how* do political actors reconstruct, transgress, and produce new scales of social organization, and with what effects? How precisely do domineering organizations confine weaker organizations to manageable scales? How do subordinated organizations liberate themselves from scale constraints imposed on them by others?

In light of such questions, in this chapter I want to argue that if we are to understand the relevance of the politics of scale for social praxis, it is crucial to develop better understandings of the linkages between, on the one hand, scale-inflected political discourse and discursive strategies and, on the other, the material conditions and outcomes of political struggle at multiple scales. As a way of examining such linkages, in what follows I draw upon Delaney and Leitner's (1997: 94–5, emphasis added) observation that scale "is not simply an external fact awaiting discovery but a way of framing conceptions of reality [such that the] politics of scale may often take the form of contending *framings.*" In presenting the case study below, then, I analyze the "framing practices" which shaped the dynamics of the dispute over the Shintech facility and which comprised the politics of scale as they related to issues of environmental racism and (in)justice. The Shintech siting dispute is particularly significant because it drew national interest – ultimately involving the United States Environmental Protection Agency – as a test case for the concept of "environmental justice," a relatively new notion which has gained widespread attention during the past decade or so. Yet, as soon became clear to those opposed to construction of the plant, operationalizing such a concept posed some difficult spatial and political problems related to geographical scale. It is this aspect of the case – the politics of geographical scale associated with actually defining what constitutes "environmental racism" and "environmental (in)justice" – that I examine here, for the geographical scale at which such issues were framed was central to the politics of the dispute, as both opponents and proponents sought to frame the debate in scalar terms which they deemed most favorable to their interests.

The Problem of Conceptualizing Environmental Justice

The problem of conceptualizing environmental justice, and how to go about achieving it, is a deeply scaled issue in contemporary politics. Calls for environmental justice suggest that the current distribution of environmental hazards (noxious industrial facilities and waste sites) among communities of color and/or low-income communities is inequitable and in need of change. The notion of an inequitable distribution of health-threatening pollution raises both distributive and procedural questions about the geographic and political scale(s) at which inequity should be measured and addressed. First, if the burden imposed on a community by a given noxious facility is argued to constitute a disparate impact, then the question must be asked, in comparison to what (Zimmerman 1994)? Across what geographic scale should environmental equity be measured (Bowen et al. 1995; Cutter et al. 1996; McMaster et al. 1996), and by what criteria? Second, if disparate burdens are imposed on particular communities, then which social, political, and/or economic processes can be implicated in the creation of those patterns on the one hand, and their mitigation or resolution on the other? At what political scale can, and should, environmental inequity be addressed and resolved (Zimmerman 1994; Lake 1996)?

Significantly, quantitative measures of environmental inequity have highlighted different axes of inequality at different scales of resolution and analysis, pointing to racial disparities at some scales and to class-based disparities at others. Such differences in findings are politically significant, because to make a claim of environmental racism is a quite different political project than to argue for the existence of class-based environmental inequities. As Pulido (1996) has pointed out, a basic legal framework exists for protecting the civil rights of racially identified groups of people. By comparison, there is little to protect the rights of poor people in quite the same way. Analytical scale, then, can be used instrumentally to represent quite different social grievances arising out of the same set of social conditions – constituting the scale of analysis at one spatial resolution may highlight racism, while constituting it at another may highlight class oppression. While a partial strategic response to these different findings has been to broaden the environmental justice movement to encompass different axes of inequality/injustice (UCC 1987, 1991), the "race versus class" debate (Pulido 1996) has nevertheless generated political tensions within the environmental justice movement and posed strategic difficulties to movement activists.

At the same time, the effect of different analytical scales on measures of environmental inequity is not the entire story of how scale matters to the politics of environmental justice. Scale also matters in the realm of environmental justice activism because, as Capek (1993: 5) notes:

> "Environmental justice" can be understood as a conceptual construction, or interpretive "frame" (Snow et al 1986), fashioned simultaneously from the bottom up (local grassroots groups discovering a pattern to their grievances) and from the top down (national organizations conveying the term to local groups).

Indeed, calls for environmental justice exhibit a complex coalescence of scale perspectives on the problem of the disparate impacts of pollution. Thus, the notion of environmental injustice juxtaposes, on the one hand, localized experiences of exposure to industrial toxins with, on the other, a recognition that broader social and political processes may be responsible for the spatial patterns of exposure to environmental hazards which are disproportionately experienced by particular vulnerable populations (Harvey 1996). Put another way, polluting industrial facilities are challenged by environmental justice activists not only because direct proximity to toxic emissions appears to have adverse effects on human health and the environment, but *also* because such adverse effects in a given locale are construed as part of a broader social and geographical pattern of discrimination against people of color and/or people of low income. At the level of grassroots environmental justice activism, neither the local nor the "larger-than-local" scale is wholly privileged over the other. Rather, we have embedded in a single concept quite differently scaled understandings of the issue.

Oddly, while the problem of scale has been raised in quantitative analyses of environmental equity (Bowen et al. 1995; Bryant and Mohai 1992; Cutter et al. 1996; Greenberg 1993; McMaster et al. 1997), it has been largely overlooked in the qualitative, or process-oriented, environmental justice research in geography (but see Lake 1996). Theorizations of the problem of environmental injustice invariably foreground social processes operating at different scales, ranging from local labor and housing markets (Pulido et al. 1996) to federal regulation regimes (Heiman 1996; see also Lake and Disch 1992), but rarely do they foreground the problem of scale itself. Yet, significantly, different interpretations of the social grievance of environmental injustice encompass conditions, events, practices, and processes operating at a range of geographic scales. That is to say, interpretations of the meaning of environmental (in)justice are subject to "contending framings" (Delaney and Leitner 1997) at different scales – what may appear just at one scale may appear quite unjust at another. The concept of frames and the process of framing is the point where my attempt to understand the politics of environmental justice and to theorize the politics of scale converge.

Of Scale Frames and Counter-scale Frames

The concept of collective action frames (Snow and Benford 1992) has been well developed in social movements research and is used to refer to framings of reality, or sets of beliefs, which guide and legitimate social movement activities and campaigns. Collective action frames serve three interrelated functions: naming, blaming, and claiming. First, they name a grievance by "underscor[ing] and embellish[ing] the seriousness and injustice of a social condition or redefin-[ing] as unjust and immoral what was previously seen as unfortunate but perhaps tolerable" (Snow and Benford 1992: 137). Second, they blame someone for the grievance, attributing blame or causality for the problem in order to mobilize a collective response to an injustice. Third, collective action frames make claims about response and recompense, suggesting one or more solutions to the problem.[1]

The recognition that social grievances are strategically constructed by social movement organizations, in conjunction with recognition that the problem of environmental justice can be framed differently at different geographic and political scales, suggests that geographic scale plays an important role in the articulation of environmental justice-related collective action frames. In the remainder of this chapter, I develop an understanding of scale-oriented collective action frames, or *scale frames*, as a central practice in the politics of environmental justice. Scale frames are conceptualized as a type of collective action frame that does the work of "naming, blaming, and claiming," all with central reference to, and differentiation by, particular geographic scales. Components of scale frames parallel components of collective action frames more generally. For each of the functions of the scale frame, the reference to scale is a significant source of the frame's effectiveness – the explanation of a social problem, the attribution of causality, and the suggestion of a remedy rely for their meaning, effectiveness, and force on the central reference to social relations organized at particular scales. For example, the very concept of environmental racism introduces the outlines of a "generic" scale frame employed in political struggles for environmental justice. In order for a protest group to claim that a potential facility siting would comprise an act of environmental racism, they must frame local conditions as part of a broader spatial distribution of disproportionate numbers of noxious facilities near people and communities of color. Their grievance cannot fully take form until and unless they reference the facility siting to patterns and/or processes that are discernible at broader spatial scales. It remains open to question, of course, which scales the authors of any given version of the generic scale frame would invoke, and in what way.

I refer to the several possibilities for invoking geographical or political scale in the construction of scale frames as multiple *expressions of scale*. Scale as an analytical category is one of these expressions of scale, and obviously plays an important role in political debates over the existence and character of environmental inequity/injustice

(McMaster et al. 1997; Bowen et al. 1995; Cutter et al. 1996). Not only can patterns of inequity be made to appear and disappear at different scales of resolution and analysis, but in the context of a given dispute some spatial characterization must be made of the affected community. While spatial analyses tend to use existing administrative and data collection districts such as counties, zip codes, and census tracts, noxious facilities are not always located conveniently at the center of either experientially or analytically identified communities. Zimmerman (1994) and Cutter (1996), for example, raise the issue of edge effects in GIS-based analysis – how does the GIS analyst proceed when a noxious facility is located at the edge of an administrative or data collection district? Likewise, how does the GIS analyst treat those people who live just beyond an administrative or data collection boundary, but who are still within a relatively short radius of a noxious facility?

Here is where it is important to move beyond the limited notion of scale as analytical category, and to situate geographic and political scales in the realm of social experience. As a second expression of scale, then, I examine the deployment of scale as a means of inclusion, exclusion, and legitimation, as introduced by Herod (1991). At the heart of many environmental justice disputes are competing efforts to characterize the impacted population in sociospatial terms of both demographic characteristics and proximity to a given noxious facility. Any given characterization of the impacted population necessarily includes some people while excluding others. Meanwhile, spatial analysts' predilection for describing disparately impacted communities in terms of administrative and data-collection districts does not always resonate with community members' own experience and characterizations of the affected community. Lived communities often stretch across the boundaries between such districts, and grassroots activists have their own rationales for drawing sociospatial lines of inclusion and exclusion in the affected community, lines which may or may not coincide neatly with spatial analyses of their circumstances. In drawing these lines, however, community activists must nonetheless engage with the spatial extent of the aggrieved community in some way or other and, in so doing, deploy an expression of scale as a means of inclusion and legitimation. In particular, the "race versus class" debates play out in this context, as community activists make strategic decisions about how to characterize both the social demographics and spatial extent of the aggrieved population.

The third expression of scale examined here is scale as a territorial framework for power within the various levels of the nation-state (or beyond). Political struggles over environmental justice take place largely within the context of environmental regulatory processes. While in the United States states have steadily achieved more authority for the enforcement of environmental laws and regulations under the "new federalism" of the past two decades, the US Environmental Protection Agency's (US EPA) 1994 Presidential mandate to address environmental justice concerns counteracts that trend, and underscores the remaining federal authority over states' regulatory actions.[2] Such a reversal creates new tensions between state and federal government agencies over both the parameters of environmental justice and the positioning of the US EPA as a potential arbiter of environmental justice siting disputes.

Significantly, any given scale frame leveraged by environmental justice activists can be contested in various ways by the protesters' opponents in political struggle. In this research, I conceptualize efforts to contest the protesters' scale frames as *counter-scale frames*. Counter-scale frames are not collective action frames *per se*, but work to counter or undermine one or more elements of the scale-oriented collective action frames. They could be targeted at one or more of the components of a scale frame and also at one or more expressions of scale that lend the scale frame its force, meaning, and effectiveness. That is to say, counter-scale frames could target and undermine activists' spatial construction of the aggrieved population, the spatial extent of the problem articulated by the frame, or the geographic scale at which a solution is suggested by the scale frame.

In this framework, several scale frames and counter-scale frames may shape key moments in a controversy. The original scale frame may have to be redefined and recast in defensive response to the deployment of counter-scale frames. Drawing upon such a conceptual framework, then, in what follows I examine how various social actors deployed, countered, and adjusted their scale frames and counter-scale frames as part of a politics of scale during the course of the Shintech siting dispute.

Scalar Praxis and the Shintech Dispute

In 1996, Shintech, Inc., the US subsidiary of the Japanese Shin-Etsu Chemical Company, announced its intentions to build a $700 million integrated PVC production facility in rural Convent, St. James Parish, Louisiana. St. James Parish is centrally located along Louisiana's 84–mile long Mississippi River Industrial Corridor, a part of the state which at the time was already home to 137 petrochemical facilities (see figure 9.1). The Convent site offered the company excellent access to raw materials, transportation, and markets for byproducts, as well as economies of scope by virtue of being in the center of the Corridor. Louisiana economic development officials were eager to woo the facility to St. James Parish and offered the company substantial tax incentives to locate there. If built, the Shintech facility would employ 2,000 construction workers for two years, and then 165 technicians to run the plant, and another 90 maintenance workers to maintain it. The company applied for parish and state environmental permits during the summer of 1996, and expected to break ground in November of the same year.

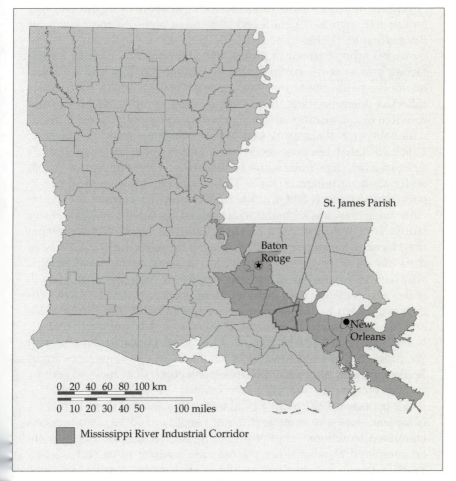

Figure 9.1 Location of Mississippi River Industrial Corridor and St. James Parish

The announcement that Shintech planned to build the plant was met with mixed reactions, spurring hope of jobs among some, and fears of environmental degradation and environmental racism/injustice among others. St. James Parish is already home to 10 major industrial facilities, 8 of which are petrochemical production facilities. The parish has ranked third highest in toxic air emissions in Louisiana's Toxic Release Inventory (TRI) for several years, and Louisiana has vied with Texas for the highest state-wide toxic releases on the federal TRI over the same period. According to the 1990 US Census, 49 percent of parish residents were African-Americans, while only 33 percent of population of the state as a whole was African-American. Parish residents were predominantly low-income, and parish unemployment levels hovered between 10 and 14 percent throughout the 1990s.

A local group formed to protest the environmental permits for the facility and took the name St. James Citizens for Jobs and Environment. From the start, the local oppositional group faced a scale-inflected dilemma. First, they were a small group, with no existing resource or organizational base, preparing to face off against a multinational chemical company that had an enormous resource base, one which included lawyers, consultants, and a public relations firm. It soon became clear that Shintech also enjoyed the support of parish and state government officials. The Louisiana Department of Environmental Quality (LDEQ) drafted environmental permits for the facility on a "fast-track" basis, while Louisiana Governor Mike Foster would later weigh in on the side of Shintech. Second, the problem they faced – the potential siting of a ninth petrochemical facility in their parish – originated in political and economic relationships which were organized at far broader scales than the parish itself, scales well beyond their control. State economic development officials were keen to add another petrochemical facility to the Corridor and the Louisiana Department of Economic Development had attracted Shintech's parent company to the St. James Parish site with the promise of tax incentives and a non-adversarial regulatory environment. Third, the local group's perception that they would be unduly burdened – indeed, overburdened – with pollution by Shintech's proposed PVC plant would eventually require them to make a comparative case of some sort. Local people would be overburdened compared to whom? The local environment would be overburdened compared to what other places? The need for some sort of comparison raised the question of the spatial extent over which such comparisons should be made. Should the people of Convent compare themselves to the rest of St. James Parish? Or should they compare themselves and their burden of pollution to the state of Louisiana as a whole? Each of these potential bases for comparison effectively constructed different decision-making problems, and had different political implications.

Significantly, by naming their protest organization "St. James Citizens for Jobs and the Environment" (henceforth, "St. James Citizens"), the local group framed the terms of the debate over the proposed facility in a way which transcended their locally experienced concerns on several levels at once. In so doing, they set the stage for discursively scaling-up the magnitude of the dispute through building strategic alliances with larger and more established organizations. The naming of the protest organization and the rhetoric with which the protesters justified their "jobs *and* the environment" stance, then, served as the initial scale frame deployed in the Shintech controversy.

The jobs and environment scale frame

> When we develop our economy based solely on petrochemicals, chemical industries that produce chemicals that are killing people, including the workers in there, we're saying "yes, you can have a job, but in order to have that you have to be willing to sacrifice your health, your lives, and the lives of your family." That's inhumane. That's not about dignity. That's stripping people of their dignity... Whoever said that economic development is synonymous with chemical, industrial development? Nobody, except the State of Louisiana and Texas! (*Interview, member, St. James Citizens*)

Opponents of the Shintech plant sought to argue that the facility's construction represented an unhealthy path of economic development which was being fostered by Louisiana economic development officials' overemphasis on the petrochemical industrial development and expansion. Expecting that state government officials would try to frame the debate in terms of "jobs *or* the environment," activists instead framed their position as one in which they asserted they were "for" both *jobs and environment*. In so doing, they sought to reject the zero-sum assumption that job creation in Louisiana must necessarily entail environmental degradation, while environmental protection must result in negative economic effects. State economic development officials had long justified any environmental and health impacts of a concentrated petrochemical sector by invoking the need to increase the number of relatively high-paying jobs in the state economy, and by denying the severity of any health or environmental impacts. In the local activists' view, state-level decision-makers could afford to make such claims because they were physically removed from the reality of a cumulative burden of industrial pollution. By arguing that the Shintech plant represented the wrong type of economic development – economic development which would exacerbate environmental pollution in their community – local activists were attempting to insert their *local* experiences of environmental degradation and lack of what they considered to be appropriate types of economic development into *state-level* policy discussions. In so doing, they sought to secure for the local community greater decision-making power over its own economic future.

In highlighting the tension between state policies and their impacts as felt at the scale of the parish, the organization's name *St. James* Citizens for Jobs and Environment drew on an expression of scale as a territorial framework for power. While the economic development policies highlighted by this frame had repercussions throughout the river corridor and in other parts of Louisiana, the frame narrowed the focus of debate over economic development to the implications for St. James Parish in particular. At the same time, focusing on the scale of the parish entailed broadening the scope of the controversy from the immediate vicinity of the proposed industrial facility. If built, the Shintech site, as are most of the existing petrochemical facilities, would be located on the east bank of the Mississippi River, in the community of Convent (Convent would be spatially represented as zip code 70723 during the controversy). The group could, then, have called itself "Convent Residents," "Citizens of Convent," or even "Mothers of Convent." But by calling itself the "*St. James* Citizens," the local group strategically referenced those dimensions of their social identities that invited broader (parish-wide) participation in the protest group. The scale frame's reference to the parish as a whole also underscored the Shintech protesters' position that adverse impacts of the facility included *both* the localized exposure to toxic industrial emissions which would be felt close to the plant site, *and* the concurrent problems of a lack of healthful opportunities for employment and economic development, a problem experienced by people throughout the entire parish.

The other part of the organization's name, the St. James *Citizens* for Jobs and Environment, located part of the solution to the problem in the rights and privileges of citizenship. The group's identification as citizens implicitly referenced the national scale at which citizenship is conferred, and resonated with the action directly available to the Shintech protesters, that being to make full use of federal provisions for citizen participation written into the environmental permitting process. As they geared up to intervene in this process, the St. James Citizens networked with a prominent statewide environmental organization (the Louisiana Environmental Action Network [LEAN]) and a community-organizing assistance group (the Labor Neighbor Project), and thereby tapped into significant technical assistance and organizing resources. In addition, members of other river parish community groups that were taking issue with corporate polluters and the Louisiana Department of Environmental Quality's (LDEQ) environmental permitting practices joined the St. James Citizens' protest campaign within the LEAN. Working closely with this network of activists, the St. James Citizens educated themselves about the environmental permitting process, kept abreast of the permits applications that Shintech filed with the LDEQ and the Coastal Zone Commission (CZC), and searched for public interest legal representation.

However, while the St. James Citizens for Jobs and Environment frame signaled the Shintech protesters' readiness to address the larger-than-local implications of siting the Shintech facility in St. James Parish, the frame also contained a fundamental limitation. Specifically, as the battle lines were forming over the state-issued environmental permits, the frame constructed the LDEQ officials as both wrongdoers and the decision-makers who could possibly provide a solution. The LDEQ was, after all, the agency responsible for fostering the state's widely touted non-adversarial regulatory environment. Yet, the jobs and environment frame did not offer a compelling reason for LDEQ officials to act on the St. James Citizens' behalf, because the siting controversy presented a problem which was beyond the administrative scope of the agency – the LDEQ routinely only dealt with environmental regulation, and not with job provision *per se*. State-level officials would remain part of the problem and would not be tempted to become a willing part of the solution sought by the protest group.

By the end of 1996, then, it had become apparent that the St. James Citizens would need legal representation in order to extend their strategy beyond the provisions for citizen participation in the environmental permitting process. In November 1996, the Tulane Environmental Law Clinic agreed to take on the St. James Citizens as a client. The St. James Citizens, their lawyers in the Clinic, and a coalition of other grassroots and environmental groups would now work to invoke formally the concept of environmental justice as a central part of their protest campaign. Doing so would enable the protest coalition to activate federal oversight of the siting dispute.

The environmental justice scale frame

The environmental justice movement has been successful at directing federal attention to environmental disparities among social groups. President Clinton's 1994 Executive Order 12898 directed the US EPA and other federal agencies to mitigate adverse health and environmental impacts on low-income and minority communities. Convent, Louisiana, actual site of the proposed Shintech facility, was just such a community. While the material implications of Executive Order 12898 remained somewhat ambiguous, federal agencies had also been directed by President Clinton to enforce their regulations under Title VI of the Civil Rights Act of 1964. Title VI mandates that no entity receiving federal funds shall engage in practices which have disparate impacts upon groups identified by race, color, or national origin. Given that state environmental agencies receive federal funds, the US EPA could review state environmental permitting decisions for their cumulative impact on groups identified by race, color, or national origin. Invoking Title VI, the Shintech protest coalition argued that the Shintech facility would exacerbate the intolerably high cumulative impacts of pollution in St. James Parish and that the LDEQ's environmental permitting practices violated Title VI, thereby abrogating community members' civil rights.

The formal articulation of an environmental justice frame in Title VI petitions for US EPA intervention represented a central attempt on the part of the Shintech protesters to overcome the scale disparities that had characterized this conflict from the outset.[3] The environmental justice frame fundamentally altered the social relationships between disputants in the case by reining in the decision-making power of state officials while enlarging the potential base of grassroots and organizational support for the Shintech protest campaign. State officials were no longer at the top of the decision-making hierarchy but, instead, were being asked to account for their actions to the US EPA. The Title VI petition identified the problem as the cumulative burden of pollution on people of color in the nearby community. With the foregrounding of racial disparities and the invocation of environmental justice, local protesters were no longer fighting a battle confined to a rural Louisiana parish. Rather, their struggle became implicated in the larger scope of social protest over environmental racism and injustice across the country. Many other existing environmental justice and civil rights organizations, as well as industry trade groups and state regulators in other states, would now have reason to take interest in the case.

An effective collective action frame would require a clear and unambiguous target of blame or causality. Formal constraints on the US EPA's involvement required this target to be the state-level environmental permitting agency. Accordingly, the environmental justice frame targeted the actions of the LDEQ and the agency's role in creating a disparate impact of pollution on St. James Parish's African-American community. If successful, the environmental justice frame would result in the state-issued permits for the facility being revoked and, very possibly, in some sort of reprimand of the LDEQ. In addition, activating US EPA oversight on the basis of environmental justice would also set an extremely important precedent for environmental justice activism across the country, a precedent which had the potential to upset the balance of power between federal and state environmental agencies, and between regulators and those sectors of industry under environmental regulation.

The environmental justice frame relied on multiple expressions of scale for its effectiveness. First, adhering to a series of scale-defined parameters required by the US EPA, the frame drew on an expression of scale as a means of delimiting inclusion and legitimacy. The Title VI petition used a four-mile buffer around the center of the proposed Shintech facility to describe the impacted community. Six facilities fall within this four-mile radius, which reported a cumulative 7,207,478 pounds of toxic air emissions to the 1996 Toxic Release Inventory.[4] Reference to these six other facilities emphasized the St. James Citizens' concern with a cumulative burden, and not simply with the emissions of the Shintech facility by itself. While maintaining a focus on the cumulative burden, the Title VI petition altered the description of the impacted community. Significantly, the use of the four-mile buffer increased the percentage of African-Americans among the people who would be impacted by the facility, compared to the Shintech protesters' earlier representation of the entire parish as the affected community. Some 81 percent of the population living within the four-mile buffer was African-American, almost twice as great as the proportion of the parish at large. While the St. James Citizens maintained a collective identity as a racially diverse group, this tactic made strategic use of the racially marked social identities of a majority of both the group's membership and of the impacted community described in the petition. Indeed, while the petition still identified the affected community as predominantly African-American and predominantly low-income, it did not suggest that the US EPA has a responsibility to act on behalf of low-income communities. Instead, the US EPA's responsibilities invoked under Title VI applied explicitly and exclusively to discrimination on the basis of race, color, or national origin (TELC 1997).

Second, the Title VI petition activated a politically scaled oversight and funding relationship between the federal and state agencies. By definition, a Title VI complaint needs to be directed against the actions of a recipient of federal funds. State-level environmental agencies receive federal funds and have been the most frequent targets of Title VI petitions with the US EPA (US EPA 1998). As with the earlier complaint, the petition addressed both the distributive effects of LDEQ's actions and procedural concerns about LDEQ's conduct during the permitting process. The petition argued that by issuing Shintech's environmental permits, it was the LDEQ which had effectively chosen the site of the proposed facility. LDEQ's actions in this regard were thus brought unequivocally back to the racial demographics of that population. The petition argued that LDEQ's permitting of the facility "in such an overburdened minority area would have the effect, if not the purpose, of discriminating against the complainants and their membership, as well as other minority individuals, because of their race or color" (TELC 1997: 3). In so doing, the LDEQ would violate the provisions of Title VI by adding to the toxic burden borne by the already disparately impacted minority community.

Third, by arguing that both the LDEQ and the US EPA should take cumulative emissions into account in order to address issues of environmental justice, the Title VI petition raised the question of the spatial scale(s) at which cumulative emissions should be measured and compared. Should the LDEQ measure and consider cumulative emissions on a parish-by-parish basis, or should it expand its evaluation to cover larger units (perhaps a parish and those adjacent to it)? If so, by which criteria should the additional parishes be included? Should cumulative emissions be measured according to administrative units at all? How should circular buffers be employed in this process? The Title VI petition did not resolve these questions but suggested, instead, that new scales of analysis needed to be produced by these state agencies.

The formalization of the environmental justice frame represented a shift from the original jobs and environment frame, a shift located largely in the differences in how the two frames drew on, and articulated, different expressions of scale. The problem represented by the jobs and environment frame was that residents of St. James Parish were experiencing a high burden of chemical emissions and few benefits in terms of employment opportunities. The scale of experience (Taylor 1982) of the problem was defined by the administrative boundaries of the parish. By contrast, the problem represented by the formal environmental justice frame was that residents of the north-western part of the parish, in the immediate vicinity of at least six existing petrochemical facilities, were disparately burdened with industrial pollution. Specifically, the concentration of chemical emissions in that area meant that industrial pollution was disproportionately felt by the low-income and predominantly African-American community. The scale of experience in this frame was defined by mathematical boundaries (the four-mile radius around the centroid of the proposed Shintech facility). Thus, while the jobs and environment frame posed the problem at the scale of the parish (227 square miles in area), the environmental justice frame scaled down the manifestation of the problem to a four-mile radius around the proposed facility in the northwestern section of St. James Parish – an area covering just 50.3 square miles (see figure 9. 2). The

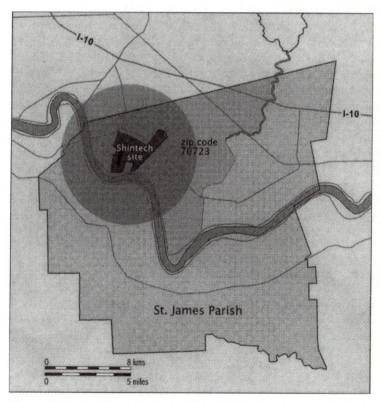

Figure 9.2 Location of proposed Shintech facility, showing 4-mile radius from center of the site

environmental justice frame also changed the demographics of the impacted community. Whereas the jobs and environment frame included all residents of the (larger) parish, the environmental justice frame prioritized the high proportion of people of color within the (smaller) area of the plant's immediate vicinity.

Significantly, however, while the environmental justice frame narrowed the spatial scope of the manifestation of the problem, it broadened the spatial scope of the implications of the problem. Whereas the jobs and environment frame invited participation in social action by all residents of the parish and others concerned about economic development practices in Louisiana, the environmental justice frame invited social action by people and organizations working against racism, for the protection of civil rights, and for environmental justice, both in Louisiana and elsewhere. Many such organizations were national in scope, if not in influence. Creating the possibility for strategic alliances with these organizations was one way in which the Shintech protesters scaled up the scope of the controversy. At the same time, the environmental justice frame no longer directly included the whole of St. James Parish in the aggrieved population. Thus, it prioritized political and decision-making relationships at larger scales over social relationships at the local scale.

In terms of the locally affected community, the shift in scale frames transposed an originally all-inclusive construction of the affected community into a demographically defined group within the protesters' originally imagined "community." Doing so gave the protesters an important edge in the larger political arena. Indeed, it expanded the political arena well beyond the confines of the Louisiana state apparatus. At the same time, though, it presented a means for the Shintech proponents to try to divide the local protest community along racial lines.

The NAACP counter-scale frame

> Now, here come Ernest Johnson. Ernest Johnson have come to our meetings. He have swore on a stack of Bibles that he's with us all the way. He would not let nothing like that happen to us. But then, he and the Governor come into the area, all of a sudden he's going to get 2.5 million dollars, for some project that he was trying to get into, then he done forgot about us. He done forgot about the little man. All he's thinking about is him getting the 2.5 million dollars! And the way it was explained on the news, he didn't have to worry about accounting for that! (*Interview, member, St. James Citizens*)

Ernest Johnson was the head of the State Chapter of the National Association for the Advancement of Colored People (NAACP). His support as the spokesperson for a longstanding civil rights organization was visibly courted by Louisiana Governor Foster during the late summer of 1997, while disputants in the case awaited the US EPA's decision on the Shintech protesters' environmental justice petition. The Shintech protesters' appeal for US EPA intervention, and the delays they created for Shintech, were an embarrassment to the Governor and to the Department of Economic Development, which had attracted the company to Louisiana in the first place. As more than one commentator noted, many in industry were watching for the outcome of the case. The fear of economic development officials was that "[s]ome people will see this and will cross off Louisiana as a state they will consider" (Secretary of Economic Development Kevin Reilly, cited in Gray 1997).

Earlier in the summer, members of the St. James Citizens and LEAN had met with Johnson and had attended a summit on environmental justice convened by the NAACP at Southern University in Baton Rouge. The Shintech protesters spoke about their concerns and their struggle over the facility. By the end of the summit, the participants had taken an informal vote in support of the Shintech protest group. The annual meeting of the NAACP was coming up in September, and it was expected that the Shintech controversy would then be taken up more formally by the organization. In early August, however, Governor Foster and Johnson toured Romeville (a small unincorporated township within Convent, immediately to the east of the proposed Shintech site), canvassing the neighborhood for support of the Shintech project. Governor Foster had been to the area without Johnson the week before. Now Romeville children reported to their grandmothers: "The Governor's back and he's got a black man with him!" In media reports, Johnson portrayed his involvement at this stage as part of a fact-finding effort, and stressed that the NAACP had not made a decision on the Shintech controversy. Instead, Johnston said he planned to meet with the local chapter of the NAACP and other local organizations and to "issue a report" by the end of the month. In contrast to Johnson's apparent reserve, however, the Governor's advisor on environmental affairs was quoted as remarking that "[Governor Foster] feels like he and Ernest Johnson are on the same page" (Gray and Wardlaw 1997).

In late August, just days before US EPA's expected decision on the Shintech protesters' complaints, Johnson held a press conference at which he averred indecision about the merits of the project. He agreed with Governor Foster that more jobs were needed in St. James

Parish, but also acknowledged that the jobs created by the Shintech facility would be out of the technical reach of the area's African-American residents (Gray and Wardlaw 1997). However, in a rather different public statement made several days later, Johnson came out in support of the Shintech project and remarked that, in his opinion, the predominantly white groups opposing Shintech had little grounds for an environmental justice complaint. A week later, the *Baton Rouge Advocate* reported that the Foster-appointed Louisiana Economic Development Council (LDEC) had approved a $2.5 million loan to the Johnson-led Louisiana Community Development Capital Fund (CAPFUND) on September 5. The news article also noted that the funding for CAPFUND was "pushed by Economic Development Secretary Kevin Reilly over LDEC staff objections to the arrangement" (Shuler 1997). The clear implication of this coverage was that the LDEC funding was used as a strong incentive for Johnson to speak out in favor of the Shintech facility and its promise of jobs for St. James Parish residents.

Governor Foster's apparent attempt to co-opt the spokesperson of a prominent state-level African-American organization was characterized as part of a larger strategy of "divide and conquer" by members of the Shintech protester group and their allies. One of the Tulane lawyers, for example, referred to Johnson's involvement with the dispute in the following way:

> I mean, what was the Governor's strategy? The Governor's strategy in Convent was to go in through enticement of Ernest Johnson, of the NAACP, and try to spin off part of the community, and try to act like, you know, the community really wanted this, and to create that split [to] split the African-American community in the town. (*Interview, Tulane lawyer*)

The significance here is that to garner the support of the head of a prominent civil rights organization was to undermine the legitimacy of the racially diverse St. James Citizens and its efforts to make a claim of environmental racism. Members of St. James Citizens and the broader Shintech protest coalition, both black and white, rejected this effort to split the Citizens. As one African-American member of the group pragmatically observed:

> They keep trying to push to make it a black-white thing. As long as the men in power keep the little black and whites fighting each other, he will stay in power. He has control. But as soon as those, that black and white down at the bottom, realize what's going on, and they join each other . . . they will do everything in the world to try and separate them,

to try to cause confusion. But the thing about it, as long as them black and white stick together, over all that other stuff, they're going to survive, they're going to make it. (*Interview, member, St. James Citizens*)

As a counter-scale frame, then, the Governor's tactic of effectively co-opting the head of the state chapter of the NAACP drew primarily on the expression of scale as a means of inclusion and legitimation. Whereas the Shintech protesters had originally constructed an affected community that was racially diverse and economically marginalized by industry-heavy economic development practices, this representation shifted during the controversy as emphasis was placed on the unwanted impacts upon African-Americans in the community. Such a change in how the St. James Citizens was represented discursively as a group presented an opportunity for proponents of the facility to make distinctions between the interests of white and black members of the protest group for their own counter purposes, and put the protest group on the defensive. The protest group then had to devote energy to maintaining the unity and focus of their group, and to justifying the racial diversity of their membership. Governor Foster's tactic also invoked to some degree a representative authority at the state level, an expression of scale as a territorial framework for power, though in an organizational rather than in a governmental sense. Thus, Johnson's personal support for the Shintech facility carried, temporarily at least, the implication of state-level authority, although the statewide chapter of the NAACP later voted not to take a stand on the Shintech dispute.

In response to this attempt to divide and conquer the racially diverse protest group and broader coalition, the St. James Citizens developed the refrain that they were working to protect "human rights, not civil rights." As a member of the St. James Citizens explained:

We're talking about human rights. I mean, if we're going to go into another country and say 'well, here's some human rights violations, and you can't be doing that' and the UN applied sanctions on another country, then my GOD, what about here? I mean, there are human rights violations here, social justice issues, or injustice, that have taken place. Don't we all have not only the right but the responsibility to speak to it? (*Interview, member, St. James Citizens*)

In drawing attention to their engagement with human rights, the Shintech protesters not only stepped up their discussion of the adverse health effects of petrochemical industry emissions but they also tried to bring the discussion back to the trade-off between poor health and economic development. The Governor's racial divide and conquer strategy had largely succeeded in removing the debate over economic development practices *per se* from center stage in the dispute. Yet the protestors' invocation of a universalist (see Harvey 2000) discourse of "human rights" to describe the disparities experienced in the parish also laid the groundwork for seeking recourse at an international political scale at which human rights abuses are monitored and addressed. However, in September 1998, before that particular tactic could be implemented, Shintech suspended its permit applications for the St. James Parish site.[5]

Conclusion

Whereas many theorizations of the problem of environmental (in)-justice are implicitly predicated on particular scales of analysis (e.g., urban, regional, national), a closer look at the dynamics of an environmental justice conflict suggests that activists themselves make sense of the problem of environmental (in)justice at overlapping geographical and political scales. The concept of scale frames and counter-scale frames provides a means to examine how they do so. In particular, examining environmental justice movement strategies as scale frames offers insight into linkages between discursive political practices and the material conditions of inequality that spur social struggle. Scale frames, as explicated here, are grounded in geographically constituted conditions of inequality. Indeed, references to material conditions at given scales lend the frames their meaning, force, and effectiveness. The discursive inclusion of different populations and geographical areas (for example, all of St. James Parish versus the immediate vicinity of the plant site) in the Shintech protesters' succession of scale frames was not ungrounded political rhetoric but, rather, a means of highlighting different aspects of the material inequalities which burden residents of Louisiana's river parishes with heavy pollution loadings and few opportunities for employment. Similarly, the Shintech proponents' use of a racially divisive counter-scale frame was grounded in a long history of geographically constituted racial divisions. At the same time, scale frames are flexible and can be adjusted to encompass shifting political circumstances in the course of a social dispute. Under the rubric of environmental justice, the articulation of social grievances at a succession of geographic scales enabled activists to draw attention to multiple facets of material inequality.

This analysis here elaborates on Jonas's (1994) formulation of scale politics, while also addressing Delaney and Leitner's (1997) concern with elucidating the social practices that comprise politics of scale. The deployment of scale frames and counter-scale frames is a social practice that grounds political discourse in particular conditions constituted at particular geographic scales. Used, as in the Shintech case, to frame a social grievance at successively "larger" geographic scales and to garner federal oversight of a siting dispute, scale frames are seen here as social practices which effectively "harness powers and instrumentalities at other scales" (Jonas 1994: 258). More generally, the concept of scale frames highlights the ways in which multiple experiences, expressions, and representations of political and geographical scale are the province not only of politicians and spatial analysts, but also of everyday social actors engaged in political struggle. In this way, scale is retheorized as an instrument of power, strategically constructed and deployed in order to reproduce some power relations while challenging others.

Meanwhile, the political implications of scale frames and counter-scale frames as tools of collective action extend beyond the Shintech case. Countless struggles for social justice around the globe question the distribution of social burdens and benefits. The "contemporary whirlpool" (Swyngedouw 1997: 167) of political, cultural, and economic transformation demands of social justice praxis that the unjust distribution of social burdens and benefits be understood in the context of tremendous scalar flux. The concepts of scale frames and counter-scale frames offer insight into how activists might pursue social justice by articulating linkages between material local conditions and the myriad social forces operating at broader geographic scales.

NOTES

1 Snow and Benford (1992: 137) refer to these two attributional functions as diagnostic and prognostic functions, wherein the diagnostic function of a collective action frame is directed at "problem identification" and the prognostic function addresses "problem resolution."
2 President Clinton's Executive Order 12898, signed February 11, 1994, directed all federal agencies to devise protocols by which to ensure that each agency's programs and policies do not contribute to a disparate burden of pollution upon low-income communities and communities of color. Of course, it remains to be seen how the new Bush administration will act in this regard.
3 The Tulane Environmental Law Clinic filed three consecutive environmental justice petitions, successively refining their environmental justice argument. When the third petition, dated July 16, 1997, was filed, the

previous petitions were effectively retracted. This discussion concerns only the July 16 Title VI petition.

4 These six facilities are Star Enterprise, Air Products, Chevron, Occidental, IMC-Agrico/Uncle Sam, and IMC-Agrico/Faustina.

5 While the company effectively pulled out of the St. James site, it subsequently successfully pursued approval for a scaled-down facility 40 miles upriver.

REFERENCES

Bowen, M., Salling, M., Haynes, K., and Cyran, E. 1995: Toward environmental justice: Spatial equity in Ohio and Cleveland. *Annals of the Association of American Geographers*, 85 (4), 641–63.

Bryant, B. and Mohai, P. 1992: *Race and the Incidence of Environmental Hazards: A Time for Discourse*. Boulder, CO: Westview.

Capek, S. 1993: The environmental justice frame: A conceptual discussion and application. *Social Problems*, 40, 5–24.

Cutter, S., Clark, L., and Holm, D. 1996: The role of geographic scale in monitoring environmental justice. *Risk Analysis*, 16 (4), 517–26.

Delaney, D. and Leitner, H. 1997: The political construction of scale. *Political Geography*, 16 (2), 93–7.

Gray, C. 1997: Law clinic under fire; Foster criticizes Tulane program. *The Times-Picayune*, Aug. 3, p. A1.

Gray, C. and Wardlaw, J. 1997: NAACP delays report on chemical plant location. *The Times-Picayune*, Aug. 22, p. A12.

Greenberg, M. 1993: Proving environmental inequity in siting locally unwanted land uses. *Risk – Issues in Health and Safety*, 4, 235–52.

Harvey, D. 1996: *Justice, Nature and the Geography of Difference*. Cambridge, MA: Blackwell.

Harvey, D. 2000: *Spaces of Hope*. Edinburgh: University of Edinburgh Press.

Heiman, M. 1996: Race, waste and class: New perspectives on environmental justice. *Antipode*, 28 (2), 111–21.

Herod, A. 1991: The production of scale in United States labour relations. *Area*, 23 (1), 82–8.

Herod, A. 1997: Labor's spatial praxis and the geography of contract bargaining in the US east coast longshore industry, 1953–89. *Political Geography*, 16 (2), 145–69.

Jonas, A. 1994: Editorial: The scale politics of spatiality. *Environment and Planning D: Society and Space*, 12, 257–64.

Lake, R. 1996: Volunteers, NIMBYs, and environmental justice: Dilemmas of democratic practice. *Antipode*, 28 (2), 160–74.

Lake, R. and Disch, L. 1992: Structural constraints and pluralist contradictions in hazardous waste regulation. *Environment and Planning A*, 24, 663–81.

Leitner, H. 1997: Reconfiguring the spatiality of power: The construction of a supranational migration framework for the European Union. *Political Geography*, 16 (2), 123–44.

McMaster, R., Leitner, H., and Sheppard, E. 1997: GIS-based environmental equity and risk assessment: Methodological problems and prospects. *Cartography and Geographic Information Systems*, 24 (3), 172–89.

Miller, B. 1994: Political empowerment, local–state relations, and geographically shifting political opportunity structures: Strategies of the Cambridge, Massachusetts peace movement. *Political Geography*, 13 (5), 393–406.

Miller, B. 1997: Political action and the geography of defense investment: Geographical scale and the representation of the Massachusetts Miracle. *Political Geography*, 16 (2), 171–85.

Pulido, L. 1996: A critical review of the methodology of environmental racism research. *Antipode*, 28 (2), 142–59.

Pulido, L., Sidawi, S., and Vos, R. 1996: An archaeology of environmental racism in Los Angeles. *Urban Geography*, 17 (5), 419–39.

Shuler, M. 1997: La. Economic Development Council made promise to Johnson. *The Advocate*, September 14.

Snow, D. and Benford, R. 1992: Master frames and cycles of protest. In A. Morris and C. Mueller (eds.), *Frontiers in Social Movement Theory*. New Haven, CT: Yale University Press, 133–55.

Snow, D., and Rochford, E. Jr., and Worden S., and Benford, R. 1986: Frame alignment process, micromobilization and movement participation. *American Sociological Review*, 51, 464–81.

Swyngedouw, E. 1997: Excluding the other: The production of scale and scaled politics. In R. Lee and J. Wills (eds.), *Geographies of Economies*. London: Arnold, 167–76.

Taylor, P. 1982: A materialist framework for political geography. *Transactions of the Institute of British Geographers*, New Series, 7, 15–34.

TELC (Tulane Environmental Law Clinic). 1997: *Amended Complaint under Title VI of the Civil Rights Act* (July 16).

UCC (United Church of Christ Commission for Racial Justice). 1987. *Toxic Wastes and Race in the United States: A National Report on the Racial and Socio-Economic Characteristics of Communities with Hazardous Waste Sites*. New York: United Church of Christ Commission for Racial Justice.

UCC (United Church of Christ Commission for Racial Justice). 1991: *Principles of Environmental Justice*. [www.igc.apc.org/saepej/Principles.html] (last accessed Nov. 27, 2001).

US EPA (United States Environmental Protection Agency). 1998: *Title VI Administrative Complaint RE: Louisiana Department of Environmental Quality/ Shintech Permit, Draft Demographic Information*. Washington, DC: United States Government.

Zimmerman, R. 1994: Issues of classification in environmental equity: How we manage is how we measure. *Fordham Urban Law Journal*, 21, 633–69.

10

Networks, Governance, and the Politics of Scale: Inter-urban Networks and the European Union

Helga Leitner, Claire Pavlik, and Eric Sheppard

Amongst the multitude of concepts that have been marshaled to try and make sense of the spatial dynamics of globalization, both "scale" and "networks" have begun to play a prominent role. With regard to the former, arguments concerning the nature of, and prospects for, globalization have often been focused around how various scales of governance are perhaps being reconstructed (Kelly 1999). Four positions on globalization and scale have been prominent. First, there are those (e.g., Ohmae 1990) who would have us believe that globalization is an inexorable process whereby nation-states will disappear as effective units of governance, and whereby local livelihoods will increasingly be dominated by global-scale processes. Such arguments, in effect, maintain that global-scale processes and institutions are coming to dominate all other scales of governance. Second, there are writers (e.g., Hirst and Thompson 1999) who, though they would not go quite this far, nevertheless do maintain that the world is becoming increasingly dominated by regionally defined, supranational entities of governance such as the European Union (EU). Third, in contrast, there are some (e.g., Weiss 1998) who argue that the nation-state remains important as a facilitator of, and an agent structuring, globalization and that the dominance of the nation-state as a scale of governance is little diminished. Finally, there are others (e.g., Jessop 1997) who suggest that globalization is creating new geographical dynamics in which localities are becoming more, rather than less, important as nation-states are "hollowed out" through the transfer of power both "upward" to supranational institutions such as the EU, and "downward" to subnational regions and cities – what Swyngedouw (1997) calls the "glocalization" of governance.

The concept of networks is also popular among globalization theorists. Manuel Castells (1996) argues that globalization is associated with no less than the "rise of the network society" (populated by distinctive social institutions such as "network firms"), which is resulting in a certain deterritorialization of governance – a replacement of the space of places with the space of flows (see also Mattelart 2000). Held et al. (1999) argue that globalization is associated with the extension, deepening, speeding up, and increased impact of global networks. Telecommunications networks, in particular, are seen as central to the global integration of finance markets and commodity chains, and are also often viewed as facilitating the global diffusion and homogenization of cultural norms and discourses (though see Barber 1995). At the other extreme (in scale terms), researchers have lauded localized networks associated with such prospering nodes of the global economy as Silicon Valley and the City of London financial district as a way of "holding down the global" (Amin and Thrift 1992, 1994). In this view, the governance and innovation provided through localized networks can guard localities against the vicissitudes of global capital flows.

Curiously, despite such parallel discussions of globalization and scale, and of globalization and networks, to date there has been little attempt to examine the relationship between networks and scale. In this chapter, we seek to remedy this neglect. We begin by summarizing the main tenets of what is now a large, multidisciplinary literature on networks – a literature which has resulted in what could be described as a current preoccupation with networks and their emancipatory possibilities as a mode of coordination and governance.[1] We then discuss how scale is a relevant aspect of networks, how the distinctive geography of networks poses challenges to current conceptualizations of the politics of scale, and whether network modes of governance can be considered an alternative to hierarchies or whether they need to be understood in relation to hierarchies. In the third section, we examine inter-urban networks in the EU to illustrate how networks are scaled and to demonstrate how network modes of governance are both articulated with hierarchical modes of governance and are part and parcel of the politics of scale.

Theorizing Networks

In the past 20 years, network perspectives have become pervasive in social science disciplines. While various perspectives have distinct histories of development within different disciplines, they are becoming increasingly intertwined as they are blended in research, analysis, and policy applications. In this section, we examine network perspectives on economic exchange, policy formation, social interaction, and the establishment of dominant discourses. In particular, we suggest that optimistic viewpoints held by proponents of economic and policy networks have been particularly influential in the promotion of transnational urban networks, while sociological perspectives on social networks and actor-networks afford relevant vantage points from which to assess the normative claims of network advocates, as well as the growth of network-based public policy initiatives.

Networks in economic geography and regional development

Since the early 1980s, attention in the economic geography and regional development literatures has shifted away from a focus on large corporations, as either linchpins of economic growth or as agents of deindustrialization, and towards small- and medium-sized business enterprises (SMEs) as sources of economic stability and growth. This shift has entailed increased interest in exploring how SMEs serve as nodes within economic networks in which firms are linked through formal business arrangements such as contracts and participation in trade organizations, as well as through informal social contacts between individuals at different firms. This representation of interfirm arrangements as networks of production has been used to study both economically robust regions as spaces in which social and cultural practices support and enable comparative economic success, as well as specific production complexes and the relationship between contractual and cooperative requirements of production and the spatial arrangement of cooperating firms.

Examinations of both robust regions and production complexes have tended to use indicators of comparative success as criteria for the selection of case studies. Regions such as Emilia-Romagna and Baden-Württemberg, for example, have stood out as areas that retained industrial employment during a period of deindustrialization and economic decline in other traditionally industrial areas (Piore and Sabel 1984; Herrigel 1993). The perceived economic durability of such regions has led to a focus on the organization of their local industrial activities, social institutions, culture, and labor practices in order to identify how they have succeeded while other regions have failed. Regions that have emerged as "technopoles" of new industrialization also have been examined as exemplars of regional success, leading to case studies of their industrial clusters and production arrangements (for example, Castells and Hall 1994). A particular emphasis in these studies has been to identify regions with higher degrees of innovation, as indicated by patents, new products, and new production technologies, and then to examine the size, arrangement, and organization of interlinkages among firms within these regions (Scott 1993). In addition, as particular organizational and production practices associated with geographical concentration have emerged as best practice standards in established industries, case studies of localized production networks have examined the exchange and production relations across firms (Kenney and Florida 1993).

Such investigations of regions and industrial complexes have principally drawn upon developments in neo-institutional and evolutionary economics, two areas of heterodoxy within the discipline. In neo-institutional economics, the transaction cost framework developed by Williamson (1985) integrates the bounded rationality of decision-makers with production-linked conditions to create a more realistic approach for the analysis of organizational choice. Directed toward the question of how to organize production, this approach presumes that decision-makers have knowledge of the costs of organizing production within the firm and that they seek to compare internal production to a small number of alternatives, such as market-based procurement and interfirm contracting. Having evaluated the costs of conducting external transactions, of implementing safeguards, and of negotiating potential hazards under each organizational alternative, decision-makers are expected to select the alternative with the lowest total cost. The transaction cost approach has been used to argue that specific features, such as proximity-linked reductions in transaction costs, changes in available communication and transportation infrastructure, or new policy regimes, lead to particular spatial patterns in production (Scott 1998) or to spatial and organizational shifts in production arrangement (Ó hUallacháin and Wasserman 1999).

Williamson's approach, however, cannot be used to explain dynamic economies linked to technological search and learning (particularly when technological change is radical in nature) because it concentrates on selecting the least-cost alternative from among known production arrangements. Thus, when technological change is radical, evolutionary economic approaches, in which search and learning are dynamic aspects of technological change, are preferable. Evolutionary approaches have been drawn upon particularly to examine and portray the conditions under which networks of SMEs are able to outperform larger rivals (Langlois and Robertson 1995; Garud and Kumaraswamy 1993). In such situations, incumbent market leaders are less likely to have relevant resources for continued market dominance. Since market incumbents are likely to select fewer search alternatives than is a group of more numerous smaller firms that are not market leaders, and because incumbents are likely to concentrate on alternatives that are linked to their existing technological capacities, the multiple and more varied searches associated with smaller, though networked, rivals are more likely to include a superior technological alternative. Under conditions of radical technological change, then, networks of smaller firms are more likely to seek out and develop wider ranges of alternative technologies. As a result, networks will tend to be the industrial organization associated with radically new technologies. Case study analyses of innovation regions, in particular, have drawn upon evolutionary arguments to link the region's industrial structure to dynamic learning advantages (see discussions in Langlois and Robertson 1995).

A general spirit of optimism has been linked to discussions of economic networks. They have been viewed as innovative, adaptive, resilient, open, and regenerative economic forms. This view, however, has been challenged by some (Lazonick 1993; Larsson and Malmberg 1999). The tendency to examine successful regions and industrial clusters has meant that traits associated with success have been determined without systematic examination of whether they are only present in successful cases (although exceptions do exist – see Grabher and Stark 1997). If less successful regions have similar characteristics, this would call into question their importance for local economic development. Unfortunately, rigorous comparative analyses of regions do not yet exist. Instead, the tendency has been to seek explanations for success *within* successful regions, rather than to evaluate how a region's embedding within larger social and geographic scales has affected its economic trajectory. Thus, cultural practices and social institutions within successful regions are cited as the explanation for a region's success, implying that the causes of success operate at the same regional scale. In addition, there has been a tendency to assume that the benefits stay within the space occupied by the network and are equitably or evenly shared by network members. Hence, networks often seem to be connected to a sense of economic fairness or economic democracy, even though in reality differences in benefits to network participants are likely to arise, with more powerful network members benefiting more. Finally, networks have been presumed to be an enduring characteristic of the new era, rather than being transitory phenomena (Castells 1996) – although this, too, has been challenged by evidence highlighting the control that large firms continue to enjoy and by their resilience in the marketplace (Harrison 1994; Larsson and Malmberg 1999; Lazonick 1993).

The widely held sense of increased competition and economic uncertainty, and the perception that a new era is emerging, have led network optimists to promote local and regional economic networks as hallmarks of the new economy. Going beyond identifying successful cases of regionally based economic networks, advocates have promoted network-based policies for regional economic development (Cooke 1995; Cooke and Morgan 1993; Scott 1998; Porter 1996). In these approaches, changing a region's economic fortune is seen as less a matter of luring investment into the region's economy from external sources, and more as an issue of identifying and mobilizing endogenous resources internal to the region itself. In so doing, proponents have adapted arguments based on advantages associated with economic networks, namely: efficiency of searching under conditions of uncertainty; ability to innovate, despite small size and lack of access to resources; and greater speed of adaptation. Because these arguments are based on attempting to recreate the characteristics of successful regions in those that are not, they are based on a presumption that the factors generating success have been correctly identified and that their translation to other regions will also result in prosperity.

Policy networks

Over the past decades the idea of policy networks as a means of conceptualizing the relationship between state and society, and of analyzing public policy formation, has gained much currency. While the idea of policy networks originated in the United States in the 1950s and 1960s, much of the recent literature on such networks has emerged in Europe (Marsh 1988a). Major questions addressed in this literature include: what are the characteristics of policy networks?; what distinguishes networks from other modes of governance?; what influences the development and form of policy networks?; and what is their impact on policy outcomes?

The policy network literature has primarily concentrated on examining how interpersonal relations among key actors, together with the structural relations among institutions, shape the way networks operate and affect policy. Much of the formal policy network analysis has concentrated on describing and mapping the components and internal dynamics of policy networks for the purpose of explaining the sectoral and subsectoral policy-making processes and outcomes at the national and supranational scale. For example, a policy network approach has been applied to explain the EU's environmental policy process and outcomes (Bomberg 1998).

Recent academic and public political discourse in Germany and Britain has conferred a variety of positive attributes upon networks, contrasting them favorably with alternative forms of organization in both operation and result. Thus, networks are frequently presented as collective and consensual, unlike hierarchical and market modes of organization and governance. Akin to arguments made by advocates of economic networks, proponents of policy networks also argue that, due to the current context of instability, flux, and contingency, network forms of governance are to be preferred as more dynamic, more flexible, and thus more efficient, modes of decision-making. For example, German scholars argue that, in a world characterized by increasing interdependence and dissolution of the distinction between the state and civil society, policy networks based on nonhierarchical, negotiated self-coordination are a superior mode of governance which are better suited to generate economic growth and resolve social problems than are traditional hierarchical relations of governance (Martin and Mayntz 1991; Mayntz 1994).

Marsh and Rhodes (1992) take a more nuanced position, acknowledging that their characterization of policy networks is an ideal type. They postulate a range of policy networks that vary along a continuum according to a set of characteristics. At one end of the continuum is the policy community which has "a limited number of participants with some groups consciously excluded;...frequent high quality interaction between all members...;...consensus, with the ideology, values and broad policy preferences shared by all participants;...balance of power, not necessarily one in which all members equally benefit but one in which all members see themselves as involved in a positive-sum game; [and in which the] structure of the participating groups is hierarchical so leaders can guarantee the compliance of their members" (Marsh 1998a: 14). At the other end of the continuum is the issue network, which is characterized by "a large number of participants, fluctuating interaction and access for the various members; the absence of consensus and the presence of conflict; interaction based on consultation rather than negotiation or bargaining; [and] an unequal power relationship in which many participants may have few resources, little access and no alternative" (Marsh 1998a: 14). This conceptualization of policy networks illustrates the problematic nature of simply equating the positive attributes mentioned above with network modes of governance. It also suggests that the tendency to present networks as distinctly different to hierarchies and markets, particularly in the German literature, is problematic. As Hay (1998: 39) points out, markets, hierarchies, and networks as different modes of governance "do not exist in isolation, but are necessarily articulated." This argument is substantiated when we confront the representations of network ideals with the practices of actual networks, for policy networks may exhibit hierarchical dominance and involve hegemonic struggles to impose a particular policy conception. Thus, policy networks are linked to, rather than separate from, hierarchical modes of governance.

Within the policy network literature two major issues have emerged: the embeddedness of policy networks in a broader societal context, and the role of network actors in shaping policy networks, their operation, and their policy impact. First, although understanding network formation, network structures, and policy outcomes requires interrogating the broader social, political, and economic context in which they operate, little attention has been paid to the relationship of policy networks to the broader context within which they are embedded (Hay 1998; Marsh 1998a). For example, policy networks often reflect and embody structural inequalities within society along class, gender, and racial lines. These inequalities not only influence who is included and who is excluded from networks, but also affect access to, and control of, resources and thus the actions of network actors. Furthermore, characteristics of a nation's political system – including state structures (e.g., degrees of centralization), organizational configurations, and political party systems – influence network formation, structures, and policy outcomes (Daugbjerg and Marsh 1998). Finally, the study of policy networks must be placed within the context of processes of globalization. Rhodes (1997: 197) identifies four processes which not only limit the autonomy of nation-states, but which also effect change in national state structures and policy networks, these being: "the internationalization of production and financial transactions, international organizations, international law, and hegemonic powers and power blocs." All these contextual factors discussed above influence the origin of networks, their structure, and policy outcomes.

Second, the role and self-understanding of network actors in shaping policy networks, together with the way they operate and affect policy outcomes, has been widely debated. While some policy network analysts have maintained that the pattern of interpersonal relations among key actors, and the bargaining among them, determines policy outcomes (Dowding 1995), others have argued that the crucial elements in policy networks are the structural relationships between institutions within which actors are situated (Rhodes and Marsh 1992). As Marsh (1998b: 194) points out, however, privileging either structures or agents is misguided. Instead, policy networks should be conceptualized "as structures within which agents operate. Agents are, in a sense, 'bearers' of those positions, but they interpret, deconstruct and reconstruct these structures; in this way the relationship between structures and agents is dialectical." Hay (1998) goes further, arguing that we need to pay greater attention to the meaning(s) of networks and networking from the perspective of network participants and the attributes conferred on networks in academic and public policy discourses, rather than imposing an analytical concept of network structures and relations. Examining "the self-understanding of network participants as to the type of organizational conduct in which they are engaged and the type of organizational form which provides the setting for such (inter)action" is important, Hay (1998: 38) suggests, because it "is in part constitutive of the process and practice of networking."

Social network analyses and actor-network approaches

While interest in, and promotion of, economic and policy networks is relatively recent, network perspectives in sociology have a longer history and are less sanguine in their view of networks. Social network perspectives are based on the assumption that human action is affected by the social relations within which actors are embedded. The argument is that social actions cannot be explained by the characteristics of individual actors, or by structural conditions that apply to all actors, but are to be explained, instead, by their relational characteristics – that is to say, how they interact with others. Three approaches have come to dominate this research: social network analysis; social network embeddedness; and actor-network theory. Each approach has posed different answers to some common questions: what is the relationship between social networks and human action?; how are social networks defined?; and what is the relationship between networks, power, and inequality?

Social network analysis was the dominant approach for many years (for a survey see Galaskiewicz and Wasserman 1994). Social network analysis uses line graphs – in which social actors are nodes and social relationships are links between actors – to portray social relationships as a network structure, employing matrix representations of network graphs to measure quantitatively network structure (cf. Chorley and Haggett 1974). Social actors may be individuals or collective social groups such as firms, and the relationships represented by links may be informal contacts or more formal ties such as business contracts. Such approaches do not, however, portray networks as consensual or democratic. Indeed, a theme throughout social network analysis has been that an actor's access to, and control over, resources (including information, people, and materials) increases as social connections increase. Actors' social power can thus be linked to the positions they occupy within the social network. Because actors' strategies are linked to access to resources, those occupying similar positions within a social network are expected to exhibit similar power relations and social behavior. Central or core actors have structural power, whereas less well-connected actors are peripheral to the social relations portrayed. This approach has been applied to a wide variety of problems, including public policy formation, social movements, labor markets, innovation diffusion, corporate interlocking, the operation of consensus and social influence, and inter-organizational dynamics (Wasserman and Faust 1994).

However, social network analysis has come under increasing criticism for its structural bent (Emirbayer and Goodwin 1994; Mizruchi 1994). Specifically, critics have argued that social network analysis treats the network as given and attempts simply to determine whether and how an individual's position within the network affects the degree of influence that can be exerted within it. Network structure, and dominance and inequality stemming from this structure, are emphasized over network change. As a result, critics maintain, social network analysts cannot explain how networks come to be structured as they are and show no interest in the role of cultural norms, discursive understandings, and broader-scale processes in network formation and operation.

Unlike the tendency in social network analysis to analyze how structural position within a single network is related to the strategic actions of each network member, network embeddedness approaches emphasize the richness and variety of multiple networks within which social actors are embedded, as well as the ways in which actors can take advantage of these networks. Granovetter in particular has drawn attention to the "strength of weak ties" by demonstrating how differences in social contact networks lead to strikingly different outcomes in job searches, due not to direct contacts but to flows of information across networks (Granovetter 1985; Granovetter and Swedberg 1992). In addition, perspectives that place actors in multiple networks point to the increased ability that individuals develop as they are embedded within greater varieties of networks. Because social interaction increases an actor's understanding of social contexts and roles, access to a broader variety of networks entails social learning and the potential to control aspects of social interaction. Thus, the dynamism and flexibility of networks is emphasized, as is the ability of individuals to manipulate and modify their networks.

Actor-network theorists take Granovetter's emphasis on flexibility and contingency several steps further (Latour 1987; Law 1992). In their view, individuals can only succeed at what they do by drawing on a complex, ever-changing, heterogeneous network of all the animate and inanimate objects and resources necessary for success. Since all individuals are embedded in such networks, they are all connected together in complex and ever-changing ways, making each co-dependent on the others. The "individuals" in this analysis are conceptualized to include not only other human actors but also the animals, resources, and machines drawn into the network. While some such networks seem so stable as to appear quite fixed, actor-network theorists stress that all such networks are constantly subject to change: "the bits and pieces assembled...into an order are constantly liable to break down, or make off on their own...[S]truggle is central to actor-network theory" (Law 1992: 386). Actor-network theorists seek to understand how such contested systems are held together in a way that makes it seem as if there is no alternative way of doing things and as if powerful individuals occupying the "center of calculation" control the network, even though they do not.

Actor-network theory has been applied to a wide variety of examples, including scientific and technological change, European exploration, nursing practices, and industrial districts. While power hierarchies may emerge, network theorists see their emergence as unpredictable and always contested. They also argue that all the elements in actor-networks are "actants" with potentially equal power to influence collective outcomes, whether these be powerful individuals, their generally overlooked minions, or even animals and machines. They conclude from this that network analysis cannot focus on, say, men, humans, power, or society to the neglect of women, animals, machines, the powerless, or nature. No such hierarchies are predetermined. Instead, they depend on the contingent forces shaping the evolution of actor-networks.[2] In this view, networks are again flexible, inclusive, evolutionary, unpredictable, and essential to the success or failure of all kinds of projects. Yet actor-network theorists make no claims for networks as an ideal form of social organization. Indeed, they have been criticized for applying actor-networks to everything, while avoiding any normative judgments which would differentiate more from less desirable outcomes (cf. Haraway 1997: 34–35).

Summary

Interest in, and use of, network perspectives for evaluating economic, social, and political interactions has grown during the past two decades. In economics, sociology, and political science this reflects increased interest in meso-level analyses and a growing concern with embedding the actions of individuals within a larger context or environment. Notwithstanding different views about the attractiveness of networks and their fixity, these approaches all demonstrate how individual action should be evaluated as connected to, and contingent upon, relative position, rather than as endogenously determined by characteristics of individuals or by macro-level conditions applying to all agents. Networks are also repeatedly invoked to account for geographic differences in the performance of places of different geographic scales (cities, regions, or nations), particularly in the economic geography and regional development literature. Yet, for all the concern for place, the *spatiality* of networks has received little attention. Two aspects in particular are neglected: uneven development and scale.

With regard to the uneven geographical development of networks, a central aspect of social network analysis has been to highlight the tendency toward asymmetric power relationships among network actors. Certain actors are centrally located and have more potential influence over the network as a whole, whereas others are more peripheral. Yet, if this is true within the *social* space of networks, it must also apply to the *geographic* space which networks (such as the EU inter-urban networks discussed below) span to link distant actors. Frequently, actors located in core geographical locations (e.g., prosperous cities and regions) are to be found at the center of the social spaces of networks, whereas those in peripheral geographic locations frequently find themselves in the social periphery. The relationship between social and geographic space also works in the other direction: places where core network actors reside are also likely to benefit more from the network than are those occupied by peripheral network actors. Much recent writing on networks has not paid much attention to network cores and peripheries, largely because the emphasis has been on thinking about networks as spaces of negotiation within which all actors have equal potential influence. However, asymmetric power relations and uneven development are nevertheless a persistent feature of social and geographic space, and are part and parcel of the ways in which actors are relationally connected. Attention to this aspect of the spatiality of networks is thus important if we are to understand social and geographic differentiation.

The second aspect of network spatiality, scale, is the focus of the remainder of this chapter.

Scaling Networks

It is clear that networks operate at different spatial scales. Economic geographers, for example, have examined both local networks (e.g., industrial districts) and global networks (e.g., international financial transactions). The former could be said to be a smaller-scale network than the latter because it is of more limited geographic extent (i.e., it spans a more restricted geographic space). But what is meant by extent? To measure extent as the physical area – for example, the diameter of a network in miles – is problematic and often misleading, for a network spanning 500 miles will often seem smaller to its members than does a network 50 miles across if the actors in the former network are able to communicate via email whereas those in the latter must communicate using the regular mail. In short, distance is a social construct and must be treated as such. In what follows, then, we seek to explore this contention through an examination of the burgeoning literature on the social construction of scale, wherein geographic scale is conceptualized as both a contingent and as an emergent property of sociospatial processes (Smith 1992; Herod 1997; Leitner 1997; Brenner 1998).

Accepting that geographic scales are both the realm and the outcome of struggles for control over economic, political, and cultural space, it becomes clear that the scale of a network is not fixed but is a consequence both of how that network evolves and of other processes shaping its territorial and social extent. Hence, in some cases a network may shift from being national to international through self-originated activities such as enrolling new members from other countries, whereas in other instances it may be external forces operating upon the network which cause it to reorganize its scale of operation –

for instance, any national network connecting Bratislava and Prague became an international network when Czechoslovakia subdivided into the Czech Republic and Slovakia. Thus, a network's scale is not fixed in advance, but is an emergent property of the sociospatial processes operating inside and beyond it. Nevertheless, at any particular point in time the scale of a particular network can be treated as equivalent to the scale of the geographic area encompassing its members. If its members happen to be from the same city it can be labeled intra-urban; if they are from the same nation-state it is national; and if its members are located all over the world it is global.

Although such labels seem similar to those applied to hierarchical modes of governance (city, region, nation-state, regional bloc, global), networks nevertheless have distinctive social and geographic attributes that make a significant difference. First, networks span space but do not cover it. Thus, they cannot be mapped as bounded territories but must be represented as spatial networks (i.e., as linked lattices of connected entities). Second, networks frequently transcend the boundaries dividing the spaces of hierarchical modes of governance (e.g., they may cross national boundaries or boundaries between individual states in a single nation), thereby making it harder for network activities to be regulated or governed from within existing political geographic spaces. Third, the flexibility of network membership means that the geographical boundary of any network, separating the places which are part of the network from those which are not, may frequently change – unlike the boundaries of hierarchical modes of governance which only sporadically shift (such as in the case of Europe after 1918, 1945, and 1989). Finally, network spaces can overlap and interpenetrate one another, unlike the non-overlapping nature of political spaces of a particular geographic scale (such as that of the "national" scale). Thus, the geographic extent of networks will frequently overlap and individual members can belong to many networks of a certain scale. For example, a city is a member of just one nation-state, but can be a member of many national and international networks.

The scaled nature of networks has two consequences of importance for theorizing about network modes of governance. First, the effectiveness of networks may be related to their scale. It is frequently suggested that network effectiveness depends closely on ease of coordination and its robustness in the face of external shocks. Those analyzing the success of such industrial districts as Emilia-Romagna or Baden-Württemberg stress their local nature, such as how the embeddedness of local economic networks within local cultural and political networks creates a mutuality and cooperative spirit that

enhances their competitiveness. However, such analysts often suggest, it may be harder for larger-scale networks to develop the rich
interactions necessary for success because such networks by their
very nature often bring together diverse cultural groups (who may
not share common values) and link together places which are far
apart in absolute terms, such that face-to-face communication is
made more difficult. Thus, cooperation in a national network spanning northern and southern Italy, or an international network embra-
cing Italy and Germany, may be more difficult to achieve than at the
local scale. This would also mean that local networks might come to
dominate larger-scale ones. Yet, there is no law linking network func-
tionality and scale. Networks make connections where none existed
before, connecting previously socially or geographically distant
actors together in ways that may potentially create new shared
understandings and collaborations. Through "folding space" (see
Latham this volume; Serres and Latour 1995) and linking seemingly
distant places in novel ways, then, the spaces created in networks
depart dramatically from those of conventional maps (Hetherington
1997; Murdoch 1997).

The second consequence of thinking about networks as scaled relates to how we conceptualize the relationship between network and
hierarchical modes of governance. As noted above, many network
proponents claim that networks are a new form of coordination, distinct from hierarchies (and markets). Our analysis of scaled networks
suggests otherwise. Networks are dialectically related to hierarchies
and markets. They are not created out of thin air as an alternative to
hierarchical modes of governance. Rather, they evolve in response to,
yet also shape, hierarchies and markets. Hence, on the one hand a
particular hierarchical mode of governance may create networks as
part of its struggle for power with other scales. For instance, as we
suggest below, the inter-urban networks of the EU were created
by EU institutions in part to strengthen their power and authority
vis-à-vis nation-states (and are contested by some nation-states for
this reason). On the other hand, networks may be created to overcome and challenge constraints posed by hierarchical modes of governance. For example, transnational inter-urban networks may help
overcome the inability of local entrepreneurialism to realize local
prosperity in the face of deregulated financial spaces and mobile
capital (Leitner and Sheppard 1999). In transcending the boundaries
of hierarchical modes of governance, networks may also challenge
the dominance of certain scale configurations – transnational local
authority networks, for instance, may confront and disturb the dominant politics of hierarchical power relations within the nation-state.

Transnational Networks among Cities and Regions and the Politics of Scale

The scalar nature of inter-urban networks

In many member states of the EU, recent restructuring of urban governance has been accompanied by the emergence of transnational networks among cities and regions.[3] Network agendas encompass a wide range of issues, including economic development, environment, energy and resources, health and social policy, urban planning, public administration, transport, technology, and research. Networks can be classified into two major categories: thematic networks and territorial networks. *Thematic networks* link together places with common concerns and problems, irrespective of their location. For example, "Demilitarised" ("Decrease in Europe of Military Investment, Logistics and Infrastructure and the Tracing of Alternative Regional Initiatives to Sustain Economic Development") is a thematic network involving 16 cities and regions in 5 member states, all of which are affected by the restructuring of defense-related industries and the closure of military bases (see figure 10.1). The "Quartiers en Crise" ("Neighborhoods in Crisis") network brings together 30 cities concerned with developing integrated approaches to combat housing and unemployment crises, together with problems of social exclusion, in urban neighborhoods. While these are all transnational networks, their geographic extent on the map of Europe varies, depending on where member cities and regions are located.

In contrast, *territorial networks* link places in a common geographic region or in particular types of regions. For example, networks of the INTERREG program exist to develop cross-border cooperation in the EU's internal and external border regions, and thus are made up of contiguous regions on either side of national boundaries. Likewise, the "Arc Atlantique" encompasses 25 regions bordering the Atlantic in France, Spain, Portugal, the UK, and Ireland. Such networks are more likely to form geographically contiguous regions, but clear exceptions exist. Networks in the ECOS-OUVERTURE programs, such as Stratour and Black Sea Ports, link EU to non-EU cities in Eastern Europe (figure 10.1).[4] These also are not mutually exclusive categories: some networks have both thematic and geographic membership criteria.

The inter-urban and inter-regional networks sponsored by the European Commission are all transnational in scale, albeit to varying degrees. With the exception of contiguous territorial networks, they

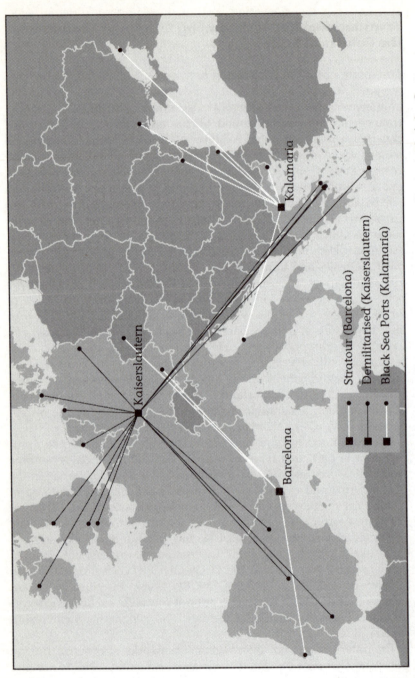

Kalamaria

Kaiserslautern

Barcelona

Stratour (Barcelona)
Demilitarised (Kaiserslautern)
Black Sea Ports (Kalamaria)

Figure 18.1 EU-sponsored transnational urban and regional networks: Stratour, Demilitarised, Black Sea Ports

span space without covering it. Thus, they imply a different geography than that of the familiar political map that organizes and divides the world into non-overlapping, spatially contiguous territories. The boundaries of these new political spaces are not fixed but are fluid and continually changing as new members join or as old members leave a network, and as networks are themselves initiated and terminated.[5] Finally, networks generally overlap and interpenetrate one another on the ground, with some cities belonging to many different networks (figure 10.2). For example, Barcelona, Lisbon, and Athens are involved with 33 other cities in the "EuroCities," "Quartiers en Crise," and "European Urban Observatory" networks.[6] In the 1990s, Birmingham City was an active member of 11 transnational networks (Collinge and Srbljanin 1997).[7] The outcome is a complex maze of transnational networks among cities and regions

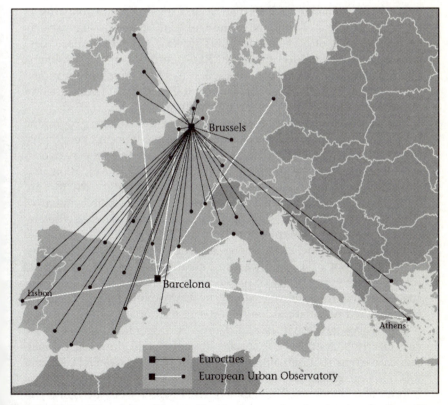

Figure 10.2   EU-sponsored transnational urban and regional networks: Eurocities, European Urban Observatory

that defies easy description and delimitation in terms of political space and geography.

Network cooperation and geographic reach

The transnational networks among cities and regions sponsored by various EU network programs show a range of degrees and forms of cooperation. The most common level, and the one easiest to implement, is the sharing of information, expertise, and "best practice" between network members which has been prevalent in the ECOS-OUVERTURE and PACTE network programs.[8] A second form of action is collective lobbying of higher-level (national and EU) state agencies for financial resources, using the collectivity of the network to leverage greater power in negotiations, and promoting the network to potential investors (as in the case of "EuroCities"). A step beyond the exchange of information and expertise and lobbying is the formulation and implementation of joint development projects (as in the case of RECITE and INTERREG).[9] For example, cross-border networks funded by INTERREG address concrete problems that arise out of cross-border interaction (such as cross-border movements of goods, services, labor, and capital) and lack of coordination of infrastructure, land-use planning, and transport.

The depth of cooperation bears some relation to the geographic reach of networks. A comparison of networks of varying geographic reach suggests that long-distance, transnational thematic networks are more likely to be oriented to simply sharing information and expertise. By contrast, spatially contiguous cross-border networks are more likely to include active cooperation and the establishment of joint projects on issues such as economic development, whereby cities develop, for example, specific plans for dividing economic activities and their benefits among network cities. These variations, while the result of a complex set of conditions and factors, suggest that geographic proximity of network actors still matters in an era of space-time compression. Proximity facilitates both complex communications and negotiations, and a sense of territorial identity.

Differences in the nature and degree of cooperation, however, are also clearly shaped by the special directives laid down in the network program requirements. For example, ECOS-OUVERTURE and PACTE were originally designed to foster primarily the exchange of information, whereas RECITE and INTERREG were designed not only to initiate cooperation but also to lead to joint projects with tangible results. This last point demonstrates that these inter-urban networks are not self-organizing – indeed, many were called into existence by the European Commission itself. Given this fact, we now turn to the issue of the relationship between inter-urban networks and hierarchical modes of governance within the EU.

Articulation between networks and hierarchies

Transnational urban and regional networks are an example of a novel form of politics, contrasting with the dominant politics and governance of vertical relations between different tiers of the state. They involve collective horizontal action among cities and regions, forged around a common agenda of mutual advantage that transcends national state boundaries. Yet, they should not be thought of as an independent development, since they are both the realm and the outcome of the politics of scale in the EU. Most of them would not have come into existence without the EU, which has its own reasons for stimulating them. Once in existence, their presence has the potential to enhance the power of cities and regions – together with that of the EU – at the expense of nation-states. In response, nation-states also have moved to circumscribe and otherwise shape the evolution of these networks.

Most currently existing transnational urban and regional networks in the EU owe their presence to the growing influence of the European Commission, which has encouraged and financially supported them. The Directorate-General for Regional Policy and Cohesion (DG XVI) alone has introduced four major networking programs (ECOS-OUVERTURE, PACTE, RECITE, INTERREG), providing funding to several thousand transnational network projects over a limited time horizon.[10] Numerous other EU Directorates also sponsor transnational urban and regional networks. For example, the Directorate-General for External Relations (DG I) sponsors networking among towns and regions in the Mediterranean area through its "Med-Urbs" program, and has also been preparing to launch programs involving local authorities and islands in Asia and Latin America.

The Commission not only financially supports networks but also uses its regulatory powers to circumscribe closely their goals, network agendas, types of cooperation, and geographic reach. This has the effect of promoting policies and policy changes which further Commission goals and institutional interests. The stated goals of networks promoted by the Directorate-General for Regional Policy and Cohesion are as follows: improving local response to challenges posed by an increasingly European and global economy; achieving a more efficient use of resources; facilitating the spread of innovative practices in economic development; and strengthening economic and social cohesion (European Commission 1995). These goals match and mirror larger EU policy concerns, namely: enhancing economic growth and the competitiveness of European cities and regions; reducing waste of public resources resulting from competitive bidding of cities for businesses and investment; and developing best practices for economic development, while at the same time reducing economic and social disparities within the EU territory. Yet, while not explicitly stated, the creation of these transnational networks also can be seen as an EU strategy to enhance its power, authority, and legitimacy *vis-à-vis* nation-states.[11] The direct provision of resources to, and the involvement of the Commission with, cities and regions not only allows EU institutions to leapfrog over the nation-state but also increases their legitimacy and helps foster greater identification of cities and regions with the EU. Thus, the Commission's promotion of transnational networks can also be seen as a strategy to stretch political identity beyond the nation-state, towards a European identity.

At the same time, transnational networks present an opportunity for cities and regions to strengthen their power and authority. With the exception of city twinning, external relations have traditionally been the domain of national authorities. The engagement of local and regional authorities in transnational networks extends their scope of action. Some member states have facilitated this through changes in the national legal framework. For example, in 1992 France passed a law "which extended the right to French regions [*Départements*] to enter into inter-regional associations beyond the scope of territorially contiguous areas and envisaged for the first time that French regions could enter into legally binding agreements with regions of other states, within the limits set by their competencies and the international obligations of the French Republic" (Weyand 1997: 168). In countries where external relations remain the exclusive domain of the central government, local authorities have found ways around such legal or statutory restrictions to become increasingly engaged in transnational activities.

In addition to providing an opportunity for local and regional authorities to engage directly in external relations, transnational networks potentially strengthen both the power of local authorities *vis-à-vis* national governments in certain policy arenas and the capacity of localities to influence directly Commission policy-making. Traditionally, particularly in highly centralized nation-states such as the UK, local and regional authorities have had little autonomy. A number of studies, though, suggest that transnational networks are enhancing the position of local and regional authorities *vis-à-vis* the national government in the area of economic policy-making. Church and Reid's (1996) analysis of three cross-border networks between French and British local authorities revealed that whereas French urban authorities (whose autonomy had been strengthened by governmental reforms of the early 1980s) did not view this potential as such an important issue, British local officials perceived that such transnational networks could strengthen their political autonomy, especially in local economic policy. Resources made available through the EU INTERREG program, in particular, were thought to permit greater local independence in economic development policy-making.

While gaining funding from the EU is an important concern in many transnational networks (especially given the reduction in national government funding for local authorities in member states), Benington and Harvey (1998) suggest that transnational networks are equally concerned with directly influencing EU policy formulation and outcomes in areas of their interest. For example, the collective efforts of the "Demilitarised" network have played an important role in the formulation of KONVER II, a Community Initiative providing EU funding for regions attempting to counter the effects of the decline in the defense industry by promoting industrial conversion and finding ways to re-use military facilities. "Demilitarised" also successfully lobbied for the eligibility and access of smaller geographic units – which have been disproportionately affected by the decline of the defense industry – to KONVER II funds (European Commission 1997). Similarly, the EURACOM and "EuroCities" networks, bypassing their respective national governments, each successfully lobbied the EU Commission and the European Parliament for the introduction of a new Community Initiative, RECHAR II and URBAN respectively.[12]

Attempts by local and regional authorities in member states and by the Commission to circumvent national governments have met with resistance, however. In particular, the British government, through a policy of opposing network initiatives and preventing direct access of local and regional authorities to EU funding, has attempted to contain the increasing power of local and regional authorities which transnational networks and the Commission are facilitating. For example, in the case of RECHAR II funding, the EU Commission proposed that funding should go directly to local and regional authorities. British government officials opposed such a set-up, though, arguing that this is not the right scale for program implementation and resource allocation because it requires expertise that is not available at the local scale. Instead, the government instituted quasi-public regional organizations that are in charge of dispensing RECHAR II funds across the country (Benington and Harvey 1998).

This example suggests that nation-states continue to be important players in the politics of scale, jostling for recognition, authority, and control alongside new forms of political power such as EU institutions and transnational urban and regional networks. Political space in respect to the locus and accountability of political power continues to be shaped by the reach of the nation-state, but not exclusively so. Rather, political power is shared, negotiated, and struggled over by diverse forces and agencies situated at local, regional, national, and supranational scales, while at the same time it operates across scales, i.e. beyond the boundaries of the traditional territorially-based political systems.

Conclusion

At the turn of the twenty-first century, globalization has become a powerful discursive construct employed "to capture a sense of heightened space-time compression, connectivity, communication and circulation in diverse processes of economic, political and cultural, and social change" (Kelly 1999: 379). Networks have been viewed as organizational expressions of globalization, with some analysts seeing globalization as no less than the "rise of the network society" (Castells 1996). Issues of scale have also been central to discourses on the nature and implications of globalization, with various discourses making competing claims about the shifting importance and power of the local, regional, national, supranational, and global scales of governance. However, the relationship between scale and networks, particularly in the context of political governance, has received scant attention.

We contend that changes in the importance of, and relationships among, different hierarchical scales cannot be understood without paying attention to the networks that connect and enable exchange between organizations and places (as well as individuals) horizontally across territorial boundaries and geographic scales, in contrast to the connections and interactions that occur vertically within traditional hierarchical governance structures. Transnational networks among cities and regions in the EU are examples of new political relations emerging across national boundaries, but situated at the subnational political scale. They involve horizontal collective action among cities and regions, forged around a common agenda of mutual advantage that crosses – and may challenge – the hierarchical relations between different scales of political governance (local, regional, national, and supranational).

While these networks are scaled (i.e., they vary in geographic extent from local to global), their spatiality is distinctive and contrasts with traditional hierarchical forms of formal territorial political organization and interaction. Transnational urban and regional networks are flexible in the entities that they include, which means that a particular city or region may participate in any number of networks. The result is that networks vary in composition and places display different degrees of network-based activity. In addition, these networks tend to be fluid in composition, with cities and regions continuously being admitted to, and departing from, specific networks, such that the spatiality of individual networks varies over time. Finally, because networks often connect noncontiguous political units, network geographies stand in contrast to the familiar political map that organizes and divides the world into spatially contiguous territories of varying geographic extent (localities, regions, nation-states, regional blocs, and the globe), with distinct boundaries and power relationships among different geographic scales. Transnational urban and regional networks thus span, but rarely cover or "fill," space – their geographies tend to leapfrog over space, connecting spatially separated territorial units as members of a network of interaction and exchange.

As a new form of governance, transnational urban and regional networks should not be seen simply as alternatives to the local, national, and global scales associated with the traditional hierarchical modes of governance. Rather, the two are dialectically related. Network modes of governance may operate to reinforce the power and importance of some scales while challenging others. Thus, networks are part of the struggles for control over economic, political, and cultural space (the politics of scale), struggles that may occur between scales, that may involve jumping scales, and/or that may involve operating on several scales simultaneously.

The increasing importance of transnational networks in shaping contemporary life and governance does not result, however, in a deterritorialization of governance and politics – that is, it does not result in the replacement of the space of places with spaces of flows. Although the relational spaces of transnational networks transcend the boundaries of local, regional, and national territories, territories remain important places of coordination and identification. The actors occupying and maintaining particular nodes and links within any network remain situated in, and retain identity with, places – cities, regions, and nations. It is from these geographically situated vantage points that they participate in transnational networks, increasing, accelerating, and deepening relations across space and time, and introducing a novel dimension to the hierarchical politics of scale.

NOTES

1 By network, we mean a group of social actors who are interrelated through economic, social, political, and cultural interactions. These connections create relationships of mutual interdependence, meaning that each actor depends in complex ways on most other actors.

2 Such networks are called actor-networks because once they are "successfully established, if all the elements act in concert, then they will take on the properties of actors" (Murdoch 1997: 361).

3 Most of these transnational networks involve local authorities as central actors. Some also include actors from the private/business sector and, in a few cases, representatives of voluntary and community sectors.

4 ECOS-OUVERTURE, initiated in 1991, aims to establish cooperative networks among regions and cities in the EU and Central and Eastern Europe in order to facilitate exchange of information on a wide range of topics.

5 Termination is often a result of the time limit imposed on EU funding of networks. In many cases the funding period also becomes the *de facto* lifespan of the network. After a network dies, some partners go on to participate in other network programs, either with the same or with new partners. Only in a few cases have partners developed a strong-enough identity with the network for it to continue without EU funding.

6 The EuroCities network was formed in 1986 to represent the interests of "second tier" cities (i.e., large and mainly non-capital cities) within the EU. With a current membership of over forty, the EuroCities network promotes member cities' joint interests by lobbying various EU Directorates and through well-publicized conferences. The European Urban Observatory network links ten cities for the purpose of developing a database and a decision-making system to be shared by its members.

7 These were: the EuroCities network; Telecities; the European Urban Observatory; the Council of European Municipalities and Regions; the International Union of Local Authorities; the Association of European Regions of Industrial Technology (which links regions with a dependence on manufacturing industry); the Association of European Regions (which brings together regional governments from across Europe); the Motor Industries Local Authority Network; POLIS (Promoting Operational Links with Integrated Services through road traffic ergomatics between European cities); the International Conference of Local Environmental Initiatives; and the European Local Authority Information Network.

8   PACTE, launched in 1989, originally sought to provide opportunities for exchange of know-how and experiences between local and regional communities of the European Union on a wide range of issues.

9   RECITE (Regions and Cities of Europe), launched in 1991, promotes collaboration among local and regional communities on economic development and sharing of experience. It has included approximately 37 different network initiatives, such as EuroCities, Demilitarised, Quartiers en Crise, and the European Urban Observatory. INTERREG, founded in 1989, aims to develop cross-border cooperation in order to help regions in the Union's internal and external frontiers to overcome the specific problems arising from their relative isolation.

10 Networks are allocated funding from a variety of different sources within the European Regional Development Fund (ERDF). Some of these funds are allocated on a competitive basis. The length of time for which networks are sponsored through the RECITE program has varied between two and six years.

11 Dang-Nguyen et al. (1993), analyzing the transnational telecommunications policy network promoted by the EU, similarly argue that transnational policy networks promoted by EU institutions are structurally "biased" towards policies strengthening the EU as a whole.

12 EURACOM (European Action for Mining Communities) is a thematic network, involving 450 local authorities in mining areas in seven EU member states and providing a platform for collective lobbying of the EU on coalfield issues. RECHAR provides EU support for areas affected by the decline of the coal industry. URBAN provides EU support to revitalize the economy and social fabric of urban areas.

REFERENCES

Amin, A. and Thrift, N. 1992: Neo-Marshallian nodes in global networks. *International Journal of Urban and Regional Research*, 16: 571–87.

Amin, A. and Thrift, N. 1994: Holding down the global. In A. Amin and N. Thrift (eds.), *Globalization, Institutions and Regional Development in Europe*. Oxford: Oxford University Press, 257–60.

Barber, B. 1995: *Jihad vs. McWorld*. New York: Ballantine.

Benington, J. and Harvey, J. 1998: Transnational local authority networking within the European Union: Passing fashion or new paradigm? In D. Marsh (ed.), *Comparing Policy Networks*. Buckingham/Philadelphia: Open University Press, 149–66.

Bomberg, E. 1998: Issue networks and the environment: Explaining European Union environmental policy. In D. Marsh (ed.), *Comparing Policy Networks*. Buckingham/Philadelphia: Open University Press, 167–84.

Brenner, N. 1998: Between fixity and motion: Accumulation, territorial organization and the historical geography of spatial scales. *Environment and Planning D: Society and Space*, 16, 459–81.

Castells, M. 1996: *The Rise of the Network Society*. Oxford: Blackwell.

Castells, M. and Hall, P. 1994: *Technopoles of the World: The Making of Twenty-First-Century Industrial Complexes*. New York: Routledge.

Chorley, R. and Haggett, P. 1974: *Network Analysis in Human Geography*. London: E. Arnold.

Church, A. and Reid, P. 1996: Urban power, international networks and competition: The example of cross-border cooperation. *Urban Studies*, 33, 1297–1318.

Collinge, C. and Srbljanin, A. 1997: Delimiting the city: Is there a "network paradigm" in urban governance? Paper presented at the EURA seminar "Governing Cities: International Perspectives," Brussels, Sept.

Cooke, P. (ed.) 1995: *The Rise of the Rustbelt*. New York: St. Martin's.

Cooke, P. and Morgan, K. 1993: The network paradigm: New departures in corporate and regional development. *Environment and Planning D: Society and Space*, 11, 543–64.

Dang-Nguyen, G., Schneider, V., and Werle, R. 1993: Networks in European policy-making: Europeification of telecommunications policy. In S. S. Andersen and K. A. Eliassen (eds.), *Making Policy in Europe: The Europeification of National Policy-Making*. London: Sage, 93–114.

Daugbjerg, C. and Marsh, D. 1998: Explaining policy outcomes: Integrating the policy network approach with macro-level and micro-level analysis. In D. Marsh (ed.), *Comparing Policy Networks*. Buckingham/Philadelphia: Open University Press, 52–74.

Dowding, K. 1994: Policy networks: Don't stretch a good idea too far. In P. Dunleavy and J. Stanyer (eds.), *Contemporary Political Studies*, vol. 1, Political Studies Association Conference Proceedings, 79–92.

Emirbayer, M. and Goodwin, J. 1994: Network analysis, culture, and the problem of agency. *American Journal of Sociology*, 99, 1411–54.

European Commission. 1995: *The European Programme for Inter-regional Cooperation and Regional Economic Innovation*. Article 10–ERDF, Luxembourg.

European Commission. 1997: *Review of Inter-regional Cooperation*. Review no. 13, DG XVI, Brussels.

Galaskiewicz, J. and Wasserman, S. (eds.) 1994: *Advances in Social Network Analysis: Research in the Social and Behavioral Sciences*. Thousand Oaks, CA: Sage.

Garud, R. and Kumaraswamy, A. 1993: Changing competitive dynamics in network industries: An exploration of Sun Microsystems. *Strategic Management Journal*, 14, 351–69.

Grabher, G. and Stark D. (eds.) 1997: *Restructuring Networks in Post-Socialism: Legacies, Linkages, and Localities*. New York: Oxford University.

Granovetter, M. 1985: Economic action and social structure: The problem of embeddedness. *American Journal of Sociology*, 91, 481–510.

Granovetter, M. and Swedberg, R., 1992: *The Sociology of Economic Life*. Boulder, CO: Westview Press.

Haraway, D. 1997: *Modest_Witness@Second_Millennium.FemaleMan©_Meets_OncoMouse^{TM}*. London: Routledge.

Harrison, B. 1994: *Lean and Mean: The Changing Landscape of Corporate Power in the Age of Flexibility*. New York: Basic Books.

Hay, C. 1998: The tangled webs we weave: The discourse, strategy and practice of networking. In D. Marsh (ed.), *Comparing Policy Networks*. Buckingham/Philadelphia: Open University Press, 33–51.

Held, D., McGrew, A., Goldblatt, D., and Perraton, J. 1999: *Global Transformations: Politics, Economics and Culture*. Stanford, CA: Stanford University Press.

Herod, A. 1997: Labor's spatial praxis and the geography of contract bargaining in the US east coast longshore industry, 1953–89. *Political Geography*, 16, 145–69.

Herrigel, G. 1993: Large firms, small firms, and the governance of flexible specialization: The case of Baden-Württemberg and socialized risk. In B. Kogut (ed.), *Country Competitiveness: Technology and the Organization of Work*. New York: Oxford University, 15–35.

Hetherington, K. 1997: In place of geometry: The materiality of place. In K. Hetherington and R. Munro (eds.), *Ideas of Difference: Social Spaces and the Labor of Division*. Oxford: Blackwell, 183–99.

Hirst, P. and Thompson, G. 1999: *Globalization in Question* (2nd ed.). Cambridge: Polity.

Jessop, R. 1997: Capitalism and its future: Remarks on regulation, government and governance. *Review of International Political Economy*, 4, 561–81.

Kelly, P. F. 1999: The geographies and politics of globalization. *Progress in Human Geography*, 23, 379–400.

Kenney, M. and Florida, R. 1993: *Beyond Mass Production: The Japanese System and its Transfer to the US*. New York: Oxford University.

Langlois, R. and Robertson, P. 1995: *Firms, Markets and Economic Change: A Dynamic Theory of Business Institutions*. New York: Routledge.

Larsson, S. and Malmberg, A. 1999: Innovations, competitiveness and local embeddedness: A study of machinery producers in Sweden. *Geografiska Annaler*, 81B, 1–18.

Latour, B. 1987: *Science in Action*. Cambridge, MA: Harvard University Press.

Law, J. 1992: Notes on the theory of the actor-network: Ordering, strategy, and heterogeneity. *Systems Practice*, 5, 379–93.

Lazonick, W. 1993: Industry clusters versus global webs: Organizational capabilities in the American economy. *Industrial and Corporate Change*, 2, 1–24.

Leitner, H. 1997: Reconfiguring the spatiality of power: The construction of a supranational migration framework for the European Union. *Political Geography*, 16, 123–44.

Leitner, H. and Sheppard, E. 1999: Transcending inter-urban competition: Conceptual issues and policy alternatives in the European Union. In D. Wilson and A. Jonas (eds.), *The Urban Growth Machine – Critical Perspectives Two Decades Later*. Albany, NY: State University of New York Press, 227–46.

Malmberg, A. 1996: Industrial geography: Agglomeration and local milieu. *Progress in Human Geography*, 20, 392–403.

Marsh, D. 1998a: The development of the policy network approach. In D. Marsh (ed.), *Comparing Policy Networks*. Buckingham/Philadelphia: Open University Press, 3–20.

Marsh, D. 1998b: The utility of policy network analysis. In D. Marsh (ed.), *Comparing Policy Networks*. Buckingham/Philadelphia: Open University Press, 185–97.

Marsh, D. and Rhodes, R. A. W. 1992: *Policy Networks in British Government*. Oxford: Clarendon.

Martin, B. and Mayntz, R. (eds.) 1991: *Policy Networks: Empirical Evidence and Theoretical Considerations*. Frankfurt: Campus.

Mattelart, A. 2000: *Networking the World, 1794–2000*. Minneapolis, MN: University of Minnesota Press.

Mayntz, R. 1994: *Modernization and the Logic of Interorganizational Networks*. MIPFG Working Paper no. 4. Köln: Max-Planck Institute für Gesellschaftsforschung.

Mizruchi, M. S. 1994: Social network analysis: Recent achievements and current controversies. *Acta Sociologica*, 37, 329–44.

Murdoch, J. 1997: The spaces of actor-network theory. *Geoforum*, 29, 357–74.

Ohmae, K. 1990: *The Borderless World*. London: Collins.

Ó hUallacháin, B. and Wasserman, D. 1999: Vertical integration in a lean supply chain: Brazilian automobile component parts. *Economic Geography*, 75, 21–42.

Piore, M. J. and Sabel, C. F. 1984: *The Second Industrial Divide: Possibilities for Prosperity*. New York: Basic Books.

Porter, M. 1996: Competitive advantage, agglomeration economies, and regional policy. *International Regional Science Review*, 19, 95–90.

Rhodes, R. A. W. 1997: *Understanding Governance – Policy Networks, Governance, Reflexivity and Accountability*. Buckingham/Philadelphia: Open University Press.

Rhodes, R. A. W. and Marsh, D. 1992: New directions in the study of policy networks. *European Journal of Political Research*, 21, 181–205.

Sabel, C. F. 1989: Flexible specialization and the re-emergence of regional economies. In P. Hirst and J. Zeitlin (eds.), *Reversing Industrial Decline?* London: Berg, 17–70.

Scott, A. J. 1993: *Technopolis: High-Technology Industry and Regional Development in Southern California*. Berkeley: University of California.

Scott, A. J. 1998: *Regions and the World Economy: The Coming Shape of Global Production, Competition, and Political Order*. New York: Oxford University.

Serres, M. and Latour, B. 1995: *Conversations on Science, Culture and Time*. Ann Arbor: Michigan University Press.

Smith, N. 1992: Geography, difference and the politics of scale. In J. Doherty, E. Graham, and M. Malek (eds.), *Postmodernism and the Social Sciences*. New York: St. Martin's Press, 57–79.

Swyngedouw, E. 1997: Neither global nor local: "Glocalization" and the politics of scale. In K. R. Cox (ed.), *Spaces of Globalization*. New York: Guilford, 137–66.

Wasserman, S. and Faust, K. 1994: *Social Network Analysis: Methods and Applications*. Cambridge: Cambridge University Press.

Weiss, L. 1998: *Globalization and the Myth of the Powerless State*. Cambridge: Polity.

Weyand, S. 1997: Inter-regional associations and the European Integration Process. In C. Jeffrey (ed.), *The Regional Dimension of the European Union – Towards a Third Level in Europe?* London: Frank Cass, 166–82.

Williamson, O. E. 1985: *The Economic Institutions of Capitalism: Firms, Markets, and Relational Contracting*. New York: Free Press.

Index

bounding properties of scale, 6–8
Bracero Program, 196
Brenner, Neil, 65, 75, 76, 107*n*,
    109*n*
Brenner, Robert, 90
bricolage, 115
Bridge, G., 148
Brody, D., 225
Buchanan, Patrick, 161, 178, 209
Burns, Milt, 235
business unionism, 225, 235, 238,
    244, 246*n*
Butler, Judith, 35
Byrne, Ken, 44

Callon, Michel, 36–7, 123, 130
Capek, S., 252
capital/capitalism: central force in
    globalization, 27; command of
    global scale, 17; in dualistic
    discourse, 19; global mobility, 1,
    17, 89–90; liberation from
    discourse of, 36, 37–8, 56*n*;
    movement between fixity and
    mobility, 93, 94–5, 100–1, 106; and
    state, 85, 89–92, 105, 106–7; *see also*
    non-capitalism
capital divisions of labor, 22, 93–5,
    98–100, 101
capitalocentrism, 56*n*
Carroll, Lewis, 183
Castells, Manuel, 64, 115–16, 120–4,
    125, 126, 129, 275
central place theory, 95, 98
Certeau, Michel de, 167
chaos theory, 28
Chicago School, 80–1*n*
Christian fundamentalism, 186
Church, A., 295
cinema: Hayes Code, 185; science-
    fiction films, 177, 178, 185, 186
cities: dualist discourse of, 19–21,
    74–7, 79–80; *see also* global cities
    literature
citizens and environmental activism,
    260–1

civil rights violations and
    environmental justice, 220–1,
    262–6, 267
class: capitalist class relations, 38–9;
    and environmental justice concept,
    252; and geographical rescaling,
    94, 104
climate change, 1, 174
closed economies, 98–9
closet metaphor, 189–90*n*
coalitions, territorially based, 95–6,
    100–4
"cogriedience," 81*n*
collective action frames, 253–4, 256,
    259–71
command and control centers, 120
communism and trades unions,
    219–20, 224–5, 235; anti-communist
    campaign, 232–4, 236–8, 239, 240–1
community economies, 41–9, 51–2,
    58*n*; identity in communities,
    41–3, 46–9; language for, 44–6,
    51–2
Community Economies Collective,
    45
Community Partnering Project, 47
computer games and back regions,
    184, 187
computer technology *see* information
    technology
concentric circles scale metaphor,
    6–7, 9
Congress of Industrial Organizations
    (CIO), 219, 227–8, 233, 237, 242
Connolly, William, 57*n*
consumption, division of, 93
context-specificity, 102
Convent, Louisiana *see* St. James
    Parish
cooperation in networks, 292–3
cooperative ventures, 26, 40, 56–7*n*
"copresence," 76–7, 81*n*
corporate cultural studies, 156
corporate promotion through VTM,
    154–70
cosmopolitanism, 119, 127, 136–7